W9-BSF-756

STRESS

Angela Patmore

Atlantic Books
LONDON

To Sidney McGee

First published in trade paperback in Great Britain in 2006 by Atlantic Books, an imprint of Grove/Atlantic Ltd.

This paperback edition published in 2009 by Atlantic Books.

Copyright © Angela Patmore, 2006

The moral right of Angela Patmore to be identified as the author of this work has been asserted by her in accordance with the Copyright, Designs and Patents Acts of 1988.

All rights reserved. No part of this publication may be reproduced, stored in a retrieval system, or transmitted in any form or by any means, electronic, mechanical, photocopying, recording, or otherwise, without the prior permission of both the copyright owner and the above publisher of this book.

Every effort has been made to trace or contact all copyright holders. The publishers will be pleased to make good any omissions or rectify any mistakes brought to their attention at the earliest opportunity.

10 9 8 7 6 5 4 3 2 1

A CIP catalogue record for this book is available from the British Library.

ISBN: 978 1 84354 236 0

Set in Monotype Sabon
Designed by Nicky Barneby @ Barneby Ltd
Printed in Great Britain by CPD Wales, Blaina.

Atlantic Books
An imprint of Grove Atlantic Ltd
Ormond House
26–27 Boswell Street
London
WC1N 3JZ

www.atlantic-books.co.uk

CONTENTS

The Truth About **STRESS**

Angela Patmore is a former University of East Anglia research fellow and International Fulbright Scholar. Her analysis of competitive pressure, *Sportsmen Under Stress* (1986), was a *Times* sports book of the year. A former *Guardian* columnist on the psychology of sport, she writes extensively for newspapers and magazines and has contributed to many television and radio programmes on stress. *The Truth About Stress* was shortlisted for the MIND Book of the Year Award 2007.

ACKNOWLEDGEMENTS

The author would particularly like to thank the Royal Literary Fund and the Russell Trust for their generous financial contributions to this project. Many thanks to Fay Weldon, to Ruth Lea, director of the Centre for Policy Studies, to Lord Brian Mackenzie of Framwellgate, and to Dr John Cooper for all their support and encouragement. Thanks to Alison Cobb and MIND for information on prescription drug-addiction; to Richard Hughes and the Department of Health for help with prescription statistics; to Boris Cetnik of Berrymans Lace Mawer, London Occupational Disease Unit for permission to quote from Dr Martin Baggaley's diagnostic guide, and to Professor David Ball and UEA's Centre for Environmental Risk for access to research data. Thanks to Rosemary Anderson, Chair of ISMA, to Dr David Wainwright, to Peter Goodwin, IHP and to Andrew Nicholls, StressCheck for granting interviews. For access to their research literature I should like to thank Dr Rob Briner, Emeritus Professor Brian Thorne, Dr Jo Rick and Professor Andrew Guppy. And grateful thanks to Toby Mundy and Louisa Joyner of Atlantic Books for editorial wisdom.

Finally, thanks for their time, help and co-operation to: Dr Dale Archer, Dr Carole Astbury, Beat the Benzos, Barry Haslam and Mike Behan, the BMA, for information on GP counselling, the British Association for Counselling and Psychotherapy, the British Heart Foundation, Belinda Linden, the British Hypertension Society, Sandra Caldwell, HSE, Marcvs Cassivs, Legion XIIII, Eric Davidson, for his translation of *La Provence en Archipel*,

Dr Martin Deahl, Dame Judi Dench, the Duke of Edinburgh Award Scheme, Dr Richard Earle, Dr Susan Hallam, Judy Leden, Dr Richard Lippin and the International Arts Medicine Association, Dr Pim van Lommel, Dr David Lorimer, the MHRA, for information on benzodiazepines, Dr Julian Miller, Dr David Murray-Bruce, Dr Michael O'Donnell, Outward Bound, Dr Reg Peart, Victims of Tranquillisers, Dr Mark Popplestone, Les Roberts, NASUWT, Brian Robinson, UKNWSN, Carole Spiers, Dr Alan Watkins, Jim Wilkes and Professor James Woudhuysen.

Whilst every effort has been made to keep facts and statistics up to date, some may have changed during the long process of publication.

IS THIS PERSON QUALIFIED?
Author's Introduction

Since you have opened this book, I hope you will also open your mind. Even if at present you very firmly believe in the term 'stress' and use it all the time, and even if you are thoroughly convinced that it is a real entity or illness, and that you or those around you are suffering from it, I would ask you to listen to the evidence presented in the following pages that you may have been deceived about your perfectly normal feelings and bodily mechanisms, and that this deception may be harming your health and happiness.

But first, let us clear up an important misunderstanding, one that is otherwise likely to prejudice you against the contents of this book. Although the author has been routinely dismissed by members of the stress industry as unsympathetic to 'stress' sufferers, this is untrue and unfair. The whole purpose of my work on this subject has been to provide information that will help them help themselves. I believe the stress mythology harms everyone, but that it harms the most vulnerable most of all.

I write from professional and personal experience and twenty-five years' research into emotional crises in the arts, in sport and in scientific literature. My book deals objectively with that research and sets it out as clearly and concisely as possible. In addition, I shall tell you about relevant events in my personal life, so you may judge to what extent my experiences have shaped my objections to the stress ideology and stress therapy.

A career in 'pressure'

Ironically, when I am not writing or advising on stress, I work in what many people consider a highly 'stressful' profession – I teach. I am a motivational trainer for the long-term unemployed in Colchester. As part of a small company, Mojo Associates, my job is to provide practical strategies and skills to help candidates overcome loss of confidence, fears, phobias and barrier beliefs. I enhance their courage by giving them techniques to improve their assertiveness, their people skills, their emotional toughness and their respect for the wonders of the brain. We have an excellent track record on getting people's lives restarted. As somebody who regularly stands up in front of a class of unemployed men and women of all ages, many of them surly and dejected, and all of them dragged kicking and screaming into my presence by the Employment Service, I would be the first to concur that teaching is a challenge. But unlike those thousands of teachers keen to retire from the profession on grounds of 'stress', I find the challenge supremely rewarding.

I have also worked as a Metropolitan Police external expert on 'workplace stress' and served on the Commissioner's panel of advisers on the subject. My role there was to suggest ways of stripping out 'medicalizing' stress psychology from our thinking in order to revert to a more credible (non-engineering) terminology. I argued against subjecting officers to a stress audit, suggesting that this might make matters worse. While everyone understands the need for supporting individual officers distressed by the horrors of the job, I felt that pre-emptive medicalizing of the psychology of policemen and women, and monitoring their heads for stress, however well-intentioned, would encourage introspection and eventually undermine their ability (and their willingness) to do frontline work.

Long before this I had written a number of books with and about people involved in emotionally taxing and difficult jobs. With Marje Proops, who for many years was the *Daily Mirror*'s 'agony aunt', I had the opportunity to analyse hundreds of the (two million) letters she had received from troubled readers, some of them with extremely serious problems, and to talk to Marje before she died about her own emotional crises and mental illness.

As a former Fulbright scholar with a couple of arts degrees I have also studied theatre, and interviewed famous actors about their sometimes disturbing but often exhilarating psychological experiences getting 'into character'. I have worked with well-known sportsmen too, discussing their emotional crises in high-level competition. In 1979, when sports psychology was still fairly new and controversial, I wrote a book on the phenomenon of 'pressure' in sport, later reissued as *Sportsmen Under Stress*. At the time of my investigations in the 1970s, many professional sportsmen had little time for the relaxation techniques now in vogue, and instead knowingly *increased* their level of arousal, a strategy they called 'psyching up'. The hardier breed of sportsmen still prefer this more traditional style of preparation, for all they might hear from sports psychologists about stress management. Some competitors would shout and scream in the locker room, slap or hit one another, and even bang their heads against the wall. At that time, like most people, I held the belief that stress was a real entity, that there was a lot of it about in professional sport, and that competitors should try to avoid it by stress management techniques, for fear that they might otherwise be harmed mentally or physically. The best way of withstanding the pressure – I assumed at that time – was for sportsmen to try to relax.

This turned out to be my first real brush with scepticism about stress. My efforts to get these sportsmen interested in relaxation exercises met with bemused indifference. In general, their awareness of arousal manipulation was developed to an unusual degree by the demands of what I have called 'the sport experiment' on their brains and bodies,[1] and they obviously knew more about the subject than I did.

But my real *anagnorisis* (Aristotle's term for 'sudden realization in a crisis') came nearly twenty years later, when in the 1990s I was invited as a University of East Anglia research fellow to carry out a meta-analysis of the clinical literature on stress with internationally renowned scientists from the Centre for Environmental and Risk Management (CERM), a World Health Organization collaborating centre. Before analysing those mountains of research papers I had had no reason to suppose there was anything wrong with the concept or the beliefs that went with it. However, once I had seen the scientific evidence that underpinned their industry, I was on a collision course with the stress professions. While writing up that review, sifting and examining literally hundreds of studies going back to the 1930s, we concluded that the term had no agreed meaning or scientific validity, and that the concept itself was bogus and illogical. Furthermore, if there were no such entity as 'stress', then the whole stress management ideology must be at best misleading, and at worst a dangerous deceit. The many serious and disqualifying flaws that we found in the research are explained in detail in the 'Science' chapters of this book. One particularly important problem is the question of what 'stress' *means*. We found that although there was no agreed definition, there were literally hundreds of *different* definitions, some of them opposites, some of them irreconcilable, and all of them felt to be 'the correct one' by somebody or other.

Another persistent flaw in the science is its heavy reliance on animal models. Even leaving aside objections to vivisection on ethical grounds (which I do not), one must surely question the logic and validity of animals modelling for human beings in all their psychological and cerebral complexity. This becomes a matter of concern when we realize that we have reached our present state of anxiety about stress, with all its dangerous pathologizing of human emotions and human biological mechanisms, by relying on just such animal studies as these.

One of the other significant problems with the stress research was its provenance, and the way in which an engineering concept has been gaily transferred, as we shall see, to human biology where it can have no possible business. Chapter 4 examines this strange grafting, and looks at the post-war origins of the stress science with due care but with modern-day scepticism. Seeing the foundations of all our present 'stress management' beliefs set out before us in the stark light of 2006 may prove disturbing for some delicate sensibilities, and the word 'gobbledegook' may quite unjustly spring to mind (it certainly sprang to mine). But then perhaps we should retain a sense of humour about all this 'stress management' and where it came from.

I am frequently asked if I hold a current stress-sufferer's licence myself. There is no right answer to this. If I say yes, the questioner assumes I don't know of any cure and am therefore not worth listening to, and if I say no, then I must be lacking in insight or 'in denial'. So I leave it to others to judge.

Sick notes bearing the s-word are all too easy to come by. Three years ago I went to my GP to ask for help because my poor mother was 'bed-locked' – unable to be discharged – in a London hospital for want of social services funding. She had been there for seven months after suffering a stroke and was becoming resigned to dying in hospital. Instead, because I was clearly upset about the matter, I was very kindly offered a sick note with the word 'stress' on it – for *myself*. I handed it back – though, to my shame, I did think of putting it in a frame for publicity purposes. Then I went away and fought with the authorities until I got my mother out of hospital.

I do not care for doctors who write 'stress' on sick notes, and although my dealings with them have been limited I am not very fond of psychiatric professionals either. I admit that ministering to the mentally ill is a heroic calling. When I was a depressed adolescent, I was referred to a psychiatrist by an ENT clinic. I became infatuated with his accent, his intelligence, his apparent interest in my life and his bright kipper ties, and when the brief course of treatment ended I felt the shock of grief numbing my extremities. It took great courage for me to thank him for his time, shake his hand, say, 'Oh sod it then,' and return to sorting out my own problems. (I might still be there, had I not been constantly insulting him about psychiatry.)

I had my share of health problems, including asthma attacks that nearly killed me and panic attacks that frightened me half to death, especially during my bachelor degree finals. Mood-altering drugs were offered for the latter but were not really an option because I saw what they had done to my father (more of which below). So I faced reality, found courage from somewhere and got a First and a scholarship to America. Because I knew I would not be able to afford expensive medical treatment there, I conquered my asthma by throwing away all my drugs and inhalers and doing breathing exercises instead (I have never had asthma since). Like most writers I toss and turn at night worrying how to meet deadlines and pay the mortgage. I have never had a partner with whom to share these difficulties and years ago I tried counselling without success. Such ordinary human troubles made me a better person and a better writer.

All of these minor problems were in any case insignificant compared with what happened to my loved ones four years ago. Six members of my family, including three small children, were burned alive in their home by an arsonist, Richard Fielding, who had a grudge against my nephew over a schoolboy prank. He told the police as a matter of official record while in custody that he intended to 'go for diminished responsibility' to avoid punishment, and convinced psychiatrists accordingly. In fact *six* different psychiatrists and psychologists came up with *nine* mental illness labels, three of them actually suggested by Fielding himself. It left the family not only very suspicious of the validity of mental health labelling, but of psychiatrists as expert witnesses in a court of law.

Fielding has never been tried or punished and is still, so far as we know, currently undergoing therapy and having canoeing lessons at Rampton Hospital where, according to fellow-inmates in tabloid press reports, he boasts about his crime. He will apparently be released soon 'if he responds well to therapy' and my family will not be informed when he is back on the streets. My cousin Brian Day, the sole survivor of the fire, refused all stress counselling. He is brave, sane, as kind as he always was, and working.

I had an interesting conversation on the subject of 'workplace trauma' with a trade union representative of the Ministry of Defence Police based in Wethersfield, Essex. He told me that although he could 'understand where I was coming from' on stress, some of his members nevertheless needed time off work and counselling 'because they had witnessed traumatic events at work'. I asked what these events were. Some members had apparently 'been involved in fires in which people died'. The union rep seemed to think it obvious, given these circumstances, that counselling was necessary. I replied that my cousin, who had survived an arson attack on his home that killed seven people including six members of his immediate family, managed without counselling to resume a sane and positive working life. Who could have presumed to 'counsel' him, or reassure him, or understand his experience? What harm might have been done to him, had he been made intensely to relive that earthly hell, as post-critical incident debriefing requires survivors to do?

Personal experience has also led me to question another branch of so-called 'stress' therapy – the use of mood-altering drugs. My father was addicted to two pacific prescription drugs. The spectacle of his suffering was hard for me to sympathize with at the time because the side effects and withdrawal symptoms seemed to his family to turn him into a monster, someone my mother and I no longer recognized – violent, unpredictable, dangerous and cruel.

After the war he had taken various jobs and become a precision engineer in a noisy factory. He suffered from sleeplessness and was always worried about money, having to support a wife and asthmatic daughter (two years before the advent of free medical treatment). One day he came home from his GP with a small bottle of pills that would 'solve all his problems'. These were phenobarbitone (Phenobarbital in the US), a barbiturate normally prescribed for epilepsy, though my father was not epileptic and had never suffered from fits. Before the advent of benzodiazepines, 'phenobarb' was also prescribed as a sleeping drug and sedative.

My father was not warned of its possible adverse effects, which included (forgive the long list): drowsiness (he drove and operated machinery), lethargy, confusion, dysarthria (impaired speech due to disturbances of muscular control resulting from damage to the central or peripheral nervous system), nystagmus (rapid involuntary eyeball movements), oversedation, depression *or* excitation of the central nervous system, respiratory depression, skin rashes, blistering over pressure points, systemic lupus (disease resulting from changes in the auto-immune mechanism that produces antibodies to body tissue and inflammation causing kidney damage, arthritis, pericarditis and vasculitis), osteomalacia (softening of the bones with pain, tenderness and muscular weakness, anorexia and weight loss), folate deficiency anaemia (metabolic deficiency), polyneuropathy (disease of the peripheral nerves), impaired judgement, dizziness, hangover effect and 'paradoxical responses, including agitation and hyperactivity', nausea, vomiting, nervousness, headache, insomnia, nightmares, hallucinations and anxiety.

Dad became addicted very quickly. If he ran out of the drugs at night my mother had to rush off in a taxi to the all-night chemists at Piccadilly Circus to get an emergency prescription filled. We lived in Walthamstow, the taxi cost a lot, and my parents were poor. But my father was now in acute mental and physical pain; he became irrational and destructive; his rages were savage and the veins stood out of his temples like small snakes. The whole house would seem to explode in noise and violence. On one occasion my mother, who was very frightened, secretly emptied the capsules and replaced the contents with flour. The results were the opposite of what she had intended, and potentially catastrophic because my father was then in chemical withdrawal. Between onslaughts Dad would sometimes sit back in his chair, exhausted, pale, sweating, trembling and scared.

The police would periodically be called to protect myself and my mother, but after a five-minute talk would go away again, leaving us to our fate. This went on for months and years.

Presumably to try to bring these symptoms under control the doctor now prescribed physeptone (methadone), a narcotic, inducing deep sleep and dulling pain. If anything, this made matters worse. Adverse reactions include agitation, disorientation, headache, insomnia, cardiac arrest, nausea, vomiting, stomach cramps, respiratory arrest, dizziness, faintness, light-headedness, visual disturbances and physical and psychological dependence. Dad was now addicted to *both* drugs. The furniture would be smashed, crockery and meals thrown about, my mother attacked. A bread knife was held at my throat. Even the most trivial incidents could set off a spiral of rage. Yet my father was a good man, a kind, imaginative, grateful, hardworking man who loved us, who was a gifted artist, adored nature and animals and had the most generous spirit of anyone I have ever known. Sometimes I caught a glimpse of this person, between the chemical rages, trying to get back to us. He never succeeded. My father's addiction continued until the end of his life in 1979. Nobody helped him, or us.

It is therefore rather ironic that years later, in my early twenties, I too became one of the millions of patients prescribed tranquillizers – in my case benzodiazepines. I was young, fresh out of university, living with my parents and trying to make my living as a writer, when I started suffering from panic attacks. I had had these attacks before, during my degree finals, but this time they were so disabling that I almost could not make the ten-minute journey on foot to the doctor's surgery to ask for help. I was very scared. Panic attacks are not anxiety about any particular thing. They are a spiral of fear about everything. They are fear of fear. I had read Freud, who said that such anxiety could 'flood the ego'. I did not want my ego flooded.

I got my prescription, but despite the waves of terror, I felt that taking these drugs would somehow weaken me. I had no way of knowing at the time that panic attacks are extremely common. I thought that I was fighting for my sanity, and that this fight needed all my strength. So I chucked the pills in the rubbish bin and did what I later learned Laurence Olivier did with his crippling stage fright – 'wearing *it* – the terror – out, and it was in that determined spirit that I got on with the job'.[2] Olivier refused to take drugs, as a lot of his fellow actors did, because he felt they would interfere with his work.

I put up with my own panic for several weeks, during which time I continued to work, researching and writing feature articles. I shook with fear and slept very badly, worrying every night that next morning I might not be able to speak to people, or identify myself any more. Apart from my doctor, I told nobody. I tried to avoid thinking about the problem. I pretended to be normal. One evening, absolutely exhausted, I went to my room, lay down and folded my arms. I thought, 'Right, whatever it is, let's have it. Madness, death, whatever. I can't stand this any more, and I can't run from it any more. Let's just have it.' And I lay there as courageously as I could, waiting for my descent into hell.

Nothing happened. Instead, I suddenly felt *fantastically good*. I am not a religious person, but this was my first and only experience of the so-called 'peace that passeth all understanding'. I went downstairs and saw my drug-addicted father, whom I had come to fear and loathe, watching a film on television, *On the Waterfront*. I was overwhelmed with a sense of love and gratitude for my father, the house, the movie, the characters in the movie, the lamp on the television, everything. This euphoria lasted about an hour. It was without question the best feeling I have ever had. It taught me a lot and altered the course of my work and my research. And I have never suffered from panic attacks since.

So my youthful experience had left me profoundly suspicious of mind therapy and mind-altering drugs, and my professional work has led me to question the research upon which the stress industry is founded. Following the CERM review, I organized the highly publicized 1998 London conference *Stress – A Change of Direction* in order to ventilate the case against the 'stress' concept, and determined to investigate the stress management industry and write this book.

An analysis of stress management websites, sales literature and direct contact information on products and packages reveals a galaxy of strategies and techniques with widely differing effects and effectiveness. Unfortunately, my delvings into the methods of individual stress outfits were constrained by the fact that most leading stress management practitioners had heard of me and regarded me with extreme suspicion as an unbeliever or worse. Attempts to repackage myself as a fellow stress management purveyor were immediately spotted and shamed. Ron Scott, corporate services director of stress consultants, the Lancaster Group, told a national newspaper: 'In effect what Patmore and her clan are saying is the old Thatcherite thing that only the fittest will survive.' And what we have clearly failed to understand is that: 'The task is to make sure managers become better managers by leadership coaching, empowerment drives and that individuals can recognize the triggers in themselves and are able to cope with it through relaxation techniques. It won't get rid of it, but it will help.'[3]

As part of my CERM research, one conference I attended[4] featured a presentation by Carole Spiers of Carole Spiers Associates, one of the market leaders in corporate stress management. In her literature Ms Spiers told us: 'Since establishing the company in 1987, I have always taken pride in high standards of ethics, excellence and professionalism.' Her 'nationwide network of professional associates and consultants' offer 'counselling, redundancy support, mediation and specialist stress consultancy.'[5]

I happened to be taping the presentation so that I could accurately quote and acknowledge this leading stress management authority in my review, when delegates suddenly had so-called 'stress dots' stuck on their hands. We were told that these measured our stress, and to watch how they changed colour from black (very stressed) to dark blue (very relaxed). As they were black to begin with and therefore inherently stress-indicating, I put my hand up. 'I understand that these dots are actually just thermometers, and that similar devices have been used to measure the temperature of water in fish-tanks.' My inquiry drew a blank, but moments later my tape recorder was seized and my recordings (including some that had nothing to do with the conference) deleted 'in case I infringed copyright'.

Despite many problems with lack of regulation, the earning of fast bucks and unproven methods that are highlighted in later chapters, it would be unjust to give readers the idea that there are not many admirable and well-intentioned people out there practising what they call 'stress management'. They work within occupational health departments, or belong to small associations with their own codes of conduct. They can show you customer testimonies ('Thank you for helping me to turn my life around' etc.) and their groups seek to ensure (though their criteria may vary) that their members, at least, are of 'the right stuff'.

I do not doubt the sincerity of leading members of the stress industry. I simply dispute their faith in the concept of stress itself, and their resulting theories and practices. No doubt there are lots of perfectly decent stress management practitioners about who are doing their best with a bogus ideology. But during the course of my research looking at some of the hundreds of thousands of 'stress-busting' organizations, I felt that practitioners tended to fall into one of four general categories: Chariters, Cheesemakers, Chancers and Charlatans.

Chariters

These are the compassionate and caring therapists who combine common sense, natural wisdom and insight with effective strategies and techniques that may help at least some of their clients to cope with their life problems. Chariters are motivated by concern for people rather than theories or ideologies, and call themselves stress practitioners simply because their clients use the term. Some start out using it themselves, and gradually abandon it as unhelpful. Such sensible practitioners would be perfectly happy if the word were abolished overnight, and would be delighted to offer their skills without the intervention of a pointless and damaging mythology that turns their clients into mental hypochondriacs and delays or disables their recovery.

Cheesemakers

Wrongly supposed in Monty Python's *Life of Brian* to have been mentioned in the Sermon on the Mount, Cheesemakers are well-intentioned people who believe that the application of sufficient amounts of stress management will leave everybody happy and smiling. Impressed by theories, these practitioners believe uncritically in the research, accept the ideology as a dogma, and see relaxation of arousal as an article of faith. They are quite unaware of the problems and dangers of the mythology because they have never either studied its provenance or examined its scientific flaws. Cheesemakers shrug off anomalies and resist discussion on definition because such questions undermine their beliefs and threaten to crack their smiles. They respond to criticism of the stress industry with moral indignation, seeing it as an attack on their clients' suffering. Like other Pythonesque characters, Cheesemakers have a firm hold on the wrong end of the stick.

Chancers

This group of stress proponents view stress management as a harmless and possibly helpful panacea that fits with current thinking, that is highly commercial and that advertises itself. They tend to be pragmatic businesspeople who are not too bothered about the niceties of the ideology or the ethics of their strategies and statements, which they have collected in a portfolio of marketable tools. To them, relaxation-based stress management is the latest money-making racket to be unleashed upon a gullible public. They reason, 'Why not just give them what they want? And anyway, sitting in a herbal bath and listening to whale song is pleasant enough, so why worry?'

Charlatans

These are the practitioners who buy accreditation and certificates, set up their premises and websites, and then practise on other people's heads in full confidence that they know better than their miserable clients how to manage their lives. They have a preference for company business as this is more profitable, and they may have impressive organizations, premises and brochures and possess qualifications from other fields that give them a patina of authority. Some may secure academic niches that attract considerable funding. Others have simply boned up on those aspects of physiology and endocrinology that serve their cause. Their knowledge of stress science and its provenance is both little and dangerous. Their chief concern is to increase 'stress awareness' as this improves their market position, but they have no power to lay the stress spectre once they have raised it, and will often leave clients worse off than before, and disabled with worry about their health. There may be little that can be done to improve the humanity of such practitioners other than to rattle them out of business by government legislation.

Angela Patmore
Gosfield, Essex
March 2005

DEFINITION?

The meaning doesn't matter
If it's only idle chatter
Of a transcendental kind.

W. S. Gilbert, *Patience*

What does the term 'stress' actually mean? The UK's Health and Safety Executive (HSE) official website should surely be able to help us. So here we have the highest authority on health and safety in Britain on the subject:

Some academics have argued that stress is an almost meaningless term and does not exist. However numerous research reports have shown that whatever you choose to call it, there is a clear link between poor work organization and subsequent ill-health. As *stress* is the most popular and commonly used term to describe this experience, HSE has chosen to retain the use of this word and define it as 'the adverse reaction people have to excessive pressure or other types of demand placed on them'.[1]

This explanation must concern us. First, academics haven't argued that stress is an almost meaningless term. We have argued that, outside of engineering, it is an entirely meaningless term. Second, we have not argued that the term does not exist. Third, numerous studies cannot be said to show anything about something that we do not know the name of. Fourth, poor work organisation may be one of the definitions of 'stress', but if it is the HSE's definition, they should say so. Fifth, any link between poor work organisation and ill-health, whatever that link may be, is not an 'experience'. Sixth, 'stress' may be a commonly used word, and it may be used for all sorts of things, but this is not a good reason for the HSE using it. And finally, the HSE's 'chosen' definition is merely one among hundreds, and for validation would need to have its own separate scientific research, based exclusively on that definition. When I drew some of these anomalies to the attention of the HSE, their Head of Health Strategy, Management and Policy, Elizabeth Gyngell, replied in writing: 'We decided some time ago that it was unhelpful to argue with people who share your view that stress does not exist, or if it does, that it is healthy.'

The authoritative literature

We must therefore now turn, in our search for the true meaning of the word 'stress', to the vast body of scientific papers that have been written on the subject.

Satirist John Dryden once famously complimented some oafish poet of his day on his ability to 'torture one poor word ten thousand ways'. Definitions of the control term are very numerous: the Appendix at the end of the book gives some of the many 'authoritative' meanings the snowball concept has so far gathered. Many researchers, scientists and psychologists have expressed their bewilderment and anger at this lack of rigour. Organizational psychologist Dr Rob Briner of Birkbeck College, University of London is one of the UK's foremost opponents of the stress concept. Not only does Dr Briner himself see no validity in the s-word, but he cites fellow scientists and academics who have expressed concern about its meaninglessness. Even without knowing the context of such complaints, it will be apparent to the reader that there is cause for concern:

- 'The simple-minded invocation of the word stress in such thinking [about disease causation] has done as much to retard research in this area as did the concepts of the miasmas at the time of the discovery of micro-organisms.' J. Cassel (1976).[2]
- 'It is likely that abandoning the stress perspective will lead to a better set of priorities for our research.' S.V. Kasl (1987).[3]
- 'There exists a widespread inconsistency in defining stress, together with an inadequate concern for meaning.' L. Haward (1960).[4]
- 'I find it difficult to express my surprise and horror that contemporary science should tolerate this confusion between stimulus and response.' G. Pickering (1961).[5]
- 'Perhaps the single most remarkable historical fact concerning the term "stress" is the almost chaotic disagreement over its definition.' J. W. Mason (1975).[6]
- 'The term has become so vacuous that it represents an obstacle rather than an aid to research.' K. Pollock (1988).[7]

Nor are these by any means the only experts to have noticed the muddle over meaning. In an analysis of stress management for athletes, for instance, concerned sports psychologist B. Wilks comments: 'The definition of stress . . . is a problem in this area of research and there are numerous opinions.'[8] Bio-behavioural psychiatrist Professor Herbert Weiner observes: 'The concept is not rigorously defined: in fact, it is a fuzzy one. Furthermore, no agreed-upon classification of stressful experience exists. The term is applied loosely; at times, it is used so generally that its meaning is lost altogether.'[9] Anaesthetist Dr Edward Hamlyn commented: 'The whole concept of stress is pseudo-scientific nonsense created with the express purpose of hiding ignorance.'[10] Even Professor Cary Cooper, the *éminence grise* of stress management in the UK, admits: 'The term is an umbrella concept.'[11]

In stress research, then, we have a wonder of sorts: a scientific concept that is itself unscientific, in that it is capable of interpretation to fit the remit of any research project undertaken to investigate it. Often that remit is to 'prove' some aspect of the stress-disease hypothesis, or to show that stress has a negative effect, for example on performance. As another sports psychologist, L. Hardy, observes: 'Although stress can be perceived as either challenging or anxiety inducing, the psychological literature on stress and performance has focused almost exclusively on the effects of anxiety upon performance.'[12]

Much of the research may well therefore have begun with a 'bad stress' bias, and gone on to augment existing negative findings. Over time the concept has been gradually overlaid with unproven meanings, most of them pejorative. Such marshmallow definition should be of concern to all scientists, but should be of extreme concern to those in the UK, where no official monitoring system exists for discovering fraudulent research data, whether deliberate or accidental.[13] Why? A lack of rigour in defining 'stress' might serve the cause of funding organizations and vested interests who seek to prove that there is a condition called stress, that this condition is harmful, and that they may be able to do something about it.

Lay definitions

Some definitions of 'stress' one comes across are actually quite amusing. For example, a nurse at a residential care home, when asked for hers, pointed the author in the direction of 94-year-old Mary, trying furtively to get up the stairs unassisted. Said the care worker: '*There's* your stress! *There!*' Yet among all the hundreds of stress studies I have read, there is not a single one using the excellent definition 'Mary'. If pressed for a meaning myself, I will answer 'dis-ease' – anything uneasy or not easy; 'life' (which covers everything referred to in everybody else's definitions); or 'a bucket of fog' – the latter vouchsafed to me by a member of the Ministry of Defence Police.

The 'science'of stress has given rise to a belief system about what stress is, or might be, or might be caused by. The credo relies to a great extent on public ignorance. Most lay definitions will include an emotional component: they will have something to do with feelings, either as they are experienced or caused. The emotional component is also strongly reflected in media coverage of the subject. Popularly, stress is a mantra for people feeling bad. Unfortunately, since so much of the scientific research on stress has not concerned itself with human feelings at all, but rather with animals, disinterested experts on the subject should really be telling their audiences that these mountains of stress studies can tell them very little about their idea of 'stress'. A favourite (anonymous) meaning doing the e-mail rounds in Britain and the US is: 'that confusion created when one's mind overrides the body's basic desire to choke the living shit out of some asshole who desperately needs it'.

Pictorial definitions are a good guide as to popular taste. An aggressive pedigree cat with enormous ears and electric shock hair bears the caption: 'Stressed out my ASS! I am going to KILL the next son of a bitch who says I look STRESSED!' A galloping or leaping man with drops of perspiration flying off his head, an eyeballs-out, hectic expression, dangerous teeth and a weapon (often an axe) is also a market leader. These are what you might call the 'stress equals anger' motifs. Then there are the 'stress equals tension' motifs: stretching cats, sometimes hanging by their claws from the ceiling, images of fraying ropes, or office workers spread-eagled between furniture or buildings. 'Stress equals cracking up' images are always popular. A man's forehead fractured into crazy paving, or exploding like an over-ripe melon, images of frag-menting office workers, breaking pens and pencils against their desks or smashing their heads through concrete blocks are of this artistic school.

At the other end of the scale we have the 'blind-'em-with-science' technical description, beloved of the stress management industry, of which many impressive examples are given in the Appendix. Stephen Palmer, of the Centre for Stress Management in London, offers: 'Stress is the psychological, physiological and behavioural response by an individual when they [sic] perceive a lack of equilibrium between the demands placed upon them and their ability to meet those demands, which, over a period of time, leads to ill-health.'[14] A complex turn of phrase for a researcher who has discovered the need for clarity on the issue. Palmer's organization polled other people on their definitions without too much success in 2000, and found that: 'When it comes to asking them what they think stress is, or how they recognize it in themselves, they have far more difficulty dealing with this. So it's a very global concept that people have been applying to many situations, but when you actually ask them what it actually means to them, they're not so clear.'[15]

The *What* test?

Stephen Palmer, also of City University, London, was featured in a BBC television series in 2004 called *The Stress Test* as one of a pair of 'stress professors' (the other being Angela Clow of the University of Westminster) on hand to diagnose and cure a case of stress – without actually letting on what it was. The opener featured QPR football manager Ian Holloway, who to his credit eventually realized, perhaps with the help of a television programme devoted to his moods, that his foul-mouthed rages were harming his family. Holloway described himself as 'a spoilt brat' and the programme contained more f-words than a Tarantino movie.

Over the brief timespan covered by the show, the outbursts were moderated by anger management, t'ai chi, painting, and turning one room of the Holloway home into a recreation zone. Had the BBC flagged *The Stress Test* as an anger-management experiment, well and good. They did not. They presented it as something to do with a condition called 'stress'. The usual truisms were trotted out:

stress is harmful to health, stress causes depression; stress causes heart attacks and so on (despite his tantrums Holloway was found to be in fine fettle by a detailed medical examination). To introduce a smattering of science, stress levels were measured (the 'only way' apparently) by monitoring cortisole in saliva swabs during the subject's various activities. Holloway's stress/cortisole levels were high during his match-watching rages (football, as can be seen in a later chapter, is notoriously tension-arousing rather than tension-resolving). But the levels were also high after scoring and when his team was winning. They were *very* high after some stress management singing and shaking therapy, and highest of all during a match at the end of the programme *after* the stress professors' treatment regimen. Ergo, his rages had improved but his 'stress levels' definitely had not.

A former chairman of the International Stress Management Association says of its own attempts to define their term: 'Since its inception in 1974, the organization has had four names, making it sound rather like a con man with a pocketful of visiting cards suitable for any eventuality.'[16] Both the British and American outfits used to have 'Tension Control' in their titles. New chairperson Rosemary Anderson told me: 'I don't want to get bogged down in definition. It's a bit like "intelligence" – that's also difficult to define.' True, but people are not incapacitated by intelligence.

There are three explicable uses of the word 'stress'. One is in its original engineering context. The second, derived from this, is as a synonym for 'laid weight on' or 'emphasized'. And the third is as an adjective in the phrase 'the stress response to threat', which is another way of referring to the fight-or-flight mechanism. For all other uses, I would maintain, the word 'stress' is best avoided altogether. Users need to think of a more specific word for the feeling or problem they are trying to describe. Researchers need to make up their minds whether they are investigating a cause or an effect, a stimulus or a response, and their studies should be placed in context with others of the same genre and not, as at present, used to cross-fertilize research of a completely different kind. Ideally, of course, researchers should be expected to examine the stress paradigm with the same rigour that they apply to the rest of their work.

Stress sensations

This definition free-for-all has both amusing and very serious consequences. On the amusing side, we get the 'stress sensations' phenomenon. Scientific research is carried out; pronouncements are made on findings; press releases are dreamt up and sensational headlines hit the streets: 'Stress makes you fat!'[17] 'Stress in pregnancy makes babies naughty!'[18] 'Kids are fed junk food to cure them of stress!'[19] 'If you thrive on stress, you will get sick!'[20] 'Lawyers are the most stressed workers!'[21] 'Miners are the most stressed workers!'[22] 'Motherhood causes more stress than a job!'[23] 'Open plan offices cause stress!'[24] 'Stress affects men more than women!'[25] 'Stress affects women more than men!'[26] 'Stress has increased over the past few decades!'[27] 'Stress was worse during the Industrial Revolution!'[28]

Then there are the headlines relating to work-volume: 'Stress is caused by overwork.' 'Unemployed people get stressed because they have no work.' 'Stress is caused by boredom.' 'Stress is caused by the pace of life', and so on, *ad infinitum*. And not forgetting this one: 'Every day the UK loses the equivalent of over 1,000 years (a millennium) of labour due to sickness absence caused by stress.'[29]

Stress and heart disease

According to BBC Radio 4's documentary *Stressed Out*, broadcast in 2000, 'A person in Britain dies every three to four minutes from a heart attack, often directly related to stress.' There are three possible reactions to this. One is, 'What an unfortunate fellow.' The second is, 'How shocking: we must all beware.' And the third is, 'Where did these figures emanate from?'

The British Heart Foundation (BHF) was invited to send a speaker to our London conference, *Stress – A Change of Direction*, or to provide a statement of clarification on whether or not stress causes heart disease. There had been some confusion in the past. A webpage of the International Stress Management Association had posted an article stating: 'The British Heart Foundation estimates that 21 per cent of all sickness absence in the UK is due to stress-related heart-disease.'[30] The source cited was a 1994 paper by S. Cartwright and Professor Cary Cooper of UMIST. As Professor Cooper is one of the best-respected authorities on stress management in the UK, I queried the figures with the BHF, who said that they had not produced any such statistics. The BHF provided its own statement, requesting that it should not be reproduced piecemeal but in full, to avoid misunderstanding on a subject so crucial to public health:

Stress encompasses a very wide range of physiological, behavioural and subjective responses to unusually disagreeable stimuli. Stress may present as an acute response (e.g. an assault), may result from one event initiating others over a period (e.g. bereavement) or may be chronic (e.g. conflict between individuals, disability).

Symptoms of stress include irritability, changes in sleep and eating patterns, lack of concentration, and anxiety about trivial issues. The physical symptoms may include atypical chest pains, and rapid heart beats, and temporary rises in blood pressure.

There is little evidence to support that stress causes heart disease in healthy individuals. However, for people with existing heart disease, certain life events and conflicts at work can aggravate angina and in very rare circumstances precipitate a heart attack.

Certain reports indicate that certain emotions such as anger, hostility, depression and mental stress are associated with coronary heart disease but it is difficult to define whether one factor can reflect a significant association. Other studies have highlighted lack of control over work organization as most important.

Some people deal with stress by indulging in tobacco, excessive alcohol, and eating too many high-fat high-sugar snack foods – all risk factors for coronary heart disease. Employing ways to counteract stress both at work and at home is therefore of paramount importance.

A range of measures is then suggested, from physical activity and a balanced diet to workplace reorganization, counselling and 'relaxation sessions'.

There are certain problems with this statement. In the first paragraph 'stress' encompasses a range of responses to disagreeable stimuli; in the second paragraph it is still a response, but it has now become a disease, because it has 'symptoms', both mental and physical; in the third paragraph we get a clear statement that whatever it is, it does not cause heart disease in healthy people, but may be a danger to those with pre-existing heart disease. However in the fourth paragraph it suddenly becomes 'mental', and may be associated with heart disease. People 'deal with it' by indulging in certain dangerous behaviours, such as smoking, alcohol and overeating. Dealing with it, or counteracting it, is of 'paramount importance', even though it does not seem to cause heart disease in healthy individuals. So stress is now a stimulus, requiring a healthy rather than an unhealthy response.

I told the BHF representative, cardiac nurse adviser Belinda Linden, that the statement might be difficult for people to understand. The BHF withdrew from the conference, but I was later contacted with the good news that they were looking carefully at their statements on stress and heart disease. The new improved version is given below, in its entirety. But as the new position statement *still* doesn't explain what stress is, the reader must do as Sir Thomas More advised and 'construe according to his wits' (my own gloss is given in italics in brackets):

Stress

Recent figures suggest that people with work stress, depression, lack of support or an angry personality may be more at risk of developing coronary heart disease.

[Recent figures suggest that people who have a lot of work to do, or who experience bad feelings about work, or who suffer from depression or lack of support or an angry personality, may be more at risk of developing coronary heart disease.]

More research is needed to find out the effects of crises (e.g. bereavement, divorce, unemployment) and how psychosocial factors may influence the process of 'furring up' of the coronary arteries.

[More research is needed to find out how bereavement, divorce, life or people problems or having no work whatsoever may influence furring up of the coronary arteries.]

In patients who already have heart disease, stress at work or in the home can bring on angina or even, very exceptionally, a heart attack.

[In patients who already have heart disease, problems or demands at work or in the home, or the person's emotional reaction to these problems or demands, can bring on angina or even, very exceptionally, a heart attack.]

However, anxious, nervous individuals often experience chest pains, which do not come from the heart. Sometimes, this kind of pain is due to overbreathing ('hyperventilation'). Reassurance and the relief of stress will often relieve this type of pain.

[However, anxious, nervous individuals often experience chest pains which do not come from the heart and which are sometimes due to hyperventilation. Reassurance and the solving of problems or soothing of negative emotions about these problems will often relieve this type of pain.]

There remains a great deal that is still unclear about the different causes and triggers associated with coronary heart disease.
[We still don't really know what causes coronary heart disease.]

The implications of stressful day-to-day living may include a less healthy lifestyle, which could contribute to the risk factors for heart disease.
[When people have a busy lifestyle, they may adopt unhealthy habits, and these habits may cause heart disease.]
For instance, stress might prevent a good night's sleep or people suffering from stress may tend to take convenient but unhealthy snacks throughout the day, rather than taking the time to eat healthy balanced meals. They may smoke more as a coping strategy for their stressful lifestyle.
[For instance, worrying or puzzling over problems may prevent a good night's sleep, or people who are very busy may eat junk food at odd times instead of eating sensibly. Being very busy may also lead some people to smoke.]

A little stress, however, is actually good for us and helps us to perform efficiently and meet challenges. However, if the balance tips into the area whereby we fail to recognize what prolonged stress is actually doing to our bodies, it may lead to insomnia, headaches, breathlessness without exertion, nail-biting etc.
[A little stimulation is good for us, but if we keep being stimulated this is bad for us.]

Learning about ways to handle stressful situations could well help encourage improved lifestyle habits such as increasing physical activity, stopping smoking and eating more fruit and vegetables.
[Learning how to cope better may well improve our lifestyle habits.][31]

Interestingly, the new statement does not mention counselling or relaxation therapy. Should these be done? More particularly, should heart patients do them? I asked cardiologist Dr Alan Watkins, an opponent of stress misinformation. He said: 'There are two different types of relaxation. One involves a positive emotional state, such as contentment or peacefulness. Alternatively relaxation can be associated with a negative emotional state, such as feeling bored, detached or indifferent. The danger of advising people to practise relaxation is that they may imagine they are doing themselves good when they are in fact generating a negative, detached and indifferent state. This may positively damage their health. I advise heart patients of the dangers of negative relaxation.'[32]

One harmful side effect of misinformation on stress and heart disease, and on stress and hypertension, is that some patients are refusing to do the exercise programmes designed to aid their recovery. These programmes may involve physical effort and exertion. Patients who fear some generalized form of arousal called 'stress' worry that such exertion may be too much for them.

Other edicts

What do the General Medical Council (whose watchword is 'protecting patients, guiding doctors') have to say about defining 'stress'? Antony Townsend, director of Standards and Education wrote to me: 'I think that the question of the definition of stress, and the medical/scientific validity of it as a diagnosis, are not really matters for the GMC.'[33] BUPA, the health insurance giant, 'prefer to let patients define stress for themselves', according to deputy assistant medical director Dr David Costain.'[34]

The British Medical Association referred me to their policy document, *Stress and the Medical Profession*, published in 1992. Here we find one of the ever-popular box-arrow-flow diagrams showing 'the stress process', 'stressor', 'state of stress' etc. (taken from Professor Cary Cooper's 1988 publication, *Living With Stress*), followed by a brief discussion on the concept and its interpretations. The BMA concludes that we should regard stress 'as resulting from a misfit between individuals and their particular environment'[35].

Life events

One of the earliest efforts to popularize the stress concept and get it into every home was the notion of 'life events'. In the 1930s, the psychiatrist Adolf Meyer (1866–1950) developed the idea of 'life charts' as a means of understanding mental illness in his patients. Meyer was reacting against diagnostic labels, and reasoned that mental illness must be understood in terms of the patient himself, and what had happened to him.[36] He devised biographical charts in which patients were asked to record their losses, disappointments and the deaths of loved ones, so that the psychiatrist could assess how life's misfortunes had affected them.

In the 1950s, Harold Wolff took up where Meyer had left off. He theorized that 'life stress' (meaning here an internal state) was a result of the individual's attempts to adapt to the demands of life.[37] Depending upon his temperament and past experiences, the stressed individual then adopts what Wolff calls 'protective reactions' – rather similar to mucus flushing out irritants from the nose.[38] Meyer's life charts were now enlisted to map biographical events against episodes of sickness to look for any connections. Inevitably, some were found. The next step was to crystallize the theory into a rock-solid set of numbers and to present it as a marketable instrument. So in 1967, T. H. Holmes and R. H. Rahe published their Social Readjustment Rating Scale (SRRS)[39], a list of forty-three life events that had been found in Wolff's studies to relate to ill-health. But now each event was assigned a set 'weighting', which the researchers termed 'life change units' or LCUs (new technical terms always add a ring to psychological testing). The higher your LCUs, the more likely you were to suffer or expire.

The life-events scale is available on the internet, and still in use. As we are seeking to understand the meaning of 'stress', and as the BMA evidently set store by this particular method and consider it 'of value', we should have a look at it. It ranks 'death of spouse' at number one, with a value of 100 points. Second comes 'divorce', with 73 points, and third, 'marital separation' with 65. Anyone not married, therefore, avoids the top three and can presumably relax and ignore studies showing single status is 'stressful' and potentially injurious to health. A 'jail term' scores 63, the same as 'death of a close family member'. 'Personal injury or illness' scores 53, raising the upsetting prospect of illness being dangerous to health (hospital superbugs?). Avoid promotion as 'change to a different line of work' scores 36, and 'change in work responsibilities' scores 29. If you get a pay rise, so much the worse: 'change in financial state' ratchets up 38. That's a total of 103 already, higher than 'death of a spouse'. Try not to extend yourself either. 'Outstanding personal achievement' earns you a far from respectable 28. Down at the bottom we have Christmas, scoring only 12 despite the high suicide rate at that time of year, and minor legal violations (such as abuse of life-event testers) with 11.

More discerning psychologists warn against such simplistic attempts to quantify people's emotional engagements with life. Drs Derek Roger and Poppy Nash of the University of York comment: 'The basic idea behind the life-event scale is that events are inherently stressful: the more events we are experiencing, the more stress we are under, and the more likely it is that our finite coping resource will crack under the strain. Believing that life events are the root cause of stress is a convenient way of attributing blame for the way we feel to some external happening ... What life-event scales ignore is that people respond to events in different ways.'[40]

A legal definition

If the medical authorities do not define stress, or see anything wrong with the science or the ideology, we may be sure that nobody else will. The trade unions are baffled but bullish. The International Stress Management Association can't help. The HSE definition leaves us guessing. So what about the courts, and all those stress compensation claims? Cases predicated on the word 'stress' are surely by definition suspect, questionable and potentially bogus. Are solicitors who bring such cases not therefore guilty of malfeasance? I asked Law Society policy adviser Anna Rowland. 'Solicitors have an overriding obligation to act in the best interests of their clients. The fact that there is not agreed definition of stress in UK law is not a prohibition for solicitors and claimants on bringing cases for injuries which they believe to have been caused by stress.'[41]

The metal man fallacy

Our efforts to find an authoritative definition of 'stress', then, appear to have ended in abject failure. We have tried the scientists, the health authorities, the stress management authorities, the lawyers and the media. We have looked at serious meanings and humorous meanings and meanings with very little sense in them at all. In the last analysis this is not simply because 'stress' is too vague to be useful in analysing living things, but because it is actually not a biological concept at all, but a mechanistic one.

Despite concept founder Hans Selye's description of the body as a machine, people really are not passive lumps of metal to be worked upon by diverse forces, any more than they are rats. A mechanistic view leads to further questionable assumptions that have bedevilled stress science from its earliest investigative efforts, as we shall see. The body is homeostatic: it reverts to a resting state. We have a finite amount of adaptive energy and this runs down, like battery life. The vital force is exhausted according to predictable laws. People undergoing distressing experiences are not responsible or self-determining; they are simply machines to be minded or mended. They can only be exposed to a certain number of 'life-events' before they crack, or wear out. Their brains are like telephone exchanges, and their nerves are like wires that jangle and then break under strain.

Of course, had the word 'stress' been used with the same precision in physiology and psychology as it is in engineering, the fallacies inherent in such a concept transplant would have become apparent at the outset. In engineering, 'stress' is pressure or tension per unit area, which causes compression or elongation ('strain'). But direct stresses are not the same as shear stresses. Direct stresses can change the volume of the material and are resisted by the body's bulk modulus. Shear stresses tend to deform the material without changing its volume, and are resisted by the body's shear modulus. Were stress researchers required to replicate this extreme precision in their experiments, along with tensors, tractions, datum planes and mutually orthogonal components, they might well wish that they had left the stress concept to the engineers.

Part One THE DISEASE

CHAPTER ONE

STRESS PHOBIA

Definition of 'Stress':
'... A purely physical condition which exists within any material because of strain or deformation by external forces or by non-uniform thermal expansion, expressed quantitatively as units of force per unit area.'

National Library of Medicine

The purpose of this book is to release people from fear.

Since the beginning of the counselling boom of the 1980s, fear of *stress* has invaded people's lives. This phobia overrides class, gender, age, education and social status. It makes its victims wary of the pressures of work, resentful of those who impose demands upon them and frightened of day-to-day problems and threats that our tougher ancestors might have laughed at. Stress phobia sends its victims to therapists who promise to soothe their fears but who, on statistical evidence, fail to do so. Angst about 'stress' prevents sufferers from working, from resting, from sleeping, from relishing parenthood, sex or holidays, from trusting their brains or their bodies, from enjoying themselves or their relationships. Stress phobia undermines their confidence and unhinges their minds.

Of course, the victims do not believe they are suffering from stress phobia. The condition they believe they have fallen prey to is 'stress'. Sufferers may in fact be deeply wounded at the suggestion that their condition is not a verifiable medical ailment. Public confidence in 'stress' is unshakeable, because a powerful ideology has convinced people of its existence. So much so that all of their problems, emotions and physical sensations are now lumped together under the scientific-sounding term 'stress'. The problems, feelings and reactions are of course real. What is *not* real is the connecting condition. Stress is a mythical malaise, based on an intellectual construct. In fact, as we shall see, stress is what we might call a designer disease, the product of vast and sophisticated research.

Unfortunately, while stress itself may be mythical, stress phobia is very real indeed, and virulent. The mental suffering and disablement it causes are on a panoramic scale, and the epidemic has struck hardest in the workplace. For example, in 2002 the European Union's Employment and Social Affairs Commission estimated that work-related stress affected at least 40 million workers in its fifteen member states and that it cost the Union at least 20 billion Euro annually.[1] The Australian National Occupational Health and Safety Commission found that in one year 47 per cent of its workers who reported sick in the financial services industry and 44 per cent of workers in the education sector complained that they suffered from stress.[2] A survey carried out for the US National Institute for Occupational Safety and Health by Northwestern National Life found that 40 per cent of workers reported their job to be 'very or extremely' stressful.[3]

This malaise would be bad enough were it spread by rat fleas, or the result of poor hygiene or malnutrition. But stress phobia has not happened by accident. It has been engendered by an ideology, and by an industry that claims to be helping people to manage their stress. The stress management industry is full of caring practitioners and well-meaning researchers who firmly believe in the concept of stress, that binds together stimuli and responses in laboratory animals, and that can be extrapolated to explain human suffering and disease. Stress management practitioners and researchers believe that their concept is serving the interests of humanity, and have not understood the ludicrous flaws or the dark dangers in what they promulgate. The industry has quite unintentionally harmed and disabled millions of people by telling them that they must be vigilant and watch out for negative emotions and physiological signs of tension or fear in their bodies. Stress managers have told the public that these emotions and mechanisms are signs of stress and will endanger their lives.

The industry has poisoned whole populations, as though it had put something in the drinking water.

The stress industry, seeming to help, has unwittingly fed its clients alive to their own demons. The ideology has transformed ordinary individuals into hypochondriacs, afraid of their own feelings and reactions to reality, fearful that these pose some threat to their survival. Stress practitioners and their researchers and 'experts' have reduced normal people to a skittish flock of helpless, joyless, spineless, self-obsessed, emotionally incompetent neurotics. Sometimes the greatest harm is done by those who believe they are doing the most good.

Stress management?

The term 'stress management' describes a system of beliefs and practices centring on the so-called fight-or-flight or 'stress' response to threat. This biological mechanism is hugely important to survival both in humans and animals. Without it nature would simply abolish us all. The theory of stress management is based on the belief that this survival response, triggered too often or for too long, is in fact most dangerous to health; that this danger has been scientifically established; that people must be warned of the perils of this latent health hazard within their bodies, and that, so far as practicably possible, they should be protected from having such a dangerous mechanism set off by themselves or others. Confusingly, the word stress is used by its believers to mean not just the mechanism itself, but all of its triggers, effects and signs, and much more besides. It is therefore quite difficult to discover exactly what dangerous thing should be managed in the first place.

Stress management is particularly seductive because the paradigm seems to fit every case, to be a credible model of the way things work, and to be based on mountains of scientific evidence. Yet the concept was actually founded in the 1930s by Viennese Canadian endocrinologist Hans Selye, whose studies focused mainly on hormonal secretions in the rat. He pointed out that the only way to avoid this 'stress' was to die.

Engineering origins

The concept, as already mentioned, was initially borrowed from engineering. Apparently Selye wanted to transfer the engineering model of 'stress and strain' to the study of living things. Epidemiologist David Phillips, speaking on BBC radio in October 2000, explained: '*Stress* in engineering terms is the force that's applied to an object, and *strain* is the deformation that that object experiences. And Selye's idea was to apply this to mammalian systems where the stress was the external event, while strain was the way that the body responded. But because of his poor English he mixed up the words *stress* and *strain*.'[4]

Of course, Selye may have been thinking of grammar, rather than just engineering. The verb 'to stress' is used to mean emphasize, accent or add weight to, as in 'he *stressed* that he was never drunk'. The idea of living things somehow *having weight added to them* may have struck Selye as darkly symbolic of the human predicament, rather like the Inquisition detainee being pressed to death.

Paul J. Rosch, Clinical Professor of medicine and psychiatry at New York Medical College, helped Selye prepare the 1951 Annual Report on Stress in the United States. He later expressed concern at what he called 'the consternation and chaos' that the subject had unleashed since Selye's *magnum opus*, *Stress*, had appeared in 1950. According to Rosch, one bemused critic had pondered how 'stress, in addition to being itself, and the result of itself, is also the cause of itself.'[5]

As might have been foreseen at the time, applying an engineering concept to human emotions and physiological mechanisms would inevitably throw darkness on the study of mankind. Indeed, the whole stress industry – its evidence, its scientific research and the findings of that research – is predicated on a metaphor: that of a living thing compressed and deformed by physical forces. Poetic and plausible though this image may be, it is not literally true that living things are exactly like inanimate objects compressed and deformed by quantifiable forces, and the model therefore cannot logically be used as a basis for scientific investigation of living things. And yet that is exactly what has happened.

Some of Selye's fellow scientists have wondered why an intensively funded 'science' has sprung up around a term with hundreds of different definitions, and at how experimental research can possibly be conducted without a credible paradigm, without proper distinction being made between cause and effect or stimulus and response – as frequently and glaringly happens in the stress experimental literature.

Two responses confused

From the point of view of public health education, one of the greatest flaws in the stress research is that it fails to distinguish between arousal and resignation. Arousal, anxiety and agitation are clearly different from resignation, desolation and despair. Though the same person may indeed suffer from both sets of feelings at different times and in different circumstances, they lie at opposite ends of the emotional spectrum. Yet the research uses the same word, 'stress', for both emotional extremes. This has had the effect of confusing two very different responses.

The galvanizing fight-or-flight response is an arousing survival mechanism that also functions as a type of burglar alarm. It is designed to spur the threatened individual into action to face the perils of life and think up solutions to save himself or herself. The mechanism enhances focus and brain functioning and accesses physical resources. But in the stress research this important response has been confused with its biological opposite – resignation.

Resignation, or 'learned helplessness', to give it its scientific name,[6] is extremely useful to a prey animal about to be torn to pieces by a predator. This response floods the brain with opiate-like substances to deaden the fear and pain of impending slaughter. It also shuts off the immune system, which is no longer required. In situations where a horrifying death is not imminent, resignation is maladaptive, that is to say, it works *against* the possibility of survival and is known to lead to disease and death both in humans and animals.

Yet under the aegis of stress management, people are being told that these dangers to health are caused not by helpless resignation but by the galvanizing fight-or-flight response. Such misinformation is dangerous. Put simply, the effect is to make people fearful of a response (fight-or-flight) that can actually save them, and virtually unaware of one (learned helplessness) that can kill them.

The research controversy

There is compelling research evidence that casts doubt on the findings of the stress science, as we shall see. Indeed, the stress research and its provenance were analysed in a lengthy report which I produced in 1997 in collaboration with University of East Anglia's scientists at the Centre for Environmental and Risk Management, a World Health Organization collaborating centre. The scathing criticisms in that report and the many very serious and invalidating flaws exposed in the research evidence, have not been challenged either by scientists or by the industry, despite the fact that a 1998 conference on the findings, which provided a platform for opponents of the stress concept from the sciences and medicine, psychology, the emergency services and the arts, raised over sixty national newspaper, radio and television features. Few people in the field of stress research could have been unaware of the debate raging over their work, yet no member of the scientific community came forward to challenge our criticisms. In fact, quite the reverse. The report and conference acted as a catalyst for other critics, already on side, to express their concerns.

The most pervasive flaw we encountered in examining the research was a major definition failure – a complete disregard for the meaning of the control term 'stress', both within the individual experiments themselves and in the context of the related clinical literature, leading to confusion and blurring of the subject under investigation. This in turn had led to adaptation of the control term to suit whatever the research remit happened to be, and this was a serious indictment of its validity. This conceptual error marred most if not all of the stress experiments under review. In the hundreds of scientific studies analysed for the UEA/CERM report we found an enormous mass carefully balanced on a single unstable term. We found poor reasoning and missing middle terms as well as errors of assumption about sequence, consequence and relatedness in many of the papers we examined. For example, one of the chief tenets of all stress research is the so-called 'stress-disease' link.

The 'stress disease' link

On the basis that disease may often follow the fight-or-flight response, it is assumed that the disease was caused by that response. Yet this is an error in logic (*post hoc ergo prompter hoc*: it followed it, therefore it was caused by it). The harm to health may not have been the result of the fight-or-flight response at all. It might have been caused by some external circumstance that triggered the survival mechanism in the first place. It might have been caused by failure to utilize or act on the response, setting in train morbid changes associated with resignation and 'learned helplessness'. And there are several other plausible explanations. Yet the stress-disease link is considered proven by many if not most stress researchers, however tenuous the logic. Confusion of arousal and resignation, leading to the fight-or-flight mechanism being blamed for health harms that were more likely to be the result of helplessness, was a recurring flaw in much of the literature we analysed.

Multiple meanings of 'stress'

We also found that the control term 'stress' may be a *cause* one minute and an *effect* the next. Conflation of cause and effect occurred surprisingly frequently, even though these are self-evidently opposites. Stress may on the one hand be a stimulus, on the other a response. For example, if an electric shock is administered to the tail of a rat, stress may refer to the tail-shock itself, to the physiological reaction of the rat, and even to the rat's emotional experience. A person may be exposed to the stress of caring for an Alzheimer's sufferer, but at the same time may be said to suffer from stress as a reaction to this exposure.

This uncertainty of meaning is rife in the stress research literature. Sometimes stress is an interaction, sometimes a transaction. For some purposes it is a verb, for others a noun; and stress may be all or any of these things within one 'scientific' paper. It may be an irksome thing in the environment, such as an enormous pile of work on one's desk, or an office bully, or having one's lawnmower stolen. But at the same time seeing the pile of work, being upset by the bully or discovering the theft may be said to stress one (or more colloquially, stress one out).

There were poor methodologies, inadequate control groups and small samples. There was a general dearth of follow-up studies, and what is known as the 'file drawer' effect – the tendency for insignificant or undesired findings to be filed away as non-typical or irrelevant, distorting overall statistics. There were interpretative difficulties, with conclusions being drawn on the basis of bias or surmise about a presumed condition called 'stress'. Reliance on cross-sectional data and self-report data, normally considered scientifically unreliable, were widely accepted: human stress studies leaned heavily on information elicited from questionnaires asking about feelings and sensations, with replies being suggested or subjective.

Then there were the problems of false extrapolation (e.g. from animal biology and from engineering to human biology), with a heavy reliance on animal models to represent people in quite dissimilar circumstances. Bias contamination and so-called 'political exaggeration' influenced the findings and conclusions of the research, so that outcomes might be predicated on research funding priorities or ideological beliefs rather than objective findings. Results might be further skewed by a whole panoply of technical errors, like predictor and outcome measures being obtained concurrently, insufficient attention paid to baseline measures, and failure to control for a placebo effect or regression to the mean, leading to false conclusions.

But by far the most serious problem with the stress research was the overall lack of definition. Such opacity of meaning undermines normal scientific protocols and in no other field of scientific endeavour would such astonishing lack of rigour be tolerated.

Overwork

Nevertheless, despite this very glaring confusion in the authoritative research and literature, many non-medical, non-academic people will insist that they know the meaning of the term, and that it has something to do with being overworked, hurried and worried.

Overwork is in itself a very serious problem. Certainly, there are studies that show overwork causes stress. Unfortunately there are also studies showing that *under*work causes stress, and that un-employment causes stress. We must ask ourselves, in instances where people are genuinely exploited and overworked – as for example, Japanese employees literally dying of exhaustion (*karoshi*) – whether their cause is best served by a concept that is notoriously imprecise, that sets people worrying about their minds and bodies and that turns a great industrial collective cause – that of fighting exploitation – into an individualized pseudo-medical one – that of shepherding through the courts lone employees reputedly injured by workplace stress.

On the evidence of occupational stress data, workers in Britain and America apparently *believe* they are working harder than ever before and that they are likely to die of exhaustion, whether they are or not, because stress 'experts' tell them so. Yet industrial historians argue that previous generations worked far longer hours in far more difficult and dangerous conditions and with far less protection from autocratic management. Until the 1940s, social welfare policy in Britain was governed by the Poor Laws. The National Trust have pre-served for posterity Thurgarton Hundred workhouse in Southall, Nottinghamshire, as a model of its type, one of approximately 600 set up in the UK under the 1834 Poor Law. The whole building was a machine for keeping people segregated and forcing families into thankless labour as punishment for their joblessness.

The visionary William Blake railed against a culture of cruelty that exploited working people in what he called 'dark Satanic mills' and that turned young children into textile workers and chimney sweeps. Daniel Defoe and Charles Dickens described the ignominy of debtors' prisons and the grinding poverty of whole communities starving and desperate for even the meanest and most arduous of jobs. Yet modern stress experts speak confidently about today's employees being more harassed than any previous generation as a result of competitive downsizing, and the so-called 2:3:2 formula: half the people doing three times the work for twice the pay, compared with some earlier period (typically, the 1980s). Employees who complain about workplace stress evidently believe all this. They also appear to believe that work is more worrying and intensive and exhausting now, and that this is an unforeseen consequence of modern technology designed to ease their plight.

Antique mental ailments

It is worth remembering that mental disorders of previous centuries, such as 'nervous debility' and 'brain fag', were also blamed on the pace of life. Fashionable in the early 1900s, these syndromes gave rise to popular remedies known as 'nerve tonics' that contained alcohol, quinine, phosphoric acid and even tiny quantities of sulphuric acid. 'Neurasthenia', a condition coined by New York neurologist Charles Beard in 1869, was thought to be a disease of civilization brought about by modern technologies such as steam power, the periodic press and the telegraph. The 'neurasthenic' appeared depressed and inert, and had identity crises. Treatment involved retreat from the hurly-burly, rest, milk diets, sea air and the application of 'revitalizing' electricity.

The growth of these fashionable nervous disorders mysteriously coincided with the emergence in the 1860s of neurology as a medical speciality in the diagnosis and treatment of nervous illness. One mental malaise of earlier origin that particularly captured the public imagination was 'nerves'. The 'nerves' epidemic of the nineteenth and early twentieth centuries was as usual blamed on the pace of life, long working hours and the new technology. Even as late as the 1950s, as we shall see, international bestsellers were being produced on how to cope with the condition. Jane Austen satirizes it in 1813 in *Pride and Prejudice* in the comic character of Mrs Bennet, whose martyrdom to her 'nerves' constantly prompts her to panic or pass out. She describes her suffering as follows: 'I am frightened out of my wits; and have such tremblings, such flutterings, all over me, such spasms in my side, and pains in my head, and such beatings at heart, that I can get no rest by night nor by day.'[7]

In his fine study of psychiatrists and soldiering, *War of Nerves*,[8] Ben Shephard gives an absorbing potted history of antique psychological complaints which he traces through popular journalism. *The Spectator* in 1894 observed that 'the nerves of modern men were often put to a heavier strain than nature intended them to bear', explaining that 'competitive examinations, luxurious indulgences, railway journeys and the daily press' compelled people to live fast rather than long, and that men were even giving up hunting or polo-playing on account of 'lost nerve'. *The Spectator* hinted darkly that overindulgent doctors might have undermined the public constitution.

Meanwhile in 1895, Sir Clifford Allbutt, a prominent medic, wrote in the *Contemporary Review*[9] that in the 1890s 'both sexes began to chant "nerves" together, to compare symptoms, to speculate together on physiological problems and to worry out their cures hand in hand'. Sir Clifford thought that people were mentally less robust than before, that they were 'set to learn of their physicians' and that this may have influenced their morbid preoccupation with mental health. The pace of life might have had somewhat less to do with it.

Oddly, the pace of modern life, technology and working very hard do not appear to trigger such nervous disorders in everybody. Today, two of the hardest working communities in the UK are Asian shopkeepers and the self-employed. Neither of these groups are known to absent themselves from work because of stress. Asian shops are open all hours, and their workers are tirelessly polite and cheerful. And those of us who are self-employed could well be accused of driving ourselves into an early grave. (We might even seek compensation from ourselves under the Health and Safety Executive's workplace regulations!)

Stress managers counter this with another argument. Stress is a result of overwork and the pace of life and the new technology and a *lack of control*. According to this reasoning, bosses, and those who choose to work long hours, don't suffer from stress because they can ease up whenever they like. Except that any boss or self-employed person who thought this way would very swiftly find themselves out of work.

A 'church' of stress

Every ideology spawns an industry. Stress management has spawned an industry that functions rather like a church, and this is part of the problem that critics face in trying to defeat it by reason alone. The stress industry is not just a commercial congress, albeit a very lucrative one. It has a pastoral role, doctrines, confessionals, and high moral ground. It has committed followers bent on protecting and helping, who set themselves up as guardians of public health. Unfortunately their beliefs and practices, disseminated through every outlet of the media, mislead ordinary people into parting with money in order to be saved or cured by devices, techniques, products and services.

The stress 'church' frightens people into thinking that they are suffering from a deadly disease that it cannot or will not accurately define. It places no limits on this chilling threat to health, backing up its claims with laboratory research costing billions, research that because of its imprecision and its funding may be unscientific, misleading, biased, bogus or even fraudulent. To be fair, the stress industry claims to be able to manage stress rather than cure it. A cure would rob the church of its benefice, and besides, founding father Hans Selye admitted that the only real 'cure' was to die.

In the world of commerce, dedicated members invite themselves into businesses large and small, with scare stories of stress litigation and vast claims for damages, and sell expensive services and techniques which they claim can alleviate stress in the workplace. A survey in 2000 of 136 UK companies by Hay Management Consultants found that stress counselling in British businesses had trebled since 1991.[10] Yet the more this church-like industry plies its trade, the worse the occupational stress problem becomes, and the more employees claim to be collapsing from stress at work.

Stress sceptics

Because the stress management industry resembles a church, its critics are sometimes referred to in the media as 'stress heretics', although we would deny that we are trying to reform stress management, or to replace one faith with another. True, some of us are suggesting a reversion to more traditional emotional education, based on time-honoured practices that served our ancestors well. But the scientists among us are simply calling for the review of a bogus concept and for restoration of normal scientific protocols, while other professionals are merely asking for more healthy scepticism, more logic and more common sense. Nevertheless, 'It seems like denying the roundness of the world, denying that stress exists, or that it is harmful,' explained the *Daily Telegraph* on the eve of our London anti-stress management conference in 1998.[11] 'But that is exactly what a new breed of stress heretics is saying about the modern world's most ubiquitous affliction. To the gentle world of therapy, it has come as Luther's 95 theses did to the primacy of Rome 480 years ago.'

Being a stress sceptic may not be quite that dramatic, but it has its moments. Organizational psychologist Dr Rob Briner of Birkbeck College, University of London, has been approached in the toilets at conferences and told to stop criticizing the stress concept because he might be damaging the livelihood of fellow psychologists. Novelist Fay Weldon, another formidable sceptic, has been criticized for attacking stress counsellors. But she believes that they nanny their clients and represent negative emotions as a disease when they are important to our survival and creativity. She deplores the harm to our love lives, our children, our brains.

Ruth Lea, former head of the policy unit at the Institute of Directors and now director of the Centre for Policy Studies, says the stress 'church' is 'one of Britain's greatest growth industries' and that it is undermining people's ability to cope in the workplace and degrading their characters. Lord Brian Mackenzie of Framwellgate, a former president of the Police Superintendents' Association, accuses the stress church of demoralizing the police force and making officers afraid to do their jobs.

Oscar-winning actress Dame Judi Dench wrote to me expressing her strong objections to the word 'stress' and allowed these views to be read out at our conference. Her comments were freely interpreted by the press to mean: 'Dame Judi, alias Elizabeth I, accuses Britain of turning into a nation of wimps.' There are indeed royal stress sceptics. Both the Princess Royal and Prince Philip have weighed in against stress counselling. The Duke of Edinburgh put forward the unfashionable view, during the VE Celebrations, that in his day people did not skedaddle to counsellors every time a gun went off.

There are prominent sceptics in the medical profession, too. Dr John Cooper, head of occupational health at Unilever, speaks eloquently of the harm of the stress ideology medicalizing the problems of people at work. Dr Carole Astbury, head of occupational health at Essex County Council, says putting 'stress' on a prescription pad should be made illegal because it damages patients. Cardiologist Dr Alan Watkins warns heart patients that relaxation has a negative side and that passivity can be debilitating and even dangerous. GP Dr Michael Fitzpatrick accuses the stress industry of creating incapacity and sending droves of people to their doctors with morbid fears about their health. Dr Michael O'Donnell, medical director of UnumProvident, warns that we are creating a climate of bogus health fears in which 'stress' is becoming a real entity.

As we shall see, many of the critics of the stress management faith are concerned that it seeks to pacify and tranquillize on a grand scale. One of the most important doctrines of the stress ideology is relaxation. If the fight-or-flight mechanism is bad, then arousal of any kind might be bad, and if arousal is bad, then relaxation must be good. Thus, Orwellian messages are piped out to embalm public emotion: calm down, chill out, de-stress, have a relaxing bath, a relaxing pill, a relaxing holiday, a relaxing car (the Omega from Vauxhall, 'a positive aid to relaxation', or the Citroen C5, 'engineered to relieve stress').

Coupled with the stress industry's teaching on the dangers of stress in the workplace, this soothing patter is seductive. Millions of people willingly submit to its messages, its massages, its manipulations, its snake oils. The stress industry lures the flock into thinking that they should really not have to work or worry at all, and that those who expect them to do either are dangerous autocrats, living in denial of this great public affliction. Best to rest: the new opium of the masses.

CHAPTER TWO

SPREADING THE INFECTION

A man who fears suffering is already suffering from what he fears.

  Michel de Montaigne, *Essays*, III, xiii

So what if we do have a stress industry? Why worry? On the face of it, stress management appears to offer the public a benign and protective panacea for life's unpleasant experiences. Unfortunately, appearances can be deceptive. For a start, the industry has signally failed to arrest spiralling stress statistics. The International Stress Management Association itself estimates that 'somewhere between 50 and 70 per cent' of workers now suffer from stress, despite the valiant efforts of many thousands of stress management personnel in the workplace. At best, one could argue, the ideology offers a prophylaxis that is failing to cure.

At its very worst, it can kill. Kava-kava, a herbal remedy still widely available on the internet and which, according to the website of producers Dashwood Direct of Fiji in October 2004, is 'medically proven to relieve stress', was recently withdrawn from the market after the Medicines Control Agency were alerted to sixty-eight cases of liver disease, several of them fatal, associated with the plant extract. As long ago as 1980 the BMA issued a warning on relaxing fringe medicine gadgets after a fifty-year-old oil executive using an electronic alpha wave relaxation device suddenly went berserk at the sound of his carpet being vacuumed and murdered his house-keeper. Benzodiazepines, regularly prescribed as so-called 'minor' tranquillizers, are implicated in road traffic accidents. These drugs are regularly given to elderly patients to calm them down and prevent insomnia, despite research evidence that they may increase confusion and falls.

Critics of the ideology would argue that such falls and fatalities are merely the tip of the stress management iceberg, and that it is the unseen bulk that will sink us all. They say the real harm of stress management lies not in individual casualties of this or that remedy but in the fact that the ideology presents perfectly normal emotions, normal arousal and normal physiological mechanisms as harmful and dangerous. It encourages people to medicalize their problems and their feelings. It tells them to diagnose stress in themselves and offers gizmos such as 'stress monitoring devices' (thermometers) and 'inventories' (self-assessment questionnaires) to help their 'diagnosis'.

Whereas previous generations faced their privations with courage and character-training designed to expose them to hardship and make them tough, post-Second World War man peeks out at life's troubles through a membrane of anxiety. Stress phobia has inspired worry over physiological mechanisms and their so-called risks to health, and about negative emotions and their so-called dangers to sanity. Phobia sufferers believe that whenever problems and pressures loom, they are about to experience a complete mental and physical melt-down. Their frantic search for relaxation, the new elixir of life, is as misguided as it is futile.

Spreading 'stress awareness'

Fear of the stress condition is disseminated by a process known as 'stress awareness': that is, by means of alarming information on the supposed links between stress and disease, and on signs and symptoms that must be 'looked out for'. For example, we are told by the Health and Safety Executive,[1] and by leading stress management gurus Professor Cary Cooper and Stephen Palmer,[2] that stress causes hypertension. Not according to the British Hypertension Society (BHS).

The BHS has stated quite clearly in its patient literature that: 'Stress is not a cause of high blood pressure although many people believe this', and that 'Contrary to popular opinion, high blood pressure is not a disease of the nervous or highly strung, nor is it caused by a stressful lifestyle.'[3] In the US, a nationwide research project set up to investigate the effects of stress management on hypertension found little evidence of benefit.[4] More recently a National Blood Pressure Survey included a question about what people believed caused high blood pressure. Respondents were asked to choose from seven options, one of which was stress. Almost two thirds incorrectly identified stress as a cause of high blood pressure.[5] The real causes are lack of exercise, too much salt, excessive alcohol intake and a family history of the condition. However, separate research has shown a link between stress *reporting* and increased risk of fatality after a stroke,[6] which would appear to indicate that fear and anxiety about the condition has a negative effect on health.

Indeed, efforts to make people 'stress aware', far from promoting public health, are evidently causing widespread hypochondria. Hypochondria focusing on physical symptoms is bad enough, but the medical profession is at least technically equipped to cope with this. A man can be shown that his heart is sound, or that his blood pressure is normal. Hypochondria focusing on psychological symptoms is altogether more disturbing. It causes anxiety that can seem limitless, and that the medical profession cannot easily assuage. In the words of Milton's Satan, it places its victim in Hell: 'Which way I fly is Hell, myself am Hell/And in the lowest deep a lower deep/Still threatening to devour me opens wide.'

Hyper-vigilance

The natural consequence of alerting people to risks posed by their own emotions and bodily mechanisms is that they become hyper-vigilant. They may be frightened, not only of real dangers but of imagined ones, and statistically very unlikely ones. They may even become phobic about life itself, which has always been a risky business. Let us look at the possible consequences of this hyper-vigilance.

Each year in the relatively safe UK, twenty people are electrocuted by a bedside light or alarm clock. Another twenty die getting out of bed. Sixty are seriously injured putting on their socks. Six hundred, almost two a day, die from falling down the stairs in their homes. In 1999, 96,000 people attended Accident & Emergency after an accident while sleeping, relaxing, sitting or lying down. Another 69,000 came a cropper in the garden. Every year home accidents account for approximately 4,000 deaths and nearly 3 million injuries needing hospital treatment. In the year 2000 the probability of death from a home accident was rated at 1 in 13,000, compared with 1 in 100,000 from murder.

Even so, life presents far less risks now than it did to our ancestors. For every person murdered in the UK today, ten were murdered in the Middle Ages. In the last 200 years the murder rate has in fact halved. For every death from infectious disease today there were 150 deaths then.

Twenty years ago, most children walked to school, or cycled. Today parents drive them to the school gates. The risk of a child being snatched by a stranger is extremely small and has remained fairly constant over the past few decades. Ninety-nine per cent of abductors are estranged parents or guardians. But driving children to school increases both pollution and volume of traffic, and places youngsters in the line of fire of a regular killer. In the UK alone over a hundred children die each year under the wheels of a car.

The Labour government think tank Demos and the Green Alliance published a report in May 2004 that concluded youngsters are less likely than ever before to 'risk' playing outside, and that their development was being stunted by this obsession with safety. Some children in the study had never seen fields, or a beach. Most preferred to stay at home because of the dangers of terrorism, paedophiles, strangers, traffic, bullying, noise, vandalism, dog mess, litter, getting lost and 'travelling on trains'. Taking this to extremes, in 2002 the parents of eleven-year-old Danielle Duval from Reading in Berkshire, had their daughter fitted with a microchip in case of abduction.

The spread of 'stress awareness' may be one of the factors implicated in the general growth of what scientists call 'risk phobia' in Britain and America – where 'zero risk' is a social goal and some screwdrivers are now sold with the warning, 'Do not insert in the ear'. The 2003 international Panic Attack conference at the Royal Institution in London explored this strange phenomenon. Scientists from many disciplines assembled to discuss why modern man – far richer, healthier, longer-lived and safer than any of his predecessors – worries constantly about statistically tiny threats posed to his well-being by eating, drinking, working and breathing. None of the eminent scientists could figure it out.

But there is a simple explanation. If one's head has been inflamed by a lot of morbid information about one's feelings and physiological mechanisms, it is very hard *not* to cower from a world where one is made to feel uncomfortable, unhappy and unstable. 'Stress awareness' may be causing the biological fight-or-flight mechanism to malfunction on a grand scale. In today's risk-averse culture, well-publicized dangers stalk the public on every side, and victims of stress phobia tremble in the face of all of them and feel they cannot cope. Perhaps they have lost the ability to reason, to gauge the magnitude of risks, or to respond to them appropriately or at all. Perhaps they only know that they are afraid.

'Gaslighting'

One of the cruellest things that one human being can do to another is to convince that person that he or she is going mad. To rob somebody of their sanity is to plunge them into a terrifying darkness where thought itself becomes a thing to be feared. This obscene form of persecution was the subject of the 1944 film *Gaslight*, directed by George Cukor and starring Charles Boyer and Ingrid Bergman. In the movie, Boyer plays a crook, Gregory Anton, who unhinges his wife's mind by tricks and accusations and by creeping about in an adjoining building and turning the gas jets up and down in their Victorian house to make her think the place is haunted. The film popularized the expression 'gaslighting' in the post-war vernacular.

There is something disturbing about suggesting that people are sick when they are not, or mad when they are simply unhappy. Marilyn Monroe, for example, had an abiding fear of madness. She was one of America's first celebrity patients of psychoanalysis – the new therapy popularized in the United States by Sigmund Freud's daughter Anna and his nephew Edward Bernays, who devised psychological testing systems both for large corporations and the CIA. After Marilyn's unsuccessful treatment and untimely death, her husband, the playwright Arthur Miller, rounded on what he saw as the disabling effects of therapism.

Miller felt that people in America were being 'gaslighted' by the very industry that claimed to be healing them: 'My argument with so much psychoanalysis is the preconception that suffering is a mistake, or a sign of weakness, or a sign even of illness, when in fact possibly the greatest truths we know have come of people's suffering. That the problem is not to undo suffering, or to wipe it off the face of the earth, but to make it inform our lives – instead of trying to cure ourselves of it constantly and avoiding it, and avoiding anything but that lobotomized sense of what they call "happiness".' [7]

The fact that stress is in the eye of the beholder augments stress phobia. Stress awareness and stress fear percolate down through all the research findings. Culture and cognition are indivisible. One recent study on work stress in America found that 'six primary American values and beliefs' actually 'biased' work stress research and urged professionals to be aware of 'cultural underpinnings'.[8] One such 'underpinning' is what we might call competitive stress, whereby individuals or groups are stress-rated and achieve 'hazard alert' status. There are even rankings for America's most stressful cities – Tacoma, Washington, Galveston, Texas, and Yuba City, California, came out on top.[9] Small comfort to inhabitants to know that their stress is not work-related. 'Most of the top-ten stress cities are grappling with high unemployment,' say Sperling's BestPlaces, who rated them. 'Today's Americans are faced with more stress than ever.'

In the UK, gaslighting is practised on a daily basis in the name of stress awareness. *Stop, Go Home* (a Channel 4 series on the dangers of workplace stress) may well have caused alarm and despondency with a depressing documentary called *The Day I Snapped* on work-place casualties. 'One person dies in the UK every three to four minutes as a result of stress,' pronounced BBC Radio 4 in its 2000 series *Patient Progress*. 'Stress triggers 89 per cent of all chronic illness,' warned the *Daily Mail* in a 2002 'Good Health' guide. 'People are beginning to crack and crumble!' suggested BBC Radio Northants in a programme entitled *Stress in the Workplace*. 'Stress takes 2.8 years off a healthy thirty-something woman's life,' announced BBC TV's evening news bulletin in June 2003. 'Stress at work is a modern epidemic,' stated a doom-laden voiceover in Channel 4's *Stop, Go Home* programme *Stressed Out*. 'Anyone can fall victim to this hidden plague. First comes psychological damage, then serious illness, and if you ignore the warning signs – death!'

Famously fit Prime Minister Tony Blair was rushed to hospital in 2003 with chest pains. His condition was reportedly diagnosed as atrial fibrillation, an abnormal heart rhythm that can be brought on by anything from overwork to drinking too much coffee. *Channel 4 News* on 20 October 2003 featured heart specialist Dr Wynn Davies of St Mary's Hospital, London, explaining that stress 'did not play a part' in this condition. Two months later Mr Blair received a Christmas present from his wife: a top-of-the-range £2,900 leather-bound Keyton Concept 'stressbuster chair' to ease away all the premier's problems. A friend told the press: 'Cherie hopes the chair will help Tony cope with the stress of his job.'[10]

A link between stress and heart attacks is prevalent in public consciousness. Consultant psychologist Dr Chris Gillespie, a member of the Trent Division of Clinical Psychology of the British Psychological Society, contributing to a Radio Northants programme on workplace stress, said that patients are now presenting with mysterious symptoms: 'Some get palpitations and chest pains, and quite a significant number turn up at their GPs and ask for a check-up in case their hearts are going ... It's quite common here for people to report chest pain which has no organic basis at all.' They are told there is nothing physically wrong, but this doesn't allay their fears. In fact, they seem to get worse, says Dr Gillespie: 'Then people start worrying that they're going mad.'

Gaslighting is not just a threat to their psychological health. It can cause harmful changes in the physiology of those subjected to it. There has long been recognized in medicine what is known as a placebo effect. If a patient is given sugar pills but believes them to be a powerful drug to aid recovery, the sugar pills will indeed often aid that patient's recovery. Unfortunately the reverse is also true. Some years ago the power of suggestion was the subject of a paper in the *Journal of the American Medical Association*, which investigated what has become known as the 'nocebo effect'. This refers to the patient's negative beliefs about his condition undermining his ability to deal with his illness. The investigation concluded: 'Poor outcomes result because patients believe the outcome will be negative.'[11]

Some therapists believe it is important actively to teach patients not to be body-phobic. Cognitive therapist Paul McLaren, while practising at UMDS Guy's Hospital and the Ladywell Unit of Lewisham Hospital, taught patients to overcome anxiety and panic attacks. The first step in this therapy was for patients to stop fearing their own bodily responses. For example, if they couldn't breathe, they were told to blow into a paper bag. By practising such simple techniques, Paul McLaren's patients learned how to override their fixation with their own physiological functioning and get better.

National nervous breakdown

Before the stress concept came along, as we have seen, worry about the body's responses was covered by the generic term 'nerves', and psychologist Dr Rob Briner has pointed out that in many ways the nerves concept was the forerunner of the stress concept. In post-war Britain millions of people worried about signs of nervousness in their own bodies. Among the medical gurus to help victims in their distress was world-renowned Sydney doctor and broadcaster Hazel Claire Weekes, MBE, who in 1962 produced her international bestseller, *Self-Help for Your Nerves*.

Dr Weekes, a kindly but pragmatic Australian, explained that 'nerves' and 'nervous breakdown' often occur when people start to fear their own normal bodily responses. In the section on anxiety neurosis, she writes: 'Many healthy people are precipitated into this type of nervous breakdown by the fear induced by some sudden, alarming, yet harmless bodily sensation.'[12] Sufferers from stress may well recognize the symptoms described in 1962: 'Sensitized involuntary nerves, sleeplessness, depression, fatigue, churning stomach, indigestion, racing heart, banging heart, shaking heart, palpitations, "missed" heartbeats, a sharp, knife-like pain under the heart, a sore feeling around the heart, sweating hands, "pins and needles" in the hands and feet, a choking feeling in the throat, an inability to take a deep breath, a tight feeling across the chest, "ants" or "worms" crawling under the skin, a tight band of pain around the head, giddiness, and strange tricks of vision such as the apparent movement of inanimate objects. Nausea, vomiting, occasional diarrhoea, and frequent desire to pass urine may be added to the picture.'

The way to defeat this spiral of fear, according to the eminently sensible Dr Weekes, was to take note of the heart palpitating, the churning stomach, the sweating hands, the trembling turns, the 'missed' heartbeats, but to accept them for what they were and then let them go. Not to fear them or worry about them. Observation and letting go would reverse the spiral of panic.

But if, as Dr Weekes and other therapists suggest, not focusing on the physiological signs of nervousness reduces fear and panic and enables nervous people to get better, what might we suppose would be the effect of the opposite? How would these same people react to being told to focus on their bodily responses, or to being given constant warnings about the dangers of such physiological mechanisms? Would not such anxiety, constantly reinforced over time by respected health authorities and broadcast to sufficiently large numbers of people, bring about a sort of national nervous breakdown?

Triggering fear

Unfortunately the biological fight-or-flight mechanism itself can be triggered repeatedly, simply by constantly worrying about it. Psychologist Derek Roger, director of the Work Skills Centre and Senior Lecturer in Psychology at the University of York, speaking on a 2002 BBC Radio programme: 'If you shock a cat and it jumps up, it exhibits fight-or-flight but then it recognizes you and becomes calm ... Whereas humans go on and on and on and on thinking about [the experience]. Every time you do so, you provoke this response in the body, so if you invite somebody to think about things that upset them, their blood pressure and heart rate go up immediately. Unlike the cat.'[13]

Derek Roger defines stress as 'preoccupation with emotional upsets' – very much in line with the hypothesis of this book that stress sufferers are actually victims of stress phobia. 'Being exposed to an event there is physical arousal, and the heart races . . . and that's a consequence of an increase in hormones like adrenalin and cortisole. That's perfectly legitimate and needs to happen. But what is critical is whether it's prolonged or not. A continued maintenance of elevations in adrenalin and cortisole have been shown to be damaging . . . the ultimate outcome is damage to the cardiovascular system and compromise of immune function. And to keep that going, you don't need to continue to be exposed to the event. You only need to think about it.' Unfortunately when people listen to the 'stress awareness' propaganda, they are compelled to think about it.

Sociologist Frank Furedi, a prominent critic of stress ideology, expresses the view that stress awareness is itself unhealthy: 'Perceptions of illness are strongly influenced by cultural norms. With so much of life and everyday human encounters interpreted as risky, it is not remarkable to find that the mere fact of feeling uncomfortable due to stress has been recast as a dangerous and threatening condition. And once a condition is defined as potentially damaging, it is bound to have a negative effect on people's health . . . Campaigns devoted to raising awareness invite people to reinterpret their problems through the language of therapy.'[14]

Critics point to the fact that there is even an annual festival of stress phobia, which takes place in early November. This date has been designated National Stress Awareness Day, with workshops, stress-busting activities and even a 'stress bus tour' snaking around central London.

People who have been made 'stress aware' naturally believe in the stress condition, and as a consequence naturally seek to avoid over-stimulating their emotions and physiological reactions. They do not consider that in so doing they may be enfeebled or robbed of life. Yet families and love relationships are abandoned in the name of 'stress avoidance'. Fay Weldon has had battles with counselling organizations over therapeutic advice to vulnerable clients to walk away from stormy or difficult relationships in order to avoid emotional pain. She argues that love is itself a notoriously troubling business, but surely natural and valuable.

Stress avoidance is difficult for people to achieve, in any case, other than by the most extreme fastidiousness about life's threats and challenges. One example is the shift towards overprotective parenting. Children are growing up hermetically sealed from contact with the world, brought home from school to gobble sugary snacks and sit in front of computers in their bedrooms away from 'stranger danger', school bullies and 'risky' games like hide-and-seek and conkers. Such parental protection is undermining children's survival competence and making them cloistered, fearful and obese. A Commons Health Select Committee warns that such children are 'choking on their own fat', and that some of them may pre-decease their parents. Department of Health statistics issued in April 2005 showed that one in four children under 11 is overweight, and that one in seven is obese. Yet parents who imprison their children in this way do so out of concern that they should avoid the 'stress' of life.

Too worried to work

The damage done by the spread of 'stress awareness' in the workplace can be measured in terms of thwarted careers, blighted CVs and early retirements. It can be seen in the introduction of radical new initiatives vainly seeking to protect workers from emotional unpleasantness of any sort. Its effects can be felt in the emergency and armed services, which are struggling to cope with recruitment shortfalls and rattled staff. Fear of stress inhibits people from doing frontline work or emotionally demanding jobs.

In fact, many people are now so nervous and miserable that they feel unable to function properly in the workplace and will go home at the first sign of emotional inflammation. This in turn becomes the 'fault' of the employer under the new workplace stress code. The employer is supposed to provide a 'psychologically safe' environment – as vouchsafed by the Health and Safety at Work Act, section 2. One might interject: What environment is that? The womb, possibly, or the grave. T. S. Eliot, a poet so sensitive that he might have had an unclosed fontanelle, once complained, 'Man cannot bear very much reality'. In second millennium industrial relations, apparently, Eliot had it all wrong. Man cannot bear any reality at all.

The TUC 2002 Focus on Services for Injury Victims showed a twelve-fold increase in stress cases on the previous year. A CBI survey showed 192 million working days lost to absence in 2000. The cost to British business, said the CBI, was £10.7 billion, and a lot of this was due to workplace stress, and the UK was not alone. According to trade union representatives in the state of Victoria, where there is no specific legislation on the subject, 'Stress is one of the major OHS [Occupational Health Service] issues confronting workers in Australian workplaces.'[15] They cite an Australian Council of Trades Unions (ACTU) survey showing one in four people took time off due to stress at work, and that more than 60 per cent reported symptoms. The Australian Chamber of Commerce and Industry therefore excited a lot of controversy with its press release in January 2002,[16] which stated: 'In spite of the substantial amount of work by academics and researchers over the last twenty years or so, we are no closer to providing proof of a linkage between so-called workplace stress and disease.'

The Australian National Occupational Health and Safety Commission nevertheless views stress as 'the most significant psychological hazard in the workplace'[17] and warns that 'a stress reaction associated with a critical incident ... will need immediate medical attention and professional counselling'. However the Commission is slightly less focused when it comes to deciding whether stress is a

Part Two THE SCIENCE THAT SPAWNED AN INDUSTRY

CHAPTER THREE

PARADIGM

'Twas thus by the glare of false science betray'd,
That leads to bewilder, and dazzles to blind.

James Beattie, *The Hermit*

Medical theories that name our ills come and go. They change by reason of what the late great science historian Thomas Kuhn called 'paradigm shifts'.[1] Old models of how the brain and body work, with all their expertise, evidence and diagrams, are debunked in favour of new ones. However, reigning paradigms have enormous intellectual power. Challenges are rebuffed, critics are dismissed, counter-evidence is filed under white noise or 'aberrant findings'. Only when the volume of counter-evidence threatens to expose the reigning paradigm and its followers to ridicule does it finally give way in favour of something else.

Great reliance is placed on scientific theories of how things work, and people do not like to have them attacked. As Erich Fromm diagnosed in *The Fear of Freedom*,[2] many – and this must include many scientific researchers – fear the responsibility of thinking for themselves. Let us look at three famous examples of scientific paradigms that have foisted ideologies (belief systems) upon us.

A sense of humours

One of the most powerful presiding paradigms in all of science and medicine was the theory of the four humours. The idea originated in Ancient Greece in about 400 BC and still influenced medical opinion as late as the seventeenth century (Charles II's physicians seem to have cured him to death on the basis of it in 1685). Its founding father was probably Hippocrates, the most celebrated physician of his day. According to the four humours model, all things were composed of four elements: earth, air, fire and water. The body contained four corresponding fluids: black bile, yellow bile, blood and phlegm.

All diseases of the mind and body were caused by imbalances in these elements, and patients were diagnosed and treated accordingly. If you were depressed, this was because you were melancholic, and had too much black bile in your constitution. You were purged, and you might well have felt better when the treatment stopped. If you had a fever, this was because you had too much blood circulating in your system, and this made your temperature rise and your heart race. So you were bled with leeches, and subjected to scarification or cupping glasses. Bleeding often reduced temperature, 'proving' the theory was sound. For hundreds of years, doctors, scholars and scientists worked on the assumption that the four humours was the only feasible model of human physiology and psychology. Patients were eventually saved from the harm of this paradigm by advances in anatomy and research. But across Europe, by sins of commission or omission, it probably killed millions.

Map-heads

Our second paradigm, or model of how things work, is less lethal but more recent. The Viennese physician Franz Joseph Gall

(1758–1828) devised a hugely influential theory of the brain as the organ of the mind. His model was also 'scientific': that is, developed by a doctor and based on anatomical and cranial research. Like the four humours, Gall's paradigm seemed to explain everything, and provided diagnoses and nostrums that satisfied the public craving for explanations of their physical and mental pain.

Gall's theory was known as phrenology. Antique shops are littered with the popular bald busts of the period, usually bearing the inscription of one of Gall's astute American followers, L. N. Fowler: 'For thirty years I have studied Crania and living heads from all parts of the world, and have found in every instance that there is a perfect correspondence between the conformation of the healthy skull of an individual and his known characteristics.' The busts are mapped out with personality traits and brain functions and with a fan-shaped array over one eye that reads: Form, Size, Weight, Colour, Order and Calculation.

The theory of phrenology was perfectly plausible. Since the mind was composed of multiple distinct faculties, and since the mind's composition could infallibly be traced back to the brain, those distinct faculties must have a separate cerebral seat or organ. The size of an organ is generally a measure of its power. So the shape of the brain must be determined by the development of its various organs. Thus far, Gall's premises have to some extent been vindicated. But now comes the characteristic imaginative leap of the medical theorist. Since the skull shape must depend upon the brain's structure, the surface of the skull can be read as an accurate map of psychological traits and tendencies.

Gall's theory sparked a new diagnostic industry among the middle classes of the 1800s, with practitioners in every town. Gall and his fellow phrenologists like J. G. Spurzheim and the American 'phrenological Fowlers' were lecturing and reading heads from London to New York, Berlin and Paris. So convincing was the new science that royals, intellectuals and employers swore by it. The workplace provided a ready market for the new expertise: 'During phrenology's first heyday in the 1820s to 1840s, many employers could demand a character reference from a local phrenologist to ensure that a prospective employee was honest and hard-working.'[3]

Thousands of people paid thousands of other people to read the lumps and bumps on their heads as a form of character divination. It was very difficult to dissuade them of the scientific value of their readings (some of my trainees feel that a vestige of truth still clings to my own map-head, 'Fran', when he is passed around the class). An *Edinburgh Review* article in 1815, exposing phrenology as bogus and condemning Spurzheim as a charlatan, merely served to make the theory more fashionable. It finally gave way, not to its numerous critics, but to advances in neurology that showed no correlation between skull extrusions and personality.

The stress paradigm

Our third and final brain–body model – because of the globalizing of information technology – is more international in its influence than the four humours and more popular than phrenology. The theory of stress governs our day-to-day perceptions of our bodily mechanisms, feelings and interactions with the world. It overarches funding, research, health education, the employer's relationship with his workers, the doctor's relationship with his patient and the individual's relationship with himself. In the twenty-first century we look for our emotional wisdom not to the works of Shakespeare, who laid bare the human soul, but to the work of a man who experimented on 1,400 rats a week in a Montreal laboratory.[4] His name was Hans Selye.

Not everyone agrees that the Canadian-Viennese Selye was the founder of the stress concept: some give the title to Harvard Professor of physiology, Walter B. Cannon. However Selye wrote some thirty books and 1,500 articles on the subject, and popularized the term across America and Europe. He says that when he was asked to lecture in France, Germany, Italy, Spain and Portugal, there was no word in their languages for 'stress', so new ones had to be coined (*le Stress, der Stress, lo Stress, el Stress and o Stress*), giving him 'forever the glory of having enriched all these languages by at least one word'. Selye has therefore become known as 'the father of stress therapy'.[5]

History and etymology

However, neither Selye nor Cannon can claim to have coined the s-word in English. It had been used for centuries as a corruption or shortened form of 'distress', and derived from the Latin *stringere*: 'to draw tight'. The word was used figuratively, usually paired with 'strain', to describe hardships or affliction as early as the fourteenth century. During the late 1700s, shadowing the development of stress laws in engineering, it was also used to mean 'force, pressure, strain or strong effort' of the individual's organs or mental power.[6] The general idea of 'strain and stress' causing disease even appeared in the work of Sir William Osler (in 1910), who thought that angina pectoris was associated with the hectic pace of life.[7] In psychology, H. Burnham[8] and Margaret Mead[9] respectively referred to the 'storm and stress' and 'stress and strain' of adolescence. But their use of the words was metaphorical rather than scientific.

This was the conceptual framework in which Selye began his research in the 1930s. He was also aware of the terms 'strain' and 'stress' in engineering, though without necessarily understanding the difference.[10] There was an obvious impetus to the work of endocrinologists like Selye and Cannon between the world wars. Soldiers had returned from the front with 'shell shock', and scientists were asked to explain it. An explosion of interest in fear and its effects upon emotional and physical competence had influenced funding and research prestige. The branch of endocrinology that investigated the adrenal cortex and the chemical messengers epinephrine (adrenalin) and norepinephrine (noradrenalin), became increasingly a focal point for government and military funding.[11]

Ben Shephard, in his definitive history of soldiers and psychiatrists, *A War of Nerves*, detects a shift from one psychosomatic term to another round about this time, and holds Hans Selye's 'determined self-promotion' responsible. He writes: 'In many ways, "Stress" filled the places vacated when "Neurathenia" finally disappeared in the 1930s in Britain and America'[12] – though perhaps without the respective labels actually assisting in curing anybody. By the Vietnam war, 'stress' had firmly established itself in the military psychologist's lexicon. Historian Russell Viner points out: 'Stress was pictured as a weapon, to be used in the waging of psychological warfare against the enemy, and stress research as a shield or vaccination against the contagious germ of fear.'[13]

And from the battle-weary soldier, his mental wounds liberally dressed with stress management ideas, it was just a short hop to the man in the street. A new paradigm had been found, one of sufficient arcane power to impress both scientist and sufferer. How they came by degrees to believe in it, we shall now consider.

CHAPTER FOUR
PROVENANCE

Quoth Hudibras: I smell a rat.

Samuel Butler, *Hudibras*, I, i, 815

Let us take a peek at Hans Selye in his laboratory at the Institute of Experimental Medicine and Surgery at the University of Montreal in 1954, in the middle of his research years (his work spans half a century from the 1930s). A row of rats are immobilized, fastened to a wooden board by means of adhesive tape. Selye calls this a 'systemic stressor'. Some of the animals have had their adrenal glands removed, but some are intact. All of the rats have had croton oil injected under their dorsal skin, which has been shaved and puffed out with air to form a convenient sac known as the granuloma pouch. The pouch can then be illuminated by a flashlight to examine the wound, its 'haemorrhagic inflammatory exudate' (bleeding and other discharges), discoloration and eventual necrosis or tissue death. Some of the rats are wriggling about (croton oil is a very painful irritant). They have also been starved for seven days. An improved method of exposure was favoured in later experiments: that of 'cold-freezing', which enabled the animals' torments to be extended over several months. Very low temperatures cause shutdown of non-essential systems as experimental subjects attempt to stay alive.

Dr Selye considers that the rats here are similar to human beings. He writes in the *British Medical Journal*: 'Since the procedure is irritating and provokes a certain amount of struggling, the condition of the rat is not unlike that occasioned by physical and mental fatigue in man.'[1] Selye believes this particular experiment shows 'that the same factor, stress, can both inhibit and facilitate the production of local disease manifestations, since it inhibits the phenomena of inflammation and aggravates those of necrosis'.

This was one of many thousands of experiments carried out by Selye, purporting to show a relationship between various forms of torture in the rat (and later the Leghorn chick, mouse, dog, cat, guinea pig, rabbit and monkey), their hormonal secretions, and the 'syndrome of just being sick' (as he calls it in his autobiographical *The Stress of Life*[2]) in human beings. Selye claims to have formulated the stress concept for beleaguered humanity in 1936, though his article in *Nature* at that time mysteriously mentions only rats, and 'a syndrome produced by diverse nocuous agents', rather than 'stress'.[3] By the time he compiled the first massive summary of his findings fourteen years later (containing well over 1,000 pages of text and 5,000 references and promoting the s-word not only in its title but its sub-title as well)[4] he admitted that he had fought shy of using the concept earlier because it had made his audiences confused and irritated.[5]

Selye, stress and sense

Selye defined his 'stress' in different ways, talking about 'the biological stress response', 'the biological stress syndrome', 'the rate of wear and tear on the body', 'the non-specific response of the body to any demand' and even, on page 407 of *The Stress of Life*, 'the tweezers of stress' (which strangely have 'three prongs'). He distinguishes between bad stress ('distress'), and good stress ('eustress'), and points out that 'sudden stress' has been used quite successfully to snap patients out of mental or physical illness, for example, by incantations, bloodletting, strong drugs, poultices, painful bandages, ECT and chucking water in the face of hysterics. He mentions the 'important discovery' of Rufus of Ephesus in AD 100, 'that strong fever can cure many diseases', and offers this as another example of 'sudden stress' being just what the doctor ordered.

In his research papers he appears to use the term to refer on some occasions to the stimulus (rat torment), and on others to the response (rat reaction), leading to conflation of these opposites in stress studies ever since. Selye was eventually alerted to his mistake by what he refers to as a 'sarcastic remark' in the *British Medical Journal* that apparently stress 'was its own cause'. He was obliged to introduce a new term 'stressor' to mean the 'causative agent', retaining 'stress' for the 'resulting condition', but by then the confusion was already endemic.

This failure to define what the research is actually about has led to much obfuscation and frankly unintelligible reasoning in the clinical literature, and to the many serious flaws and failings that have earned stress research the sobriquet 'sloppy science'. Words convey meaning and sense. Without some precision in their use, the organization of thoughts and concepts in pursuit of scientific truth wanders off with its gas jars (or its granuloma pouches) into the hills. Selye refers by turns to 'topical stress', 'systemic stress', 'non-specific stress', 'state of stress', the 'stress syndrome', 'stress-producing factors', 'stress status', 'stress quotient' and 'stress machinery'. In a section worryingly entitled 'Abstractions and Definitions' in *The Stress of Life*, being unable to tell us clearly what stress is, Seyle tells us what it is *not*. Stress is 'not simply nervous tension', and it is 'not an emergency discharge of hormones from the adrenal medulla'; nor is it 'everything that causes a secretion by the adrenal cortex of its hormones, the corticoids'.

Seyle continues that stress is 'not always the nonspecific result of damage', nor is it 'the same as deviation from homeostasis'. For Selye, 'stress is not anything that causes an alarm reaction' either, nor is it 'identical with the alarm reaction'. But there may be a few people out there still not sufficiently confused, so Selye gives it to us straight: 'Stress is not a nonspecific reaction', but on the other hand, 'stress is not a specific reaction' either. Don't worry, though, for whatever stress is, it 'is not necessarily something bad'. Furthermore, it 'cannot and should not be avoided . . . Stress can be avoided only by dying.' Thank God. Although we don't know what exactly we should be avoiding, even if we did know, we wouldn't be able to avoid it.

Selye theorized that what he called 'stressors' might vary, but that 'they all produce essentially the same biological response'. He also believed that he had glimpsed in this biological response the secret of sickness, although the excitement of discovering this unfathomable condition caused him to suffer it himself: 'The urge to share with others the thrill of adventure which comes from penetrating, even if ever so slightly, into hitherto unknown depths of life can become a major source of stress in itself.'[6]

The secret of sickness

He found that exposing his laboratory rats to extreme and over-whelming stimuli – pain, infection, radiation, intense heat, months of extreme cold, fractures and wounds, life-threats and starvation, without any possibility of survival, adaptation or escape – produced three stages of response which he called the General Adaptation Syndrome or GAS. These were the alarm phase, in which there is tension, depression and shock; the defence or resistant phase, in which (galvanized by the response to threat mechanism) the subject puts up a struggle for its life and adapts to the conditions as best it can; and finally the exhaustion phase, in which the subject (no doubt realising that it can never escape from Dr Seyle's laboratory) gives up and resigns itself to its fate.

Critics have pointed out that his GAS, even were it based on more discriminating methodological evidence, would be of little survival value to the organism and that nature would long since have evolved it out.

Helpless against such painful and deliberately damaging agents, Selye's dying rats exhibited gastric erosions, enlargement of the adrenal cortex, and atrophy of and haemorrhaging into the thymus gland, spleen and lymph nodes of the immune system. Selye called the changes 'diseases of adaptation', although his critics have called them diseases of *mal*adaptation. And thus began the stress-disease perplex, with Selye's work inspiring six decades of subsequent research to investigate the puzzling link he had apparently found between the General Adaptation Syndrome, the stress response, stress hormones, stress or stressors – and harm to health.

Herbert Weiner, Professor of Psychiatry and Bio-behavioural Sciences at the University of California, Los Angeles, is one of Selye's most formidable critics. He analyses the provenance and development of stress research and summarizes its founder's influence as follows: 'For years thereafter, the connection between stress and disease was, and has continued to be, sought. He assumed that the corticosteroids mediated the anatomical damage he described, despite the fact that it had been demonstrated by the time of his first report that corticosteroids may actually protect animals against injury and infection.'[7]

The work of some of Selye's contemporaries like Dr Phillip Hench into corticosteroids suppressing disease in rheumatoid arthritis patients confirmed this,[8] and newer research has shown that adrenalectomized animals are more susceptible to injury and infection.[9] Selye himself, in his section on cancer in *The Stress of Life*, refers to 'general stress' suppressing cancerous growth. Besides, by the 1970s even Selye had to admit that his GAS was not quite the reliable phenomenon he had rested his case on – it varied in different animals and different circumstances. This necessitated the introduction of a new concept – the LAS or Local Adaptation Syndrome, to deal with such anomalies.[10]

Selye's translation

The notions of 'stress' and GAS left most of Hans Selye's fellow endocrinologists underwhelmed. For about forty years they failed to grasp their scientific significance, or predict that his concept would one day rule the world. Even if his 'nocuous agents' did produce a syndrome, and even if this could be conceptualized scientifically, they could not see how it 'translated' (or could be extrapolated) to the human species. Rats, even terrified, starved rats taped to boards in laboratories and injected with irritants, are not people.

Selye's 'translation', like Elijah's, was eventually achieved outside the laboratory. According to Russell Viner of the University of London, it 'was brought about by Selye's recruitment of a broadly based constituency outside of academic physiology, whose members each saw in stress a validation of their pre-existing ideas of the relationship of the human mind and body in industrial civilization'.[11] The Canadian Institute of Stress was founded in 1979 by Selye himself in partnership with Alvin Toffler, author (in 1970) of *Future Shock*. Thus began a very profitable alliance between a sociologist predicting disaster for mankind from the fast growth of technology and the modern world, and an endocrinologist keen to apply the effects of laboratory experiments on rats to the complex emotional pain of humanity. Those who sought in Selye's work a solution to the riddle of human sickness and suffering flocked to support and imitate his endeavours as potentially helpful to technophobic mankind.

In the latter years of his life, Selye's laboratory work fanned out into what seems, for a scientist, a bizarre utopianism. He philosophized about what he called 'altruistic egoism', or building up a stock of gratitude in others, as a means of self-preservation. This 'maximizes eustress and minimizes distress'. It is 'not so much the stressor agent but your preparedness to meet it that counts'; indeed, he warned that we should not talk glibly about '*being under stress*' at all, as this is just as vague and non-medical as saying one 'has a temperature'. Oddly, one should nevertheless look out for signs of stress in oneself before it is too late, although 'even the best' scientific measures of stress cannot distinguish 'between eustress and distress'. At the same time, one must conserve one's limited amount of survival power or 'adaptive energy' by avoiding 'overexertion' at one activity. The best remedy is 'deviation' from that activity, or 'general stress' – activating the whole body, or thinking about some other problem instead. However, deep relaxation will not work because we are all really no more than machines: 'Just as any inanimate machine gradually wears out, so does the human machine sooner or later become the victim of constant "wear and tear".'[12]

Hans Selye has been called many things in his time, including the Father of Stress Therapy and the Einstein of Medicine.[13] However one of his critics, E. S. Deevey, prefers something a bit saltier, referring to him as 'a modern haruspex'.[14] The haruspex was an Etruscan priest who could divine the fate of man in the entrails of domestic animals.

Dealing with disturbances – W. B. Cannon

Apart from Selye, two other scientists figure prominently in the history of stress research: W. B. Cannon and J. W. Mason. Harvard Professor of Physiology Walter Bradford Cannon, the man Selye called his 'first critic', started out investigating the mechanism of swallowing and noticed that the digestive system of his experimental animals stopped functioning when they were upset. So he applied himself to researching bodily states of excitement, from 'emotional' stress[15] to voodoo death (the result of being ceremonially cursed using a 'bone pointer').[16] Selye, a fine one to talk, observed that Cannon 'never proposed the term *stress* as a scientific name for anything in particular'. On the plus side, Cannon's work focused on the 'normal' physiology of defence, both in humans and animals, rather than on the kind of morbid changes going on in Selye's laboratory. On the downside, although he wrote about the 'wisdom' of the body,[17] Cannon evidently viewed the response to threat as a sort of energetic bouncer outside a gentlemen's club, dealing with disturbances and restoring the normal 'steady state' within.

Cannon found that during exposure to cold, asphyxia, injury, rage, pain, hunger, fear or excitement, an experimental animal's body went through a physiological pattern that prepared it for 'fighting' or 'fleeing'. Like Selye, he relied heavily on the evidence of vivisection, and for eighteen years was chairman of a defence committee set up to fight the anti-vivisection movement. He described his subjects as 'under stress', though he was equally imprecise with his terminology and was no better than Selye at distinguishing between 'stress' and 'strain'. He was particularly interested in the adrenal medulla and adrenalin (which he calls 'adrenin') and demonstrated their connection with high emotional states. He became so adept at isolating the physiological system concerned that he could surgically remove the entire sympathetic nervous system of animals under study, and exhibit the creatures at conferences. He designed experiments to discover how extreme physical and emotional exigencies disturbed some normal range within which he presumed the body operated. As he puts it in *The Wisdom of the Body* (p. 24): 'The co-ordinated physiological processes which maintain most of the steady states in the organism are so complex and so peculiar to living things ... that I have suggested a special designation for these states: *homeostasis*.' In the course of this work, 'stress' gradually came to mean 'disturbances, whether internal or external, of homeostasis'. This would lack precision if the body were indeed homeostatic, but becomes even less rigorous if, as more modern research suggests, it is not.

The 'fight-or-flight' response may owe its fame to Cannon, though it is by no means unanimously agreed that any single such mechanism exists. The physiological reaction to threat may well be more discriminating. Cannon's notion of homeostasis (or Claude

Bernard's notion of it)[18] has annoyed his scientific critics, but has helped to establish as a cliché of stress research the idea of 'steady state disturbances' in the body. This in turn has led to the fight-or-flight mechanism being viewed as a hard-wired, primitive, malfunctioning sort of bodily self-destruct system, that is even referred to in some of the literature as 'the fight-or-flight *syndrome*', as though the survival mechanism were an illness. Actually few 'steady states' exist in the body. They tend to oscillate because they are regulated by negative and positive or mixed feedback loops.[19] More importantly, complex organisms undergoing distressing experiences do not simply revert to a previous condition, like a spring. They develop and adapt.

Mason's monkeys

Professor John Wayne Mason[20] is one of the big guns of Selye criticism. During his tenure as neuroendocrinologist and later head of endocrinology at Washington's Walter Reed Army Institute of Research from 1953 to 1974, he carried out research of his own on the organization of hormonal mechanisms and found that Selye's theory of General Adaptation Syndrome and Cannon's theory of homeostasis could not be reconciled. The same hormonal response in the organism would not be appropriate for opposite stimuli, such as heat and cold, which require different metabolic adjustments. Mason himself had discovered much more intricate variables in hormonal regulation, keenly sensitive to different psychological states. In the 1970s, both Mason and L. E. Hinkle[21] published GAS attacks, arguing that no organism could survive if its responses to danger and damage were so crude.

Picking up Selye's 'stress' in inverted commas as though using rubber gloves, Mason gives his idea of GAS a ruthless pounding. For twenty years Mason had carried out experimental procedures to explore the psychoendocrine mechanisms: in his case using monkeys, and measuring variables in their blood and urine.[22] These monkeys were subjected to heat experiments and to seventy-two-hour aversion experiments, strapped in laboratory primate-restraint chairs. In one experimental series they were given electric shocks to their feet if they failed to depress a hand lever when they saw a red light. Yet Mason found no sign of any GAS in his monkeys. On the other hand, what Selye had called 'mere emotional stress', however induced or interpreted, could cause striking changes in the animals' individual responses to their laboratory ordeals.

Mason felt that emotional subtleties had been overlooked by Selye. He argued that stress was really a behavioural concept rather than a physiological one. He reviewed the research, both human and animal, showing the importance of psychological factors in hormonal regulation – from studies of schizophrenic patients and sportsmen, to rats with their legs tied together or blasted with air or ringing bells. Mason's own experimental monkeys responded differently according to subtle variations in their torments and according to their different psychological coping abilities. If a starved animal had to watch other animals being fed, it responded differently from being starved in a group ('the deprived animals often vocalized in apparent protest'). 'Naïve' monkeys, unused to handling, gave different results from more experienced monkeys. Over time, as they became accustomed to their repeated ordeals, their hormonal regulation altered and adapted. In some cases its patterns were actually reversed.[23] If it is acceptable to extrapolate from animal research, such findings must surely have far-reaching implications for emotional education in humans repeatedly exposed to threats.

Noting these differences, and observing even wider variations in human responses, Mason offered endocrinologists some very sensible advice: 'If we think along these lines, it seems likely that we shall find increasingly little need or use for "stress" concepts or terminology.'[24] He felt that they needed to stop such crude and confused experiments and start asking sounder questions about the interface between the purposeful, survival-orientated, organized and mutually regulating hormonal mechanisms – and the brain. More recent research[25] has confirmed such dissimilarities of response between different strains of the same animal and between different animals. Some distressing experiences elicit the same hormonal patterns in the rat; others evoke different ones.[26] Generally speaking, only animals that are completely overwhelmed and prevented from defending themselves produce Selye's reaction.

Mason's monkeys were constrained in unnatural surroundings and made to perform unnatural tasks. Yet like Selye, he needed to suggest that his animals' responses had relevance not only to normal animal physiology but to normal human responses as well. Mason goes further: he links hormonal responses to psychological ones. Emotions occur, hormonal changes occur, but one does not necessarily *cause* the other. However, in the mind of the observer of such experiments, emotions may well occur, with or without hormonal changes, at the idea of pitiful monkeys, strapped in chairs, modelling for free human beings in all their emotional complexity. Indeed, in a passage that cries out to be framed on stress lab walls, Mason himself observed: 'Unless one is extremely mindful of the exquisite sensitivity of the pituitary-adrenal cortical system to psychological influences, one is likely to subject animals or humans to stimuli such as exercise, fasting, cold, heat, etc. under conditions in which either considerable pain, discomfort, or emotional reaction is simultaneously elicited.'[27] Mason warned that these uncontrolled factors may influence results, though he does not ask how it is possible to discover *natural* hormonal reactions in subjects alarmed by being used in experiments.

The spread of the stress bug

The concept of stress, once it had gained scientific legitimacy, escaped from the laboratories of Selye and Cannon in the 1930s and

1940s and began to infect work at other sites, particularly military ones, where its vague neuro-psycho-physio-lingo appealed to anyone of professional standing with a taste for psychobabble.

In 1945 Roy Grinker, a neurologist who had been psychoanalysed (and indeed by his own account leaned over and dribbled upon) by Freud himself in Vienna, joined forces with Dr John Spiegel to produce a weighty record of their interventions with convalescent flyers and North African US army casualties. Although their work had little to do with Selye's rat research, using as it did a combination of the barbiturate Pentothal (thiopental sodium) and psychoanalysis with mixed results, Grinker and Spiegel chose to call their book *Men Under Stress*.[28] (Publishers tend to like the pithy term as one of my own books, a study of the experimental nature of sport, proved: it was originally called something else but was later reissued as *Sportsmen Under Stress*, to more acclaim.) In the culture dish of the clinical literature, the stress bacillus was now growing fast. Between 1936 and 1945, only eight abstracts were published bearing the term. Over the next four years, there were thirty-two; between 1951 and 1955, 207.[29] Selye's own vast library of stress literature, which he carefully itemized and coded, reveals that between 1950 and 1976 (when he revised *The Stress of Life*), between 2,500 and 7,700 publications had appeared each year. The epidemic had begun.

Psychologist Dr David Brown, whose Reading University doctoral thesis mercilessly dissects the body of stress science, comments on the ramifications in the military sphere. Wartime psychologists searched for 'a scientific basis for military triage', and a means of identifying combat fitness and fatigue: 'The US Office of Strategic Services, for example, used a practice known as the "stress interview" to select intelligence agents capable of maintaining "deep cover".'[30] Intelligence operatives were routinely subjected to realistic interrogation to prepare them for working behind enemy lines and this field provided rich soil for early military stress studies. War also afforded well-funded opportunities for psychologists offering various forms of 'stress therapy' that could swivel in peacetime towards the civilian population.

Just as the word 'Martian' entered the vernacular via science fiction in the 1950s as a scientific-sounding term for 'little green man in space', so the term 'stress' gradually established itself in the public consciousness through tabloid journalism as a scientific-sounding condition. Dr Rob Briner has spent many years tracking the concept. Here he is, in humorous vein, speaking at the 1997 London conference, *Stress: a Change of Direction*:

The nearest bit of history I can give you is the concept of 'nerves'. When people used to go to the GP perhaps 40 or 50 years ago, and even more recently, they'd say in a kind of Ealing Comedy fashion: 'I've got a problem with me nerves', and the doctor would duly write 'nerves' on a sick note and off they would go, perfectly happy. This is a book written in 1913 entitled simply *Nerves*, and apparently what happened was that your nerves just sort of went 'jangly', and then they would 'go', and when they had 'gone', you were in big trouble. This was followed by *Mastering Nerves*, *How to Conquer Your Nerves*, and *Self-Help for Your Nerves*, published in 1962. Around this time, books about nerves stopped being published: the latest I could find was the early 1970s. Interestingly around the same time, you've got the rise of the concept of 'stress'.

The Canadian Institute of Stress, founded in 1979 in Ontario, began a remorseless campaign to publicize not only Selye's work, but the syndrome he had evidently discovered. The American Institute of Stress had opened for business the year before, 'at the request of Hans Selye to serve as a clearing house for information on all stress-related subjects', thus bringing the concept to the attention not only of the therapeutic community, who would be keen to take it up, but also, via the Institutes' websites and campaigning literature, to the international media, where it would be presented by social commentators and lifestyle gurus as a means of helping and understanding humanity. Stress was now famous. Nobel prize-winners and

Bob Hope were on the American Institute's board of trustees.

In the 1980s and 1990s, further work with animal models, combined with a general dearth of precision on terms and methodologies, paved the way for a new development – that of 'therapism'. If 'stress' were a syndrome, then something should be done to cure it. However, nobody could 'cure' a nebulous thing like 'stress', whose meaning and corporeal identity had eluded even the researchers who had discovered it. There had to be a biological target for all the new psychological, physiological and pharmaceutical interventions.

And so it was that the fight-or-flight response to threat, the normal and natural survival mechanism that had been the subject of much of the original research of Selye and Cannon, itself became the focus of therapeutic efforts. Nobody seemed to notice the way in which it had been subtly pathologized. The response to threat, now pejoratively referred to as the stress response, was in the line of fire for 'magic bullets'. Stress therapism erupted across Britain and North America. An ever-expanding pool of 'consultants', with or without qualifications, offered their highly paid but largely unregulated services to deal with the perceived new threat to public health. The 1980s were a period of social unrest, downsizing of companies, increasing workloads, social and marital breakdown, high crime and normlessness. There were no quick fix solutions to these problems. But by means of 'stress management' theory, the fight-or-flight mechanism could become the perceived threat to well-being, rather than the serious problems that set it off.

The science that spawned the global stress management industry has attracted enormus sums in research funding across Europe and the US (no official figure exists). Those who stand to profit from the concept of stress as a vague disease terror – by offering technical, strategic or medical 'cures' and prophylactics – have been liberal with their resources and these vested interests are big stakeholders in the stress ideology. If there were a clearer case of conflict of interests in scientific research, it would be difficult to imagine what it might be.

CHAPTER FIVE

PSYCHONEUROIMMUNOLOGY

Any sufficiently advanced technology is indistinguishable from magic.

Arthur C. Clarke, *Profiles of the Future*

The last chapter looked at the bold anomalies and curious assumptions of some of the pioneering stress research. But surely, you say, stress science is not like that now. It must have progressed, it must be more exact and sophisticated.

Indeed, a new science has developed over the past thirty years: that of psychoneuroimmunology or PNI. This shiny new stress science examines the interactions between stress, the brain (or mind) and the immune system. It enters the micro-world of the bone marrow, the lymph nodes, thymus and spleen to observe macrophages (mothership cells that can fire off enzymes and, if necessary, 'eat' antigens or foreign bodies), NK cells (natural killer lymphocytes for dealing with tumours and virally infected cells), T and B cells (lymphocytes that recognize and bind to antigens), cytokines (soluble proteins released by immune cells) and even tinier entities derived from these, all swimming and wiggling to war under high magnification.

PNI sounds and is complex, so much so, in fact, that some critics think it may have become detached from reality altogether. PNI scientists conduct many of their experiments outside the body, using minutely coded chemical components, cells and actants from a variety of human and animal sources to do battle with bacteria and viruses in dishes, tubes and computer programmes. Psychologist Dr

Steven Brown: 'It literally fragments the body under stress and distributes it across a bewildering variety of proprietary technics ... PNI, with its wholesale shuffling of entities and mediators, disrupts the most secure place of all, embodiment itself.'[1]

In 1975 Dr Robert Ader of New York's University of Rochester School of Medicine and Dentistry and his colleague Nick Cohen were examining conditioned responses in rats and how these could be influenced.[2] Dr Ader gave his rats drinks of saccharine water immediately followed by injections of the immunosuppressive drug cyclophosphamide, which is fairly toxic. It made the rats want to vomit. Once they had got used to this combination he gave them saccharine water alone, to see if they now associated the drink with the drug, and if they had been conditioned to dislike saccharine. The rats, which had been given a toxic immunosuppressant earlier, began to die.

Ader's colleague, immunologist Nick Cohen, joined him in replicating the experiment. They concluded that the rats were dying because their immune systems had been undermined, just by drinking the saccharine water. Could this be because the rats mentally connected the sweet drink with the immune-suppressing drug? Did it show that the rats' brains had altered their immune response and assisted in their demise? Or did the vomiting rats simply give up their small ghosts? Ader and Cohen's results met with scientific scorn. The brain could not undermine the immune system. There was no interface between the two. White blood cells or lymphocytes of the immune system can attack bacteria and viruses in a petri dish, no brain involved.

The University of Rochester, New York, responded with more findings. Dr Suzanne Felten, looking through a microscope at blood vessels, came across a small nerve terminal in close proximity to a lymphocyte cell membrane. 'It was tremendously exciting. There it was. You could see it. It was right up next to the lymphocyte and there had to be talk between the two cells.'[3] Here was further apparent proof that the brain – and hence psychological reactions

– could interfere with the immune system. Meanwhile, at the University of Alabama, neuroimmunology Professor J. Edwin ('Ed') Blalock investigated white blood cells making antibodies to fight off infection. He took human blood cells and put them into a culture, to which he added a brain hormone, ACTH (adreno-corticotrophic hormone). This slowed the ability of the white blood cells to grow and make antibodies, and appeared to show that a brain hormone, albeit out of its human context, can alter immune functioning.[4]

'Enormous assumptions'

Though most of the scientific community was yet to be convinced, PNI was gathering momentum. If the brain could influence the immune system, why then, mood could moderate resistance to disease. Upsetting events must undermine immunity. Positive thinking or relaxation exercises must make you healthy. Suddenly lab-loads of scientists were keen to explore the (presumed negative) impact of the stress response to threat on the immune system, and New Age gurus were proclaiming that positive thoughts could cure cancer. Professor Stafford Lightman of the University of Bristol: 'It was absolutely appalling. I mean basically they took what was a little bit of knowledge and they turned this into enormous assumptions ... Of course we never had that evidence.'[5]

PNI experiments 'proved' that hormones involved in the stress response had a negative effect on the immune system. But on the other hand, PNI research on adventure activities such as sky-diving, parachuting and bungee jumping 'proved' that adrenalin, a key factor in the stress response, causes an increase in NK-cell activity, and thereby gives a positive boost to immune functioning. Indeed, the immune response was found to produce the equivalent of a stress response.[6] Stimulators of immune cells (for example, macro-phages) can produce behaviours identical to those of anxiety and fear. Confusing indeed for anyone wishing to generalize about stress and immune functioning.

Professor Steven Maier, of the University of Colorado's department of psychology, warns other PNI researchers of the dangers of simplistic stress-mongering: 'Not infrequently, investigators have drawn sweeping conclusions such as "stress suppresses immune function" from studies that have measured but one aspect of immunity at one point in time. This is akin to measuring a single aspect of neural function ... and making claims about what "stress does to the brain".'[7]

Like so many of their fellow stress scientists, PNI investigators placed great reliance on research using rodents. Acute exposure to electric shocks, maternal separation, rotation, injection of saline, immersion in cold water, loud noise, crowding and other torments caused a variety of immune response variables in animal subjects. When PNI researchers studied human beings at all, it was usually under extreme conditions: space missions, prolonged exposure to noise and sleep deprivation, earthquakes, recent bereavement and so on. Critics questioned the relevance to everyday life of these studies, and how they could actually be useful.

PNI and 'long-term stress'

Then in the 1980s, PNI turned its attention to that favourite (though notoriously ill-defined) topic – 'chronic', 'everyday', or 'long-term' stress in humans. Professor Jan Kiecolt-Glaser, of the Department of Psychiatry, Medical Microbiology and Immunology, Psychology and Medicine, Ohio State University College of Medicine, and her husband Ron Glaser, Professor of Medical Microbiology and Immunology, looked at 'marital stress' and its effects on endocrinology and health. Newlywed couples were lured out of their love nests and admitted to a hospital research unit for twenty-four hours to study the effects of rows and 'conflict resolution behaviours'. The ninety otherwise 'happy' couples were required to discuss their differences under scientific scrutiny, while body language was studied and blood drawn. The results showed changes in immune functioning, particularly among the women.[8]

The Glasers had become interested in the effects of psychological stress after Ron's father died. Ron had taken it very badly, and wondered about the impact of bereavement on health. Here is his psychologist wife Jan, talking on a BBC TV *Horizon* documentary in February 2000:

When Ron said 'Does stress affect health?' I said 'Of course it does'. We already had good data – we knew from a number of studies that stressful episodes were associated with greater incidence of illness. People who had life events in the prior year, like death or a move or loss of a job were more likely to get sick. Those were interesting, but what we knew immuno-logically was pretty limited.

The Glasers now launched into their very influential experiments on stress and the immune system. Medical students undergoing exams had catheters inserted in their arms so that blood could be drawn hourly. They were found to have 'a very wide range of immunological functions' affected. Particularly noted was a decline in gamma interferon, which stimulates the activity of NK (natural killer) cells. Also their T-cells could not perform properly in a test tube.[9] But these changes might be a temporary effect. What the Glasers really wanted was data on long-term stress. They had tried replicating marital rows in the laboratory, and put catheters in the arms of combatants so they could draw blood regularly. But this may not have been a good model of long-term stress either.

The answer came in a series of Glaser-team studies of the 'carers' of Alzheimer's disease patients and their 'affective, sympathetic, and neuroendocrine tonus'.[10] The research team made 'small punch biopsy wounds' in the arms of the carers, and found that these took longer to heal than the same wounds in 'non-stressed' people. They also measured the antibody and virus-specific T-cell response to influenza vaccine. They measured a wound-healing cytokine (IL-1) in blood samples and found that the count was down. They measured the production of another pro-inflammatory cytokine, IL-6, and found that the count was up. Conclusion: the stress of caring for an Alzheimer's sufferer causes potentially unhealthy alterations in immune functioning.

There are important considerations here that researchers appear to have overlooked in their concern to investigate and assuage human suffering. Having a catheter in one's arm, and being monitored by scientists while one cares for one's brain-diseased spouse, may well affect one's emotions, and these emotions in turn may affect the minute legionaries of the immune system in a variety of ways. But does this mean that the galvanizing stress response to threat is responsible for these changes? Or if the changes are mediated by emotions, *which* emotions? Are people who care for Alzheimer's sufferers for years at risk from the ill effects of arousal, or are they actually at risk from despondency, resignation, self-destruction and despair? People looking after elderly helpless loved ones often have their sleep interrupted and their social and sex lives curtailed. They may not eat properly or groom themselves. Indeed, their own health may be their last consideration. I once watched an elderly uncle, caring for his bedridden wife, standing eating beans out of a saucepan because he could not be bothered to prepare his own meals. He consoled himself with small rewards like cigarettes and cream buns eaten directly out of the paper bag. He did not survive my aunt very long. I have no idea what happened to his immune system, but one suspects that it wasn't pretty.

Psychoneuroimmunology is now Big Science, and those who promulgate it must assume considerable responsibility for informing the public on 'stress' and disease. Oddly, the Glasers themselves had misgivings about the way their work has been extrapolated. Jan Glaser said in an interview in 2000: 'Part of the popular press, some of the New Age gurus have made it seem as though we know all the answers and that we can translate what we have seen in the laboratory directly into important health outcomes; that the way you act and think will automatically translate into huge differences in health. We are certainly not at that point.'[11]

If the label falls off, call it stress

Unfortunately researchers in the fledgling discipline are no better than were their forebears at defining stress or spotting flaws in the stress paradigm. Steven Maier, Linda Watkins and Monika Fleshner, in their review of the new science,[12] showed enormous faith in its rationale: 'In our discussion of stress and immunity we will not provide extensive documentation that stress can alter immune function – that is well known and has often been reviewed.' They offer no definition of the said 'stress', but set out to show why the effect of stress on immunity may have been 'adaptive in evolution, rather than simply being a curiosity'. They explain that 'numerous studies conducted over the past thirty or so years have demonstrated that a wide variety of stressors can alter many aspects of the immune response', and go on to list various frightening and painful rat torments. So stress must mean 'extreme arousal' then? But no. They also mention 'social defeat' experiments on resignation and helplessness in male rats, lumping these together with the other procedures under the label 'stressors', as though they were all the same. They are not. Arousal and resignation are opposites.

Another reviewer of the PNI literature, A. O'Leary,[13] doubts that a vast paradigm like stress can be useful in explaining anything. And Ader and Cohen, the men whose work set the PNI ball rolling, offer us this: 'In the present context, "stress" refers to any natural or experimentally contrived circumstances that (intuitively, at least) pose an actual or perceived threat to the psychobiological unity of the individual.'[14]

The billions of research dollars currently poured into investigating stress and immunity in order to develop more pharmaceutical products might be better spent looking at a far more obvious threat to the immune system – the one posed by everyday painkillers and anti-inflammatory drugs and their potential hazard to public health. It has become fashionable to think of fever, pain and inflammation as mere symptoms to be drugged down, and proprietary products are routinely swallowed to prevent them. Yet PNI scientists are better qualified than anyone else to understand that these are part of a highly regulated and intelligent system for dealing with infection and invasion, and that we medicalize fever, pain and inflammation at great potential cost to our immune systems.

Above all, questions must be asked about the relevance of PNI stress research to our society. Even on its own terms, how does this new science actually help people? Does it enable the carer of someone with Alzheimer's disease to bear up under the strain of watching a loved one sink into mental degradation and decay? Even if such research *did* establish that the carer's immune system was at risk from such thankless labours (and using the present paradigm this must be a matter for conjecture), would it help that carer not to fall sick?

PNI stress research is extremely useful to three groups: PNI researchers, stress management purveyors, and those trying to invent a magic bullet to 'cure' whatever they might mean by stress. One of these is Professor Stafford Lightman, talking excitedly on a Channel 4 science documentary about the latest developments. Note that 'stress' is treated here *both* as a stimulus and as a response:[15]

We've been involved in an intensive programme to design a pill which can counter the effects of stress. And the way to do this is to block the first chemical made by the hypothalamus in the brain which actually controls the whole of the *stress response*, and it's a chemical which we call CRH [corticotropin-releasing hormone] which is made by the hypothalamus.

And what we have done, together with the drug companies, is to design a drug that can actually block the effect of CRH. So if we can do this, the whole part of the cascade starting in the hypothalamus, which causes you to *respond to stress* – by producing cortisole, for instance – can be blocked right at the central level in the brain. [My italics.]

In other words, they want to shut down your stress response to threat.

CHAPTER SIX

PATHOLOGISING EMOTIONS

I am not an animal.

John Merrick, *The Elephant Man*

Of mice and men

The reader will have noticed that almost all of the stress research so far discussed made use of animal subjects: vivisection is the seabed upon which the Leviathan stress science rests. As Hans Selye put it: 'Naturally, the thing to do was to give enormous amounts of corticoids to normal experimental animals and just see what happened.'[1] Humans cannot lawfully be subjected to very painful and distressing stimuli in laboratories to investigate stress or anything else, though perhaps stress researchers could follow the example of some of their more heroic predecessors and conduct their trials on themselves.

Investigators who favour animal models argue that the physiology of animals and humans is much the same, so valid inferences may be drawn from one to the other. That this is at least questionable is evident from the number of pharmaceutical preparations later withdrawn from the market or found harmful to humans after having been proven safe on animals, such as Eraldine, Opren and Thalidomide. Morphine wakes up cats and penicillin is toxic to guinea pigs. Animals and humans react very differently to phenyl-butazone. Aspirin causes birth defects in rats, mice, monkeys, cats and dogs, but not in humans. Saccharine causes bladder cancer in rats.

Animals are therefore not necessarily valid analogues of human physiology. Results are potentially misleading and hazardous to public health, and this is why, despite the financial and political might of the vivisection industry, there is now a growing body of objectors within the sphere of medical and scientific research. The international pressure group Doctors and Lawyers for Responsible Medicine (DLRM), for example, whose members are all medically and professionally qualified, states as its objective 'the immediate and unconditional abolition of all animal experiments on medical and scientific grounds'. For the same reasons in 1984 the Italian Congress voted to outlaw vivisection, and in 1989 the International Congress of Doctors Against Vivisection was held at the Italian Parliament.

The appropriateness of animals as models for human psychology, as is so often the case in stress experiments, is even more dubious unless the agreed point of analogy is 'ability to suffer'. If laboratory animals are analogous, then they must be presumed to experience the same anguish as human beings undergoing similar procedures. If laboratory animals are not psychologically analogous, then the stress experimental results are of course worthless scientifically and wasteful of funding, and objections on these grounds have nothing whatever to do with sentiment.

Human responses

A besetting flaw in the stress science has been its disregard and disrespect for humanity and the complexity of human conscious-ness. Human response to distressing or challenging experiences is not general but individual. It is based on different percep-tions, different arousal preferences, different levels of intelligence, experience and self-confidence, different coping skills, education, information and desire for control, and above all, different interior constructs of reality. Investigators such as Viktor Frankl, J. B. Rotter,[3] S. C. Kobasa[4] and Aaron Antonovsky[5] have studied such variants in human perception, health and survival and they offer useful and relevant concepts with which to try to understand why some people get sick during the trials of life and others do not. Their work, which spans a gigantic field beyond the remit of this book, pays homage to human complexity, courage and imagination, and in so doing perhaps comes closer to fathoming human arousal experiences than do misleading laboratory studies of stress and animal physiology.

In humans, cognition is not just another thing. It is everything. Even speech plays a significant part in human arousal, and scientists in this specialist field suspect that vivisection may have skewed the research. J. J. Lynch, K. E. Lynch and E. Friedmann have written: 'It is widely accepted that animal models can be used to fully understand the development of various stress-induced illnesses in human beings ... [This] has also had the unfortunate effect of encouraging investigators to minimize or completely overlook the unique interactions of human speech on bodily functions, particularly the human cardiovascular system'.[6] These interactions are complex and remarkable, and for anyone interested in the fascinating speech–physiology link, a selection of studies is given in the Notes.[7] For example, simply talking about feelings of hopelessness and despair can cause life-threatening changes in blood pressure. This is one of the reasons why so-called links between stress and blood pressure, and between stress and cardiovascular disease, need to be examined with a gimlet eye. Using crude concepts like 'stress', and crude methods like vivisection, the human brain is factored out, and human physiological phenomena may be completely misconstrued.

A good example is provided by the work of an American scientist who ironically serves on the board of the American Institute of Stress, but whose own study of emotions and physiology is much more precise and discriminating than that vague concept. Professor James L. Lynch is director of the Life Care Health Centre in Baltimore, Maryland. His groundbreaking research has high-lighted the role of loneliness, hopelessness and despair in heart disease and increased morbidity. By carefully combining cardio-vascular monitoring with interview techniques he has been able to pick up 'sudden precipitous drops' in blood pressure when his patients attempt to describe feelings of helplessness, despite the fact that none of those monitored were even aware of these danger-ous physiological changes. Lynch hypothesizes that the act of attempting to communicate utter helplessness connects people to the physiology of their very early childhood, when such feelings may have threatened to overwhelm them. Indeed he suggests that such cardiovascular changes are the 'living embodiment' of hope-lessness itself.[8]

Normal emotions as disease

Other researchers who have focused their efforts on their own species attack the assumption that 'arousal causes disease' as a simplistic falsehood. In the original work of Selye and Cannon, no allowance was made for the coping skills or otherwise of the animal subjects. Their laboratory situations bore little resemblance to life in nature, let alone to that of self-determining individuals capable of exercising the powers of speech and influence over their threatening circumstances. Yet their work has exerted such in-fluence that frequent explicit and implicit reference is made in the scientific literature to the 'pathophysiology of arousal', as though emotions themselves were a morbid change.

Critics argue that this has not only led science up a blind alley, but that it has done grave disservice to humanity. Stress researchers are suspected of trying to meddle unnecessarily with the human emotions by studying and doctoring the physiology of laboratory animals. Such pathologizing of emotional arousal should not surprise us, when so much else natural and normal to humanity is being subtly turned into a disease. Tonsils and wisdom teeth are removed on the smallest medical pretext. The delivery of babies is treated as a surgical procedure in the form of caesareans (one in four babies, at a cost to the NHS of £250 million a year). Obesity is not a matter of overeating or alcohol abuse, but a 'disease' caused by insufficient appetite-suppressant hormones. Disruptive children are not simply naughty, but victims of a hyperactivity disorder. So then anxiety or arousal in response to a perceived threat is not a normal and useful reaction, but an illness to be eradicated by anodynes or mood-altering drugs. Anger must be managed; grieving must be mediated; surviving distressing events must be manipulated; having relationships, or not having relationships, must be counselled.

The *Lancet* and American medical journals now refer poe-faced to such conditions as Bingo Brain, Oyster Shuckers Keratitis, Body Builders Psychosis, Expresso Wrist, Panty Girdle Syndrome and Yoga Foot Drop. Shropshire County Council's Occupational Health Physician, Dr Dale Archer, drew my attention to another such gem – 'Post Traumatic Embitterment Disorder'. 'I'm told this is a disorder of people passed over for promotion, humiliated by a superior or made redundant . . . Is this an attempt at Teutonic humour or is it yet another non-disease to add to "stress" etc.? I think we should be told. When I see PTED on a medical certificate I'll know satire has finally been laid to rest.'[9]

How did all this begin? Why should we now perceive ourselves as victims of nature rather than natural survivors? According to those who believe in stress management, Mother Nature has foisted on us this pathetically primitive device, the fight-or-flight response, suitable for dealing with sabre-tooth tigers and suchlike but wholly inappropriate for the second millennium traffic jam or busy office environment. According to stress researchers, this woefully outdated mechanism goes off like a car alarm every time we are in trouble and makes everybody sick, and the best thing would be if we could stop it with a 'magic bullet' or have it surgically removed. According to stress ideologists, Mother Nature is trying to kill us.

Survival mechanism

There is another related physiological mechanism, not beloved of stress researchers but extremely important if you happen to be a duck. This is the so-called diving (or face immersion) response, the ultimate defence of the submerged vertebrate against asphyxia. It involves a gross redistribution of the circulation in order to concentrate oxygen in the brain and the heart and enables the domestic duck to remain submerged for fifteen minutes, the sea-lion for thirty minutes, and the whale for two hours. The three key elements of this response are: cessation of breathing (apnoea), reduction of heart rate, and extensive constriction of non-coronary and non-cranial blood vessels. In other words, there is a massive vasoconstriction of the entire arterial tree, so that the circulation becomes in effect a heart–brain circuit. When the animal surfaces, these changes are reversed in seconds. But while it is submerged, its heart needs to pump and its brain needs to think.

The fight-or-flight or stress response is similarly remarkable. Threats to survival, whether mental or physical, cause the body and brain to activate a defence mechanism, triggered by the hypo-thalamus at the back of the skull as it galvanizes the body into action. The hypothalamus transmits electrical and chemical signals (using a substance labelled CRF or corticotrophin-releasing factor) to the pituitary gland, which relays the exciting news to the adrenal glands just above the kidneys, using the hormone ACTH or adreno-corticotrophic hormone (also referred to as 'corticotrophin').

The sequence that follows reveals this awe-inspiring survival mechanism – dismissed by stress management theory as a bringer of disease and death – in all its magnificent complexity. Over thirty chemical messengers suddenly cascade from the adrenal medulla (inside the adrenal glands) and adrenal cortex (outside the glands) and are sent round the body. Those from inside the adrenals are called catecholamines (epinephrine and norepinephrine – adrenalin and noradrenalin to us). Those from the cortex are steroid hormones known as corticosteroids or corticoids ('things from the cortex'), and these include cortisone, the focus of much of the stress research. Under certain conditions, some of the corticoids can increase inflammation, while others can inhibit it (cortisone is used as an anti-inflammatory to treat rheumatoid arthritis, for example). Their tiny tasks are exceedingly complex, even to specialist scientists. They can alter mineral metabolism, alter blood pressure, alter the pigmentation of the skin and raise blood sugar. For this reason Hans Selye suggested calling them 'glucocorticoids' (from glucose). The adrenal cortex also makes its own sex hormones, the focus of Selye's original research.

Although these chemical messengers have diverse miniature missions, depending on the nature of the challenge perceived by the brain's higher command centres, their grand effects are palpable. The heart rate increases, metabolism of sugars increases, digestion slows down and blood thickens. The body is preparing for fight or flight. Blood supply is diverted away from the extremities, and from non-essential systems like digestion. The blood is needed elsewhere. It goes to the large muscles, which may be needed for fighting or fleeing, and – significantly – it flows to the brain. The body may be preparing for action, but the brain is preparing for something else. It is readying itself to work in a high gear, to focus, connect, create, crystallize and come up with appropriate solutions to the emergency.

Experiencing these normal physiological changes may be disquieting and unpleasant. The response was designed to galvanize the threatened individual to take urgent action, or make urgent plans, to solve the riddle of the situation in order to save himself. The mechanism also functions as a burglar alarm, and is not meant to be ignored, or endured. If we ignore or endure it, we are like the small boy on the burning deck, standing eating a banana. Physiological changes include increased heartbeat, increased blood pressure, cold hands and cold feet, sweating, dry mouth, muscle tension, 'butterflies', diarrhoea and nausea. There may also be strange alterations of perception, such as feelings of being about to explode, burst or fragment, and feelings of being stretched, strained or pulled apart.

Such physical and perceptual changes, though normal and explicable, lend themselves very readily to presentation as 'symptoms' of some catastrophic disorder. We have only to name this disorder 'stress' and we are well on the way to engendering fear, both of the disorder and the survival mechanism itself. In other words, of unleashing stress phobia.

CHAPTER SEVEN
PERPLEX

My heart aches, and a drowsy numbness pains
My sense, as though of hemlock I had drunk,
Or emptied some dull opiate to the drains
One minute past, and Lethe-wards had sunk ...

John Keats, 'Ode to a Nightingale'

We have looked briefly at the so-called 'pathophysiology of arousal' as a means of presenting normal emotions as a disease, and we have seen where this idea came from, and where it has led. But the girder that bears most of the weight of the stress therapy industry is the stress-disease perplex – the puzzling and perplexing idea that the stress response to distressing stimuli, though meant to aid survival, impacts negatively on health. Without the perplex, stress management would not exist, as there would be little call for it. Stress absenteeism would not exist, since there would be nothing to be feared or gained by using the term 'stress': workers would simply be absent by reason of a particular illness, or because they could not handle some particular workplace situation. Stress consultants would not exist. Stress diagnosis would not exist. Stress compensation would not exist.

Since Selye's work on the General Adaptation Syndrome and Meyer's theory that distressing events cause mental illness, the idea that the stress response to threat directly causes disease has been scientifically respectable. Few have sought to disprove such an absorbing and plausible theory. Unhappiness and distress are self-evidently connected in some way with illness, since they often occur when it occurs. But scientists who customarily expect and exert precision in their work have somehow allowed the concept of stress, which they cannot clearly define, to escape their usual rigour. Because they have allowed the concept such licence, it has attached itself to every negative life event, and to every disease and disorder, as leeches cling to everything in the pond.

Evacuation sickness

Our researchers have apparently not asked themselves one rather obvious question about illness: could sickness itself become a form of survival strategy? In combat psychology and in professional sport, this phenomenon is well recognized.

Lord (Charles Wilson) Moran wrote an extraordinary book[1] about his experiences as a medical officer in the First World War trenches, for example in the Ypres salient, where he had weathered bombardment and controlled his own terror. Though full of compassion for his men, he observed a catastrophic loss of the glue that holds soldiers together under fire:

When the name shell shock was coined, the number of men leaving the trenches with no bodily wound leapt up. The pressure of opinion in the battalion – the idea stronger than fear – was eased by giving fear a respectable name ... The resolve to stay with the battalion had been weakened, the conscience relaxed, the path out of danger was made easy. The hospitals at the base were said to be choked with these people though the doctors could find nothing wrong with them. Men in France were weary. Unable or unwilling? It was no longer a private anxiety, it had become a public menace.[2]

When the term 'shell shock' was coined, Lord Moran noticed, the medical tents were suddenly full of terrified and battle-weary soldiers complaining of it. Arguably, no human being should be expected to endure what they had endured, and for the most part their 'symptoms' were not consistent with malingering. But a valve had evidently been opened inside their heads.

In professional sport, those who have studied competitive psychology quickly become familiar with complex 'defensive' illnesses that save nervous competitors from enduring pressure situations. A competitor who secretly does not wish to face a gruelling championship final develops a bad back, a 'syndrome' or an injury. He cannot, for all sorts of professional and social reasons, say, 'Sorry, folks – I know I've qualified for this match through a lot of hard work and sponsorship, and with the support of my family, friends and fans, and I know I said I wanted to be a champion, but the thought of this final now fills me with dread and I would rather avoid it.' Instead he gets sick. It is important to realize that he may not even know himself that his sickness is a strategy, as self-deception plays an important role in it. He is not malingering; his emergency illness is just as real as any other incapacity, and the symptoms just as genuine. Over the years working with professional sportsmen, the author came across this 'evacuation sickness' time and again.[3] Why should we not suppose therefore that physical incapacity could come to the rescue of the overworked employee or the desperate carer, without the sufferer necessarily realizing the cause?

According to those who believe in the stress ideology, people who face distressing circumstances, even if they do not actually become physically ill, succumb to mental illness. Such casualties may of course be victims of stress phobia, in which the sufferer focuses on normal physiological changes and as a result experiences petrifying anxiety, but there may be another explanation. In his bestseller *The Road Less Travelled*, psychiatrist M. Scott Peck writes:

What makes life difficult is that the process of confronting and solving problems is a painful one. Problems, depending upon their nature, evoke in us frustration or grief or sadness or loneliness or guilt or regret or anger or fear or anxiety or anguish or despair. These are uncomfortable feelings, often very uncomfortable, often as painful as any kind of physical pain, sometimes equalling the very worst kind of physical pain ... Yet it is in this whole process of meeting and solving problems that life has its meaning ... Fearing the pain involved, almost all of us, to a greater or lesser degree, attempt to avoid problems ... This tendency to avoid problems and the emotional suffering inherent in them is the primary basis of all mental illness.[4]

So problems and mental illness may be connected and coincidental without one necessarily 'causing' the other.

Disease list

What are the alleged risks of 'stress' to health? The following list is a combination of lists published by various stress management and health authorities, some of which readers may have seen already. Among the health risks enumerated are: diseases of the cardio-vascular system including coronary heart disease, hypertension, strokes and migraine, diseases of the digestive system including indigestion, nausea and heartburn, stomach and duodenal ulcers, ulcerative colitis, irritable bowel syndrome, diarrhoea, constipation and flatulence, diseases of the muscles and joints including back pain, neck pain and cramps, as well as allergies, skin conditions, cancer, diabetes, rheumatoid arthritis, asthma, sexual dysfunction and sleep disorders, emotional illnesses including anxiety, phobias and obsessions, depression, aggression, hyperactivity, eating dis-orders, excessive drinking, excessive smoking, irritability, drug abuse and nervous breakdown.

It is an impressive list. It freely mixes organic diseases with functional disorders (which are not actually diseases at all, but simply changes in the body's rhythmic functions). It is also a frightening list. Similar disease anxieties were conjured in the past by those claiming to treat 'imbalances of the humours' (earth, air, fire and water, the four elements believed to govern life), 'vapours' (fainting, often due to tight corsets), possession by demons, witchcraft, miasmas (harmful 'exhalations' in the environment, e.g. from marshes), 'railway spine' (caused by the travelling at unnatural speeds of up to 25 mph in the new trains), 'nervous debility' (general nervousness), 'brain fag' and 'neurasthenia' (discussed earlier) and 'hysteria' (emotional problems of deep origin, giving rise to sudden outbursts). Freudian 'neuroses', and also 'nerves', popular until recently, have seemingly lost ground to 'stress'.

Flaws in the stress–disease Link

Many researchers, both from within and outside the stress science, even if they accept the stress concept and are broadly sympathetic to the aims of stress investigation, have queried the so-called 'stress–disease link' itself. For example, if the link is genuine, healthy individuals should be those who are subject to relatively few distressing experiences, or none at all, and this is not the case. Similarly, the majority of people exposed to distressing experiences do not develop mental illness; if they did most of the population, rather than just a minority, would be mentally ill. The fact is, individuals have different levels of vulnerability and emotional maturity, different worry thresholds and different buffers that protect them from mischance.

The stress–disease theory holds that stress undermines the immune system. However, objectors point out that 'stress' is used to mean different emotional states, and these cannot all have the same immunological consequences. Positive life events are just as significant in their hormonal impact as negative ones.

Some researchers who believe the stress–disease link is fallacious object to the use of animal models in stress research and claim it fails to represent human beings in all their linguistic and meta-physical complexity. Furthermore they say the hydraulic feedback system formulated by Descartes, Darwin and Cannon cannot be used to conceptualize the human body in arousal and despair, or to evolve suitable therapies for it.

Other objectors point out that emotionally upsetting episodes may have negative, neutral or salutary health effects; they may actually be beneficial in the long term. This group of critics argues that the biological response to threat gives access to enhanced mental and physical resources, and mediates neural adaptation and learning. The response can be fifty times as potent in its pain-killing action as morphine. Critics of the statistical data, however compiled, observe that the stress–illness relationship (however defined), although significant, is consistently low (for the technically minded the typical range is from 0.12 to 0.35). More importantly, the stress response, and distressing experience, do not generally, linearly or by themselves produce disease, and this is widely accepted, even within the stress research itself. Much depends on predisposition and coping skills.

Methodologies, semantics, sample sizes and bias have all been questioned by critics of the presumed link between stress and disease. In studies where 'stress' refers to levels of arousal, magnitude of arousal is another niggling issue. Wide agreement exists that some (unspecified) level of arousal is beneficial, but that above this level its effects are harmful to health and performance. This theory is usually illustrated by a simple parabolic graph known as the Yerkes-Dodson curve (after the psychologists who formulated it), indicating the rise, peak and fall of efficiency under growing levels of arousal. This looks plausible enough, until we remember that individuals vary widely in their levels of activation towards the same threatening stimulus, and in their pursuit of – or aversion to – arousal. Some hate being nervous and will do anything to avoid it. Some thrive on what they call 'pressure' and go in search of it. Sensation-seeking has been shown to enhance coping skills, and it may therefore be suggested that 'optimum levels of arousal' may be *learned* through experience and exposure.

'Long-term stress'

To be fair, even stress scientists themselves do not generally believe that 'stress' is an *immediate* cause of disease. There is a very broad consensus that 'health dysfunctional phenomena', however these are established or defined, are caused by what they call *'long-term* stress'. 'Short-term stress' is not usually seen as the culprit. This qualification alone should have alerted stress researchers to the fallacious logic of the Perplex. Harmful health consequences may frequently occur *after* the stress response to threat has been triggered, or triggered repeatedly. It is deduced that the stress response therefore caused the harm to health, but this is not necessarily so. The harm to health may have been caused by some mediating condition.

The stress response to threat is a survival mechanism, activated by danger or emergency. It is by its very nature short-term and, perhaps to sharpen its spur, physically unpleasant. If this galvanizing response is ignored or endured, harmful health consequences may indeed ensue. But why? Logically, there are three possibilities. They either happen as a result of the stress response itself sabotaging the body's defences (Selye's idea), or as a result of the threatening stimulus, or as a result of some new and morbid change in the organism subjected to long-term threat.

In animal-based experiments using inescapable threat (prolonged and repeated tail shock, forced swim, water restraint, hot plate contact and other ordeals dreamed up by researchers), long-term inability to respond to perceived danger results in a syndrome that is the biological *opposite* of the galvanizing stress response. In this quite different response, which has nothing at all to do with survival, the subject gives up the struggle for its life and resigns itself to its fate. This is the so-called 'third phase' of Selye's GAS, but it is important to realize, as Selye evidently did not, that the animal may do this in return for a degree of neural tranquillization, and that its brain may now release pentapeptides and other opiate-like substances to dull the pain and horror of its situation. The resigned animal then succumbs to morbid physiological changes.

A very robust causal link between resignation and disease is established in the clinical literature, and because it is so important we shall be returning to it in chapter 17 on 'Nation Sedation'. 'Ode to a Nightingale' by John Keats, briefly quoted at the start of this chapter, is one of the most famous descriptions we have of this resignation that soothes while it kills. The victim is sick of 'the weariness, the fever and the fret', and 'half in love with easeful death'. Keats was a young man who had been diagnosed with consumption. In the poem he longs to let go, to give up, to escape into the sound of the nightingale singing in the distance, but is called back to his 'sole self' by a tolling bell. With enormous courage Keats fought his resignation and his illness and committed his genius to paper before he died.

Giving up may buffer you from reality, but at considerable cost. Resignation causes the suppression or shutting down of the immune system. If you've given up, why would you need an immune system anyway? The link between resignation and disease (or death) has been found not only in animal-based work, but much more importantly, in human studies involving prisoners of war, concentration camp survival, spouse bereavement and long-term disability.

So here we have an alternative solution to the mystery of why people who have distressing experiences get sick. The harmful health effects so often associated with the stress response to threat may relate to one particular aspect of that response, namely the failure to act upon it. If this is the case, then the harm to health is due, not to the threat mechanism, but to resignation. The former is a life force; the latter a death wish. Resignation is a maladaptive behaviour, which disrupts the body's defences and exposes it to pathogens. It is of central importance to our understanding of the stress mythology. Resignation is potentially not only dangerous to health, but lethal. Consider a real-life example.

In 1997, twenty-seven-year-old Andrew Thomas of Glamorgan died after being made redundant. Pathologist Dr David Stock said Mr Thomas appeared to have been a 'completely healthy young man' and the cause of death was 'unascertainable'. After initial attempts to find work, Mr Thomas had begun getting up late and spending every day watching videos and television. He even gave up getting dressed, and would sit all day in his pyjamas. His father Gwilym was reported to have said at the hearing: 'I believe he lost the will to live.'[6]

In my work as a trainer rehabilitating the long-term unemployed, I come across this tragic syndrome on almost every course. I call it the dole sleeping sickness. People who have endured a lot of career rejections go into apathy mode, which dulls the pain. They sleep a lot, daydream a lot, and lie in bed. They stop trying and failing because these rejections hurt, and they simply wait for Godot, or a lottery win, or a miracle. For them, the war of survival is over. Ironically, a lot of them claim to be suffering from stress, or think that arousal is the cause of their problems. If only that were the case.

Resignation – the research evidence

Why do people and laboratory animals give up? Failure to initiate responses in the face of threat or challenge was famously explored in the work of Martin Seligman and Steven Maier (in the late 1960s),[7] in experiments using rats and dogs. Whatever the rights and wrongs of vivisection, the results were certainly not what the researchers expected.

Dogs were subjected to painful electric shocks while being

strapped down or prevented from avoiding them. The shocks were then continued, but under different conditions. The dogs were put into compartmentalized boxes with barriers that could be jumped, but some animals still did not try to escape their ordeal. After an initial search for exits they simply gave up, whimpering pathetically while further shocks were administered. These dogs had evidently 'learned' that their actions could not save them, so gave up taking any. Subsequent research showed that animals that behave in this helpless way succumb to very harmful physiological changes. They get sick, and they die.

Perhaps wary of false extrapolation from animals to humans, Seligman and his colleagues turned their attention to students, shutting them in a room with loud unpleasant noise, and various knobs that might or might not control the volume. Some continued to turn the knobs, even if they appeared not to alter the sound levels. Others gave up. By now Seligman had developed a model of depression based on his experimental work.[8] His concept of learned helplessness – resigned failure to act in the face of threat – has become a fulcrum of psychological research.

The poet and visionary William Blake diagnosed this same psychological state in the poor of London in the 1780s. He watched the infant chimney sweeps and their weeping, starving parents and saw that their helplessness was more effective in keeping them subjugated than any constraint of their harsh employers. Their despair was destroying their spirit. His remarkable poems, including 'Jerusalem' ('I will not cease from mental fight . . .'), seek to inject passion, anger, joy and inspiration in hopeless lives. The alternative was too terrible to contemplate, but Blake contemplated it all the same, in his poem 'London':

In every cry of every Man,
In every Infant's cry of fear,
In every voice; in every ban,
The mind-forg'd manacles I hear.[9]

The poet's powerful observations are not without relevance to our modern epidemic of helplessness. The same 'mind-forg'd manacles' arguably imprison many a 'stressed' worker now who avoids confrontation with an oppressive employer for fear of losing his job, to many an overworked housewife afraid to establish her rights in the home for fear of appearing lazy or selfish, and many a frantic parent reluctant to read the riot act to wayward children for fear that love will be lost for ever.

Learned helplessness and control

Those who wear such mental shackles are said to suffer from 'learned helplessness', a perceived inability to influence or control an outcome, which results in the suppression of overt behaviour. The helpless person believes that his or her actions will be futile, and that he/she cannot possibly alter the situation. He/she believes that the 'locus of control' is outside the self, in the hands of others, of authorities, even of destiny.

Helpless people will tend to have poor self-esteem, and poor coping skills. Faced with a serious threat to well-being, they will avoid scenes, resort to escapist habits like smoking, drinking and other anodynes (even though these are known to be harmful), and try to ignore the problem in the hope that it will go away. The sense of self-worth and competence will suffer accordingly. They may not exhibit aggression or frustration, even though the situation might warrant both. If bullied at work, they will not fight back, or complain. According to research cited in a 2004 HSE technical report[10], 40 per cent of victims do not even turn to anyone for support. They simply resign themselves, or leave. They may vent their anger on minor annoyances, or people unconnected with the source of suffering. They may appear placid, even bleakly cheerful, in the face of unacceptable reality. Yet as we have seen, such people are at considerable risk of infection, disease and even death.

A number of key studies in the stress literature have highlighted the importance of *control* in vulnerability to illness from distressing experiences. Here we plainly see why this is so. Those who act to help themselves assume control. Those who fail to act relinquish it. Helpless people believe they have no control, and their passivity confirms them in their faith. Control was a key variable in the HSE Report on 'Work, environment, alcohol consumption and ill health', the so-called *Whitehall II study*,[11] and some of the other evidence on the importance of control is reviewed in the CERM/UEA report.[12] For example, S. C. Kobasa[13] in the 1970s, found that people who believe they can control events remain healthier during distressing experiences than those who believe they are powerless.

Viktor Frankl studied (at first hand, for he survived four Nazi concentration camps) the behaviour and susceptibilities of the victims of Auschwitz and Dachau, and formulated a theory of survival that he called the 'will to meaning'.[14] Of immense significance was self-determination. As Frankl observes: 'Everything can be taken from a man but one thing: the last of the human freedoms – to choose one's own way.' Taking action based on personal choice, whatever the crucible in which one burns, ensures a degree of control over one's fate. It may also send vital messages from the brain to the body to keep fighting and not fall sick.

Distress and disease – a new model

So now we are in a position to suggest a new theory, based on studies of humans rather than animals, to explain the relationship between distress and disease. It is this:

When the response to threat is activated by a perceived danger, inadequate coping skills, an external locus of control, poor self-esteem and fear or misunderstanding of the stress phenomenon may result in failure to act or adapt in order to deal with the threat, thus setting in train morbid changes associated with resignation, and consequent harm to health.

According to this reasoning, Selye was wrong. The distress–disease link that he formulated was not the direct, simple bond that he envisaged, but a complex sequence of events dependent on each individual's psychological make-up, courage and coping skills. According to this alternative theory, disease strikes not as a direct result of the response to threat, but as a result of resignation, helplessness and failure to act. More rigorous and modern research than Selye's work on GAS has shown that his so-called 'third phase' – resignation – by itself can shut off the immune system both in humans and animals and cause disease.

Misrepresentation of the stress response as the threat to health may have occurred purely by accident, through want of definition in the authoritative literature, and through inexact science in which the stress response has been confused with the very environmental threats it is designed to address. But it may also have been reinforced through the influence of a powerful, lucrative and unregulated industry with a vested interest in presenting stress as a disease in need of the treatment it provides.

CHAPTER EIGHT
PROOF POSITIVE

The great tragedy of science – the slaying of a beautiful hypothesis
by an ugly fact.

Thomas H. Huxley

So far, we have looked at flaws in the stress science that give us
reason in principle to doubt its findings. We now need to investigate
the counter-evidence, the research findings that show positive
beneficial effects of the stress response mechanism itself, and
positive benefits of other phenomena that currently go by the name
of 'stress'. There are, after all, reasons to be cheerful.

We are all descended from ancestors who endured and survived
far greater hardship than we can ever imagine, who were not wiped
out by virulent diseases that swept Europe and America, who did
not perish in the war or the workhouse, the madhouse, the mines
or the mills. If survival of the fittest were all, we should do well, for
we are their progeny. Nature has gifted us with brains and bodies
that may serve our turn, if only we respect them.

The late Charles Rycroft was a reforming psychoanalyst and one
of Freud's most influential critics. His book *Anxiety and Neurosis*
set out to dispel the notion that anxiety is always merely irrational
or neurotic, arguing instead that anxiety is a biological necessity, a
form of vigilance vital for human survival.[1] It alerts the brain to
unexplained data and threatening phenomena. Today, anxiety
often goes by the name of 'stress', as do anger, fear, exhilaration,

grief. But as the poet William Wordsworth has observed in his 'Ode: Intimations of Immortality', these emotions are bound up in our humanity. If we should strip them out, what would be left of us?

Thanks to the human heart by which we live;
Thanks to its tenderness, its joys, and fears:
To me, the meanest flower that blows can give
Thoughts that do often lie too deep for tears.

We can respect human emotions; we can also respect half-understood human physiological responses. Professor Herbert Weiner, in his review of the stress science[2], considers the 'integrated, discriminated, patterned biological responses to stressful experiences' have a purpose: 'ultimately to ensure survival, reproduction and health. When they fail, injury, ill health, disease and death ensue.' He objects to the popular definition of stress as 'demands that tax or exceed the resources of the system', explaining: 'This definition implies that stressful experience entails or forecasts a failure of adaptation. A definition of stressful experience must get away from focusing only on adverse effects.'[3] The following sampler from the research literature includes studies that may use the word 'stress' to discuss the mechanism, but that disclose some aspects of its positive value.

Take, for example, research evaluating the effects of 'stressors' (as laboratory torments are usually called) and anti-depressants on different strains of mice. This has found that 'stressors cause neurochemical changes which may be of adaptive value', failure of which 'may engender behavioural disturbances'.[4] Other studies found that 'stress' exposure, even 'inescapable stress' exposure, 'persistently facilitates associative and non-associative learning' in rats.[5] Neurons associated with the release of noradrenalin are widely thought to act as an alarm system, alerting the organism to threat. In pharmacological research investigating adaptation in the brain and its limbic system, researchers have found that laboratory 'stressors' increase the activity of these particular neurons, but that 'when the stress is repeated, as frequently happens in everyday life . . . neurons produce more molecules of the enzymes needed to synthesize noradrenalin, enabling the cells to manufacture and release more of this neurotransmitter. Such changes, which show that neurons are adaptable cells, may underlie the ability to cope with stress.'[6]

More interestingly, although a single exposure produces unpredictable changes in receptor cells, 'When the stress is repeated, more consistent changes appear. In particular, the number of b-adrenoceptors in the brain falls.' Repeated exposure reduces the function of these target cells, and this important adaptive change appears in laboratory rats that are 'tamed' by handling. Progressively the animal becomes less alarmed. Its brain learns and adapts. The relevance of this 'toughening up', as it is called, will be discussed in the chapter on Inurement.

There is consensus among the stress scientists that although what they call '*long-term* stress' is an unhealthy thing, the stress response itself is not. Indeed, in the short term, they concede, it may be positively useful. Even Hans Selye admitted that a certain amount of 'stress' (however sloppily defined) is required by the body for well-being, and that 'It is only in the heat of stress that individuality can be perfectly molded.'[7] Elsewhere the fight-or-flight mechanism is credited with facilitating *resistance* to environmental threats referred to as 'stress'.[8]

Oxford University Professor of Physiology Colin Blakemore explains why the response to threat is vital to survival: 'The natural environment of an animal in the wild is full of problems that we would call stressful – the attacks of predators, shortages of food, extremes of climate. In such situations, the brain acts on the body to enable it to cope: endorphins, released from the pituitary gland, help the animal to avoid pain; adrenalin and noradrenalin, produced as a result of activity in the nerves reaching the central core of the adrenal gland, tone up the heart and direct blood towards the muscles; another hormone from the pituitary stimulates the outer rind of the adrenal glands to produce corticosteroid hormones, which help to mobilize reserves of fat and carbohydrate in the body. All of these reactions are protective, indeed essential, for an animal in a demanding situation.'[9] He goes on to state the case for harm from 'long-term stress'/learned helplessness.

The role of arousal in performance

In professional sport, arousal is crucial to a 'keyed-up' display. Indeed, some sports psychologists reject the many different stress management techniques currently available, because of the positive role arousal can play in performance.[10] There is persuasive evidence for a connection between extreme (and even distressing) arousal, and feelings of elation or what we might call 'soul-sensing' in high-level sport.[11] A link between arousal, catharsis and 'highs' is investigated in the work of psychologists J. Heider[12] and Abraham Maslow, who saw 'peak experiences' as 'acute identity experiences',[13] and indeed, this soul-sensing or visioning may be one of the motivating factors in risk-taking generally and sensation-seeking in particular.

Neurologist Michael Persinger[14] investigates what he calls the 'God experience' or 'sense of profound knowing' produced by the brain under certain extreme conditions. So-called 'near death experiences' (or NDEs) belong to this group of phenomena. Such patterns, says Persinger, are exhibited by 'temporal lobe patients' between seizures, but they are also experienced by 'average people during the peaks of frustration, stress, and personal crisis'. To the bewilderment of some of his human subjects, Persinger can duplicate these beatific experiences in the laboratory, simply by stimulating certain regions of the brain.

Wellness and work

Even the normal strife of life can be interesting, important, motivating. The *Health & Safety Practitioner* (April 1996) found surprising the results of a readers' survey that asked: 'Can you see a need to introduce stress into the workplace in order to act as a motivator?' Ignoring stress management dogma, 55 per cent of respondents agreed in whole or in part. Without some driving force, there can be no drive. Brian Simpson,[15] an associate fellow of the British Psychological Society, says: 'Stress is not just a pathological symptom: it is an essential feature of the mechanism that drives people ... Absence of stress may seem safe, even desirable, but it is actually quite dangerous. Those who suddenly lose their sense of challenge frequently enter a period of mental and physical decline.' Dr Anthony Daniels agrees: 'Man needs problems, he needs anxiety, he needs stress, he needs excitement, he needs security, he needs peace of mind. These are contradictory, but that does not make them any the less necessary.'[16]

In 1998 a movement was underway in America known as 'Thank God it's Monday', in which employees bucked the pressure-phobic trend and expressed their exhilaration at the thought of starting another demanding working week. In the civil service, statistics show, the healthiest employees are those with the most responsibility.[17] According to organizational psychologist Dr Rob Briner, multi-task work and responsibility are not sick-making but salutary: 'There is some evidence that people who have a lot of responsibilities and goals – juggling families and work – actually thrive more than others who are focused on one goal.'[18]

The European Agency for Safety and Health at Work, who view occupational stress as a priority issue, commissioned the Institute of Work, Health and Organizations at Nottingham University Business School to review the European research data. Findings were published in 2000. The research team found that stress didn't translate to ill-health as had been supposed, and that any physiological changes were mainly minor and reversible. Although stress might adversely alter the way a worker feels, opinions on stress effects varied widely. Some even thought it improved performance and health.

A recent Royal Economic Society annual conference paper highlighted new research using data from the International Social Survey Programme on fifteen OECD (Organization for Economic Co-operation and Development) countries. Respondents were asked to assess whether they were 'always stressed', 'often stressed', 'sometimes stressed', 'hardly ever stressed' or 'never stressed' at work. (Self-report questionnaires are the stock-in-trade of stress researchers, even though such inventories are based on subjective feelings and perceptions.) The study found that UK respondents ranked themselves *moderately* stressed compared with other countries. Canadian, Swedish and Portuguese workers ranked themselves higher. Yet one in four of the UK employees planned to leave work in the next twelve months because of stress, while one in two reported being absent for the same reason.[19]

A team of psychologists in 2003 polled 3,000 people in the UK on their attitude to stress, and found that nearly half of those interviewed felt they worked more effectively when under pressure, while only 7 per cent reported signs of slowing down when they felt 'stressed'. Those who found pressure stimulating felt that work time passed more quickly and they were more focused. Four out of five thought that working to a tight deadline produced work of average to high quality.[20] In fact, 77 per cent believed that work stress increases job satisfaction.

A joint US/Canadian twenty-five-year study of working adults from over 5,000 households published its results in 2002, showing that time-pressured hard work prolongs life and lack of such pressure shortens life. Workers who faced few pressures or responsibilities were found to be up to 50 per cent more likely to die within ten years of retirement than were people who had had major responsibilities. No significant effects were found for 'high-strain work' (high demand and low control) or for 'psycho-social or physical job demands, job security, or work-related social support'. But 'passive work' (compare helplessness) was linked to higher mortality.[21]

Worklessness

Despite all the cant on workplace stress being harmful to health, there is no shortage of research evidence that unemployment can be bad for our mental and physical well-being, and that retirement can polish us off. Some of this evidence was reviewed in the CERM/UEA report.[22] For example, *under*work is seen in some of the research as a significant cause of stress. At a 1996 London conference on workplace stress organized by Euro Forum, senior occupational health physician Dr Mark Popplestone of Nestlé UK told a packed audience how one of their managers had a nervous breakdown in the early 1990s due to underwork, and how this had prompted the company to introduce its stress management programme. Dr Popplestone explained later: 'Underwork was one of the main factors, yes. This very nice chap was put in charge of a new department before I came to the company, and for the first three or four months there was nothing much for him to do. Astonishingly enough, the first thing that was affected was his ability to play golf, and this was noticed by one or two of his colleagues. I think stress is a balance. If you didn't have any pressure at all you'd never get out of bed in the mornings.'[23]

Boredom (defined as 'a state of being wearied by insufficient interest or pace'), far from being a pacific state of mind, is actively harmful. In zoos, bored animals are distressed animals, perpetually pacing the length of their cages, mutilating fur or feathers, or swinging their heads monotonously from side to side. Human boredom can be equally distressing. Psychologist Dr Stephen

Vodanovich of St Louis University and Dr Jennifer Sommers from the University of West Florida discovered that employees who were prone to boredom at work were more likely to suffer from 'stress' and were more vulnerable to heart attacks.[24] Boredom, hitherto an under-researched topic, has been found to contribute to marital breakdown, poor academic performance, clinical depression, overeating, obesity, lack of job satisfaction, vandalism, crime, drug use and gambling.[25]

This has great relevance for the so-called link between stress and work. Because if too much work causes stress, and boredom, insufficient or no work also cause stress, then the disease must be presumed to strike all populations not engaged in ideal and totally satisfactory levels of work. Such a 'disease' would by definition cease to be a disorder, since the majority of the population would normally experience it.

The wonders of work and its beneficial health effects have been highlighted by the so-called 'healthy worker syndrome' in epidemio-logical studies. For example, in one such study of staff at a nuclear plant, when past and present employees at the facility were assessed for possible work-related stress, it was found that despite their 'worrying' occupations they registered better health and lower mortality risks than the general population. Some experts believe this is because companies recruit healthy workers in the first place; others think that work itself has a salutary effect. 'There is good, well-documented evidence that on aggregate the unemployed suffer worse psychological health than the employed',[26] although some investigators suggest that job insecurity may present an additional threat.

The late Marie Jahoda, one of the most influential of social psychologists and emeritas Professor at the University of Sussex, studied prolonged mass unemployment in the 1920s and 1930s. She and her researchers found that regular work was a fundamental need for most people, not just for economic reasons, but because work gives people a personal sense of identity and worth, a structure for their day, and social contacts.[27] Workless people often suffer from a malaise of isolation and despair.

The retirement–mortality statistics are often skewed by the fact that people may quit work because of poor health. Research that takes this into account therefore carries more weight. A study published in the *British Medical Journal* in 1994 found that men who experienced unemployment in the five years after initial screening were twice as likely to die during the following 5.5 years as men who remained continuously employed. This study concluded: 'Even men who lost employment for reasons unrelated to health were at raised risk of dying, after adjustment for factors such as smoking, drinking and social class, suggesting a causal effect.'[28] In a Canadian study, newly retired pensioners were found to have an increased risk of suicide, with the first month after retirement a critical period.[29] People who go on working beyond retirement age do seem to live longer, according to statistics from the Continuous Mortality Investigation Bureau of the Institute of Actuaries.[30]

Professor Siegfried Lehrl of the University of Erlangen-Nürnberg's psychiatric clinic in Germany is a medical psychologist and intelligence expert. He has found that inactivity is bad for one's brain. He has measured the IQ (intelligence quotient) of politicians during and after polling, of people idling in saunas, and holidaymakers. Apparently, prolonged periods of relaxation can cause the nerve cells of the frontal lobes to atrophy, and this cell death is irreversible. Professor Lehrl subjected German holiday-makers to a battery of IQ tests. After a week their average IQ dropped by 5 per cent, and after three weeks, worse. 'Through the lack of intellectual activity during a holiday, when most Germans prefer to lie on a towel at the beach, nerve cells in the frontal lobe begin to shrink. A three-week trip to the seaside lowers the IQ of the average holidaymaker by about 20 points.'[31] Lehrl thinks we have to fight every day to keep our intelligence, suggesting the brain needs a workout as much as the body.

Stressing the positive

University of Strathclyde lecturer Michael Cavanagh, examining both the positive and negative aspects of stress, comments: 'It's helpful to understand that stress is not inherently destructive, but necessary for both physical and psychological growth. Therefore stress should not be avoided and in fact, it often should be judiciously sought out.'[32] Michael Bland, managing director of Michael Bland Communication Consultancy in London, agrees: 'Increasingly, the failure of traditional stress management methods and a better understanding of the subject . . . are leading to a new way of tackling stress. The first task here is to help people recognize stress as a good and necessary thing.'[33]

Particularly for women, apparently. A 2002 UCLA study revealed that women 'respond to stress' with brain chemicals that cause them to make and maintain friendships with other women. One of the researchers, Laura Cousino Klein, now Assistant Professor of biobehavioral health at Pennsylvania State University, comments: 'Until this study was published, scientists generally believed that when people experience stress, they trigger a hormonal cascade that revs the body to either stand and fight or flee as fast as possible.'[34] In women, this is not so. It seems that during female crises, the hormone oxytocin modifies the fight-or-flight response and encourages women to tend children and gather with other women. The effects of this calming hormone are neutralized by male testosterone, which is why men don't experience the same thing when they respond to threat.

Another rather remarkable side effect of the response to threat was seen in Northern Ireland. During the early years of the Troubles, scientists noticed a fall in the number of suicides and cases of self-harm.[35] They suggested that perhaps self-aggression had been somehow externalized. It is of course possible to speculate that in war and civil strife, the struggle simply to survive may focus the mind on immediate dangers, reducing to some extent the opportunity for morbid introspection and self-doubt. In wartime, social norms and objectives, often in the form of propaganda, at least provide the individual with a matrix in which to operate and think. He or she may utterly reject these norms, as our great anti-war writers and poets have done. But war provides an opportunity to review and clarify our individual values whatever they may be, and the chance to fight for them. Wartime camaraderie may also serve to reduce social isolation and self-destructive thoughts.

'Stress' and longevity

But the best news of all is that, in spite of all we have heard about stress and its negative health effects, life expectancy is set to soar. According to experts like Jim Oeppen, from Cambridge University, and Dr James Vaupel from the Max Plank Institute for Demography in Rostock, Germany, reaching the age of 100 will soon be 'commonplace'.[36] Based on patterns since 1840, the highest average life expectancy has improved by a quarter of a year every year. Average lifespan around the world is around double what it was 200 years ago.

Better still, the Japanese, reputedly among the world's most stressed workers, fare well in the wrinkle stakes. Despite death from overwork, high urbanization, overcrowding, financial crashes, techno-shock and such indignities as being stuffed into hotel sleeping compartments the size of luggage lockers and forced on to rush-hour underground trains with poles, Japanese men rank second highest in the world for longevity, while Japanese women are currently top wrinkle queens. The improvement in their life expectancy is among the fastest on the planet.

In fact, at an Anti-Ageing Conference held at the Royal College of Physicians in May 2005, new evidence began to emerge that is changing the whole scientific perspective on 'stress'. At that conference

Dr Marios Kyriazis, president of the British Longevity Society and a medical specialist in anti-ageing, presented new findings that the strains of life can actually protect our brains and bodies from the ravages of time. Over the past decade the process, known as *hormesis*, has been the focus of growing scientific interest and research, and this year experts from around the world have formed the International Society for Hormesis to promote its study.

Pressure and challenges increase the production of so-called 'heatshock proteins' that repair and strengthen damaged cells in the body and brain and enable them to function at peak capacity. This self-repair mechanism slows down as we age, but experts like Dr Kyriazis say that the best way to keep it working efficiently is to seek out challenges and short bursts of 'stressful' experience: hurrying over a task, 'going outside your comfort zone' and even short-term sleep or food deprivation are recommended. Such challenges 'exercise' the repair mechanism that protects the body from age-related conditions such as Alzheimer's, arthritis and heart disease. Says Dr Kyriazis: 'Stress is vital to survival. If you don't get enough, you could be doing yourself more harm than good.'[37]

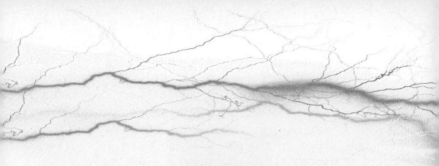

Part Three COSTS

CHAPTER NINE

WORK SICKNESS

What it was that was actually the matter with us, we none of us could be sure of; but the unanimous opinion was that it – whatever it was – had been brought on by overwork.

Jerome K. Jerome, *Three Men in a Boat*

A 1996 World Health Organization Survey referred to stress as 'a world-wide epidemic.' A *Time* magazine cover story in June 1983 called it 'the epidemic of the eighties', whereas for *The Times* in October 1998 'The Age of Stress' was the nineties. A 1992 United Nations report labelled stress 'the twentieth century disease', and Nigel de Gruchy, General Secretary of the National Association of Schoolmasters and Union of Women Teachers (NASUWT), warns that it could become 'the cancer and chief killer of the twenty-first century'.

In this chapter we shall examine some of the truly alarming statistics on the stress pandemic, in particular that most costly of stress phenomena – workplace stress. As we crunch the numbers we need to remain alert, for the effect of such preponderous statistics can be daunting and may stifle our critical faculties. We need to notice what is actually being measured by the figures, what assumptions are being made, whether the different sets of data agree, how the statistics have been compiled and interpreted, and whether in fact the figures quantify a real entity called 'stress' or an anxiety called stress phobia. In either case the cost may still be great, but the cause and treatment will be very different.

Workplace stress in the US

Workplace stress is a global phenomenon. The American Institute of Stress (AIOS) is one of numerous organizations to have created a test for measuring stress. Using this instrument Harris Interactive, together with the Marlin Company, carried out a telephone survey of the American workforce in 2001. They found that 82 per cent of workers reported being 'at least a little stressed at work' while 35 per cent said that work was negatively affecting their physical or emotional well-being.[1] The AIOS calculated that each day one million employees in the United States were absent because of stress or stress-related conditions. Since then, things have deteriorated. According to the AIOS and MSNBC News in 2003, the estimated cost to American industry of all this job stress is $300 billion annually in absenteeism, health costs and 'programs to help workers manage their stress'.[2]

In October 2001 the informative Symbiosis On Line (symbiosisonline.com) ranked stress as 'America's #1 Health Problem', citing research reports over the past two decades that show 43 per cent of American adults suffer adverse health effects due to stress; that between 75 and 90 per cent of all visits to primary care physicians are for stress-related complaints; that an estimated one million workers are absent on an average workday because of stress, and that stress is responsible for more than half of the 550 million working days lost annually. Another three-year study suggested that 60 per cent of employee absences were due to psychological problems such as stress.

The American NIOSH Stress at Work report cites studies showing 40 per cent of American workers considered their job to be very or extremely stressful, 25 per cent viewed their jobs as the number one 'stressor' in their lives and 26 per cent of workers said that they were 'often or very often burned out or stressed' by their work. The 2000 annual Attitudes in the American Workplace Gallup Poll found that 80 per cent of workers felt they were suffering from stress, and 25 per cent said it made them feel like screaming or shouting.

In 2000 Integra Realty Resources, a real estate advisory and appraisal firm with offices in forty-three US cities, conducted a survey on workplace stress. It reported that 65 per cent of workers said that workplace stress had caused them difficulties and 19 per cent had quit a previous position because of stress. Forty-four per cent complained of 'stressed-out eyes', nearly one in four had been driven to tears by stress, 29 per cent had 'yelled' and 2 per cent had attacked a colleague. Eleven per cent said that workplace stress was a major problem for them, and two thirds thought it was a problem for them at least occasionally. One in eight workers (12 per cent) had called in sick, and 26 per cent had been driven to eat chocolate.

The overriding assumption underpinning this sort of research data is that workplace stress equates to overwork. American employees apparently think they 'work longer hours than medieval peasants'. Friday, 24 October 2003 was the first annual Take Back Your Time Day, a nationwide initiative 'to challenge the epidemic of overwork, overscheduling, and time famine that now threatens our health...'[3] The date fell nine weeks before the end of the year, symbolizing 'the fact that the average American now works a full nine weeks longer than the average Western European worker'. Enough to make anybody heave his desk out of the window.

American workplace stress equates not only to overwork, but to aggression. Stories with the theme of 'stress equals aggression' appeared in *USA Today* and the *Wall Street Journal* under the headline 'Increasing Incidents of "Desk Rage" Disrupt Offices'. Rob Walker, writing for the *Slate* website in 2003, comments: 'Actually there was an earlier bout of publicity about desk rage as well, stemming from an earlier survey in the UK.'[4] Stress overwork and stress aggression equal absence from work. A poll of 800,000 workers in over 300 American companies found the number of employees calling in sick because of stress had tripled between 1996 and 2000.[5] According to an online newsletter of the Institute for Management Excellence, executives alone cost the US economy more than $10 billion annually in lost workdays, hospitalization and 'early death from stress'.[6]

Workplace stress in Australia

In Australia in 1994 the Federal Assistant Minister for Industrial Relations estimated the cost of occupational stress to be around A$30 million.[7] That same year, in an issue of *NSW Doctor*, the journal of the New South Wales branch of the Australian Medical Association, Sydney psychiatrist Jean Lennane blamed employers for all this. She explained that they were victimizing whistleblowers and industrial complainants and railroading them through medical consultations to make them appear psychologically weak and unreliable in order to get rid of them: 'Employees in these situations commonly become anxious, depressed and develop other somatic symptoms of stress.'[8] They then took time off work because of these symptoms, fulfilling expectations that they were psychologically infirm. The psychiatrist found herself in the unusual position of pleading with fellow psychiatrists and doctors to word medical certificates carefully concerning this 'anxiety and depression caused by the stress', as such certificates might be used by bosses to pathologize troubled employees. How different Australians were in 1994 in this respect. In 2005, some of the more delicate employees hang their hopes on being pathologized at the earliest opportunity.

Since Dr Lennane's alert, workplace stress reporting down under has increased, and Australians have come to think of themselves as overworked and out of their minds with worry. 'Working hours in Australia are now longer than in almost all other countries,' announced a report by the Australian Institute's executive director Clive Hamilton in 2002. 'Among full-time workers, 30 per cent are working more than 48 hours a week.'[9] Evidently this may have less to do with pressure from bosses than with 'affluenza' – the fever to get a bigger barbie. The same source continues: 'It is fair to conclude that a substantial majority of Australians who experience no real hardship, and indeed live lives of abundance, believe they are "doing it tough" ... As a result, the little Aussie battler has become the great Australian whinger.'

Workplace stress in the EU

The European Agency for Safety and Health at Work (EASHW) estimate that half of all sickness absence in Europe is now stress-related.[10] An earlier International Labour Organization (ILO) study of mental health policies and programmes affecting the workforces of Finland, Germany, Poland, the UK and the United States showed one in ten workers in these countries now suffer from stress, depression, anxiety, or burnout. The report estimates that 3–4 per cent of GNP is spent on such mental health problems in the European Union. In Finland over 50 per cent of the workforce experiences stress-related symptoms. In Germany absenteeism related to mental health disorders is estimated at over 5 billion DM annually.[11]

An ILO review[12] suggests that 'approximately 30 per cent of the workforce in developed countries, and possibly even a higher proportion in newly industrialized and developing countries, suffer from work-related stress' and that 'on the basis of figures from a number of countries we estimate that in total stress and violence at work may account for 1–3.5 per cent of GDP'.

EASHW estimated during European Week 2002 that nearly one in three of Europe's workers – more than 40 million people – believed that they were suffering from stress at work.[13] The cost to businesses in the fifteen member states then was at least Euro 20 billion annually. However, the EASHW also referred to Dublin European Foundation's Second European Survey on Working Conditions 1997, which showed that 28 per cent of workers reported stress-related health problems, and that this amounted to 'about 41 million EU workers affected by work-related stress each year'.[14]

The UK – sick note epidemic?

The fact that stress is not recognized as abnormal in law, and the fact that, even according to the HSE, stress is a 'natural reaction' and not a disease,[15] does raise the question, what is the word doing on medical certificates entitling the bearer to paid absence from work, absence that is costing the economy billions? Since medical doctors are trained in pathology, and since stress is not pathological, it surely has no place in the medical lexicon of 'reasons for absence'. 'Exhaustion due to overwork', 'depression' or 'anxiety' – these are feasible explanations for a patient being unable to work. But 'stress' certainly is not.

Although the real overall cost of 'stress' phobia to the NHS is unknown, we may be sure that it is ruinous, and particularly so with respect to general practice. The stress management ideology actively encourages people to look for signs and symptoms, and persuades them that they are in need of psychological and other treatment, when in fact they may simply be experiencing normal emotions and reactions. Stress sufferers may lack coping skills; they may face real practical problems at home or at work. But the ideology itself sends them to the doctor and the therapist. It is therefore a direct burden on the NHS.

The 'stress' word stands at the interface between GPs and their patients. GPs interpret patients' complaints and decide treatment. They are very busy. Many of them believe that they themselves suffer from stress and the BMA provides them with counselling. It is all too easy for these doctors to write 'stress' on a sick note rather than investigate further, or examine non-medical aspects of their patients' feelings and difficulties (they used to write 'nerves' for the same reason). They must, if possible, be asked to stop. In 2003, press reports appeared about the case of a forty-year-old father of four, Paul Boddon, who was sent home by his own doctor, and three times from accident and emergency departments, with analgesics for his crippling stomach pains. He was told that he was suffering from stress. Eight weeks later he was dead – from undiagnosed lymphatic cancer.

Workplace absenteeism in the UK, therefore, provides only a conservative estimate of the scale of 'stress' costs to Britain's economy. It will not reveal the full toll on the National Health Service because some sufferers may report to GPs and receive treatment but continue to go to work. The true price of whatever we are calling 'stress' would include GP time, drug prescription (including mood-altering drugs), referrals to psychiatric services, referral to stress management and counselling services and so on. Stress treatment frequently involves long- and medium-term prescription of mood-adapting drugs. Concerns have been raised about over-prescription, dependence and side effects by the mental health charity MIND's Yellow Card Scheme investigation, and by other groups such as Victims of Tranquillizers (VOT), an organization representing prescription drug users who have suffered serious side effects. VOT say that since 1960 there have been over 700 million prescriptions for benzodiazepines in the UK, and that these drugs are dangerous and disabling. This 'disease', whatever it is, costs people, and not just money.

Absenteeism

Let us look first at the overall cost of absenteeism in the UK, and then at the significance of the stress phenomenon within these statistics. A CBI survey in 2001 showed 192 million working days lost to absence in 2000 – the equivalent of 861,000 people, or the entire working populations of Nottingham and Merseyside, not working for a year. The cost to British business, said the CBI, was £10.7 billion.[16] A more recent CBI survey put the figure at £11.8 billion. In May 2004, the CBI and Axa Insurance polled 500 companies and discovered public sector workers were by far the worst absenters. Overall around 25 million sick days were regarded as 'suspicious', at an estimated cost of £1.75 billion in wages and cover. Stress was felt to be part of this scam. Because of its limitless vagueness, the condition self-evidently provides a ready excuse for dubious days off. Supermarket giant Tesco announced its own clampdown, saying the first three 'sickie' days would no longer be paid.

In July 2000, ministers had announced a clampdown on the '£1 billion a year' bill for early retirement in the public sector and a review of the 'scandal' of 25,000 public sector staff retiring early every year. A Treasury inquiry had shown the rate of ill-health retirement among workers on the state payroll was a third higher than in the private sector. The investigation covered five years up to 1999, and had shown that 68 per cent of all fire-fighters who retired did so early on grounds of ill-health. In the police force – where £1 in every £7 spent went on pensions – the rate was 49 per cent and in local government 39 per cent. (The armed forces figure was just 6 per cent.) The figures embarrassed Tony Blair, who in 1996 had announced to a Labour party conference: 'I vow that we will reduce the proportion we spend on the welfare bills of social failure. This is my covenant with the British people. Judge me upon it.'

More blushes were to follow. In 2003, according to Treasury figures, the cost of sickness and disability payouts had nearly doubled, growing by 41 per cent since the Labour party took office. Treasury figures then forecast sickness payments would rise to £23 billion before the end of the year and hit £25 billion before the next election.

Stress and the statistics

What part does 'stress' play in these shocking statistics? In the UK the Health and Safety Executive estimated in 2000 that the stress epidemic was damaging the economy to the extent of 6.7 million lost working days a year, at a cost of between £3.7 billion and £3.8 billion to the nation (1995–96 prices), and that 5 million people (one in five) were 'very' or 'extremely stressed' by their work.[17] About half a million of these workers believed that their stress was making them ill. The cost to British employers was estimated by the HSE in 1999 to be between £353 million and £381 million per annum (again at 1995–96 prices). Since these assessments were carried out, the estimated number of days lost due to stress has more than doubled.[18] In 2004, according to the HSE and TUC, the startling cost of workplace stress to the UK economy in sick pay, lost productivity and NHS bills had risen to £7 billion a year.

In December 2004 the Department of Work and Pensions issued a sorry set of figures showing that the number of Britons on incapacity benefit and unable to work had reached 2.7 million. Many of these claimants were young (159,100 of them under twenty-five), and of these, six out of ten (92,600) had been on the benefit for more than a year. Worse, the number of people claiming this benefit who were unable to work because of emotional problems – 'depression, anxiety or other neuroses' – had for the first time breached the one million mark (1,028,300). Compared with just over 700,000 who were on incapacity benefit for these reasons in 1997 when Tony Blair took office, this represented a 45 per cent rise. In some areas, one in four men of working age was now claiming the benefit for emotional incapacity. The cost to the taxpayer of these mental and behavioural disorders is reckoned at £2.4 billion a year.

Apparently, white-collar workers feel much worse than hair-dressers or plumbers. In March 2004, a City and Guilds survey of

1,054 employees revealed that, while half of the professionals regarded themselves as stressed, hands-on employees rather enjoyed their work. This phenomenon of stress susceptibility had already been highlighted in an occupational analysis the previous year, showing public sector workers like teachers, civil servants and police officers were far more likely to absent themselves from work with stress and other mood disorders than even the most high-pressured private sector workers like commercial tradesmen and restaurant staff. A TUC survey of almost 5,000 health and safety staff in October 2004 cited 'stress' as the major cause of complaints according to 58 per cent of their representatives, with public sector workers far more likely to complain of it than private sector workers. The TUC blamed the threat of redundancies and cruel office workloads. According to General Secretary Brendan Barber: 'We know that long hours and dense workloads are stressful ... Yet some employers insist on trying to squeeze every last drop of sweat out of their workforce.'[19]

In 2002 the Health and Safety Commission (HSC) found 33 million days were lost in the previous year from work-related sickness, nearly twice the 18 million in its last comparable survey in 1995. The HSC had discovered that 'a lot of employees were taking off more than six months a year because managers were reluctant to challenge their claims or help "rehabilitate genuine sufferers"'. *Sign Up*, a joint HSE/Department of Health booklet, put the annual Europe-wide cost in 2002 at £20 billion.[20] The same publication in 2001 referred to a Department of Health estimate that stress absence costs £5 billion annually, 'which doesn't include hidden costs like low staff morale, problems with recruitment and retention, early retirement, cover for colleagues and complaints and litigation'.[21]

The figures on absence due to stress are mind-boggling. On 25 February 2004, a BBC2 *Money Programme* special investigation ('Burnt Out Britain'), put the absence figure 'over the past twelve months' at 13 million lost working days; in the *Observer* on 12 October 2003 (in a feature entitled 'Life makes you sick'), the same

13 million figure was given for the number of days lost to stress during *that* past year. Both figures derived from HSE data.

When the HSC's disturbing 2002 figures were published, co-director of the HSE's health directorate policy group Sandra Caldwell was reported as saying: 'At the moment we are not 100 per cent sure whether this is an actual increase in stress or whether there are technical issues such as over-reporting.'[22] She told me: 'If you look at the technical notes that accompany the latest statistics you will note that the multifactorial nature of ill-health (and this is certainly the case for stress) makes it difficult to attribute individual cases of ill-health to causation by work factors. But we are confident that there has been an increase in the association made by people between ill health and work-related stress. I am also concerned that HSC/E are not perceived as driving a campaign which promotes "stress" as a common workplace condition when this is not soundly based on evidence.'

However this may be, an HSC/E Priority Programme which began in 2000–2001 will apparently bring the figures into even sharper focus: 'Our statisticians have predicted that as the Priority Programme gets underway we can expect an increase over these figures in coming years.' This will be due to 'increased awareness of the issue, a growing "acceptability" of reporting the condition, and possibly increased prevalence'.

A Chartered Institute of Personnel and Development survey in July 2004 showed that absenteeism in the public sector is costing the taxpayer £4 billion a year. On average, public sector workers took nearly 11 days off sick in 2003, almost 50 per cent more than employees in the private sector (Welsh workers, for some reason, were off sick more than anybody else, averaging 10.7 days). Overall, according to the CIPD, workers were laid low for an average of 9.12 days in 2003, raising the cost of sickness absence to £567 per worker, with stress an increasing pain in the employer's pocket. Among non-manual workers, stress was the second most common reason for not turning up.

In April 2005 the CIPD issued figures that were even worse. Absenteeism, especially in the public sector, had risen again, with employees claiming an average of 10.7 sickness days a year. The average cost of absence now stood at £588 annually per worker, and stress played a significant part in this cost, with stress-related conditions accounting for a third of the 11.6 billion total sickness bill on lost productivity and healthcare costs as estimated by the Department of Work and Pensions.

The Work Foundation, which was perhaps thinking of renaming itself the Absent from Work Foundation, found that absenteeism in the public sector had almost trebled in twelve months, at a cost to the nation of £8 billion annually. The average public sector worker took more than three weeks off sick a year, most commonly with stress, minor ailments and back pain. Business leaders reacted angrily. Ruth Lea, then policy director at the Institute of Directors, commented: 'This is a national scandal and a huge cost to the nation. Stress has been medicalized and as a result it has opened up a can of worms. Anybody now can claim to be stressed and not turn up for work, whereas ten or twenty years ago they had to get on with it.'[23] The IOD thought things were pretty bad. Tim Field, who runs the UK's bullying advice network, thought the end was nigh. As far back as July 1999 his *Bully OnLine* website carried the confident assertion: 'Every day the UK loses the equivalent of 1,000 YEARS (a millennium) of labour due to sickness absence caused by stress.'

Inflating the figures – the role of propaganda

For Britain's unions particularly, stress is the number one health concern for the nation's workers, with four in every five union representatives, according to the TUC, 'raising fears' (their words) about its effects in a survey of 5,300 union officials published in November 2002. Eighty per cent of union health and safety reps told the TUC that stress was a problem in their workplace. This represents an awful lot of anxiety about stress, and the unions are naturally keen to protect the health of their members. Between 2000 and 2001 the unions started almost 9,000 new stress compensation cases.[24] The TUC 2002 *Focus on Services for Injury Victims* showed a *twelve-fold* increase in stress cases since the previous year, with 6,428 new cases reported, compared to just 516 in 2001. TUC General Secretary John Monks told the press, 'Unions took slightly less [personal injury] cases than the year before but the rise in stress cases is very worrying indeed. I do not want to join the "blame race" [*sic*] over stress at work ... Trade Unions want to be part of the solution where stress is concerned, not part of the problem.'

Evidently he had not had the opportunity to peruse issue 40 of the TUC newsletter (9 February 2002), *Risks*, which announced: 'Unions must promote understanding of the stress syndrome ... They should include awareness-building exercises in their activities to enable their members to demand that employers take the necessary measures upstream and that prevention prevails over cure [*sic*].' A recent (2002) Court of Appeal ruling which overturned three stress compensation claims may have dismayed members. However, the TUC's Owen Tudor said bad employers should take no comfort from the rulings: 'Unions will certainly make sure that employers know that they must assess the risks of stressful occupations. We will make sure our members know that the Court of Appeal has urged them not to suffer in silence.'

One employer with burning ears might well have been Unison, the largest union in the UK. An internal Unison report on stress levels in October 1997 found that 63 per cent of union officials were 'anxious' at work and 53 per cent were 'sometimes depressed'. Almost 60 per cent felt they were overworked (as distinct from merely 'stressed').[25] These figures were made public after Gordon Brown's election campaign chauffeur, senior Unison official Jim Waller, died of a heart attack in April 1999. Two weeks before his death he had been working up to twenty-one hours a day and complaining about attempts to increase his workload. His widow accused the Labour party and trade union bosses of 'driving him to his death'.[26]

A bulletin issued by the TUC in August 2003 warned: 'Workers exposed to stress for at least half their working lives are 25 per cent more likely to die from a heart attack, and have 50 per cent higher odds of suffering a fatal stroke. Also blue collar workers are more prone to such illnesses than executives.'

The TUC perspective

These statistics are certainly alarming, and they were widely publicized in the national press. If the figures gave a true impression, then the cost to the UK workforce would be awesome indeed. But if we are to be objective about workplace stress statistics we need to look more closely at the TUC's evidence.

An editorial by Rory O'Neill under the bannerhead *Drop Dead*, in the union-backed *Hazards* online magazine, cites studies that allegedly show: 'Workers with stressful jobs are more than twice as likely to die from heart disease' and that: 'Workers are smoking, drinking and "slobbing out" to deal with workplace stress.'[27] Also that 'Long term work-related stress is worse for the heart than aging [*sic*] 30 years or gaining 40 lbs in weight,' and 'Working for unreasonable and unfair bosses leads to dangerously high blood pressure.' I queried the latter finding with Mr O'Neill, pointing out that the British Hypertension Society say high blood pressure is not caused by stress. The editor of *Hazards* responded: 'There's a mountain of evidence on stress and increases in blood pressure. That BHS [*sic*] doesn't accept it is alarming.'[28] It is odd that the highest authority on high blood pressure in the UK should misunderstand the research evidence, but then blood pressure and 'stress' often cause confusion. The fight-or-flight or stress response does indeed involve a temporary rise in blood pressure but this is quite normal, and not to be confused with hypertension, an abnormal condition in which blood pressure levels are elevated over a prolonged period.

The research evidence cited by *Hazards* is interesting but hardly alarming. The most authoritative research in this field, the HSE *Whitehall II Studies*, are a very long, very complex ongoing investigation of the statistical relationship between disease (including coronary heart disease) and work-related factors such as job demands, degree of control and effort-reward in 10,308 civil servants. Nowhere within them do the authors make sweeping or alarmist statements about their findings. They say that although 'both job demands and job strain predict CHD [coronary heart disease] events', other variables such as low pay, job insecurity, coping skills and need for control influence these statistics. They also point out that people who find their jobs upsetting and difficult may console themselves with smoking and other lifestyle habits that place them at risk.[29] The HSE describes 'the effects of change in work characteristics on physical health and coronary heart disease' as 'modest'.[30]

Other research has reached very different conclusions about workplace stress and health. In 2002, for example, a joint study by researchers from Birmingham, Glasgow and Bristol of 5,600 men from twenty-seven different workplaces in Scotland, led by Professor John McLeod of Birmingham University's Department of Primary Care and General Practice, found a *lower* incidence of heart disease and mortality among workers complaining of stress. The stressed workers were thought to be more likely to present themselves with chest pains and therefore to receive regular medical check-ups and monitoring of their hearts.

It seems, then, that any research purporting to be about workplace stress and heart problems needs to be viewed with prudence. Increasing evidence has emerged, during the last decade particularly, linking heart disease with bacterial and viral infection: with periodontal disease, with the sexually transmitted diseases, herpes and *chlamydia trachomatis*, with *cytomegalovirus*, and with the 'ulcer bug' *helicobacter pylori*. Separate studies have shown that patients treated with antibiotics are less prone to heart attacks. Such variables would need to be 'factored out' before firm conclusions could be drawn about the effects of negative emotions upon the heart.

Of the other studies cited by the TUC publication *Hazards*, one is based on blood pressure readings of 213 New York men who were asked to fill in questionnaires about their previous jobs; one is a small study of female healthcare assistants on their perceptions of two different supervisors' styles; and the other is a study of 812 employees in the metal industry in Finland which used self-assessment scales on their perceptions of work relative to the national mortality index.

Based on this rather underwhelming evidence, *Hazards* claims that British workers are dropping like flies from workplace stress, at great cost to the nation. The TUC make the common assumption that job stress is more or less equivalent to overwork. As already acknowledged, overwork is a very serious industrial problem, and we may wonder why the unions' role in helping their members should have changed from one of demonstrating outside coking plants on such fundamental issues, to one of chaperoning stress victims through the courts.

The *Hazards* article refers to the national tragedy of exploited workers in Japan, where compensation is awarded to families of those who have died of *karoshi* (exhaustion from overwork) and *karojisatsu* (suicide from overwork) 'after regularly working overtime of 80 plus hours per month ... Less than 45 hours overtime in each month prior to death is considered "weak" evidence.' The TUC bulletin sounds a note of doom for British workers: 'The problem may not be quite so bad in the UK – yet.' It refers us to a Department of Trade and Industry survey in 2002, which discovered that 16 per cent of employees surveyed were working over 60 hours a week, up from 12 per cent in 2000. This would certainly indicate overwork in a relatively small minority of UK employees, although we do not know the reasons for their long hours and cannot necessarily assume coercion. The DTI also found that 19 per cent of those surveyed had visited the doctor complaining of stress, rising to 23 per cent in the over forties. Again, the *Hazards* article seeks to conflate the overwork and the stress, as though they were one and the same thing.

Hazards' other evidence is a 2003 Samaritans survey on stress. This survey asked respondents to choose 'the biggest source of stress for you personally at the moment'. Thirty-six per cent replied 'Job/Workplace'. However, in another part of the survey not quoted, the same percentage reported that they experienced stress 'never' or 'less than once a month'.[31] This is why it is foolish and misleading to assume that stress and overwork are interlinked.

The 'long hours' culture

Supporters of the stress ideology, when interpreting workplace stress statistics and the cost to public health, often refer to a phenomenon known as 'presenteeism' – the idea that workers are remaining at their desks and overworking themselves for fear that they will otherwise lose their jobs. Again, there are problems with such an interpretation. For a start, we need to remember that research shows underwork may itself be considered a source of occupational stress, particularly in workplaces where there is a culture of job insecurity. As we have seen, one of the earliest stress management programmes in the UK was introduced at Nestlé's after a manager had a 'nervous breakdown' from not having much to do.[32] In a survey of 2,000 executives carried out by *Management Today* and Ceridian Performance Partners in 1999, nearly a third said they felt stressed if they were *not* constantly under pressure at work, fearing that they might be 'no longer needed'.[33]

The suggestion that workers are remaining at their desks through oppression and fear needs to be reviewed. There may be other explanations for those extended hours. The 1999 government-funded *Britain at Work* survey interviewed more than 30,000 employees and found that 37 per cent of male managers were regularly working well past the forty-eight hours a week imposed by the Brussels Working Time Directive. Why? Some may have felt insecure and were trying to make themselves indispensable; some might have been coerced; others might simply have been conscientious and keen on their jobs. Common sense suggests that not every white-collar male looks forward to an evening at home with the wife and children. Some actually revel in their work, find home life relatively dull, and enjoy the company of their colleagues.

A survey of senior HR professionals published by *Personnel Today* magazine and the HSE in October 2003 suggested another reason for those long hours. Britain's productivity is 20 per cent lower than France or Germany and well below the European average. The report stated: 'The only reason Britain has kept pace at all is because we work the longest hours in Europe.' In fact it was worse than that. UK productivity was 40 per cent lower than the USA and sixteenth in the world league of competitiveness.

The Institute of Directors, in *Work-Life Balance Revisited* (May 2003), offer some counter-evidence on the 'long hours culture'. They point out that according to official figures, 'the average actual weekly hours was 39.6 hours for a full-time man and 34.4 hours for a full-time woman in 2002. These data hardly support the notion that the UK is a nation of frantic workaholics. Moreover, average hours worked have been remarkably steady since the early 1980s.' On long hours and sickness, the IOD refers us to an Institute of Personnel and Development report (*Living to work?* August 1999), which says: 'there appears to be little distinct correlation between ill-health and long hours up to 48 or 50 hours a week'.

Presenteeism, or staying late at work without being required to do so, was again highlighted in 2001, when companies like British Telecom and Microsoft UK began introducing schemes to persuade their employees to go home at the normal time. To have tired and stale workers staying late for the sake of it was seen by these employers as counterproductive. Microsoft UK even promised a donation to the children's charity NSPCC if only workers would clear off at 5.30 p.m. An earlier investigation of long working hours in 1995 had concluded: 'Britain is recognized as having the longest working week in Europe (while still being one of the least productive countries).'[34]

One reason why workers may feel duty-bound to stay late at the office is 'Afternoon Apathy Syndrome' or AAS, thought to affect 12 million British workers or over 40 per cent of the UK workforce. In research on healthy eating commissioned by Ryvita and conducted by ICM Polls in 2003, workers reported eating high-carbohydrate snacks that increased levels of serotonin in the brain and left them drowsy in the afternoons. If all the workers affected suffered a drop in efficiency of even 10 per cent between 3 p.m. and 4 p.m., it would cost the British economy £3.93 billion a year. Liquid lunches and long working lunches are another potential cause of afternoon despond. So there may be slightly more to 'overworked Britain' than statistics on office hours seem to suggest.

Interpreting the evidence

When surveys measure stress, or stress absenteeism, what is it that is being measured or suffered from? HSC's Sandra Caldwell expained: 'I think we have common ground in concerns about what "stress" means and how people choose to tackle it. For the HSC/E it has been a fundamental principle to get a common under-standing ourselves of what the term means, and this is now being widely accepted.'[35] Unfortunately, as can be seen from a glance at the Appendix, by no means all authorities agree with the HSC/E's definition. There is also the rather embarrassing problem of the HSC/E's own research evidence on workplace stress. For this evidence to be valid, the new chosen meaning would need to inform all of the research and statistics the HSE/C choose to draw upon, and this is certainly not the case at present.

Bamboozled by statistics

We also need to remember that people are often bamboozled by statistics, and liable to be persuaded and even brainwashed by them. I can offer an obvious example of this 'stress stats' gullibility. At the start of my classes and presentations, I get a volunteer to read out a list of stress statistics from a printed sheet. The sheet has a lot of gaps, for example:

These are figures for 2004 (the latest year for which statistics are available). The cost of stress to British industry that year was £......... in lost productivity, £......... in absenteeism and £......... in early retirements. The number of deaths due to work-related stress in the UK was .... Among high-risk occupations, ... ranked highest nationally. In the year 2004, ... people died from stress-related heart attacks, a further ..... from stress-related hypertension (etc. etc.)

The volunteer is asked to insert the missing figures from his or her imagination. For the 'occupations most at risk' they will generally insert that of the audience, one assumes out of mischief. My unemployed trainees, for example, insert 'unemployed people'.

At the end of the reading there is a *rapt silence*. Nobody ever questions the figures, however preposterous. Nobody ever says, 'Where did these statistics come from? How were they compiled? How are you defining "stress"?' Definitions, as the reader will notice from the relevant section at the back of the book, will often begin with the words, 'Stress *is when* so-and-so'. This is not a definition. The definition of 'cat' is not '*when* something is furry'.

Reading through all the stress stats in this chapter, what does the reader notice? Well first, there are a lot of them. Stress is one of the most measured phenomena in the social sciences. Second, the figures are *very* large and rising *very* fast. Thirdly, one notices that, even within the same national remit, the figures are *different*. They appear to be measuring different things, or sets of things.

Since there is no agreed definition of the control term in science or out of it, every data-collecting organization or agency assumes that it knows what stress means, and that this meaning will also govern data collected by other organizations and agencies. A great deal of the data on stress is from self-report surveys and inventories in which respondents are offered multiple choice questions or asked to grade their feelings and perceptions (using such scales as extremely–very–moderately–hardly–not at all, and always–often–occasionally–rarely–never).

Because 'stress' can be used to describe any negative emotional state or external circumstance, results depend upon the minutiae of personal feelings and reactions, on perceptions of working environments, management styles and relationships, and on domestic life, belief systems, culture and coping strategies.

According to a report by the Work Foundation (or the Industrial Society as it was then called): 'Stress audits, now offered by a growing number of commercial as well as non-profitmaking organizations, present major problems of their own. They typically use self-report measures of stress ... They do not necessarily identify real hazards or show the associated harm that is likely to occur. So they are limited in the extent to which they can be used to carry out accurate and useful risk assessments.'[36] Stress audits administered by profit-making stress management firms are self-evidently not designed to show that no intervention is needed. They must be framed in such a way that miscellaneous problems and perceptions can be interpreted using stress terminology, that respondents are seen proportionately to suffer from stress, and that the audit instruments are measuring 'hot spots' where this suffering is focused. Questions are often designed like Venus fly-traps to catch the buzz-word 'stress'.

Often implicit in such stress questionnaires is a 'there there' factor: the respondent feels someone somewhere is taking an interest in him and allowing him in confidence to unburden himself of all his cares. Some respondents weep as they fill in the forms, and express dread at hearing the findings. Leeds Council workers were televised waiting for the results of their pressure management indicator questionnaires. Comments included: 'Am I one of the casualties?' 'I'm quite scared of what it's going to show me,' 'I'm really scared – I've got butterflies!' and 'I just hope no one's going to be carted off to the lunatic asylum.'[37] Apart from being potentially upsetting and damaging to self-esteem, a stress survey implies that because a person is busy he is suffering; that his suffering is unnatural and dangerous to sanity and health; that it is pitied by some benevolent authority, and that the survey will infallibly result in his 'suffering' being recorded, recognized and remedied.

In the stress statistics such subjective data are freely mixed and matched with other more tangible variables like the number of working hours, overtime, number of customer interactions, decision latitude, job demands, resources, etc., which seek to measure the length, intensity and control of the working day, based on the false assumption that stress is reliably a factor of overwork (rather than underwork or no work at all) and that it has to do with feelings of being supported, appreciated or self-determining, or with the relationship between effort and reward. The results are a mass and the result is a mess.

In fact, the *least* anomalous and most certain outcome of all of these stress statistics is that they measure concern about the stress phenomenon and fear of the stress phenomenon. In other words, they measure stress phobia.

CHAPTER TEN
LITIGATION

A lawyer with his briefcase can steal more than a hundred men with guns.

Mario Puzo, *The Godfather*

While employees may be anxious – and even phobic – about their 'workplace stress', employers are positively unnerved by the threat of stress litigation. Stress is a fuzzy word that lends itself to lawsuits.

One of Australia's largest employer organizations, the Chamber of Commerce and Industry, argued in 2002 that there was still no proof of any 'linkage between so-called workplace stress and disease'. Meanwhile, a South Australian court has ruled that an employee's fatal bowel cancer was partly the result of workplace stress.[1]

According to the American Institute of Stress,[2] a significant part of the estimated $300 billion annual cost of stress to the American economy comes in the form of legal and insurance costs, and compensation awards. The same source tells us that 'In California, the number of workers' compensation claims for mental stress has increased by almost 700 per cent over eight years and 90 per cent were successful.' Symbiosis On Line, also monitoring the situation, records: 'Workers' compensation awards for job stress, rare two decades ago, have skyrocketed and threaten to bankrupt the system in some states. California employers shelled out almost $1 billion for medical and legal fees alone. Nine out of ten job stress suits are successful, with an average payout more than four times that for regular injury claims.' A study by the California Workers' Compensation Institute showed that between 1980 and 1986, the number of stress claims rose by 430 per cent, but worse was to come. Total compensation costs for Californian employers increased from $11 billion in 1998 to $29 billion in 2003 – eight times the gross domestic product of Haiti – prompting Governor Arnold Schwarzenegger to get tough and sign a bill in June 2004 to reform the whole compensation system.

Some states require more proof of job stress than others. Attorney at Law Jon L. Gelman offers a professional analysis:[3] Wisconsin, for instance, takes an 'objective' approach, requiring 'out of the ordinary' workplace stress to qualify. New Jersey has adopted a 'middle of the road' stance, requiring some evidence over and above the personal perceptions and feelings of the claimant. A woman bookkeeper with a history of hypertension who failed to balance her books was awarded compensation after she suffered a coronary infarction. Her heart attack was deemed to be work-related. But in Michigan, an employee's purely subjective reactions may form the basis of a claim. A perfectionist employee who became irritable and nervous about his co-worker's efforts suffered 'psychoneurosis' and was awarded compensation. And in California a baker who had rowed with her supervisor and who, the court heard, wrongly felt that she had been bullied, was said to have had 'an honest misperception of job harassment'. She too was awarded compensation, as was a fire-fighter who became preoccupied with heart disease after years of exposure to fumes and smoke. He was compensated for a syndrome known as 'cardiac neurosis'.

Stress and UK regulation

According to TUC figures for 2002 the highest regional bill for personal injury and stress compensation claims was for the South-

East and East of England with £61 million, compared with £16.05 million for the North-East. The total cost to employers and, in the public sector, the taxpayer, for stress and personal injury claims was around £321 million.

Now in Britain, 'safety first' has become the watchword of employment legislation. At a time when frightened elderly residents are being evicted from their care homes for want of funding and NHS patients lie groaning on hospital trolleys waiting for a bed or death, whichever might come sooner, the Health and Safety Executive, employing 4,050 staff, receives an annual net income from the government of £219 million. Its income from publications and services boosts this to £262 million. Thus larded, the HSE in 2003 introduced a tough new code, which for the first time will put employers on notice of legal action if they ignore the issue of workplace stress. (Hitherto, actions have been brought under existing legislation.) The new standards are to be fine-tuned, and the code was formally launched in November 2004. In 'Real Solutions Real People' the HSE sets out six guidelines:

- **demands** – 85 % of employees must feel they can cope with the demands of the job
- **control** – 85% must consider they have an adequate say in how they do their work
- **support** – 85% must feel they get adequate support from colleagues and superiors
- **relationships** – 65% must feel they are not subjected to unacceptable behaviour
- **role** – 65% must consider they understand their role and responsibilities
- **change** – 65% of workers must feel they are involved in organizational changes.

The HSE announced: 'The management standards will be what we expect companies to do to manage the stress in their workplace.

They will be equivalent to the Highway Code. It will make it easier for employees to bring actions.' Employers who fail this 'stress litmus test' will be given five months to comply with the code or face criminal charges. The first Enforcement Notice was issued in August 2003 against West Dorset Hospitals, a National Health Service Trust. And according to the TUC's Tom Mellish (interviewed for BBC2's *Money Programme* in February 2004), there are some 6,400 work stress claims currently waiting to go to court.

Compensation cases

Stress compensation cases make grim reading. They are the stuff of nightmares, both for employers being sued, and for employees having the gory details of their mental suffering read out in court and then picked over in the tabloid newspapers. Below I have summarized press reports of ten of the UK's most highly publicized cases. Although 'workplace stress' is the umbrella term covering all such claims, the interpretation of what constitutes 'stress' in each particular case varies considerably. Sometimes the employee felt bullied or abused, on other occasions there was difficulty with a particular aspect of the job. Sometimes the claimant felt exploited or overextended and in one case the degree of work was felt to be 'traumatic'. The lay term 'nervous breakdown' is in inverted commas because the condition, however distressing, varies very much from person to person.

1. In 1996, Unison-backed social services officer John Walker was awarded £175,000 from the taxpayer and Northumberland County Council, for two 'nervous breakdowns' occasioned by his work, with legal fees, sick pay and pension bringing the total costs of the case to nearly £500,000.
2. The same local authority was obliged to pay another £100,000 of taxpayers' money to teacher Christine Browell after she was

bullied by the former head of Mowbray First School in Guide Post, near Morpeth.

3. Deputy head teacher Anthony Ratcliffe was awarded £101,000 from the taxpayer and Pembrokeshire County Council in 1998 for two 'nervous breakdowns' suffered during his tenure at Sageston County primary school near Tenby, Wales. Mr Ratcliffe, who had been made to feel 'ashamed and humiliated' by the behaviour of colleagues at a Christmas party and by his headmistress, commented: 'One morning I was so stressed I literally couldn't open the front door.'

4. Beverley Lancaster received £76,000 in compensation in 1999 from the taxpayer and Birmingham City Council for distress caused by insufficient training and changes to her part-time job. Unison, the public service union that backed the claim, said they had 7,000 similar cases pending, at least 2,000 of which were likely to go to court.

5. Head of year teacher Muriel Benson received £47,000 in October 1999, for the distress of her long hours at a school in Birkenhead, Merseyside.

6. Unison-backed 'traveller' Randy Ingram won an uncontested £203,000, more than twenty times his salary, in January 2000 from the taxpayer and Worcestershire County Council for abuse suffered as a gypsy site warden.

7. £300,000 from the taxpayer and Shropshire County Council was awarded to an unnamed male teacher in May 2000, after the appointment of a woman head at his school who 'allowed discipline to break down and continually undermined his position'.

8. Bank worker Leslie North received £100,000 in August 2000 from Lloyds Bank for distress caused when staff cuts led to a workload that reduced him to tears. Unusually for a workplace stress case this one hinged upon the controversial after-shock diagnosis 'post traumatic stress disorder' (more of which in a later chapter).

9. In December 2000 primary school teacher Janice Howell was awarded £254,000 from the taxpayer and Newport County Council for two 'nervous breakdowns' said to be the result of dealing with disruptive pupils. The fact that Mrs Howell had also had severe financial worries and a husband on remand for serious drug offences featured in widespread tabloid press criticism of the award.

10. Unison-backed social worker Thelma Conway received £140,000 from the taxpayer and Worcester County Council in 2001 for promoting her from deputy manager to manager of a residential home for adults with learning difficulties in Redditch, despite her protests that she could not cope. Mrs Conway's union representative said she was now only fit for a job with 'nil stress'.

Others making stress-related claims include: former civilian police worker Wendy Johnson (2001), seeking £100,000 for having worked on the 1993 James Bulger murder case; two policewomen, Catriona Ewing and Suzanne Ogg, seeking £400,000 each for attending the scene of the 1996 Dunblane school shootings and for 'not receiving proper stress counselling'; the nine Stansted airport hijackers (May 2003), suing the Home Office for 'up to £1 million' for their 'ordeal' during arrest and trial; and not forgetting a horse called Tilly, whose owner in 2002 received £1,700 from a motorist after a collision left Tilly 'hesitant and nervy'.

Several of the highest awards have gone to victims who evidently suffered two 'nervous breakdowns' as a result of their jobs. In other words, they not only continued in a position that allegedly drove them mad, but went back to it after a period of mental illness. Under the Health and Safety at Work legislation, 'Employees are themselves under a general statutory duty to take reasonable care for their own (physical and mental) health and safety (section 7 of the Health and Safety at Work Act).'[4] So that if employees consider that a particular job might pose a foreseeable risk to their mental health, it surely cannot be reasonable for them either to apply for that post in the first place, or to continue in such a job when they feel themselves to be at risk, with or without absence from work. Under the law as it exists, employees also have 'a duty to inform their employer ... of any work situation which they consider reasonably represents a serious and immediate danger to health and safety'.[5]

In any civilized society, adults who are not under the most severe coercion (as, for example, in war or political internment) must normally be expected to take responsibility for their actions and for their own mental and physical health. This was the view, at least, of some of Britain's most senior judges in August 2003, in a case unconnected with workplace stress. The Appellate Committee of the House of Lords unanimously demanded an end to 'the culture of blame and compensation' as an 'evil' that interferes with freedom of will and civil liberties. The five law lords had ruled against a litigant, John Tomlinson, who was paralysed after diving into a lake at Brereton Heath County Park in Cheshire. He had ignored warning signs telling him not to dive into the lake, and had sued the council for failing to prevent him from diving into the lake.

Appeal court ruling

The costly flood of UK stress compensation cases in 2002 met a formidable obstacle in the shape of a landmark Court of Appeal ruling now being studied by employment lawyers all over the country. In February 2002, the Court of Appeal found against Penelope Hatton, a teacher at St Thomas Becket RC High School in Merseyside who had won £90,765, Mervyn Bishop, a graphite blower, who had received £7,000 in damages from Baker Refractories, and Leon Barber, a teacher at East Bridgwater School in Somerset, who had been awarded £101,041. It was found that Ms Hatton had had serious marital problems that could have contributed to her 'work-related' depression. Messrs Bishop and Barber had not made their bosses sufficiently aware of their plight and therefore their breakdowns were not 'reasonably foreseeable'. The judges also blocked the claimants from taking their cases to the House of Lords.

The press greeted these decisions with headlines suggesting the law had been changed. In fact it had simply been clarified. 'Reports by some of the tabloid press that the judgement represents the end for stress at work claims is misleading,' warned Boris Cetnik, a partner at law firm Berrymans Lace Mawer.[6] The judgement of Lady Justice Hale[8] rejected the proposition that some jobs are intrinsically dangerous to mental health and emphasized that mere 'occupational stress' is not itself a 'psychiatric injury'. Absence from work with stress was not in itself sufficient reason for an employer to foresee his worker was about to collapse with mental illness. Furthermore, an employer is usually entitled to assume that the employee can withstand the normal pressures of the job unless he knows of some particular problem or vulnerability. And there was another important clarification. If the only reasonable step would have been to dismiss or demote the employee, the employer will not be in breach of duty by allowing a willing worker to continue in the job.

The unions were furious. They promised to get their members to complain loudly in future about their stress and write everything down. Since then a number of other appeals have reached court. In January 2005, six claims for damages for psychiatric injury caused by workplace stress were heard consecutively by the Court of Appeal, where Lord Justice Scott Baker ruled that claimants must prove that their psychiatric injury was 'foreseeable'. It was insufficient, in seeking to establish a claim in negligence, to show that a claimant had suffered stress at work and that the employer was in breach of duty of care in allowing this to occur. Lord Justice Scott Baker said that there were other similar cases in the pipeline. Yet despite the principles laid down in the Hatton case ruling and a decision in the House of Lords on a claim against Somerset County Council in 2004,[8] it was apparent that judges were still finding difficulty in determining on claims arising from workplace stress.[9]

The counselling safety valve

One curious upshot of the Appeal Court ruling, which may have a direct bearing on the cost of workplace stress in future litigation, was that it enshrined in legal annals the principle of introducing counselling into the workplace as a safety valve to guard against stress claims: 'An employer who offers a confidential advice service, with referral to appropriate counselling or treatment services, is unlikely to be found in breach of duty.'[10] As we shall see, expenditure on stress counselling by employers is already extremely high, and not everyone agrees that this money is wisely spent.

The reference to counselling is particularly odd, since the HSE itself and some international authorities have cast doubt on the usefulness of counselling services in dealing with workplace stress. In fact the HSE sees the efficacy of such 'first aid' as one of the myths that it is keen to expose: *'All you need to do is go for counselling to stop work-related stress.* **Wrong** – counselling may help individuals who are suffering from work-related stress, but it is unlikely to tackle the source of the problem.'[11] They expand on this, saying: 'An in-depth study of the provision of workplace counselling and employee assistance schemes concluded that many had been introduced without any consideration as to how effective they could be at meeting the organization's needs ... Employment [*sic*] Assistance Programmes (EAPs) were often purchased for public relations reasons to try to demonstrate employers cared for employees ...'[12] Even more precise on this point was HSE Head of Strategy Elizabeth Gyngell in a letter to the author: 'We also say that training, counselling and other forms of individually-focused "treatments" are insufficient alone to discharge employers' legal obligations.'

This opens a can of worms for two reasons. First, some employment liability insurers who have so far bankrolled the stress compensation jamboree are now considering discriminating between employers who introduce stress management programmes and counselling and those who do not; and second, according to the Appeal Court ruling: 'An employer can only reasonably be expected to take steps which are likely to do some good.'[13] Will a huge increase in employer-funded counselling 'do some good' on workplace stress, or simply replace one species of stress cost with another? The jury is out.

CHAPTER ELEVEN
DAMAGED WORKERS

Indeed, the over-enthusiastic psychiatric diagnostician can find evidence of psychiatric ill-health in most human beings.

Lord Taylor and Sidney Chave, *Mental Health and Environment*

The cost of stress phobia to national economies and businesses is great, as we have seen. In this chapter we shall be considering how employers can withstand the onslaught of stress compensation claims that may otherwise put them beyond health insurance cover and (in some cases) out of business.

However, by far the greatest cost is not to economies or businesses, but in the form of damaged employees, whose minds have been disturbed and whose anxiety and fear for their own physical health and sanity are both real and lasting. Many of these people believe their illness has been caused by work. A growing minority of them go so far as to seek compensation for work-place stress because they are convinced that this is the root of their problem. It was for these people, and others like them, who think they are sick from 'stress', that this book was chiefly written.

Workers disabled by anxiety about 'workplace stress' may absent themselves from work, at great cost to their employers and the tax-payer and the most severely incapacitated may also sue. Once they embark on legal proceedings, they place themselves at considerable risk of being turned into 'victims', because their minds become the subject of lengthy argument, diagnostics and mental illness labelling.

Psychiatric injury

There is a good deal of misunderstanding of the law regarding workplace stress. The landmark *Sutherland v Hatton* Court of Appeal ruling corrected one of the most widely held beliefs in stress mythology: that stress per se is an actionable injury. It is not. Nor are 'distress, sadness, grief, or stress responses short of physical or mental illness'. These are considered 'normal human emotions'.[1]

Actions on workplace stress prior to the new HSE Code were all brought under the law of contract (breach of contract) or the law of tort (the tort of negligence). A common law 'duty of care' is owed by an employer to his workers, to take all reasonable steps to protect them from foreseeable risk of injury, while they are acting in the course of their employment. Straightforward enough, but where does it say this duty extends to the contents of an employee's mind?

One of the crucial judgements that extended this duty of care derived from a House of Lords ruling in *Page v Smith* [1996],[2] in which a traffic accident was deemed to have caused 'foreseeable psychiatric injury'. Mr Page, the claimant, suffered no apparent physical injury as a result of the accident. He was in fact away from work, with ME. However his lawyers argued that the collision had had such a devastating effect upon Mr Page's ME that it prevented him from returning to work. The law lords were shown complex evidence on adrenalin flow, chemicals in the body and their relationship with arterial problems and hormonal changes, after which three out of five found in favour of the claimant.

To succeed in a stress-related claim, therefore, the claimant must first establish that there is a duty of care, and that the duty has been breached; that he or she is suffering from a medically recognized psychiatric illness, that the risk was foreseeable, and that the breach itself materially contributed to the 'psychiatric injury'.

Let us suppose that an anxious worker is considering making a claim on grounds of workplace stress. First, it is insufficient to claim that work has caused him or her to suffer 'stress' and to expect to be financially compensated for this. It must be established in court that the 'stress', whatever this condition may be, has made the worker mentally ill. This is because, in law, 'stress' is not itself a recognized psychiatric condition, but thought to *cause* recognized psychiatric conditions.

This opens Pandora's Box, as mental illnesses are much harder to define and classify than physical conditions. Psychiatrists do not always agree on what mental illnesses are, or how best to treat them, or even that mental illness labels should be used at all. In a desiccating attack on his erstwhile profession, former psychiatrist and project director of the Freud Archives, Professor Jeffrey Masson, says of mental illness labels: 'None of the terms refer to real, objective entities. They are more like flags waved to indicate the user's intellectual allegiance.'[3] He believes that the labels have been used to harm and mislead and humiliate people and now sees no cure or comfort in 'therapy'.

Yet psychiatrists and psychotherapists are routinely called as expert witnesses to give evidence in courts of law, and must determine, based on the theories they espouse, and often upon the briefest acquaintance with the persons concerned (or their doctors' notes) what their symptoms 'mean', and whether or not they are genuine. In workplace stress compensation claims, this process of legal 'diagnosis' may by its imprecision hinder justice. Worse, it may influence anxious and vulnerable litigants and convince them that they are suffering from a psychiatric illness even when they are not. In other words, it may serve to medicalize normal emotions and worries and turn the stress phobic worker into a damaged worker.

For the following insights I am indebted to Dr Martin Baggaley's diagnostic guide in Berryman Lace Mawer's excellent Occupational Disease Series.[4] Legal practitioners and medical experts rely in workplace stress cases as elsewhere on two main textbooks: *ICD-10 (International Classification of Mental and Behavioural Disorders; Clinical Descriptions and Diagnostic Guidelines,*[5] and *DSM-IV (Diagnostic and Statistical Manual of Mental Disorders).*[6] The former is favoured in Britain and Europe, the latter in the United States. But as Dr Baggaley explains: 'The distinction between what constitutes mere mental stress and symptoms that amount to a recognizable psychiatric illness is not always clear or well-defined.' He lists the following:

- **mixed anxiety and depressive disorder**: 'This type of disorder is on the borderline of a normal response to events ...'
- **adjustment disorder**: 'Typically a mixture of anxiety and depressive symptoms in response to a specific adverse life event ... sometimes also used to describe symptoms in response to a traumatic event, which are not sufficient to be classified as post traumatic stress disorder.'
- **anxiety disorder**: 'Usually present in depressive disorders, so if it is possible to diagnose a depressive disorder one would not classify an anxiety disorder in addition.' Subtypes include generalized anxiety disorder, social phobia, agoraphobia with or without panic attacks, and obsessive compulsive disorder. 'Although the above conditions may be precipitated by stress at work, they are more usually understood to be due to individual vulnerability.'
- **depressive disorder**: 'Depression is a very common psychiatric disorder (the 'common cold' of psychiatry).'
- **alcohol and drug misuse**: 'Work-related stress can lead to increased use of drugs including alcohol ... However alcohol and other substance misuse can itself be the cause of other psychiatric disorders such as depression or anxiety.'
- **psychotic illness**: '"Psychotic" equates to the lay view of madness and is associated with such things as hearing voices (auditory

hallucinations) and abnormal beliefs (delusions). The commonest disorders associated with such symptoms are schizophrenia or bipolar affective disorder (also known as manic depression).'

- **post traumatic stress disorder**: 'Although events at work can lead to post traumatic stress disorder, this would not normally be considered work related stress … Individuals who become depressed for whatever reason, and who have been exposed to traumatic events in the past, may develop symptoms of apparent post traumatic stress disorder.'

These extracts give some idea of the difficulty of classifying mental illnesses. No wonder psychiatrists called as expert witnesses do not always agree. They also recognize the possibility of fraud, of which there are two main categories:

- **factitious disorder**: 'This is feigning illness without there being an obvious external gain and is probably done for complex psychological reasons, for example for attention.'
- **malingering**: 'Feigning illness for obvious material gain.'

Worker angst

Employers under threat of costly 'stress' litigation, and some sections of the tabloid press, may feel that those who present themselves in court as suffering from mental illness through workplace stress are fakers, malingerers or gold-diggers. Whereas those fighting for justice for the claimants, including their lawyers and union representatives, feel that these workers are suffering from mental illness. In fact the truth may lie somewhere in between. When people believe that workplace stress has made them ill, stress phobia may play a very significant part in their condition, and this anxiety may produce symptoms and signs of mental illness that confirm them in their belief and reinforce their fears.

What is the employer currently being told to do to protect himself and his workers from stress that is thought to cause 'psychiatric injuries'? The International Stress Management Association recommends that, to avoid being sued, employers should take 'a more proactive stance' on workplace stress. They should introduce 'stress awareness' (which arguably spreads stress phobia), provide employer assisted programmes, often in the form of one-to-one counselling (which the HSE says doesn't solve the problem), carry out risk assessment in the form of stress questionnaires (even though self-report data are not valid scientifically), and provide stress management training.

Whereas doctors can scribble 'stress' on medical certificates with great facility, employers are expected to be jolly good at foreseeing and recognizing signs of 'stress' or mental illness in their staff *before* they become incapacitated. This places them in a 'diagnostic' role. They are also expected to understand the many and complex laws governing their relationship with their workers' minds and bodies. Significant litigation include the Health and Safety at Work Act 1974, particularly section 2 (1), which requires employers to ensure the health, safety and welfare at work of employees; the Management of Health and Safety at Work Regulations 1992 and 1999, which impose an obligation on the employer to carry out a hazard analysis (risk assessment) of the workplace and provide health surveillance; and the Working Time Regulations 1998. The latter, passed under Article 118a of the Treaty of Rome, limits the number of hours that employees can be expected to work in a week and lays down minimum obligations on breaks, holidays and rest periods. There is also the 1995 Disability Discrimination Act, designed to protect the employee from bullying, oppressive management or 'any other detriment'. Mental health problems, including those thought to have been caused by workplace stress, constitute a protected disability under the Act. And employers should certainly not forget the right of constructive dismissal under the Employment Rights Act 1996, which vouchsafes protection of an employee forced to resign by a fundamental breach of his employment contract, namely breach of the duty of mutual trust and confidence.

At a London conference in 1998, barrister Andrew Buchan, who with Brian Langstaff QC appeared for the plaintiff in the landmark *Walker v Northumberland County Council* [1995], admitted that the HSE guidelines are actually unworkable. He said: 'The fact that it is impossible to comply with the HSE Guidelines is the reason for the existence of all these conferences.'[7] Indeed, there is an overwhelming volume of guidance and other papers issued by the HSE. Texts include: *Stress at Work: A Guide for Employers* (1995, HSG 116), *Help on Work-Related Stress: a Short Guide* (1998, INDG 281), *Managing Occupational Stress: a guide for managers and teachers in the schools sector* (1990), *Stress in the Public Sector: nurses, police, social workers and teachers* (1998) and *Tackling Work-Related Stress: a manager's guide to improving and maintaining employee health and well-being* (1999, HSG 218). The Loss Prevention Council also provide guides for bosses: *Work Stress: A Brief Guide for Line Managers*, and *Work Stress: Advice on its Prevention and Management*.

Before all this impressive literature on workplace stress prevention appeared, employers might have thought that workers could not sustain damage from desk jobs, or hurt themselves badly, as they might do, for example, if they fell off a crane or into a loom, just by doing their work. Bosses might have imagined that asking people to work hard in jobs that were demanding, even emotionally demanding, was fair enough, so long as these workers applied for the post and so long as they were paid. In 1995, however, employers discovered they were wrong.

A landmark case

Fundamental to our understanding of the 'damaged worker' is the 1995 case of *Walker v Northumberland County Council*.[8] In many ways the case is a monument to the true cost of the stress ideology, which is not to be measured in statistics however gigantic, or in pounds or dollars, but in blighted people.

Walker v Northumberland CC has proved a landmark in stress litigation. Decided on grounds of negligence, it was the first successful claim for psychiatric injury arising from stress at work in the UK. Previously, 'psychiatric injury' was seen as a complication of physical injury, as for example 'nervous shock' as a result of an accident. The *Walker* case, which was backed by Unison, opened the floodgates for aggrieved workers who felt, or whose union representatives and lawyers felt, that they had been made to suffer from workplace stress.

Mr Walker was employed by Northumberland County Council as an area social services officer, responsible for managing four teams of social services field workers dealing with child care and abuse cases. He himself was a middle manager who did not deal with cases directly. According to a colleague he was a conscientious man, a non-delegating, involved perfectionist who 'could not shrug his shoulders and say stuff it' when job demands became unrealistic. His hours were not onerous: he worked from 8 a.m. until 5 p.m. or 5.30 p.m., with a break for lunch. He did not normally work in the evenings or at weekends. He had a full life outside his job. A father of four, at weekends he ran the touchline for a church soccer team, and was an active member of the charismatic New Life Christian Fellowship Church. At work, though, he faced worrying problems.

His department was understaffed pending restructuring. The volume of cases had soared but the number of staff had not. Mr Walker complained about his workload and made suggestions on restructuring, but nothing happened because of the Council's budgetary constraints. In September 1984 he had written asking for a week's additional leave because in four months he had 'worked 130 hours extra' (which averages out at 32 hours a month) and had suffered from hay fever and asthma. He said, 'I am exhausted, and need a break, without using up too much leave.' He was given an extra two days. By the end of November 1986, things were at crisis point. Here is John Walker himself, talking on BBC2 in 1998 as part of a *Money Programme* item, 'Stress in the Workplace':

I suddenly developed a bad back. And I went to the doctor's with a bad back, sat down in the surgery and he said 'What's the matter?' and I burst into tears. And that was really a sign that it wasn't just the back; that it was really a lot of other things that had all come together, and that was the beginning of a breakdown. I had to go straight on the sick.

According to the *Journal of the Royal Society of Health*, Mr Walker 'was found to suffer from clinical depression, and had what is known as a "nervous breakdown" at this time'.[9] Mr Walker had by now consulted a psychiatrist, Dr D. A. Stephens, with whom he had professional contact. Dr Stephens had known Mr Walker 'as a stable, industrious and committed colleague for many years'. His advice was to prove crucial to the case. The psychiatrist *'took the view that Walker's breakdown was caused by the pressure of his work and advised Walker that he should not return to the same level of work responsibility as before* [my italics].'[10]

Mr Walker was away from work for four months from November 1986 to March 1987. On 10 March, just days after he resumed his duties, he faced what for many people is a personal watershed – his fiftieth birthday. Nothing has been made of this. Dr Stephens had told him that his symptoms had been caused by his work, and warned him not to face those pressures again. So after extensive discussions with his boss, Mr Walker agreed to remain at his post, provided he had less work and more help. He was promised more support but did not get it. When he returned he had a temporary assistant who was soon seconded elsewhere.

There was now a backlog and Mr Walker began to experience 'stress symptoms' again. After two weeks' holiday in August, he briefly went back to work but on 8 September told his boss that he could not cope any more. On 16 September he was diagnosed as suffering from a 'stress-related anxiety state' and advised to go on sick leave, after which there followed a 'second nervous break-down', and in February 1988 he was dismissed by the Council on grounds of permanent ill health.

In his televised interview John Walker stated:

At first all I wanted to do was get out of it. I was very distressed about having to lose my job, at a relatively young age of 50. I suppose I thought 'Let me get out of this.' But as I began to reflect I thought this isn't right. I was promised things that weren't given. And I wouldn't have had this breakdown if those things that had been promised had been done.

In the High Court Mr Justice Coleman, finding in his favour, observed: 'there is no logical reason why risk of psychiatric damage should be excluded from the scope of an employer's duty of care', even though physical and mental 'injuries' are self-evidently very different. He considered that Northumberland County Council had 'exposed [Mr Walker] ... to increasing stress and that because excessive stress causes mental illness, a "real risk" of psychiatric injury' must have been foreseeable. His summing up makes re-peated mention of 'the inherently stress-creating nature of social services work', and 'the intrinsically stressful character of child abuse cases': 'I am satisfied that although sheer volume of work often imposes stress which can cause psychiatric damage to a norm-ally robust personality, the character of the work can itself impose stresses capable of causing such psychiatric damage, regardless of volume of work.'[11]

The court ruled that Mr Walker's second 'nervous breakdown'

was 'foreseeable' and therefore liable for compensation, but that his first was not. The award of £175,000 stunned the business world. Whether it adequately compensates someone who feels that the citadel of his sanity has been breached is doubtful. After his win, a grey and ashen-faced John Walker told the media: 'I don't think I could ever hold down a job where there was a lot of stress and pressure. That part of me has been permanently damaged.'[12] He now works as a self-employed painter and decorator. Even working for himself, he admits that he sometimes feels 'stressed'. This tragic waste of a valuable, dedicated professional is pitiable, but not unique.

Because of the size and significance of his award, there has been a great deal of speculation in the media about what happened to Mr Walker, the first 'damaged worker' to be compensated financially for workplace stress. Since it was such a landmark in industrial relations, and since it has been widely analysed and commented upon already, it may be helpful to look at Mr Walker's case once more and this time ask the question: could anxiety about the physiological mechanisms of arousal and the so-called dangers of hard work to mental health cause the kind of suffering that Mr Walker experienced? Mr Walker went to his doctor with a 'bad back', wept, and emerged a 'stress sufferer'. He had described his own state of mind as 'exhausted' and in need of a break, rather than 'stressed'. Would he have been classified as 'stressed', or mentally ill, were it not for the prevailing stress ideology, full of warnings and prognostications about the pressures of work and ill-health? Would he have been so anxious, had it not been for a psychiatrist's warning of the risk of mental breakdown posed by the pressures of his job? Would he have had a second 'nervous breakdown' – the 'foreseeable' mental collapse that resulted in his award for damages – had it not been for this anxiety?

Would Mr Walker have absented himself from work had he not been 'advised' to do so, or might he have taken a more assertive stance and threatened to resign if he did not get more staff? Most important of all, would he be, as he calls it, 'permanently damaged' in his ability to withstand workplace pressure, were it not for the warnings of the stress management industry in general and his psychiatrist in particular that these put him at risk of mental illness? These questions need to be asked, not because of Mr Walker's damages, but because of his damage.

There are other more pragmatic questions about what an employee in this situation might do to help himself. Why did Mr Walker not immediately look for another post within the organization or outside of it? Why did he not see his highly serviceable Unison representative, lay down the law, or lay down his pen and walk out, before he became a victim, a casualty, a man whose name must forever be synonymous with compensation and 'nervous breakdowns'?

Anxiety about stress has downloaded like a killer virus into the psyche of vulnerable people. The fact that they are suing their employers for causing them workplace stress is actually unsurprising. They spend a lot of their lives in the workplace, they experience a lot of emotions there, and some of these emotions are negative. Those who pay are ultimately not the ones who are sued, but the ones who do the suing.

Part Four THE INDUSTRY

CHAPTER TWELVE

HEAD-HELP HONCHOS

They answered, as they took their fees,
'There is no cure for this disease'.

Hilaire Belloc, *Cautionary Tales*

Head-help honchos – therapists of whatever theoretical persuasion with perceived authority and power to help people's minds – enjoy not only the confidence of large sections of the public, but often impressive business kudos as well. There are an awful lot of these authoritative practitioners helping people with their heads, and 'stress' fuels their trade, as well as the public show of faith in their skills.

No one knows, even within the industry, how many 'stress' therapists there are in Britain, let alone the United States, Asia, Australia or the European Union. Estimates vary because of the industry's amorphous structure and the reluctance of some organizations to disclose the nature of their membership statistics (as, for example, where members simply pay a fee for accreditation). Practitioners are not required to register with any organization and there is no central system of qualification, ethical control or statistical data.

Global business

There are over 11,200,000 websites on the internet devoted to stress.[1] A random search one day in 2003 for UK organizations offering help with stress brought up a handy list of 246,391 company and individual sites selling stress management, stress control, stress education, stress counselling, post-traumatic stress counselling, stress conferences, services, surveys, products and packages. Many of these websites belong to marketing and information networks. For example, just one with links to other UK stress management sites listed 1,453 organizations. A 'Stress Homepage' is offered by the Health and Safety Executive, and the International Stress Management Association (UK) runs lists and links of its own. Indeed, in 2004 the ISMA itself, concerned about the global mushroom cloud of stress businesses, started reorganizing the validation and regulation of its own membership.

Canada, where Hans Selye's Canadian Institute of Stress started it all, offered 186,526 sites, and a search for Australian stress management outfits produced 134,839. By comparison, the Asian stress management industry boasted a mere 93,792 online that day. The American Institute of Stress declined to divulge the size of its membership. A spokesperson said there are 'various membership options – fellow, associate, sustaining etc, in addition to subscribers to *Health and Stress*, the Newsletter of the American Institute of Stress.'[2] The Canadian Institute of Stress/Hans Selye Foundation was more forthcoming. Managing Director Dr Richard Earle told me: 'The answer very much depends on how you define "stress management" and "practitioner". If loosely, there are probably hundreds of thousands. If more rigorously, then perhaps several tens of thousands in North America. Yet more stringently, as admitted to full practitioner membership in CIS, 230 in Canada, perhaps 2,000 in the US.'[3]

There is even a secondary industry selling information on the leviathan stress industry. For example, a 1996 survey by Market-Research.com custom-mailed over 1,000 American stress service providers, including stress clinics, biofeedback centres, psychiatrists and psychologists, therapists, wellness programmes, hospitals and the anti-anxiety drugs market. Its online report, which runs to 158 pages, 'contains provider-operating data to an extent not available elsewhere' and can be 'added to your cart' for £646.86 or $1,195.00. The word 'stress' appears 819 times in that report and the word 'definition' four times, but a definition of stress is not among them.[4] In March 2003 MarketResearch.com announced publication of another report, *Stress Management*, this time by Datamonitor, on the 'many areas that CPG [consumer packaged goods] players can target' and 'how better to position products in order to target this phenomenon'. Add this to your cart for a mere £376.21 or $695.

Licensing and certification outside the UK

Where did all this stress therapy come from? Is there a case for protecting members of the public from those offering to 'help' their minds? Some would argue yes, and point to recent history in the United States, where therapy has achieved quasi-religious status. According to a 2002 British television investigative series by Adam Curtis entitled *Century of the Self*,[5] winner of Best Documentary Series and Historical Film of the Year awards, psychotherapy and corporate PR in America originally went hand in hand. Indeed, in the 1920s Freud's nephew, Edward ('Eddie') Bernays, worked with the CIA and invented PR as a means of manipulating the consumer. Amid fears of economic unrest and post-war demons, psychoanalysis and psychological testing were regarded as government tools that could be used to change and pacify 'dangerous' elements in the human mind.

The lack of regulation and potential for harm of mind-remodelling in the US has attracted much criticism. Reasoned attacks like Bruce Wiseman's *Psychiatry – The Ultimate Betrayal*,[6] Peter Braggin's *Toxic Psychiatry: a psychiatrist speaks out*[7] and Jeffrey Masson's *Against Therapy*[8] have highlighted the controversy. Mentally ill and anguished people are totally vulnerable to theoreticians and experimenters. In 1949 the Nobel Prize for Medicine was awarded to neuropsychiatrist Egas Moniz for the leucotomy or pre-frontal lobotomy – the deliberate destruction of part of the brain's frontal lobes. It turned many people into gaping ghosts. The first person forced to undergo electroconvulsive therapy, a man found jabbering on a Rome railway station in 1938, sat up after his convulsions and pleaded: 'Not a second time!' But ECT pioneer Professor Ugo Cerletti disagreed, and reapplied the current.[9] Just because something is called therapy does not necessarily mean it is 'for the patient's own good'.

In December 1997 the prestigious *Harvard Mental Health Letter* expressed concern that: 'Monitoring of the therapeutic professions in general has always been inadequate. Mental health professionals have not educated the public about the difference between acceptable practice and quackery. Too little attention is paid to the conduct (whether illegal, harmful, or just plain bizarre) of the impaired, quirky, or insufficiently trained therapist.' Or as R. Christopher Barden, a psychologist, lawyer and president of the American National Association for Consumer Protection in Mental Health Practices, put it: 'It is indeed shocking that many, if not most, forms of psychotherapy currently offered to consumers are not supported by credible scientific evidence.'[10]

Britain holds the dubious distinction of having the world's most unregulated national stress management industry. In America now, the American Association of State Counselling Boards (AASCB) is an association of bodies legally responsible for the registration, licensing and certification of counsellors in the USA. The AASCB, which grew out of a Los Angeles convention in 1986, is dedicated to developing standards of qualification and competence and to protecting the public from charlatanism. In Canada, where the Health Professions Regulatory Advisory Council (HPRAC) is pressing for changes in the Regulated Health Professions Act, moves are also underway to put the entire stress counselling industry under licence, threatening the status even of non-statutory self-regulated professionals who already hold Masters-level qualifications.[11] At present, in Ontario, where hundreds of thousands of employees are covered by Employer Assisted (counselling) Programmes, most EAPs are provided by non-statutory self-regulated counsellors and therapists.

In Australia, where a ten-year review of empirical research evidence of effectiveness traced only one 'gold standard' evidence-based study, the paucity of 'published information regarding what works'[12] has led to calls to tighten up on stress management delivery in the Australian workplace. The Psychotherapy and Counselling Federation of Australia Inc. (PACFA), a self-regulating 'professional peak body' comprising more than forty major professional associations for counselling and psychotherapy across many different modalities, tabled its own best practice model for psychotherapy and counselling in Australia in January 2004.[13]

Regulation and accreditation in the UK

In the UK counsellors and stress practitioners are thought to out-number members of our armed forces or GPs. According to a Department for Education and Science (DFES) mapping exercise carried out ten years ago, Britain had around a quarter of a million therapists. A lot has happened since then. 'Accreditation of members' by the British Association for Counselling and Psychotherapy alone, according to BACP's Philip Hodson, has 'grown by 710 per cent in the last eleven years and its *actual* membership by 160 per cent'. Membership now stands at 'just shy of 24,000', according to a different press spokesperson. In fact, the BACP's own published figures show that despite the 'more stringent' joining rules in place since it unwittingly welcomed comedian Bernard Manning into its ranks, between 1991 and 2003 the Association increased its accredited membership by a total of 804 per cent.[14] If the rest of the therapeutic industry has expanded at the same rate, the number of head-help honchos in the UK would be in excess of two million, and given the fact that many therapists belong to no organization or body, the numbers are likely to be far greater. The BACP is undertaking a statistical survey on the nation's counselling population, 'but given the enormity [sic] of this process, it will be some time before accurate figures are available'.[15]

Other counselling organizations include the British Psychological Society, the UK Council for Psychotherapy, the British Association of Psychotherapy, the British Confederation for Psychotherapy and the CPN (Community Psychiatric Nurses). Not all the members of these organizations focus on stress counselling, but according to a BACP spokesperson, 'most counselling would include a stress component'. 60 per cent of the primary care practices in England now offer some form of counselling: the figures rose between 1992 and 1998 from 31 per cent to 51 per cent of all GP practices.[16] Given that the average caseload for each counsellor is 3.5 clients a week,[17] this represents a staggering amount of therapy. In the case of the BACP alone it represents almost 4,000,000 client sessions a year.

Moves are afoot to regulate counselling in the UK. In September 2004, representatives of nineteen accrediting organizations assembled to discuss with the Department of Health the setting up of a national register for counsellors in Britain. The steering group, which has been promised government funding, has been appointed the task of working out criteria for therapists who want to be included in a national register. It is hoped that the register may be up and running by 2008, although the endeavour may be hampered by profound theoretical differences between the various disciplines. This laudable initiative comes not a moment before time, but will apparently be aimed at regulating the counselling professions only.

It will not seek to regulate the much larger army of head help honchos of all descriptions that make up the gigantic stress management industry.

Stress management organizations are laws unto themselves. Quite apart from the International Stress Management Association (UK), there are many authorizing or overarching bodies with 'stress' in their titles, such as the Society of Stress Managers, the Confederation of Stress Managers, the Centre for Stress Management, the Association of Stress Management, the UK National Work Stress Network, the Association of Stress Therapists, the Association of Stress Consultants, the Stress Counsellors' Association, the Stress Management Counsellors' Association and so on, any of which may include stress counselling within their remit and which certainly market and federate stress expertise. These organizations may confer registration, qualifications and diplomas. But stress business is hectic, and authorizing outfits vanish from the pool and regroup faster than researchers can track their bubbles. Competition is fierce and stress bodies do not necessarily speak kindly of each other.

Among all the hundreds of thousands of scientific papers on stress, only a tiny minority seek to discover whether or not stress management makes sense in theory or works in practice, and in the UK, certainly, no government agency appears to accept responsibility for monitoring stress service providers or products. In fact, the industry does its business all over the country without let or hindrance. Department of Trade and Industry? 'No, we don't regulate it: sorry.' N.I.C.E? 'No. Topics are set by the Department of Health.' Department of Health? 'No. We recommend that you try the UK National Work Stress Network.'

The UKNWSN turns out to be a trade union organization investigating workplace stress. Network co-ordinator Brian Robinson explained to me that he is a former teaching professional and union man who used to shepherd 'stressed' teaching staff through tribunals. One day it struck him that perhaps this medicalizing, individualizing approach might not be serving his teachers well. Evidently they had an industrial problem, and what they needed was someone to fight their corner. Mr Robinson set out to do this with the UKNWSN. So far, so laudable. But then we got round to the subject of stress management. Although the UKNWSN does not itself provide counselling, it refers inquirers to websites of those that do. In fact, it leads the browser to over 200 sites. The Co-ordinator seemed taken aback to learn that there were 11,200,000 such sites, and when I asked about definition, the conversation went thus:

BR: We are a group of basically trade unionists. Certainly we approach it from a worker's point of view, and our aim is to gather information and spread it as far as we can, and make it available to people working on the shop floor, basically to health and safety workers at shop floor level and through trade unions. We work with the Hazards Campaign and run seminars and workshops dealing with workplace stress, both in Europe and the UK.

AP: There are many definitions of stress. What definition are you using?

BR: I'm a little hesitant because I'm not quite sure what you're looking for as a definition of stress.

AP: What it means.

BR: Well bear in mind that we approach stress as workplace stress. We look into the causes of stress.

AP: Yes but I'm sorry, Mr Robinson: you haven't said what it is that you are looking for.

BR: No nor have you quite asked me a question which it is possible to answer in the sense that you have. I can give you a definition of the standard metre and the standard litre. But we're dealing with something here that has got a highly subjective element and which varies from workplace to workplace. I'm not altogether sure of your background and the angle that you're coming from, which makes it extremely difficult to answer the question in a meaningful manner.[18]

Needless to say, the UKNWSN does not regulate the industry either. Nor does the Health Professional Council: 'The HPC do not currently regulate stress management staff, nor have we been approached by any organisation or body regarding an application for statutory regulation.'

What about the Medicines and Health products Regulatory Agency (MHRA)? They regulate pharmaceutical products such as homoeopathic remedies tested in laboratories, but the stress industry and its methods? 'Not us. Try the Health and Safety Executive'. HSE Stress Policy Unit's Martin Jones: 'Nobody regulates it.' Why not? 'It just doesn't happen to be regulated.' How about Tony Blair's new Healthcare Commission, set up in 2004? 'No, we wouldn't regulate stress management. You could write in.' Last hope was the Confederation of British Industry. The CBI actually has stress management persons among its membership. Would they take responsibility? A spokeswoman for the Policy Unit told me: 'No. That would be the HSE.'

We can only assume that the stress management industry is viewed by government departments as belonging to the realms of alternative medicine. One in three Britons consult alternative therapists,[19] and although the situation is changing, much of this treatment falls outside the remit of scientific or medical scrutiny. So, in the absence of any controls from above, there are literally hundreds of organizations doing the appointing and accrediting. Variously accredited counsellors may boast BAC, BACP, CPS, EAC, FMA, FPC, FSMCA, NAADAC, NACHP, SCA, SMCA or UKRC on their business cards, though they may freely practise without any of the above. 'Stressed out' members of the public, wishing to entrust themselves to the powers of hypnotists will naturally be reassured by the wealth of licensed hypnotherapy qualifications, including:

APHP	CHP	GCH	LHS	NCH
APCH	CRAH	GHR	MACH	NHR
ACH	DCH	HPG	MAHH	NRAH
BAThH	Dip.THP	HRS	MAPHP	NRHP
BHA	ESMH	IAH	MCAHyp	SOCH
BHR	FCRAH	ICH	MHS	UKCH
BSCH	FHRS	ICHP	MIAH	WFHyp
BSH	FHS	IRPH	MICHP	WIPH[20]
BSMDH	FIHP	ISH	MNCH	
CAHyp	FOH	LHRS	NACHP	

However, if you prefer something less hypnotic for your 'stress', no worries. For example, the Complementary Health and Alternative Medicine Information Service website lists some of the impressive sounding abbreviations used by therapists after their names. At the time of going to press there were 317, although the Information Service's Pascal Bourguignon tells me: 'There are many more than the ones we have published. These are only the ones we could gather.'

Charges

What do stress management firms charge? Although some sales literature mentions prices, the standard answer is the one given by Dave Coleman of the Ridgewalk Consultancy, *bona fide* members of the International Stress Management Association: 'Our charges vary enormously depending on what service the customer is buying. We have no fixed prices.'[21] Many stress managers prefer to come into one's company (or home) to undertake an audit and 'find out what is required' or 'find out the size of the problem'. Given this degree of evasion and the undoubted needs of client confidentiality, it is difficult to pin down what firms may actually end up forking out.

But one televized stress management intervention in 1999, at Leeds Council's One-Stop Centre, gives us some idea. The One-Stop treatment plan began with an audit by 'leading experts in stress at work', Stephen Williams and Lesley Cooper. Things were found to be very bad. Additional external counselling costs alone were originally expected to 'top £6,000'. But after further recommended measures such as in-house de-stressing, staff reorganization, training and a hotel workshop, the stress-busting bill was revised upwards – first to £61,000 and later to £100,000, presumably of taxpayers' money.[22] The programme did at least end on a positive note. One member of staff who attributed her 'recovery' to counselling handed in her resignation.

Market leaders Carole Spiers Associates (CSA) run corporate and public training courses. Carole is a Relate-trained counsellor of twenty years' standing. She prides herself on her corporate after-sales service, such as personal tutorials four to six weeks later, included in the fee. 'After the course has bedded down, all delegates also have the opportunity to take part in a teleconference,' says Ms Spiers. Ballpark figures for public courses would be £335 plus VAT for a single day and £535 plus VAT for a two-day course, both held in London. An in-house corporate day with the lady herself, however, might set your company back around £1,850 plus VAT for about ten to twelve delegates, although charities and public companies receive concessions and preferential rates because Carole is as she puts it, 'spreading the word'. CSA boasts a 'research bureau' that passes on the latest information on stress (though without analysis), and produces books on 'aligned subjects'. 'We are continually researching and that goes out to all our clients on a regular basis.' And what definition does CSA favour? 'We use the HSE definition. It's the safest and we know where we are with it.'[23] A 'keynote' conference speech by Ms Spiers, perhaps? 'Between £2,000 and £2,500' plus VAT. Her website, for those interested, is www.carolespiersgroup.com.

Urban Life Support offers 'a strategic, holistic approach to stress management and workplace wellbeing'. They come into one's office and carry out a 'contentment' audit, followed by workshops and a company stress MOT. How much? Individual sessions from £280 plus VAT. Workshops (for fifteen people) from £980. Or you might prefer a 'confidential assessment' of your company's stress-ors from Clarion, based in Dukinfield, Cheshire, and 'Delivering Analysis of Work Related Stress-ors'. A Clarion audit and analysis costs between £5 and £7 a head plus VAT. Why so cheap? 'We deal in companies with hundreds and thousands.' Or you might plump for Roger Mead Associates, whose motto is : 'Taking the Stress out of Stress Management'. They offer an audit, followed if necessary by stress awareness training and then a counselling contract or pay per use arrangement. The cost varies – 'It's how long is a piece of string.' But the audit comes in at between £8 and £15 a head plus VAT, depending on numbers. A hundred staff would cost between £800 and £1,500 plus VAT, plus consultancy costs, plus postage. Consultancy costs? A pre-audit management briefing, to ensure that they 'don't have a problem' with some comedian who thinks stress does not exist.

Karen Guy, based in Tiverton, Devon, provides a six-day OCR (Oxford Cambridge and RSA) accredited stress management course called 'Training the Trainers', at just £850 plus VAT, whereas Living With Stress, 'The Stress Management Training Company', charge £1,150 plus VAT for a six-day OCR-certificated course. Or, if you're a bit flush, why not try Taunton-based BalanceCare? Executive chairman Robert Sharpe says that for a full corporate day's course they charge just £2,250 plus VAT.

A spokesperson for the mental health charity MIND confirmed: 'We've double checked and there is no price regulation.' Former ISMA chair Janet Williams told me: 'We haven't any way of establishing fees at present – as far as I know nobody's done a survey.'[24] As there is no regulation, stress management organ-izations can charge whatever the market will bear. And it will bear both stress and strain. The outlay by businesses is set against the comparative expense of possible stress litigation. Stress management, it is argued, is cheaper in the long run than costly stress litigation and stress absenteeism.

Can anyone practise?

In contrast, it can cost next to nothing to establish oneself as a practitioner. Take for example, the Therapists UK registration Site Map. For just £15 plus VAT, I was able to register online and 'enter our active directory of UK Therapists', thereby joining the ranks of thousands of member practitioners of this organization plying their wares to UK companies and members of the public in search of stress relief. An additional £60 would have bought me 'full entry' and a five-page website on which to advertise my services. Nobody asked me what kind of service I would provide, or what qualifications I had, much less if my methods actually worked. Internet regulation is notoriously lax and such breaches of protocol may apply to other professions, and not just to stress management. Buyers should beware.

I also applied for the post of 'trainee hypnotherapist/stress counsellor' with an organization called IHP, whose London office is in Chadwell Health, Romford. No previous experience was required as training would be given. This training would apparently be one day a month, during which time the rate of pay was £10 an hour (rising to £20 after completion of training). I was required to have a suitable interview room and a fax machine because I would be working largely from home. I sent off my CV like a shot, and back came the reply from director Peter Goodwin: 'Thank you for your recent application. Unfortunately your criteria do not meet the requirements for the Trainee Position advertised. Your CV would meet the requirements for a Case Supervisor. All those positions are full at this time.'

A critical mass

Even within the stress industry itself, lack of regulation or scientific validation of stress management methods have prompted queries. Professor Cary Cooper, the high priest of stress management in the UK, formerly of the University of Manchester Institute of Science and Technology and now Professor of Organizational Psychology and Health at Lancaster University's Management School: 'We've been doing the science [on stress] for twenty years, a range of us. So we know the issues. What we *don't* know is, what do we do about them? We don't know what stress management interventions work and which ones don't work. And we need to get the science around those.'[25]

Another UK stress professor, Stephen Palmer of the Centre for Stress Management, admits that stress management outfits often go into companies with 'head-help' in mind, rather than any practical agenda: 'Sadly, instead of saying, they've got too much work, or we've got bullying employers, they don't change that at all. All they suggest is helping the individual – "send the individual for stress counselling", "send them for stress management or time-management workshops" ... They're not focusing on changing the organization. No. They're focusing on changing the individual.'[26] The London Hazards Centre has warned against corporate stress management packages. 'Despite a lack of evidence supporting the effectiveness of such programmes, a large proportion of stress management activity in the UK and US is individually focused.'[27] Stress management training was viewed as 'another popular method of palming off responsibility for stress management on to individual employees' which 'consists largely of training in such techniques as meditation and relaxation'.

Consultant psychiatrist, writer and broadcaster Dr Raj Persaud agrees that the stress industry pre-packs its therapy: 'I think it's a very worrying thing for many reasons. This industry doesn't attempt to understand your particular problem. They offer a panacea.'[28] Ruth Lea, director of the Centre for Policy Studies and, when I met her, Head of Policy at the Institute of Directors, puts it more bluntly: 'The stress industry is one of Britain's great growth industries, and why? Because there are huge vested interests involved here.' For Ruth Lea, the stress business is 'egregious and insidious'. She asks: 'When will more people realize that pandering to this self-interested and selfish "industry" not merely undermines business but also robs people of individual resilience and adult responsibility? The industry is parasitical, exploitative and cynical. It should be "closed down".'

There have been numerous television debates in which critics have locked horns with proponents of stress management. One of these was BBC's *Heart of the Matter*, presented in 1999 by Joan Bakewell. Taking part was Professor Cary Cooper who is now so widely consulted on workplace stress that he has become a sort of 'stress guru' to the UK business world and a prolific writer on the subject. In February 2004 Amazon listed 47 titles under his individual or joint authorship or editorship, including *Theories of Organizational Stress* (OUP, 1998), *Living With Stress* (Penguin, 1988), *A Brief History of Stress* (Blackwell, 2004), *Managing the Risk of Workplace Stress* (Routledge, 2003), *Preventing Stress, Improving Productivity* (Routledge, 1999), *Strategic Stress Management* (Macmillan Business, 2000) and *Managing Workplaces* (Sage, 1997). His masterclass video *Stress*, produced by Melrose Film Productions Limited, was distributed by Resource Systems management consultancy services, and his CD package *Under Pressure* is marketed by StressCheck, the UK's main industry product outlet. It offers advice that is 'comprehensive and learner centred' in an 'engaging format', complete with 'clear navigation, printable checklists, assessment quizzes and booklet'. The cost? £695.

During this particular televised debate on the pros and cons of stress management, Prof. Cooper, with his usual persuasive charm, was defending the stress ideology when Joan Bakewell suddenly turned to me and asked: 'But do we really *need* more stress management?' 'No', I suggested. 'What we need is management of stress management.' There followed a rather surprising exchange:

Prof. Cooper: I totally agree with Angela that there is a stress management industry and that we have to control it and we have to get proper standards.

Joan Bakewell: You're part of it!

Prof. Cooper: I'm a researcher but I'm not involved in actually delivering it.[29]

Product testing?

Those offering their services for 'tackling stress' may be very powerful and persuasive. They are evidently hugely successful at marketing their wares to UK companies. But just how good are they? What evidence do consumers and clients have that all this 'stress management' actually works? The statistics on rising workplace stress casualties are hardly reassuring.

At the opposite end of the academic spectrum from Cary Cooper stands senior lecturer in organizational psychology Dr Rob Briner of Birkbeck College, University of London. Mere mention of his name can strike terror in the hearts of people he calls 'stressologists' and send them scuttling for their stress balls. Dr Briner has produced a number of critical reviews and reports on stress management. He and psychologist Shirley Reynolds (then of the University of Sheffield) were among the first to subject stress interventions in the UK workplace to scientific scrutiny and showcase academic criticism of the industry and its methods. Their work, citing other critics, highlighted: 'the puzzling and ever-increasing gap between vigorous practitioner activity in the domain of stress management and the limited evidence that such interventions are effective'.[30] Another study investigating the 'fashionable notion' of occupational stress programmes found that 'Stress management training ... is typically directed at unselected, heterogenous groups of workers who are seldom experiencing elevated levels of psychological distress. It is not surprising therefore that there is no evidence that such training has any long-term benefit', though like many interventions it may produce a temporary 'feel-good' factor. The report concludes: '... expectations that occupational stress interventions will somehow magically remove all organizational ills will not be met.'[31]

More recently, in the *Employee Health Bulletin* in December 2000, Dr Briner asserts that stress management has become the uncritical knee-jerk reaction to workplace problems. Interventions are often ill-conceived and hastily implemented and very little evidence of their efficacy is valid or reliable, since much is based on self-report data. The latter is so discredited that a number of professional journals now refuse to publish it. Other 'proofs' of effectiveness are marred by poor methodologies, lack of definition, unclear objectives and questionable assumptions. One of these is that stress interventions work at all, and Dr Briner concludes that much of what passes for stress management at present is actually not worth doing. He told *BBC News* that such endeavours are 'often an extremely unfocused ragbag of ideas and techniques which are of little long-term benefit to employees or employers'.[32]

As my own UEA/CERM meta-analysis also discovered, 'validating' studies of occupational stress interventions are often subjective, devoid of follow-ups and lacking in rigour. But in one very carefully constructed three-year government-funded stress management intervention study involving four organizations, stress management was found to have no effect whatsoever on overall stress levels of the organizations concerned.[33]

What is the product *for*?

One reason for retaining a healthy scepticism on the efficacy of the 'product' provided by the vast stress management industry is its name. 'Stress management', in order to be of use to the public and to businesses, must 'manage' something. But what? We have already seen how difficult it is to pin down 'stress'. Clearly we are not talking here about some simple identifiable problem like vermin or asbestos, that may be eradicated by suitable operatives and never seen again.

Even if we suppose the target of the practitioners is 'stress suffering' in the workplace or elsewhere, it would be hard to monitor the industry's success. This is because, even among practitioners themselves, there is no agreement on what victims of stress are actually suffering *from*. Medical experts find it tricky to distinguish between stress and anxiety. 'There is inherent conceptual confusion which makes stress potentially difficult to discriminate from general anxiety.'[34] There again, experts also find it difficult to distinguish between stress and depression. Bristol Royal Infirmary's Professor Stafford Lightman, of the University Research Centre for Neuro-endocrinology: 'There are very close correlations between chronic stress and depression ... The chemistry of the brain is very similar in patients who are depressed and patients who have chronic stress.'[35] As Briner and Reynolds pointed out a decade ago: 'Most importantly, we need to establish a clearer understanding of *exactly* what it is that stress management training is attempting to manage.'[36]

Outside the workplace, clinical studies of stress management techniques highlight flaws and pitfalls. Canadian trials of stress management in relation to hypertension are a good example. Initial studies suggested that stress interventions lowered blood pressure in hypertension, but there was concern over methodologies. Many of the early trials were hampered by small samples, lack of control groups, inadequate methods of blood pressure measurement and ignorance of baseline readings. An evaluation of the Canadian literature on cognitive behavioural techniques for hypertension treatment found 800 published works, of which only twenty-six studies met the criteria of random assignment to an experimental or control group. In a meta-analysis involving 1,264 patients, stress management techniques did not produce a greater decrease in BP than a credible sham technique in a control group or self-monitoring alone.[37] The review concluded: 'There are few data to recommend stress management for the treatment of hypertension.'

Other investigators found that 'Illness itself is a potent stressor and there is a continuing debate about whether high stress levels in individuals with, for example, inflammatory bowel disease, are due to the condition itself or are causal agents.'[38] A study of stress management on rheumatoid arthritis gave no support to the use of stress management in this condition.[39] Long-term benefit is difficult to demonstrate because of the self-limiting nature of many psychological problems. The American NIH's Hypertension Pooling Project[40] was negative about the effectiveness of stress management techniques in treating hypertension. Another study concluded that the techniques produced the greatest reductions in blood pressure among patients to whom the treatments were novel.[41]

The stress management toolbox

Many, if not most, things in the stress toolkit – from dolphin clicks, aroma pillows and 'squeezy water knobbled key rings' to exercises, 'self-entrainment' devices, CDs and tapes – are intended to produce the stress industry's great panacea: relaxation. The argument runs like this: techniques and products designed to produce relaxation help those of a nervous disposition to take a more dispassionate view of their problems and calmly assess what action they can take to improve their lot. Unfortunately, calm-downs may also lull the senses, for example whilst working or driving, and expose people to danger and death. And because passivity is so seductive, they may anaesthetize people with serious and urgent problems from taking immediate action to help themselves.

Methods and remedies for achieving stresslessness are very numerous. They include (and this list is by no means inclusive): PMR or progressive muscle relaxation, biofeedback, desensitization and stress inoculation training, neuro-linguistic programming (NLP), cognitive restructuring, counselling, psychiatry, psychotherapy and family therapy, autogenic therapy (AT), hypnosis, deep breathing relaxation, music relaxation, isolation or flotation tanking, crystal therapy, aromatherapy, kinesiology, stress mapping, visualization and visuo-motor behavioural rehearsal; various types of massage including reflexology or foot massage, reiki, Indian head massage and shiatsu; yoga, transcendental meditation (TM), t'ai chi and feng shui; binaural brainwave entrainment technology, herbal and embrocation remedies including kava kava, St John's wort, Roman chamomile, lavender, clary sage, cypress, sweet marjoram and mandarin; flower remedies such as larch, oak, crab apple, rock rose, mimulus, red chestnut, gorse and walnut; homoeopathic remedies including aconite, colocynthis, ignatia, sepia and lycopodium; acupuncture and acupressure, zero-balancing, postural relaxation (such as those methods advocated by Alexander and by Feldenkrais) and various forms of aerobic exercise.

There may be nothing wrong with many of these techniques and remedies in themselves, but some have been borrowed from Eastern religious disciplines or clinical settings where their use is strictly supervised and controlled. When these same techniques, arts and remedies are commandeered by an unregulated industry and pressed into action against 'stress' (or arousal, or human emotions generally) by self-proclaimed experts with a smattering of know-ledge, we are in very serious trouble indeed.

A good example is that of hypnotism. In clinical use, it has produced potent and lasting effects that have dug sufferers out of the most profound depression, and helped people to give up smoking and overcome fear and pain. The musical genius Sergei Rachmaninov, suicidal after the public failure of his First Symphony, went on to produce one of the world's most famous pieces of music, his Second Piano Concerto in A minor, after hypnotic suggestion by Dr Nikolay Dahl that he would 'write with great facility'. But in the wrong hands, hypnosis can be ruinously harmful. By its very nature it places one person's mind in the hands of another, and a complete stranger at that. American hypnotherapist Robert Ferrago, speaking on television about his arachnophobia treatment programme at the London Zoo: 'All hypnosis is, is subconscious domination of the subject. It's not a very politically correct thing to say, but the point is that the hypnotist is the authority figure.'[42]

In 1995, a Home Office report called for tougher guidelines on stage hypnotism. Twenty-four-year-old Sharron Tabarn had died from a fit hours after being put into a stage trance. Ann Hazard, twenty-five, had broken a leg whilst under hypnosis and received £20,000 compensation in an out-of-court settlement. Celebrity hypnotist Paul McKenna, who gave evidence to the inquiry panel, commented: 'there are cowboys out there who carry out hypnotism.[43] During my research for the UEA/CERM report, the then ISMA chair Janet Williams told me in a phone interview: 'A lot of the clients who call us in do so because they have had some previous disastrous contact with untrained stress management practitioners using techniques such as hypnotism. We then have to go in and put it right.' Her concerns are shared by her successor Rosemary Anderson, and substantiated by the alarming proliferation of hypnotherapy accreditations listed earlier.

Autogenic therapy, developed by Berlin psychiatrist and neurologist Johannes Schultz from research by Oskar Vogt of the Berlin Neurobiological Institute in the 1880s, is a powerful self-hypnotic system based on the theory that, given the right inducements, the brain can synthesize and resolve its own data better than any therapist. The training happens to include deep relaxation and attention-focusing techniques, which make it attractive to stress management merchants. Autogenic therapy proper requires an expert on hand to deal with potentially disturbing experiences as the patient undergoes what are known as autogenic discharges,[44] during which he or she may violently sob or become hysterical. Yet autogenic training is frequently offered piecemeal as part of workplace stress management packages and is available at chemists and health food outlets in the form of cassette 'relaxation' tape recordings for unsupervised use.

Another stock-in-trade, biofeedback, has demonstrable value in clinical settings but should be dabbled in with caution, especially by anyone suffering from some form of mental illness. The system evolved out of self-hypnosis and relaxation techniques but incorporates the use of electronic equipment designed to monitor respiration rates, skin temperature, conductivity and blood flow and then 'feed back' this information to the brain, via visual or audible signals, to enable it to regulate relaxation. Alpha wave sound devices have been known to trigger violent outbursts, and some clinicians have noted increased hallucinations with biofeedback training given to schizophrenic patients.[45] The wide application of such techniques by untrained persons practising on unsuspecting members of the public or random groups of UK employees raises extreme concern.

CHAPTER THIRTEEN

GADGETS AND GIZMOS

It has become appallingly obvious that our technology has exceeded
our humanity.

Albert Einstein

Stress management consultants do not generally meet prospective
clients empty-handed: they bear with them the latest glossy
marketing, advertising and PR, and the latest technological and
'scientific' gadgetry by way of proof that stress is all about us. In
this chapter we shall be looking at some of the impressive array of
high-tech gizmos for managing, monitoring or measuring something called stress. Although stress management experts may carry
or sell these gadgets, the products may also be bought direct from
independent outlets and manufactured by those who do not
themselves profess stress management skills. The equipment itself
is therefore a separate issue.

Many popular stress products and devices lie within a (very
large) grey area, monitored neither by the Department of Health,
the Department of Trade and Industry nor the Medicines and
Health Products Regulatory Agency. According to an MHRA
spokesman, stress products are seen as 'borderline' and 'not strictly
medical devices' because stress is not strictly a medical condition.
However, stress products are marketed on the understanding that
they will monitor, measure, ameliorate or cure something called
'stress'. While many may simply be toys – desktop Minis, stress

mugs, squeezy balls, silly putty, stress-popping bubble wrap and stress dolls featuring rip-off Velcro limbs, for example – some are not, and we are not just talking about the odd calming fish tank.

Computerized stress business

One recent innovation is computer software packages. Quite apart from the dazzle of 11,200,000 websites offering stress management of every persuasion, there are now software packages for stress and cyber stress services. The UEA/CERM research in 1997 turned up a computerized, telephone-based stress management programme, offered free of charge to the public in the US, via an 800 telephone number. It employed an interactive phone system and a natural-sounding, digitized voice and it made assessments of the user's 'stress levels', based on touch tone recognition of a caller's previous responses. A study of the programme by the Human Investigations Committee of Yale University School of Medicine found subjects viewed themselves as being under a great deal of stress. Over the course of the programme, however, there were no statistically significant changes in self-reported degree of stress, which cast doubt on the programme's effectiveness.

We also discovered a computer software programme available in the UK, called Stress Counsellor. Marketed by Fitech and Business-health Group Limited of London, it provides 'personal stress assessment, highly personalized reports and group analysis reporting'. Fitech explain that: 'The primary purpose of this unique interactive program is to provide an opportunity for people to understand their present state of mind and reflect constructively upon it. At the heart of the stress counsellor is an onscreen questionnaire which take about 20 minutes to complete.' The programme interviews clients and provides them with a 'personalized report' on proneness to stress, stress levels and 'coping strategies used'.[1]

Phone counselling is set to take off in the UK, as it has

done in the US. Whereas the Samaritans charge nothing, this new breed of phone counsellor has acumen. For example, 1to1phonecounselling.com arranges the first half-hour session free, after which they charge £40 an hour. Spokesman Conor McKenna explained: 'If finance is a problem, we often come to an arrangement that suits both yourself and 1to1phonecounselling.'[2]

Then there is cyber counselling. In 2000 the *Evening Standard* discovered 200,000 counselling websites operating worldwide, most of them in America, 'virtually all of them unregulated and unlicensed'. Unlimited online stress sessions are to be piloted by the NSPCC to counsel vulnerable children. The charity is thrilled about cyber therapy. 'It is definitely going to happen soon and we are very excited about pioneering such a potentially dynamic breakthrough in the way children can reach out to us,' says an NSPCC spokesperson.[3] The British Association for Counselling and Psychotherapy (BACP) predicted that a third of its members will be working in cyberspace by 2005. While recognizing the risks and hoping that one day there may be a suitable monitoring body, BACP Chief Executive Ken Lewis said: 'We believe there is an exciting future for counselling on the internet. Just as the arrival of telephone counselling added an important tool to the work of therapists, so "cyber counselling" could bring a major new service to millions.'

Not everyone shares his optimism. The computer stands at the interface between the user and the most sophisticated global marketing known to man, serving every psychological need. Many users are children, whose needs are very great but whose judgement is very green.

Stress hormone testing

Aside from the power of the PC, many stress gadgets are, like audits, intended as diagnostic tools to alert people to their 'stress levels' and excite desire for stress management therapy. Stress hormone tests are an example. One such test, the Adrenal Stress Index Test, costs £66 and measures cortisol (the corticosteroid hormone hydrocortisone) and DHEA (dehydroepiandrosterone) in saliva in order to assess your daily 'stress hormone cycle'. Adam Carey, a senior registrar in obstetrics and gynaecology at Queen Charlotte's hospital in Chelsea set up the Natural Health Clinic in London where the tests are analysed. He advises patients on the results. DHEA and cortisol apparently peak at mid-morning to wake us up, and then dip at night. Dr Carey explained: 'We see a lot of stressed executives who make their problems worse by poor diet. They can't get up in the morning and need four cups of coffee to get them going. By mid-morning they're flaked out, so they have more coffee and choco-late.'[4] The clinic admirably advises on sensible nutrition and exercise. But what of the stress hormone tests themselves? Neuro-endocrinologist Professor Stafford Lightman: 'Although the test can give an indication of someone's hormonal stress response, hormones vary from person to person, depending on how their hor-mone system is set.'[5] And depending, too, on whether they have swallowed a lot of DHEA capsules, sold on the internet for their 'anti-ageing' properties.

StressDots

One of the most popular and successful stress gadgets on the market in 2004 was a product called StressDots. StressCheck Limited mar-keted and distributed them from a farm at Bordesley Park Farm, Boeley, Worcestershire. According to StressCheck's catalogue it was 'The UK's only stress training product company'. It sold stress relief books, stress monitors, stress training packs, stress monitoring packs, stress tapes and CDs, stress squeezers, stress fun toys, stress massagers, relaxation pillows, fragrance gift sets, stress posters, stress training toys 'and much more!' Its thirty-two-page *Stress Check Book* sold over 95,000 copies and came with 'a card of ten

StressDots for use as personal stress monitors' that 'give an accurate and instant reading of personal stress levels', and a number of 'simple, personal quizzes that create an awareness of stress in the user's work place and lifestyle'.

The StressDots were also marketed separately – 'ideal for health promotion days' – ten dots per card at £2.25. These 'Personal Stress Monitors' are black paper circles of liquid crystals with adhesive backing that change colour to deep blue through green and brown in response to 'changing stress levels' and feature a cartoon character. StressCheck also sold the dots in plain strips, each containing ten of the black detachable circles. Over 250,000 strips have been sold in the last ten years to hospitals, government organizations and stress trainers. Similar devices for measuring stress have been marketed in the US and on the internet as Stress Points or BioDots. BioDots, manufactured at that time by the UK firm Stresswise, were tried out at a 'health fair' in 1999 on staff at Stirling University. Senior occupational health nurse Aileen Brown explained: 'As someone gets stressed, their veins contract and the body cools down . . . The dots are a fun way to show people how tense they are because it can be very difficult to recognize.'[6] Other related products include Stress Film Stickers and Mood Cards, all of which change colour as temperature changes.

In 2004 StressCheck also sold what they called a 'Stress Test' which it advertised as: 'An effective way of getting the stress message across.' The test takes the form of a card and costs £39.95. It is printed with the message: 'Warm hands are relaxed. Cold hands are tense!' The card contains a sensor and is taped to the finger or held between the fingertips and the reading is compared with the 'stress range' written on the card. 'Below 79 degrees – tense. 80 to 90 degrees – nervous. 90 to 94 degrees – calm. Over 95 degrees – relaxed.'

In 2004, StressCheck's then-managing director Andrew Nicholls expressed pleasant surprise at the news that there are now over eleven million stress websites. I asked him who StressCheck's main customers were. Mr Nicholls explained that their customer base consisted mainly of 'companies that can afford occupational thera-pists – health authorities, those sort of people', as well as individual trainers. Business had presumably grown astronomically in the last few years. 'Yes, we have all the brand names and everything, and we thought the market would increase,' said Mr Nicholls. What was the StressCheck MD's background – was he a doctor? 'No, I am a busi-nessman,' he replied. 'I run several businesses and this is one of them.' We turned to one particular product – the Stress Test – and what differentiates it from the StressDots. Both products measure temperature but the difference between them lies in the way they do so. The test works 'digitally':

AP: You also sell the Stress Test, but that's different [from StressDots] isn't it?

AN: Yes, that's digital and we do a lot of those for Health Days and that kind of thing.

AP: I am slightly confused because the dots measure temperature.

AN: Well yes, you are measuring temperature with a Stress Dot – that's what you're doing anyway, measuring the skin temperature and detecting changes in the skin temperature.

AP: But what's the connection with stress?

AN: It's skin conductivity. When you get stressed your body temperature reduces. You will see all that stuff on there.

AP: On the Card it says warm hands are relaxed and cold hands are tense.

AN: Yes, that is the general theme; that's a little bit black and white. But that's the biofeedback machine. We do two different ones. One is very accurate, the other one is sort of an indicator. There is one cheap one that we do for about £40 which is used on Health Days to help draw people to the stand, and then we have got the proper ones.

The 'proper ones' turn out to be 'medical biofeedback devices' that appear in the sales catalogue. Mr Nicholls goes on to explain what the 'medical biofeedback devices' measure:

AN: They are measuring the electrical impulses across the hand as opposed to the temperature. At the end of the day it is not an exact science. To get a fully accurate situation you need to be measuring the impulses across the hand as opposed to the temperature, but the temperature would indicate, but obviously a lot of these are indicators of the issue and that is why they are such an effective training tool. In terms of long-term accurate stress reading they are not designed really; well, they are designed to some degree for that, but obviously they are relatively cheap and cheerful, so people use them, get the message, between the body and stress, therefore they are very good training tools.

So in other words, these products are intended to promote 'stress awareness'?

AN: Exactly. Which is how they are sold as opposed to being sold as the ultimate accurate monitoring of stress levels.

Here we have two rather worrying issues. One is the promotion of 'stress awareness' which fuels public anxiety about physiological signs of arousal and prompts people to try to investigate their 'stress levels' in case they are at risk. The other concerns what StressCheck's devices, impressively high-tech though they are, actually monitor or measure. If the 'stress' is not the same thing as temperature or galvanic skin response, what did the readings or levels indicated by the products signify? I asked Mr Nicholls: What does 'the UK's only stress training product company' mean when it says 'stress'?

AN: Well, we don't define it. Other people define it in a hundred ways.
AP: Six hundred.
AN: OK, six hundred. It's like defining sex – it's pretty impossible really. That's why our Stress Check Book is a generalist book. It covers and touches on the different aspects of stress, but it doesn't go into huge detail . . . Certainly, putting our book together, nobody would agree: you get an educational view, a medical view, you go round in ever-decreasing

circles, but we are the main suppliers of stress products. People take large or small volumes depending on where they are coming from, what the circumstances are. There are not many hospitals that we don't supply in the UK.

AP: Does it bother you that people wishing to make a fast buck would buy your products and offer them to people and delude people into thinking they have got some psychological illness when they haven't, when they are just perhaps worried or just normal or have had a bad day?

What worried him, he responded, was that a large multinational:

Can order a thousand books for £4,000 – which is a nice order thank you in one week – and then three months later you read that they have made half the staff in that particular office redundant. The only reason that we get good orders from big companies is because now they have to do stress because the lawyers tell them to. If lawyers didn't tell them they wouldn't bother at all. They do that just to placate the staff and then they sack them. That's reality time. We do a lot of shows, and people come out with all sorts of angles, but we deal with reality. Our end of the game is we supply helpful products which people can use to get the message of stress across to people. How they do it, or whether they do it well or not is not my problem. At least I am not purporting to be some intellectual organization who don't give a damn about whether or not there are any standards in the industry. Because there aren't any standards.

This is quite right – there aren't any standards. Mr Nicholls went on: 'Really the HSE should get to grips with it and accredit people, because it is a dangerous subject to teach.' He believes that StressCheck do help people. They deal with cost-pressed occupational health departments who can't afford '£400 or £1000 a day on a stress consultant' but who are careful and painstaking and 'use our products on a selected basis. They have got enough nous to take a view and get it right, and that's fine.'[7]

CHAPTER FOURTEEN

WORKPLACE INTERVENTIONS

Where facts are few, experts are many.

Donald R. Gannon

There is now unanimous agreement that the problem of workplace stress costs a staggering amount of money, and this has naturally created a hot market for intervention, particularly in the business sector. What is this market, how does it work, and what is it worth? More important, does such intervention deliver?

The American appetite for stress management programmes, products and services in 1995, according to US website Symbiosis OnLine, was worth US$9.4 billion. The 1999 market was estimated to hit US$11.31 billion.[1] For 2006 and beyond, name your squillions. Projected growth is 22 per cent annually[2] based on the fact that Americans are the world's biggest spenders on healthcare, forking out close to $4,000 per person per year and an estimated $27.2 billion in 2000 on alternative medicines and nutritional supplements.[3] The Australian Broadcasting Corporation reported in June 2000 that the Royal Australian College of General Practitioners is now supporting Medicare coverage for alternative therapies. Apparently 44 per cent of Australians are willing to try everything from acupuncture to spiritual healing for their *Weltschmertz*.

In Britain, spending on yoga and Pilates classes, massage, acupuncture, aromatherapy etc. was estimated to have reached

£670 million in 2003.[4] In the workplace the UK stress management industry received a fantastic boost in 2003 both to its market and prestige. At its head now stands the government's own watchdog, the Health and Safety Executive, ably supported by the International Stress Management Association (UK) whose literature now carries the logo: 'working in partnership with HSE'.[5] It should be emphasized here that the UK is now in some respects the stress capital of the world, and that what happens here resonates round the planet. British research sends out signals to American workers, who come down with similar syndromes. British stress compensation cases are closely monitored across Europe. Britain boasts the *International* Stress Management Association. Where the UK moves on stress, other countries are likely to follow.

In October 2003, the HSE moved majestically into the workplace with new standards to 'tackle the problem of stress', which it currently defines as: 'the adverse reaction a person has to excessive pressure or other types of demand placed upon them'. A stress-busting organization that may once have had difficulty getting a foot in the door of UK companies will now be gliding in carrying HSE literature packs and HSE Stress Management Standards.

The HSE has identified six clusters of risk factors that may cause work-related stress: Demands, Control, Support, Relationships, Role and Change. Employees will in future be audited on these aspects, and if between 65 per cent and 85 per cent are not satisfied, their employers will be deemed to have failed in their efforts to tackle stress in the workplace and punished accordingly.

Things to be tackled

Under 'Demands' the HSE bullet-points issues such as whether or not the organization has designed jobs with realistic goals in mind, whether employees have sufficient resources to carry out their jobs effectively, and whether they face threats of public violence or abuse. Under 'Control' it raises questions about pace of work and whether or not employees have a say in the way work is undertaken, or *'feel that they are able to air concerns'*. 'Support' refers not only to managerial support and support from colleagues, but to the need for *'systems in place to help employees cope with work or home-related issues'*. The code asks: *'Are employees encouraged to seek support at an early stage?'* 'Relationships' refers to resolving work-place conflict, dealing with unacceptable behaviour and whether or not employees *'feel able to report their concerns'*. 'Role' categorizes issues surrounding conflicting demands, induction, job description and plans of work. 'Change' covers whether or not employees 'understand the reasons for changes' and the likely impact on their jobs, and whether they have been consulted. Employers must ask themselves: *'Are special arrangements made to support employees through the change process?'*

The history of industrial relations has traditionally focused on workers' rights. Now it seems, parts of the HSE code, and particularly those parts of it highlighted above, focus on workers' feelings.

Chief medical director of income protection insurers Unum-Provident Dr Michael O'Donnell expressed his concerns about the new code to the *Observer*: 'Stress is not a traditional hazard like asbestos or lead. You cannot measure exposure and then define an acceptable limit because stress is a subjective phenomenon.'[6] When I spoke to him, Dr O'Donnell was even more emphatic, saying that this effort to pathologize normal emotions was feeding a culture of fear. 'We are *creating* a climate where stress is real,' he said. 'People are being predisposed.'[7] Stephen Bevan of the Work Foundation was another expert underwhelmed by the code: 'It's based on the false premise that you can measure and regulate it. You can't.'[8] The Federation of Small Businesses complained that the new Standards could facilitate an outbreak of unjust claims against employers and that the HSE needed to do more work on its 'stress' research.

Technical know-how

The HSE sets out its case for intervention in a lengthy technical document,[9] which discusses at great length the tackling of stress, without troubling too much over the identity of what is to be tackled. True, it refers to 'difficulties' such as 'disagreements about terminology and theory' and the dearth of studies 'of the effectiveness of interventions'. The Standards had been produced 'in the face of these obstacles'.[10] The paper states that the aim is 'to shift the working population under consideration to a more desirable or better state'. Shifting populations is always hazardous. Why is one shifting them? Apparently because one has a *notion*: 'In particular there is the notion that stress entails a sequence of events that include the presence of demand, a set of evaluative processes through which that demand is perceived as significant (in terms of threat, and in terms of its impact on individual resources or requiring of the individual something other than normal functioning), and the generation of a response that typically affects the well-being of the individual.'[11] (This last defining moment evidently derives from Professor Cary Cooper and colleagues, who consider that 'There is now good agreement on the key features of the stress process.'[12]) Put another way, says the HSE, there is 'a perceived imbalance or discrepancy between preferred or desired levels of particular environmental features and actual or reported levels themselves'.[13] Or put *another* way: things are not as people would wish.

We march confidently on to a 'taxonomy', to 'seven stressor areas', and a 'five-steps approach' as follows:

STEP 1 – Look for the hazards
STEP 2 – Decide who might be harmed and how
STEP 3 – Evaluate the risks and decide whether the existing precautions are adequate

STEP 4 – Record your findings

STEP 5 – Review your assessment and revise it if necessary.

One is struck by the similarity to the 'ORDER OF LOOKING FOR THINGS' in Winnie the Pooh's 'Search for Small', one of Rabbit's friends-and-relations:

ORDER OF LOOKING FOR THINGS
1. Special Place (To find Piglet)
2. Piglet (To find who Small is)
3. Small (To find Small)
4. Rabbit (To tell him I've found Small)
5. Small again (To tell him I've found Rabbit).[14]

The HSE paper tells us that there are 'a number of systems that set out a series of criteria for gauging the strength of evidence supporting the associations between risk factors and disease.'[15] There are apparently seven 'main candidate mechanisms' whereby these biological harms take place and data on each of these mechanisms that support 'a link between work and dysfunction'. Unfortunately the 'plentiful' data are difficult to interpret because of 'numerous well-documented methodological problems', with the result that 'causation ... is difficult to demonstrate' and interventions may therefore not lead to any discernible improvement in population health. But still, 'the absence of such high quality data in the public health sphere should not be an excuse not to take action'. Translation: 'Even if we don't have proper evidence for what we're doing, we had better not *not* do anything.'

Research evidence testing the much-favoured demand-control model of stress[16] 'tends to be derived from cross sectional level studies'. Not so good. We learn that the 'very many published studies of links between workplace psychosocial stressors and health and related outcomes have been the subject of a number of recent systematic reviews'. Three are mentioned, the last of which was commissioned by the HSE itself to examine the scientific evidence. This review[17] concluded 'that there is insufficient evidence' but that 'the relative lack of evidence that applies across all contexts' suggested a 'bottom-up' approach, dealing with local issues in particular organizations. This news delights the HSE because they know all about bottom-up approaches: 'Recent HSE-funded work on organizational interventions describes both process-based approaches and standards based approaches for achieving a bottom-up approach.'[18]

Risk assessment and control standards applied to physical hazards have proven practical advantages. But can they be used for psychosocial hazards in workplace situations? A 1998 study by Professor Tom Cox[19] suggests they can. A study in 2000 by Dr Jo Rick and Dr Rob Briner suggests they can't.[20] But no matter: let us get into the fine tuning of each of our six Standards. Each 'has a title and a platform statement that represents conformity with that standard ... This is represented as the percentage of the workgroup who agree that a certain state of affairs exists.'[21] There follows a list of 'states to be achieved' (one possibility being a state of confusion). We progress to 'an indicator tool' and the need for work groups of sufficient size 'to allow a meaningful response to the Indicator Tool'. To what purpose? 'The aim is to shift the population to a more desirable or better state. The aim is not to focus on particular individuals who might be considered to represent a high risk by virtue of the fact that they disagree with many items in a risk assessment questionnaire.' The identity of these 'particular individuals' is unclear (they may possibly be Jo Rick and Rob Briner).

The paper goes on to consider whether organizational stress intervention actually works. For the HSE apparently: 'Taken together the totality of evidence drawn from the evaluation of organizational interventions presents a mixed picture.'[22] Briner and Reynolds[23] had apparently drawn 'unnecessarily pessimistic' conclusions: 'there are many positive findings, many null effects, but not many negative ones – although intervening in complex organizations will always run the risk of the last of these'[24] (in other words, the Standards might make matters worse). Some studies, like the one in 2000 by Shirley Reynolds,[25] 'have seen the evidence on the effectiveness of organizational interventions as problematic'.

In the light of the HSE's own evidence, was a management standards approach really justified? 'As in many areas of health and safety, the data are incomplete.' Nevertheless, the Standards have been cobbled together, the HSE has worked mighty hard on them, and here they are. In summary, 'Each of the six Management Standards consists of a series of statements that, together, define a desirable state to be achieved.' Unfortunately, 'These are necessarily generic and thus represent a "top-down" approach'[26]. Oh dear. And we thought they wanted it *bottom-up*.

Standards launched

At a launch of the new Standards in October 2003, hundreds of delegates like myself were crammed into the Millennium Conference Centre at London's Gloucester Hotel and treated to glossy literature and even glossier speeches on 'Real solutions, real people', performance indicators and beacons of excellence. Des Browne, Minister of State for Work and Pensions, announced that he was proud to be the minister responsible for developing the new code. Professor Cary Cooper's colleague, Joe Jordan of Robertson Cooper, was thankful that: 'We've gotten over the problems of "does stress exist?" and we're onto prevention.' Elizabeth Gyngell, who heads up the HSE stress team, described a 'ghastly meeting' at which they 'started with a blank piece of paper and ended up with it'. Of the final Standards she explained: 'We decided that we should base them on perceptions' – which might be perceived as purely subjective. Only Bill Callaghan, Chair of the HSC, sounded anything like a warning note. He said, 'We are not out to create a scrounger's charter'; that they were looking for 'practical solutions' and that stress was 'not an issue that should be medicalized'.

Mr Callaghan had already expressed his views in a letter to me in 1999:

I understand some of the concerns you have about some aspects of stress management. You are probably aware that the Health and Safety Commission and Executive are interested in preventing problems from happening in the first place. Therefore, we would like to see employers taking steps to reduce the risk of their employees being made ill by work-related stress, which may in turn reduce the need of employees to seek some of the coping strategies you refer to.[27]

What the HSC Chairman and the HSE appear to be saying is this: prevention of stress is better than cure, so how can we intervene in the workplace to prevent employees feeling that they are suffering from stress, or suffering illness as a result of feeling stress? Clearly, their remit must be very ambitious. They must introduce a code to ensure that employees a) never have anything to complain about and b) that they do not experience unpleasant feelings at work, or if possible, at all. If they experience unpleasant feelings, then they must be supported and cherished, and their employers must be hammered and fined. How can all causes of bad feelings at work be removed? By ensuring that the workplace is impeccably managed, and that all conceivable difficulties, disputes, cares and concerns are ironed out. In fact, the Standards admirably endeavour to make the workplace heaven on earth. In no other industrialized nation in the world have such idyllic working conditions been enshrined in regulation.

However because 'stress' is such a vague and subjective term, the new Standards must go even further. They must tackle *all* possible causes of bad feeling. They must deal with problems from home that are brought into the workplace and foist this responsibility on to the employer, and they must tackle problems that do not arise directly from the job, but that depend on attitudes towards work per se. A 2002 European Values Survey[28] revealed that UK workers these days attach more importance to their leisure than to their jobs. This contrasted not only with former attitudes in the UK (a similar survey in 1990 showed the opposite) but with the rest of Europe, where the majority of workers in fourteen other states rated work as more important than leisure. It might therefore be construed as upsetting (and therefore a trigger of 'stress') for these work-shy Britons, wrenched away from their leisure, to pitch up at the workplace week after week and remain there all day, enduring demands upon them, when they would prefer to be doing something else. Even in their own terms, the Standards would surely need to address this source of emotional unpleasantness, were they to be consistent. If a code is devised that seeks to mollify employees' feelings, its remit must take account of all of these issues in order to 'prevent problems from happening in the first place'.

Such an intervention is therefore doomed to failure, and even the HSE admitted in an earlier publication in 1995 that it would be unrealistic and unworkable: 'There is no such thing as a pressure-free job. Every job brings its own set of tasks, responsibilities and day-to-day problems, and the pressures and demands these place on us are an unavoidable part of working life. We are, after all, paid to work and to work hard, and accept the reasonable pressures that go with that.'[29]

Critics of the new code submit that the HSE, trying to help, has missed the point. No one would dispute that workers should be protected from overwork, exploitation and autocratic management styles. We should otherwise sink back into the dark satanic industrial landscape of mill serfdom, match-girls and child boot-blackers. This protection is already vouchsafed in a forest of employment legislation, and so it should be. Redress is available through the tribunal system and the courts for workers exposed to such oppressive, unjust and health-endangering management practices.

But disavowers believe that this is not the nub of the stress problem at all. We submit that one of the main reasons why workers complain about stress, and feel that they are suffering from stress, and fear their work may be causing them stress, is that they have been told a lot of medicalizing twaddle about their brains and bodies by an industry poised with its audits and its potted endocrinology lessons, its thermometers and squeezy balls, stress counselling and its expensive calming courses to 'cure' them. And what has the HSE done to tackle this particular source of stress? Nothing.

Workplace therapeutics

Professor James Woudhuysen of the Innovation department at De Montfort University, Leicester, emailed me a 'Comment' in *The Times* in which he warns: 'We face a burgeoning demand for therapeutic intervention, both on the job and back home. Bring in the Feng Shui merchants, as British Airways has done in its new HQ, and spread chill-out zones in every office.'[30] Says Profesor Woudhuysen: 'Frustration and hostility. That's just what I feel toward the stressbusters.'

Dr David Wainwright, senior lecturer in Health Services Research at the Centre for Health Services Studies, University of Kent, agrees: 'There has been an industrial transformation. In the 1970s, if you were having problems at work, you went to your union rep and you went on strike, or took industrial action or whatever. Whereas now, because perhaps other avenues have been closed off, I think the pressure is on to individualize the problem and treat it as a health issue.'[31] So in come the therapists, whose stock in trade is suggesting perceptual changes anyway, to reinterpret a worker's real grievances in terms of stress. This has not, in Dr Wainwright's opinion, been in the best interests of the employee. He or she has been 'reconstituted as a feeble individual, a weak, vulnerable, inadequate person who needs to be protected from the employer by the state'. In field work, Dr Wainwright told me that he and his team have come across sad cases of employees blighted by stress medicalization, such as nurses in their thirties, diagnosed as suffering from stress, who will never work again. Expectations of emotional resilience plummet. Yet those of us who criticize this degradation of human psychology are viewed as unsympathetic to workers. According to Dr Wainwright: 'It's now seen as grossly immoral even to question the ideology of stress. If you do you are an extreme right-wing government lacky or something. Bizarre.' Indeed, one high-ranking TUC official told me: 'You're on the side of the employer, aren't you?'

An Institute of Directors report, whilst recognizing the devastating effects of severe depression and anxiety from whatever cause, considers: 'it is clear that stress in the workplace should be treated as a management issue.' Where 'employers have brought counsellors and therapists into the workplace, they have weakened their own management control'.[32] Indeed, 'some commentators . . . would go further and say that, as many HR training courses, for example, focus on problems and symptoms in the workplace, they can themselves create workforce problems and lessen management's ability to manage. Managers may believe they are doing the right thing by their employees by introducing these programmes – but the programmes could be counterproductive.'[33]

A review in 2000 by the European Agency for Safety and Health at Work of Europe's stress data undertaken by the Institute of Work, Health and Organizations at Nottingham University's Business School was lukewarm about most stress management interventions. It concluded: 'Whilst it seems logical that such interventions should promote employee health, there are not yet sufficient data to be confident that they do.' A Chartered Institute of Personnel and Development (CIPD) survey in July 2004 revealed not only mournful rises in stress prevalence and absenteeism among British workers, but that half the 1,100 employers surveyed had already introduced audits and professional stress expertise to tackle their stress.

Indeed, rocketing stress absenteeism itself raises an embarrassing question for our corporate stressbusters. Does it mean that workplace stress interventions, despite their huge cost and proliferation, have failed? Or does it perhaps mean that firms offering stress management for workers are helping to create a work disease culture? Another stress ideology critic, Professor Frank Furedi of the department of sociology at the University of Kent, talks about the trend towards therapizing workers and medicalizing their difficulties as 'diseasing the workplace.'[34] His recent analysis of this malaise, *Therapy Culture: Cultivating Vulnerability in an Uncertain Age* (Routledge, 2003), presents powerful evidence that the therapeutic culture is not for the benefit of public health at all. It is 'primarily aimed at imposing a new conformity through the management of people's emotions', and one of the themes of Prof. Furedi's research is that the workplace has become a seminary for this insidious process.

Of course, such 'workplace diseasing' may not be confined to the therapeutic interventions themselves. Scaremongering journalism must bear some responsibility. One recent example was a documentary in the Channel 4 series *Stop – Go Home!* called 'The Day I Snapped',[35] about people who had suffered emotional crises. The programme presented all of these cases as examples of some homogeneous condition called 'stress', which it associated with overwork. The theme of the programme was that if you work hard, eventually something will 'snap' – as though you were composed of electrical wires and cables. The series title suggested the solution: Stop work and go home. Yet people of all ages have crises for all kinds of reasons, including worry about work, overwork, underwork, people at work and not having any work. For a programme to suggest that all of these conditions are the same serves no useful purpose. Indeed, it may actually 'disease' some of its viewers, who might sit before their television sets and think, 'I'm having an emotional crisis, so I must have this disease as well! I had better not go to work tomorrow, or if I do and anything upsets me, I must go home.' And they will use the word 'stress' to describe their condition, and join the absence statistics.

Evidence of effectiveness

In 1998, the BBC's flagship *Money Programme* interviewed Rob Briner on the growing volume of corporate stress business. He said 'Stress management has been around for ten to fifteen years, but in the last five we've seen a huge increase in the number of companies offering services . . . One reason is simply that they are creating the demand themselves. Managers are now bombarded with literature telling them they must do something about stress.'[36] Programme journalist Nils Blythe commented: 'What worries some observers is not just the unproven nature of the gadgets; it's the lack of any evidence that any of these quick fix stress-busting techniques have any lasting effect . . . But the bandwagon is already rolling and the challenge for those on it is to prove that stress management can make a real difference to a serious problem, not just peddle gobbledegook and gizmos.'

Apart from the evidence cited earlier by the HSE, what other research is there on the sort of workplace initiatives stress management purveyors are offering? Are their interventions really beneficial to the employee? Are they ethical? And not least important, where is the evidence, other than from the stress managers trying to sell them, that they work? A landmark HSE review carried out by Professor Tom Cox of Nottingham University[37] criticized Stress Management Interventions (SMIs) on the grounds that they place too much emphasis on altering the perceptions of workers and not enough on adapting the working environment. Professor Cox also queried the weak theoretical base of many such packages and questioned the validity of their supporting evidence.

Dr Rob Briner,[38] in one of his numerous reviews, found that SMIs fall into certain distinct categories. Stress Management Training (SMT) is, on a relative cost basis, the most common intervention. Then there are Employer Assisted Programmes (EAPs) involving counselling, psychotherapy and hypnotherapy. The latter is offered to workers on an individual basis either on site or elsewhere, and may deal with distresses quite unrelated to the workplace. Other interventions analysed involve job redesign (with variable results), audits (usually self-report and with sparse evidence of success), risk management (very little current proof of effectiveness), health and fitness interventions (which may work on their own terms) and management standards for managing stress (little evidence yet available).

Workshops and training courses

The mainstay of corporate stress management is the workshop or stress management training course, the SMT. Stress management programmes are often given robust, macho or aggressive titles to attract prospective clients and users. 'Stress-beating' and 'stress-busting' are popular course names. 'StressBusters', an allusion to the movie *Ghostbusters*, implies gung-ho fearlessness in the face of the spooky and intangible. One stress management incentive programme for nursing staff during Operation Desert Storm (also imaginatively entitled 'StressBusters') offered participants prizes for completing the course.[39]

Current knowledge of the effectiveness of stress management training is gleaned largely from positive profiling by organizations seeking to market their wares, anecdotal and self-report data, and other weak methodologies. The UEA/CERM report cites a number of more objective studies: controlled trials that have shown a reduction in anxiety among those participating in SMT but no reduction in either stress or blood pressure readings; a study that found two forms of stress management training to have little impact, another that concluded there were no grounds for recommending the widespread adoption of SMT, and so on.

Stress management training is generally offered as a pre-packaged group course, consisting of 'stress awareness' and a portfolio of snippets, saws and strategies for 'reappraising one's situation', often including at-a-glance endocrinology facts and box-arrow-flow diagrams. Relaxation exercises, typically borrowed from various clinical and meditative disciplines, form a key part of the training, on the assumption that stress and arousal are pretty similar types of things. Trainees often end up lying on the floor imagining their limbs are heavy or picturing calm scenes. Hypnosis is a distinct possibility. There are also likely to be gizmos and gadgets that add a techno-scientific illusion of 'proof' to the plenary material. And finally there are the after-sales – books, audiotapes, CDs and other support products – to keep the stress management message alive in the weeks ahead. Individual counselling or therapy may be offered as part of the package or as a bolt-on accessory. There may even be follow-up phone conferences, all-expenses paid hotel sojourns, or exotic week-end retreats.

The SMT course is typically directed at healthy, non-distressed, heterogeneous groups of workers on a voluntary basis,[40] who may welcome the training, valid or otherwise, as a change from normal work. Somebody suddenly cares about them, and here are experts able to understand and help! Unfortunately trainers may be completely unregulated and unqualified. As Briner and Reynolds concluded in one of their studies: 'It is not surprising therefore that there is no evidence that such training has any long-term benefit . . . It does seem to be the case that these courses do have small short-term beneficial effects on well-being, but this is likely to be the consequence of non-specific factors (e.g., the 'feel-good' factor) which are common to many training courses.'

No doubt some stress management courses, gadgets and gizmos help some of the people some of the time. But this must remain largely accidental. Because so long as such courses and products peddle a concept – stress – that has no agreed meaning or discernible usefulness, and a theory – stress management – that has no logical or credible scientific pedigree, they must ultimately be misleading, or worse.

In terms of industrial action over workers' rights, stress management ideology, taken to its logical conclusion, may sound the death knell. If workers *en masse* are taught to fear hard work and made afraid of their own bodily mechanisms, they will all need soothing and comforting. They will be far too sick to strike. Rather than industrial action, they will be taking industrial *in*action. Of course, things probably won't go that far. Because the present situation, with one in three workers saying they are stressed and millions absenting themselves from work, cannot continue. The reason has to do with harsh economic and political realities. The majority who go into work, despite their own serious problems, worries and negative feelings, are currently paying taxes to subsidize the work absences of their less robust peers. And it can only be a matter of time before this is pointed out to them.

Creating the 'can't cope' worker

Critics claim that therapists let loose in British businesses may be medicalizing employment problems. But there is another even graver possibility – that stress management intervention in the workplace could actually be disabling workers. We have already seen the potential harm of learned helplessness to public health, and that this danger may be compounded by the relaxation culture that anodyne stress management so often encourages. In the workplace such effects may be particularly disastrous. Soothed and mollified workers are not great problem-tacklers and do not complain. Avoidance of underlying problems is a recipe for disaster, but one that calming workplace stress interventions may actually encourage. Worse, employees who seek, as they see it, to avoid the 'stress' of 'tackling the issue', or bringing their grievances to the attention of management, tend to lose any coping expertise they may once have possessed. This disablement then sends the helpless and uncomplaining worker in search of medical treatment, either to a GP or to his or her occupational health department. Senior OH experts are well aware of this disempowering process and that their surgeries are full of people suffering the effects of it. One OH chief, in charge of a local authority workforce I spoke to diagnosed an outbreak of *a-copeia* – a 'can't cope' mentality – among British employees.

In a landmark study of the coping strategies of hundreds of white-collar workers published in the influential *European Work and Organizational Psychologist*, '... use of avoidant coping methods was significantly associated with perceived problems with coping at work, with lower job satisfaction, and with poorer levels of general mental health'. Whereas 'problem-focused methods' were 'significantly associated with fewer problems with coping at work, higher job satisfaction, and better levels of general mental health'.[41] The same study pointed out that 'relaxation-related methods' have 'no obvious relationship with well-being from the presented results.' The study talks about mere 'symptom management' being increasingly advertised as a way of 'combating stress', and showed that 'palliative coping' is 'positively related to health complaints'. On the other hand, facing up to the problem showed significant 'buffering effects' on the individual's coping abilities. None of which augurs well for stress management experts offering to relax the workforce.

One of the authors of this study, Dr Jo Rick, then of the Institute of Employment Studies (IES) at the University of Sussex, later led a team of scientists examining stress management interventions themselves, and gave a summary of this research at the London conference *Stress – A Change of Direction*: 'The approach we took was to try and stick with the more familiar and better known aspects of the stress literature etc. and raise questions about how much use they are in an organizational context.' The first stumbling block they encountered was the stress concept itself. Dr Rick found that when the word stress was used in organizations, it tends to 'take one's eye off the ball'. Their report conclusions move away 'from traditional and sometimes vague concepts of stress and stress management, to propose a pragmatic, problem-solving framework'.[42] The IES scientists found that the relative merits of different stress management approaches were difficult to establish because 'quality research evidence is limited'. They recommended that anyone seeking to introduce stress management within the workplace should ask two essential questions: first, 'Why do [they] think they have a problem with stress (what is the evidence)?' and second, 'What do they mean by stress (what is the specific problem)?'

Indeed, stress management interventions can actually refract a direct beam of light on workplace problems and focus it all over the place. 'Because stress has become such a big issue in itself, and such a confused issue in terms of definition, the concept can get in the way of looking at what is actually going on.' Taking our lead from Dr Rick, let us look at three examples of jobs with a high stress management profile, to see whether workplace stress interventions have been sensible and successful, and if not, to ask what might be tried instead.

Stress-busting the teachers

In 2000, a *Guardian* opinion poll revealed that half of England's teachers expect to quit the profession within ten years.[43] More than 200,000 are planning either to retire or seek alternative employment because of stress, bureaucracy and overwork, thus posing a serious recruitment problem for the government. I consulted a leading authority on the problem, Les Roberts, assistant secretary of the NASUWT. He wrote back: 'You will be aware that "stress" at work has been identified as the priority health and safety issue by the TUC and its affiliates. NASUWT was instrumental in the founding of the UK National Work Stress Network ... The Association will continue to press the claims of members who have been damaged by the unreasonable demands placed upon them. When we meet members and their families whose lives have been destroyed by excessive workplace pressures we need no further convincing that, far from being a figment of imagination, "occupational stress" is alive and well in the UK education service.'[44]

Like a lot of people, Mr Roberts here assumes that overwork and 'occupational stress' are one and the same problem. But he does concede that stress management is not necessarily the solution, and quoted as an example 'correspondence from one of our members in Northern Ireland who described how his employer organized "half-hour courses in juggling, shiatsu and aromatherapy" as the answer to a stressed-out workforce. The Association believes that the detrimental psychological and physical manifestations of workplace pressures have organizational causes and must have organizational solutions.' In other words, *overwork* is best dealt with directly as an organizational problem rather than a 'stress management' one. There are lessons to be learned from these teachers.

The stress-busted police

Stress interventions in the British police Force have been given added impetus since 1997. In that year, Her Majesty's Inspector of Constabulary (HMIC), the National Audit Office and the Metropolitan Police Service highlighted concern over increasing sickness absence levels. Analysis revealed that 17.5 per cent of total absence was attributed to stress at a nominal value of more than £4.5 million in sick pay, excluding the costs of early retirement and compensation claims. A 1997 HMIC Thematic Inspection Report investigated the problem, one aspect of which it called 'the medicalization of dissatisfaction'.[45] It cited evidence like this: 'Many officers remarked on the widespread abuse of ill-health retirement provisions, whereby significant numbers of officers were leaving the Service early on medical grounds with full pensions, but were widely regarded as simply using the system to avoid facing the stress and strain of police work.'[46]

Compared with traditional policing, there is now an extremely high level of psychological maintenance in the Force. For example, regional crime squads have a requirement 'that undercover officers meet with a clinical psychologist at least four times a year'.[47] Many Forces now have access to counselling and Employer Assisted Programmes (EAPs), a tradition long established in the US. In addition, in August 2003, senior detectives in North Wales Constabulary were given added help – stress balls to squeeze. The force's monthly clear-up rate on burglaries had fallen to 18 cases out of 296. Their Chief Constable, Richard Brunstrom, announced his intentions of getting tough – on speeding motorists. He was also spearheading an offensive on what you might term emotional infringement. In future, according to a mouse mat specially printed, officers must avoid 'using offensive language', 'making hurtful remarks' and 'using nicknames which cause upset'.[48]

Not everyone believes that officers have benefited from such emotional protection, particularly as the job is getting tougher by the day. Crime, and particularly gun crime, is escalating. Morale has slumped in the wake of 'institutionalized racism' claims, and there is now a serious 3,000-man recruitment shortfall in the Met, while several provincial forces, according to the Superintendents' Association, are 'haemorrhaging' officers. Others have apparently gone missing, buried under piles of paperwork. In 1999, Shadow Home Secretary Ann Widdecombe complained: 'We find today a police service so starved of resources and dispirited that sickness and absenteeism are running out of control and a culture of fear lurks within our police stations.'[49]

According to some, this 'culture of fear' has evolved, not through insufficient psychological protection, but through a great deal too much of it.

Lord Brian Mackenzie was a chief superintendent in the Durham Constabulary and is a former president of the Police Superintendents' Association and a graduate of the FBI National Academy. He was a police officer for thirty-five years. He spoke at our London conference calling for a reappraisal of stress management in the Police Force, and argued that it is disabling to those on the frontline of police work to have their emotions constantly reviewed and medicalized when they are expected to deal with distressing and horrifying incidents on a daily basis. A House of Lords ruling on the 1989 Hillsborough disaster,[50] in which officers tried to help dying football spectators trapped and crushed by surging crowds, supports this more robust view of police work. 'So far as rescue was concerned, police officers must be regarded as professional rescuers. They will not be persons of ordinary phlegm, but of extraordinary phlegm hardened to events which would to ordinary persons cause distress.'

In two American states, a principle of policy has developed known as the 'fireman's rule', under which it is held that there is no 'duty owed to the fireman to exercise care so as not to require the special services for which he is trained and paid'. Likewise, those who reached judgement in the Hillsborough case took the view that the police officer 'may by reason of his training and experience be expected to have more resilience in the face of tragic events in which he is involved, or which he witnesses, than an ordinary member of the public'.[51]

In 2000, in the wake of growing concern about stress absenteeism, early retirements and compensation, the then Metropolitan Police Commissioner Sir John Stevens and his occupational health and HR staff assembled a think tank, the External Experts' Advisory Group on Stress, on which I also served. Other members included stress management guru Cary Cooper, HSE stress chief Elizabeth Gyngell,

David Alexander, a mental health clinician and trauma expert, and psychiatrist Gordon Turnbull, also a trauma expert. The project manager was (until recently) Christie Rainbird, then Met Head of Counselling. Surrounded by so much stress management and therapeutic expertise in 2000, the 'non-medicalizing' viewpoint indicated in the 1997 HMIC Report appeared at times to be either eccentric or redundant.

There are user-friendly alternatives to stress management in the Force. The following ten-point plan, drawn up by the author, is offered for consideration, one theme of which is to provide officers with information on the stress ideology itself. That way they could make up their own minds whether or not it is in their best interests:

NON-THERAPEUTIC POLICE SERVICE STRATEGIES
1. Judicious recruitment
2. Inurement (realistic exposure) training
3. Stress ideology briefing
4. Moral and professional support
5. Respect for the right to privacy of feelings and opinions
6. Mixed deployment (seasoned officers with new recruits)
7. Praise and honour for courage and self-management
8. Normalizing activities (competitive, cultural and social)
9. Delegation of paperwork to support staff
10. Help on request with specific grievances and problems.

Using this simple plan would alert officers to the harm of a 'stress' mentality, raise their expectations of emotional robustness and reduce the need for stress management interventions. It would prevent what might be referred to as 'institutionalized stress phobia' within the Force. The 'stress' culture has led in recent years to dozens of officers suing for compensation under the impression that disturbing emotions felt in the line of duty should result in a lump sum from the taxpayer's pocket. The bottom line must be that police work, like armed combat, is extremely tough. Its thrills, its comradeship and its public esteem have always been what they are, because it is tough. Those who feel they cannot face the experience should either not join up, or leave, with dignity but without compensation, as soon as they realize they have made a genuine career mistake.

Stress-busting the BBC

Another emotionally challenging profession, with a lot of tight deadlines, late nights, editorial bullying and time-driven mental work, is journalism. Back in the 1980s, the mantra was: 'Give me the deadline and I'll write you the piece.' It was assumed no piece could possibly be produced without a time-whip. But things have changed since then. A fifty-seven-page glossy brochure entitled *Distressed? How to Avoid Problems*, allegedly issued to BBC staff by their occupational health unit, told them how to control their workplace stress by dabbing their hands with lavender, taking up origami, or staring at a picture of the Alps. Whilst at the computer, the brochure advises, 'ensure you sit on the cheeks of your bottom' – rather than, presumably, on other cheeks, BBC equipment or personnel.

Shadow Culture Secretary Peter Ainsworth commented: 'Most people at the BBC might find this funny if it weren't so expensive. I'm not sure that this is the sort of thing the licence fee is supposed to fund.'[52] A Corporation spokesman hit back: 'If employees recognize stress is making people less productive, it is sensible and responsible to offer sound advice on ways to combat it.' BBC occupational health expert Dr Rob Morrison told me: 'We already have good mechanisms for helping people who are distressed. Contrary to your assertion that the current ideology is failing those who come to OH for help, I am confident that I can show effective assistance and appropriate preventive strategies for the future are being provided. I hope you are not being led to confuse the professional work of the department with the way in which "stress" may be presented by programmes, or in the press, over which we really have no control whatever.'[53] Mr Ainsworth's comment 'is quite inappropriate if it is true, and would seem to indicate a poor understanding of the obligations imposed upon employers.'[54] One 'appropriate preventive strategy' provided by the Corporation for its staff is counselling, more of which later. For the moment, deadline writers, make sure you sit on those cheeks.

CHAPTER FIFTEEN
COUNSELLING

Who is this that darkeneth counsel by words without knowledge?

Job (38:2)

The stress mythology spawns wherever painful emotions are likely to be felt, and influences those wishing to be helped and those wishing to help them. Nowhere is this more apparent than in the field of counselling. The effectiveness of 'stress counselling' and 'debriefing', even for emergency workers, combat troops and the survivors of disasters, is the subject of heated debate.

Today the field of stress counselling is open to practitioners from many different disciplines; from those qualified in one of the numerous schools of psychiatry, psychoanalysis, psychotherapy, psychology and counselling, to those who call themselves therapists and counsellors without any of these forms of training at all. CounsellingResource.com, who in partnership with *Psychology Today* publish an online directory of therapists covering several US states with credentials independently verified by that journal, advise: 'Regulation of the profession varies greatly between and within countries, and in the UK, for instance, there is no statutory regulation of counsellors at all: quite literally, anyone can set up shop.'[1] The excellent CounsellingResource.com warns, of directories generally: 'It is worth keeping in mind, however, that practitioners pay to have themselves listed in such directories, and the information provided ... is just whatever is reported by the practitioners themselves.' The information website points out that there is 'significant debate' over the merits of different professional accreditation schemes, and that:

The degree of medical or psychiatric knowledge which counsellors or psychotherapists can bring to bear on their work varies greatly between individuals and between countries, and in the UK, for instance, most counsellors have either very limited medical or psychiatric knowledge or none at all. So while a competent counsellor will urge you to consult a doctor if he or she suspects your distress may have an organic cause, it is entirely possible that even with the best intentions, he or she won't recognize the symptoms ... There will often be little or no choice as to the theoretical orientation of counselling which can be accessed through medical referrals, and in the UK at least, there may be long waiting lists.[2]

Figures publicised in the UK in October 2003 showed that officially more than 250,000 people use counselling skills as part of their job – more than belong to the armed forces – and that, in any given month in Britain, these people are conducting 1,231,000 counselling sessions.[3] This figure, of course, excludes all unaffiliated counsellors in private practice and recent exponential rises in accreditation.

Yet 'counselling' did not have an entry in the *Penguin Dictionary of Psychology* when it was first published in 1952, nor did it appear in the reprints of 1953, 1955, 1956, 1958, 1960, 1962 or 1963. Neither, come to that, did 'stress'. Clearly, a shift of geological proportions has happened in the world of therapy, and as we shall see, the workplace and emergency service work have become the proving grounds for some of the new ideas.

A British Association for Counselling and Psychotherapy (BACP) leaflet on counselling states that: 'It is always at the request of the client as no one can properly be "sent" for counselling'.[4] This is not strictly true. Medical counselling is mandatory before abortion, genetic screening and HIV/AIDS testing.[5] It is also compulsory in certain branches of the police service.[6] Distressed individuals may have counselling thrust upon them by medical and other authorities as the 'only sensible option' following certain incidents. Why would members of the public question such advice? Schoolchildren exposed to disasters, or attending schools where a pupil has been attacked or murdered, are now routinely provided with counselling as 'the right thing to do'. Abused children, rape victims and under-cover police officers have all been targeted by therapeutic zeal.

Even within the counselling professions themselves, this zeal is sometimes questioned. First principles are queried. Colin Feltham, in his capacity as senior lecturer in Counselling at Sheffield Hallam University writes:

It seems astonishing that in a field like counselling and psychotherapy, with all its psychological, socio-economic, epistemological and other ramifications, few people stand back and ask, 'What's going on here?' You only have to ask a few counsellors or counsellors-in-training, for example, 'What is counselling?' to discover that any answers that may be forthcoming are quite likely to be muddled, vague, uncertain or defensive. If, as a client, you ask your counsellor or psychotherapist, 'What is counselling/psychotherapy?' you may well meet (a) an 'analytic' silence, (b) a 'rabbinic' question: 'What do *you* think it is?', (c) a negative reply: 'It's not me telling you what to do', or (d) a vague statement such as 'Well, it's an opportunity for you to explore any issues of concern to you.'[7]

Some critics, like former head of Abertay-Fife University Centre's Department of Trauma Management and Victim Assistance, Yvonne McEwen,[8] condemn the whole counselling industry on the grounds that it encourages a sense of victimhood, rather than self-determination, survival and pursuit of rights. Such critics certainly have a point. On the other hand, well-regulated, well-qualified, experienced and compassionate counsellors who somehow help people to help themselves, or help them to overcome a sense of abnormality after a shocking event, may be of great value to their clients' lives. This is particularly true where clients have turned to them in desperation, have no one else to talk to, and imagine that they are going mad.

Nor is it even true that because an 'emotional adviser' lacks paper qualifications, he or she is necessarily unskilful. The author once wrote a biography of *Daily Mirror* agony aunt Marje Proops, who never had any qualifications (she had a network of advisers and latterly an in-house team), but received over two million letters from troubled readers, some of them enough to reduce a tyrant to tears. All the letters were carefully replied to and filed away in Marje's archives. There can be no doubt that her no-nonsense humour, compassion, originality and common sense helped a lot of these people to show courage and sort themselves out, as they acknowledged in their letters. So as the poet W. B. Yeats warned, one needs to guard against 'intellectual hatred'.

Some 'stress counsellors' are surely above reproach. These are the therapists who use the term 'stress' simply because their clients use it, and wean them off it as soon as possible. These are the counsellors whose intervention is at the request of individual clients rather than of organizations or authorities, who base their advice on common sense rather than theories, who do not prolong treatment for economic reasons, who do not pathologize their clients' emotions or their problems, who treat them with personal kindness and respect, and who steady them to accept the fact that pain and fear are part of life. Since we have become accustomed to hear of stress counsellors descending en masse on every misfortune ('like locusts', according to some critics), it may surprise many to know that such laudable aims were the impetus behind counselling as a profession.

Britain's largest bereavement counselling service, Cruse, was founded in 1959 to support a group of grieving young widows. It now has over 7,000 volunteers and 45 per cent of its referrals are from medical professionals. One of its counsellors, Caroline Morcom, explains: 'One thing we do remind people of who come in for counselling, feeling as though they are going off their heads, is that almost any reaction is "normal" in grief.'[9]

Person-centred counselling

Emeritus Professor Brian Thorne of the University of East Anglia is director of student counselling and a former Chair of Counselling and Fellow of the College of Preceptors, making him one of the highest-ranking counsellors in the UK. Brian Thorne worked with the American psychologist widely regarded as the father of counselling, Carl Rogers, and has dedicated forty years of his life to helping his clients. Yet this very senior counsellor endorsed my UEA/CERM meta-analysis on the pathologizing of the stress response. This is what he said in his report about 'stress':

What is much more debatable ... is the almost universal assumption that it is the individual's responsibility to master his or her stress, to 'manage' it and, as a result, to become a more resilient and productive worker. This assumption is badly flawed. It leaves out of account the fact that debilitating stress (there is a positive form which motivates and inspires) is invariably a warning sign. It is telling the individual not that there is something wrong with him or her but that there is danger around, which is a threat to health and well-being. Once this perspective is adopted, it becomes immediately evident that enabling an individual to control or 'domesticate' his or her stress may be performing a gross disservice. We need our 'warning signals' for our self-preservation and to be diddled out of them by learning stress management skills and techniques may be rendering us more vulnerable ...[10]

The 'person-centred' or 'client-centred' school of counselling or psychotherapy to which Brian Thorne belongs derives from the work of Dr Carl Rogers (1902–87), a founding figure in the development, in the 1940s and 1950s, of counselling as a significant wing of clinical psychology. Rogers believed that human beings have two basic needs: the need for positive regard from others, and the need to realize one's own individuality, which he called 'self-actualization'. But whereas Freud let slip to a close friend that his patients were 'only riff-raff',[11] Carl Rogers did not look down on his clients, or wish to pathologize their emotions, or see himself as an authority figure or rescuer. In Rogers' view, not only should the therapist modestly listen to the client and unconditionally respect him, but the client must remain, ultimately and entirely, responsible for his own fate.

Rogers' work began in the US and percolated into British therapy, mainly through the work of the Marriage Guidance Council (now called Relate). Brian Thorne says that 'Those coming for help were no longer referred to as patients, but as "clients", with the inference that they were self-responsible human beings, not objects for treatment.'[12] When Rogers started working in the US in the 1920s, psychologists were not permitted under American law to practice psychotherapy. Rogers therefore called himself a 'counsellor'. The person-centred counsellor aimed to shuck aside academic labelling and diagnosis, and any other mystique or pretence at 'expertise' on the part of the counsellor. Instead he worked in an atmosphere of trust and kindness with the client, encouraging the person's own dynamic power to get better.

In one of his books, Rogers recalled a boyhood memory of a bin of potatoes stored in a cellar for the winter, several feet below a small window. He noticed that these pathetic potatoes sent out spindly shoots towards the light, and thought that if potatoes could do this, human beings must have it in them. He believed 'that the individual has within himself vast resources for self-understanding, for altering his self-concept, his attitudes and his self-directed behavior.'[13] It was the good therapist's job to facilitate this process.

Of course, even the finest person-centred counselling is not without its critics. In his indicting exposé, *Against Therapy*, Jeffrey Masson says: 'Reading Rogers is such a bland experience that I found myself recalling the old adage that psychotherapy is the process whereby the bland teach the unbland to be bland.'[14] Masson argues that Rogerian therapy appeals by its very simplicity to therapists who do not wish to have lots of training, and that it pretends to be friendship but isn't, as it is paid for by the hour. He says that when it came to dealing with real mental illness, for example at the Mendota State Hospital in Wisconsin where Rogers was allowed to practise with patients, the counselling failed. It failed either to recognize or change the horror, violence and degradation of those patients' lives.

Hazards of the therapeutic bond

Even Brian Thorne's work at UEA, conducted in an atmosphere of trust, illustrates how the relationship between client and counsellor can be – perhaps must be – a risky business. With one client, he admits, that relationship was controversial in its emotional intimacy: 'The work with this client began and ended before the Code of Ethics and Practice of the British Association for Counselling (BAC) appeared in 1984 prohibiting sexual activity with clients ... I should wish, of course, strongly to challenge this interpretation for I am firmly in agreement with the Code that "sexual activity" with clients is unethical, but do not believe that my behaviour with my client could at any point be so described.'[15]

Thorne is referring here to the case of 'Sally', a married client who had come to him in 1980 with her husband and who for sixteen years had been frozen with fear about her own sexuality. Like Brian Thorne the couple were devout Christians, and placed their trust in him partly on this account. Thorne always consulted Sally's husband on how best to help her, and explains in his book that sensitivity and control were key to the process of unveiling as Sally disclosed her damaging experiences. But sensing that this client needed something more than empathic words, the therapist had used physical caress, gentle massage, hand-holding, hugging and even nakedness. Brian Thorne emphasizes in his account that at no time did he ever break trust with his client or have sexual intercourse with her. Over many months of interaction, the relationship helped Sally to understand and respect the body in which she resided and her role as a woman in her marriage. Yet Brian Thorne was aware how controversial his therapeutic style had been and how close he came to jeopardizing his reputation.

His remarks highlight the dangers of such a therapeutic bond, both for therapist and client, but Thorne argues that a therapist with a head full of theories but no heart can't actually help anybody anyway. 'I doubt if a therapist who is incapable of loving or of allowing himself to be loved can do much good. Therapeutic technicians may perform an effective service for robots or computers but they threaten to finish off human beings who already have little enough sense of belonging to the species.'[16]

Another hazard of Rogerian method, so much beloved of stress counsellors, arises from its central precept, that of empathy. The following description comes from a recent bestseller on person-centred counselling:

Empathy is a continuing process whereby the counsellor lays aside her own way of experiencing and perceiving reality, preferring to sense and respond to the experiences and perceptions of her client. This sensing may be intense and enduring with the counsellor actually experiencing her client's thoughts and feelings as powerfully as if they had originated in herself.[17]

Unfortunately, empathy of this intensity is a perilous sacrifice. For many practising within the therapeutic professions, the greatest genius among them was the late lamented psychiatrist R. D. (Ronnie) Laing, who did so much to humanize and normalize serious mental illness. *The Divided Self*, his 1960s odyssey into the world of schizophrenics, is one of the most moving and remarkable books you are ever likely to read, and one of the most painful and shocking. Such intimacy with his patients is widely recognized to have cost the therapist dear, for Laing was himself institutionalized.

Indeed, Marje Proops once told me that her empathy with her distressed readers, though by no means so intimate, had contributed to her own mental illness, panic attacks and depression.

Empathy with clients' anguish is not for the faint-hearted, and may not be to every weekend certificated 'stress counsellor's' taste.

The 'listening ear'

Dr Bruce Charlton[18] of the Department of Psychology at Newcastle upon Tyne University describes confessional counselling and psychotherapy as sentimental professions that function in the same way as religious confessions. The client/sinner 'unburdens himself' before the listening ear of the therapist who is 'non value judgemental'. The harm lies not in the catharsis of 'getting it off the chest', but in the notion that therapists can solve problems when they cannot. The vain hope of help undermines natural survival and stoicism.

Charlton does not go so far as to suggest that many 'listening ear' therapists (including those that take the client's money and remain completely silent so as not to interfere with the client's mental processes) could usefully be replaced with a tape-recorder at a fraction of the cost. An essential part of this do-it-yourself method, of course, would be to play back the tapes with an interval between recording and listening, to facilitate some reasonably objective analysis. Troubled people can and do help themselves by all sorts of methods. That most wise and gifted of therapists – the human brain – stands ever ready and waiting for its user to consult its arsenal of skills.

However, not all counselling is of the 'confessional' type. Cognitive and behavioural counselling seek to structure a programme of self-help, whereby the client makes alterations in his physical and perceptual routines and learns to cope better with reality. Counselling that works along these lines relies greatly on the client's own willingness to change, and on his or her determination to help him/herself. These can by no means be guaranteed. Confessional counselling – the listening ear – is less demanding, but also much less likely to influence the client's characteristic ways of dealing with crises that go by the name of 'stress'. It may therefore not make any inroads into his sense of helplessness, psychological sickness or victimhood. The so-called 'talking cure' may end up being simply that – talking. And confessional counselling is by far the most common form of counsel on offer.

Celebrities and talking 'cures'

As part of an overall review of the effectiveness of counselling in 1996 (there is no more recent Government data of such breadth), the Department of Health commissioned a review of the evidence on psychotherapy, published the same year in book form.[19] One chapter focused on counselling and primary care interventions and concluded that, based upon studies published between 1975 and 1994, there is no evidence for the efficacy of counselling.

Pro-counsellors naturally claim that this review was unfair, and that other studies have shown different results. Anti-counsellors hit back that while advocates of 'talking cures' may highlight their successes, there have been some very conspicuous failures. In an interview with chat-show host Michael Parkinson, Woody Allen, perhaps the most analysed man in Hollywood, denounced his forty years on the couch as 'an irrelevance' and a waste of his time.

The plight of another intensely therapized client is detailed in Ingrid Seward's revealing biography of the late Diana, Princess of Wales, based on personal interviews with Diana herself and members of the royal household. In it the Princess recalls: 'All the analysts and psychiatrists you could ever dream of came plodding in trying to sort me out.'[20] Among the head doctors who 'plodded in' were Jungian psychotherapist Dr Allan McGlashan, David

Mitchell, and Maurice Lipsedge of Guy's Hospital in London. Seward comments: 'None of them was able to offer an optimistic prognosis, and the pills they fed her did little more than dampen down the symptoms without getting to its root cause.'[21] The Princess apparently had 'a medicine cabinet of anti-depressants, and also Valium'. Diana complained that the pills were really for the therapists' benefit: 'They could go to bed at night knowing that the Princess of Wales wasn't going to stab anyone.'[22]

Diana's mother, the late Frances Shand Kydd, vouchsafed in a newspaper interview her own belief that therapists did the Princess lasting damage. 'They did make Diana truly unhappy about "being a disappointment" because she wasn't born a boy. It was put into her mind by a counsellor, a helper supposedly, when she was unhappy. If you're a bit down with yourself, you're receptive to that sort of thing ... I'm unforgiving of that – unforgetting and unforgiving of the damage done and the pain it caused her.'[23]

The umbilical cord

Stress counselling is a growth industry. In order to justify its existence it must guarantee a supply of clients. Is this more likely to be achieved by normalizing clients' feelings, or by explicitly or implicitly pathologizing them? Some would say the latter, and that even if counselling ultimately strives to make the client independent of therapy, the umbilical cord is way too long. According to psychotherapist Dr Dorothy Rowe[24], for anyone in private practice there is 'an increasing temptation to hang on to clients' for commercial and professional reasons, and this may prolong therapy beyond its natural usefulness.

One factor in this 'prolonging' is that the client may form an attachment to the therapist, and may even become deeply infatuated with him or her. This emotional dependence, and the client's own anger, confusion and resentment about such an inherently artificial 'love affair', are often viewed as part of the therapeutic process. 'Transference' – to use Freud's term for the irrational grafting of powerful feelings from key figures in the patient's past on to the revered therapist – has the potential to cause great pain, not only to the patient but to his or her family.

There are estimated to be 415 different forms of therapy and counselling on offer in the UK and elsewhere.[25] Even if we discount as irrelevant many of the criticisms cited above, given that most of the 415 will, to quote the British Association for Counselling and Psychotherapy, 'include a stress component', this leaves an awful lot of scope for the spread of stress awareness, mythology and misinformation. It provides 415 possible trade routes to the medicalization of emotions and difficulties. It sets up 415 types of psychological authority dispensing stress nostrums to the troubled client.

Counselling the worker

A chapter that focuses on the efficacy of stress counselling would not be complete without an analysis of one of its key growth areas: in the workplace, stress counselling has boomed.

The reasons for this are obvious. We have already looked at the new HSE code which obliges employers to provide 'stress-free' workplaces, and at the interpretation of the law that appears to recognize stress management and counselling provisions as valid employer initiatives in this context and a firewall against possible stress litigation. We have seen how stress management experts have capitalized in the corporate sector using their training programmes, aids and audits. Counselling simply provides another string to their bow. Workplace counselling is essentially little different from any other type of counselling, except that it is funded by the employer and provided either on site or at some external clinic. The treatment and its merits depend upon the validity of counselling per se. If stress counselling works, then workplace stress counselling will work. If not, then employers and workers need to review their options.

Is it enlightened to provide workplace stress counselling? Cheshire County Council think so. They spend between £30,000 and £40,000 a year on counselling for their staff. Kent County Council spend 'significantly more than that' on their in-house EAP (Employer Assisted Programme) service. Wiltshire County Council have had in-house counselling for ten years, although staff counsellors can also refer externally. Spending last year was £79,500. Suffolk County Council have had an in-house service for twenty years, although they recently externalized their provision. Norfolk County Council have a self-referral system with an external provider, costing £120,000 per annum. Even Midlands Fire Brigade have brought in a full-time counsellor. Chief fire officer Ken Knight and welfare officer Nick Aylett consider they are 'looking for caring fire-fighters'.[26]

A survey of 136 UK organizations showed that stress counselling in the workplace has trebled since 1991.[27] Cleveland County Council offered 'bereavement counselling' to staff in 1995 after a staff reshuffle meant that they might have to relocate.[28] According to a former BBC director, television crews were given counselling after the 'disturbing experience' of filming the Normandy Landing reunion in 1994 and watching veterans' grief. After the shooting of presenter Jill Dando, even BBC colleagues who had never met her were offered therapy by a team of counsellors specially drafted in.

Employer Assisted Programmes (EAPs)

Employer Assisted Programmes or EAPs have been around, certainly in America, for over seventy years, with a significant increase in the mid-1960s. They originated in the classic non-psychiatric Hawthorne programmes designed to facilitate changes in attitude both of employee and management. But gradually there was a shift towards treating 'troubled' employees, particularly those with drink problems. By the 1980s, EAPs had spread their wings to enfold many troubled workers' issues, including stress and post-incident reaction, anger management, sexual and racial harassment, domestic worries, relationship worries, financial and legal problems, childcare and elderly care problems, and drugs.

With this shift towards paternalism, the EAP has focused on changing the employee, rather than the organization. Organizational matters and performance-related issues were thought to be the province of human resource management or HRM. The EAP has therefore tended to provide management with information on employees and their difficulties, and to provide employees with therapeutic and stress management techniques. These include, in particular, one-to-one counselling, either on site or elsewhere.

According to figures released in 1999 by the EAP Association, the industry's trade body in the UK, one third of the US workforce is now believed to be covered by more than 50,000 such programmes, including 80 per cent of *Fortune 500* companies. The value of the market generated among programme providers is estimated to be in excess of $1 billion per annum.[29] Other countries have taken America's lead. Apart from the UK, Ireland, Hong Kong, Brazil, South Africa, Australia and the West Indies also now drip-feed counselling to workers via EAPs. Belgium, Holland and Sweden are introducing such programmes. Many involve external providers, and many of these will profess stress management or stress counselling skills.

The UK at first favoured EAPs in the form of internal programmes, supervised by occupational health departments. But since the 1980s 'an external provider marketplace developed . . . and has expanded rapidly since then – there are now more than a dozen companies, which together provide external EAPs to more than 600 organizations covering in excess of 1.2 million employees and their families, or roughly 5 per cent of the UK's workforce.'[30] About

400,000 employees are covered by internal programmes, where the counsellor is actually on the company payroll. Although the counselling is paid for by the employer, only 21 per cent of problems aired will tend to be work-related. The rest are mainly personal, family, financial or legal. Costs vary, but the EAPA claims such interventions have 'contributed significantly to the control of escalating healthcare costs' and that 'an EAP pays for itself and usually several times over'. Such claims have been disputed, not only by the HSE, who say such counselling programmes may be introduced without a great deal of forethought, but by academics seeking evidence of effectiveness.

Evidence of effectiveness?

Among those studies, workplace counselling EAPs have had mixed reviews. Two early studies discussed in the UEA/CERM report[31] showed that EAPs were effective in helping employees with their personal problems and distresses, whether connected with the workplace or not, but that such therapies work in their own terms, rather than in terms of 'stress management'. A later, larger and more critical review[32] contradicts 'the traditional anodyne image of stress management, wherein it is seen as an impartial practice which can be applied by a caring progressive management'.

The HSE advises employers that they are not legally obliged to provide EAPs, and that client confidentiality may in any case prevent them from taking action to tackle the problems complained of. So stress counselling in the workplace may not have any effect on your actual stress. Interestingly the take-up of the service is, according to EAP Association figures, on average fairly low: counselling is likely to be used by 3 to 5 per cent of employees in any given year. This is partly because a stigma attaches to counselling at work, but may also reflect employee desire not to be medicalized.

Shropshire County Council's Occupational Health physician, Dr Dale Archer says: 'Some commercial EAPs are in my view snake-oil salesmen selling what they've got instead of meeting our needs, and at vastly inflated costs with overblown claims of effectiveness.'[33] Dr Archer sets out very strict criteria for such services, which must be 'solution-focused'. Dr John Cooper, senior medical adviser to Unilever UK, was one of the first health chiefs in Britain to introduce EAPs for the benefit of staff. 'I spent huge amounts of my previous employer's money investing in taking on people trained in counselling skills, and making sure employees had access to counsellors and putting in an Employer Assisted Programme. We were the first company to put in an EAP to cover the offshore workforce in the North Sea and, perhaps more significantly, the families left behind, as they say, on the beach. I firmly believed this was the right thing to do.'

But Dr Cooper's faith in workplace counselling, and particularly *stress* counselling, has diminished. 'I don't believe for one minute that stress will be prevented by counselling and I say this with regret because like a lot of other people I've put time, effort and energy into developing counselling services: the input has been enormous. What has started to concern me over the years has been the output – the results – and although I'm quite sure that people have been helped individually by counselling, I don't see any evidence of the reduction in the whole area of *stress*. The more we look at our workplace to try to tackle whatever this "s" substance is, the less I find counselling the answer to it.' The answer may not be, in Dr Cooper's view, a medical one, with occupational health teams struggling to 'reduce the distress' of staff; rather it might be at the other end of the spectrum – 'to increase the coping skills'.

Professor Brian Thorne, though committed to the cause of employee/student counselling, is nevertheless aware of its pitfalls. Providing the service as part of employment policy may be seen as a substitute for tackling organizational problems and grievances: 'If a counselling service is simply acting as a band-aid, it is not good enough, and could even become collusive.'[34] The function of workplace counsellors was not simply 'to return the walking wounded to the front line'. They should be prepared to talk to management about necessary changes.

It should also be noted that stress itself has become big business. The market place, it seems, abounds with stress counsellors, stress consultants and stress management teachers. Indeed, nothing is more irritating for a professional counsellor, who has probably been three years in training, than to discover a so-called stress counsellor commanding a lucrative income after a few intensive weekends of preparation for the role.[35]

In view of the HSE's reservations, negative research results and the fact that even the most caring occupational health chiefs are having second thoughts, do workers who go to workplace counsellors need to have their heads examined? Ruth Lea of the Centre for Policy Studies (and late the IOD) looks with extreme suspicion on the therapeutic professions that have insinuated themselves into the workplace. This tough, successful woman believes they are softening us up: 'Insofar as we are less happy people than we were forty years ago, and more depressed . . . one cannot help but wonder how much arises from the influence these professions have over people and the tendency to "medicalize" the general ups and downs of life as "depression" and "stress".'[36] She cites a number of negative studies on counselling, including a York University investigation that found no evidence that counselling works. Indeed, the NHS Centre for Reviews and Dissemination report concluded that: 'counselling, by itself, has not been shown to produce sustained benefit in a variety of groups at risk.'

At all events, the idea of vulnerable employees or patients being obliged to have counselling whether they like it or not seems to Ruth Lea not only futile but a dereliction of care. 'Yet they have counselling forced upon them in a flagrant flouting of the basic principles of medical ethics. Patient autonomy is ignored, "informed consent" is ignored and, insofar as counselling can do more harm than good, the principles of beneficence and non-maleficence (non-malfeasance) are ignored.'

But perhaps, amid all this discussion of talking cures that may not cure and Employer Assisted Programmes that may not assist, we are not seeing stress counselling in its truest colours. Perhaps such stress therapy works best for those who have endured the most – the victims of disaster.

CHAPTER SIXTEEN

'TRAUMA' STRESS COUNSELLING

You gain strength, courage and confidence by every experience in which you really stop to look fear in the face. You are able to say to yourself: 'I have lived through this horror. I can take the next thing that comes along.' You must do the thing you think you cannot do.

  Eleanor Roosevelt

Where 'stress' ends and 'post traumatic stress disorder' begins is shrouded in mystery. Since they are connected and clearly overlap, and since 'stress' and 'trauma' are often used interchangeably in the media, a book on stress must at least address the subject of PTSD. Whereas the term 'stress' acts as a cloaking device for otherwise normal emotions and physiological mechanisms, PTSD is, at the moment at least, a recognized form of mental illness. (Stress is not.) But the British Medical Association now regard PTSD as an 'everyday phenomenon', which suggests that the term's former specialist use, for referring to sufferers from shell shock and survivors of disasters, has now been generalized to refer to the victims of any upsetting event. This places PTSD well within the remit of this book. One very good reason for including it, of course, is that if 'stress' is not a valid or helpful term, then PTSD as a syndrome must also be called in question. This becomes particularly important when we consider that the term PTSD may have the power to cause anxiety, and to 'disease' the victim in exactly the same way as the single word 'stress'.

In 1992 the BMA published a report on stress and the medical profession, in which it is estimated that 1 per cent of the general population experience signs and symptoms of PTSD, and that among certain groups the incidence will be higher.[1] This would represent at least 600,000 civilian so-called 'PTSD sufferers' in the UK.

Before the Vietnam war, when the condition began to be either diagnosed or designated (depending upon your point of view), nobody had heard of it. Then in 1972 an article by psychiatrist Chaim Shatan appeared in the *New York Times* which coined the phrase 'post-Vietnam syndrome' to refer to the plight of war veterans, their sacrifice brushed aside by politicians, who had subsequently committed acts of violence on themselves or others. Dr Shatan became one of the formulators of the concept of PTSD as a 'service-connected disability' which enabled veterans to claim invalidity benefit and compensation. In Britain the concept gained acceptance after the 1985 Bradford Stadium fire that killed thirty-six football spectators. Some of the fire-fighters attending the blaze were diagnosed with PTSD.

A Law Commission Report[2] describes the nature of PTSD, its causes and effects:

The phrase 'post traumatic stress disorder' was coined in the 1970s and was officially recognized with the publication of DSM-III [the American Diagnostic and Statistical Manual of Mental Disorders] in 1980. Veterans returning from the Vietnam War were found to be suffering from severe stress and in need of treatment, yet there was no diagnosis to fit their syndrome. PTSD was a concept created to meet that need. However, the acceptance of PTSD among psychiatrists has not been universal and the diagnosis remains controversial.

Be that as it may, an increasing number of people have since been diagnosed as suffering from PTSD, raising several disturbing issues, both for those offering to help and for those diagnosed. The potential for an emotional 'syndrome' to provide scope for fraud and hypochondria is fairly obvious and must concern national health authorities. But the potential for such a diagnosis to add to the suffering of those exposed to distress must concern us all. The following examples, taken from three countries where PTSD is widely accepted as a diagnosis (the US, the UK and Australia), serve to highlight some of the concerns of those who would like to see a review of the designation and treatment of PTSD.

Problem one – 'symptoms of financial benefit'

In America, where the syndrome originated, there are 124 special PTSD clinics dotted around the states. There are also a number of websites offering diagnosis and help for 'Nam vets'. Typically, they start out like this: 'Are you a combat veteran, law enforcement officer, rescue worker, first responder? If you have seen action, it's possible that you could be suffering from Post Traumatic Stress Disorder (PTSD).'[3] They go on to list the symptoms, and offer technical help on the protocols for applying for compensation and disability pensions: particularly useful in assisting an application are combat medals. 'Regulation 38 CFR 3.304(f), 19 May 1993 provides the mechanism whereby the VA [Department of Veterans' Affairs] must consider veterans who possess such an award(s) or decoration(s) as having experienced a combat stressor.'[4] Disability is determined by the Compensation and Pension Service, a division of the Veteran Benefits Administration. As of March 1998, 101,978 American veterans were successful in their applications.

Veterans Benefits News and Resources, the official website of Vietnam Veterans of America, follows the typical pattern of claim assistance and diagnosis, emphasizing 'STEP 4: GET EVIDENCE OF STRESSOR'. It lists 1999 monthly disability compensation rates as follows (depending upon the disability rating, allowances for a spouse range from $34 to $112 and for each child, $18 to $60):

10 per cent	$96
20 per cent	$184
30 per cent	$282
40 per cent	$404
50 per cent	$576
60 per cent	£726
70 per cent	£916
80 per cent	$1,062
90 per cent	$1,196
100 per cent	£1,989

The level of impairment is determined by a schedule of ratings, from 'a mental condition has been formally diagnosed, but symptoms are not severe enough either to interfere with occupational and social functioning or to require continuous medication' (10 per cent) up to 'total occupational and social impairment' (100 per cent).[5] American technical reports evaluating serving soldiers' PTSD abound. Typical is NTIS Order Number ADA388582, US Soldier Peacekeeping Experiences and Wellbeing After Returning from Deployment in Kosovo. Soldiers stationed in Germany were surveyed: 'using a 15-item peacekeeping experiences scale, the 17-item Post Traumatic Stress Checklist, a 10-item revised Conflict-Tactics Scale, and three wellness behaviours (alcohol consumption, sick days and sleep'.[6] Unsurprisingly there was a lot of PTSD about.

After the Vietnam war, veterans were treated shamefully. Now, overrun by stress researchers, US service personnel are dealt with technically and financially. Whether this approach remedies the suffering of those affected, or whether it simply draws former servicemen into a vortex of emotional analysis, diagnosis and pathology is a moot point. Rewarding symptoms is a dangerous precept.

Problem two – the 'perpetual victim'

The Australian government's recent decision to review veterans' compensation and benefits, based on the Clarke Committee's Report, resulted in a package worth $267 million over five years. Nevertheless this met with a very angry rebuff on the website of Australian servicemen and veterans, the Aussie Digger: 'This tricky and mean government should be thrown out'. Particularly threatened were TPIs (Totally and Permanently Incapacitated), whose disabilities render them incapable of working longer than eight hours per week. Their compensation 'has steadily eroded over the last 29 years or so'. The Aussie Digger protests: 'You probably thought when a medical specialist declared that the war had rendered you totally and permanently disabled, the Department would accept that judgement, pay you a pension and leave you alone. Think again.'[7] Rehabilitation, or at least an assessment for it, was now a distinct possibility. Apparently the government suspects that some TPIs could be working:

One of the reasons they give for suspecting this is that lots of TPIs don't go to the doctor a lot; they don't have ongoing treatment. Now, we know that lots of TPIs manage their condition themselves, especially those with PTSD. They try to avoid stress, and just do what they can cope with. And for many, going to the doctor is one of those stresses to be avoided. A lot even go bush in an attempt to avoid stress and be left alone . . . There are simply no grounds for forcing these TPIs into some compulsory rehabilitation regime. Indeed, doing so, or even the possibility of doing so, could cause just the sort of stress these veterans are so vulnerable to.[8]

War can certainly blight people's lives. But rehabilitation might hold out the hope of a cure, or at least some form of treatment to improve the lot of those affected. That the suggestion of a return to normality should arouse such outrage surely demonstrates how belief in a stress-related disease can harm sufferers further. People who accept diagnoses of 'stress' and 'PTSD' may, by their beliefs, be turned into perpetual victims of these syndromes.

Problem three – 'psyches and damages'

PTSD awards are apt to cause great public anger in the UK, particularly among those who remember that British soldiers in the Second World War who could not face the Front bore the disgrace of the letters LMF ('lacking moral fibre') on their service records, and that 3,083 death sentences were passed on British Empire servicemen during the First World War. Although most of these sentences were commuted, 351 terrified men were shot for cowardice.

In 1994, Falklands veteran Alexander Findlay, a lance sergeant in the Scots Guards, became the first man successfully to sue the UK government for his PTSD. He had seen comrades killed at Mount Tumbledown by a mortar bomb in 1982, and had used a bayonet to perform a tracheotomy on a fellow soldier. He was awarded £100,000 in an out-of-court settlement in which the Ministry of Defence accepted no liability. It was feared that the case would open the floodgates on claims from hundreds of thousands of service personnel and emergency workers, who, because of their horrific professional experiences, believed themselves to be suffering from the disorder. Initially at least, the courts have dammed the flood. A compensation claim for 'inadequate training and treatment resulting in PTSD and Combat Stress Reaction' – a claim that could have cost over £100 million of taxpayers' money – had been pursued by 350 former army veterans from the Falklands, the Gulf, Northern Ireland and Bosnia. Although that particular battle was lost, the fight for compensation by aggrieved war veterans is set to continue.

The BMA's '1 per cent of the general population' have also been very active in pursuing justice for their damaged psyches. In July

1999, for example, former NHS paramedic Gary Maddock, forty-seven, announced his intention of suing his ex-employers, Cleveland and Merseyside NHS Trusts, for £400,000 for PTSD and for failure to provide trauma counselling. He claimed that his twenty years as an ambulance man had left him an emotional cripple. Clinical psychologist Dr Gillian Mezey of St George's Hospital, London, diagnosed PTSD in Maddock and two of his colleagues, despite the fact that Mr Maddock himself was now running his own Templar Private Ambulance Service from his semi in Middlesbrough. Apparently Mr Maddock still thought ambulance-driving a worth-while profession, despite its undoubted horrors.

In April 2004, computer consultant Amanda Luscombe smiled for the press as she walked from the courts having won £1.5 million in compensation for PTSD suffered as a result of the Paddington rail crash which claimed thirty-one lives. The amount far eclipsed awards to victims' relatives and was thought to exceed even the compensation paid to Pam Warren, whose horrific burns had required twenty-two operations and two years in a plastic mask. Some subtle shift had evidently taken place in the law, whereby psychological stress was now seen as worse than the death of a loved one, and worse even than the worst possible physical injury.

In 2001 a thirty-two-year-old nightclub bouncer from Romford in Essex, Mark Cooper, injured a four-year-old deaf and dumb girl, Sarah Sykes, when she jumped out of a minicab in front of his car. He successfully sued the minicab firm for £476,500 for his PTSD, as he thought initially that he had killed the child. That same year another motorist, Leona Mudd, knocked down and injured thirteen-year-old Hayley Greasley, and sued for PTSD. Mudd was an off-duty policewoman. Another policewoman, WPC Lynne Schofield, in 1998 won £151,000 in damages for PTSD after a colleague nearby discharged a gun into some bedding. The court heard that the woman officer felt no fear at the time, but that her ears rang. Two more WPCs, Suzanne Ogg and Catriona Ewing, are each suing Stirling Central Police for £400,000. They were on duty at the school gates after the Dunblane Massacre. Prison warder Lynn Armstrong wants a modest £50,000 for her ordeal in guarding mass murderess Rosemary West. Those not personally involved in disturbing events may contract PTSD at one remove. Prison typist Joyce Errington is suing the Home Office for the trauma of typing up interview transcripts with sex offenders.

Fourteen police officers attending the 1989 Hillsborough disaster, in which ninety-six football fans were crushed to death in the spectator pens at Sheffield Wednesday stadium, went to court to argue that they had been negligently exposed to PTSD as a result of their duties in the carnage. They were initially awarded £1.2 million in compensation and the decision was upheld in the Court of Appeal, but two years later the Law Lords overturned the ruling.

Problem four – 'medicalizing' normal reactions

The problem here is one of distinguishing between 'normal' and 'pathological' reactions. PTSD 'symptoms' vary from person to person. Some psychiatrists argue that PTSD, characterized by re-experiencing the disturbing event ('flashbacks'), general avoidance of the subject, and hyper-arousal (which may include anything from panic attacks to outbursts of aggression), is not actually an abnormal reaction at all – at least not initially.

Indeed, they consider that it may be positively debilitating to the vulnerable survivors of shocking events for therapists to step in and medicalize emotional responses to those experiences, when the ones who endured them are at their most suggestible. In other words, 'Generally "treating" people who are reacting normally is not considered good practice.'[9] According to an excellent information leaflet issued to NatWest Bank staff by its occupational health department (then under the directorship of group senior medical officer Dr David Murray-Bruce), the best help is to normalize the situation as swiftly as possible, and to tell the survivor:

It is normal to experience recurrent, painful and intrusive thoughts of the incident and what might have happened. You cannot stop these, but do not dwell upon them. They are necessary to achieve acceptance of the incident and will gradually fade. Stress hormones, like adrenalin, can cause temporary physical symptoms when there is nothing physically wrong ... To help you get over the experience as soon as possible, you should carry on with your normal routine and return to work as soon as possible.[10]

Problem five – 'groundhog day' stress therapy

The opposite of this so-called 'diffusing' (or de-fusing) approach is to treat the survivors as potential wreckage, and to put them through a psychological procedure known as 'debriefing', whereby they must intensely re-experience the ordeal and discuss reactions with a trained Post Traumatic Stress Disorder Critical Incident Debriefing Person.

The original idea behind debriefing was no doubt sound enough. A recognized 'symptom' of PTSD, or feature of Post-Incident Reaction, is avoidance. People who have endured horrifying experiences naturally prefer not to think about them. 'There is a paralysing avoidance of anything – people, places, things – that may trigger anxiety,' explains Dr James Thompson, co-director of the Traumatic Stress Clinic, set up after the 1987 King's Cross fire. Re-exposure to the memory is therefore the conventional treatment, in the hope that: 'This will help this patient to habituate himself to anxiety, rather than trying to avoid any stimulus that may provoke it.'[11]

However, looked at without a psychiatric slant, suppressing or censoring thought about a distressing incident may leave the brain no recourse *but* to repeat and re-present this data to the conscious mind for resolution and processing. Indeed, this may need to happen before the experience can be filed away in the brain's 'understood memory' circuits. Debriefing was undoubtedly designed to address this issue of natural flashback prompting. But helping the survivor face up to and resolve his experience is one thing, and giving him a nightmarish Groundhog Day, in which he repeatedly relives it, is quite another. Besides, debriefing is often completely artificial. It does not re-expose the patient to the original incident, but to his or her emotional reactions to that incident. This circular process can hardly be inuring and any improvement may simply come about through the patient's own will to recover. Arguably all debriefing does is to make the survivor's battle with the past harder than it would otherwise be.

Dr Jo Rick, in her capacity as a leading researcher at the Institute for Employment Studies in Sussex, reviewed the evidence on trauma stress debriefing. Of PTSD she writes: 'This is considered a normal reaction in the short term and in most people such symptoms will diminish over the next few weeks. PTSD or Adjustment Disorder is only considered as a diagnosis if symptoms persist for over four weeks. Only in a minority of cases will individuals go on to experience PTSD.'[12] Yet Critical Incident Stress Debriefing (CISD) is routinely given to groups of people involved in disaster incidents, often immediately after the event.

Mental 'wounding'

All of the serious problems we have so far discussed with relation to PTSD have arisen because of an influential theory – that the mind can be wounded. This theory may in fact be wrong. The word 'trauma', which has slipped so readily into the vernacular on critical incidents, is Greek for 'injury'. That the psyche (more Greek) may be said to suffer injury when it has no corporeal form is metaphorically useful. It is poetically descriptive. It helps others who have not shared a particular dreadful experience to understand the intensity of mental suffering involved, and to treat the sufferer with compassion and respect. But whether it is literally true that the psyche can be injured is very much a matter for conjecture.

To describe someone as 'traumatized' presupposes that painful emotions and experiences are wounds or abrasions in need of medical treatment; that they are not normal to life; that human beings cannot absorb and respond to them quite successfully; that they cannot recover, learn and grow. Such talk outrages the therapeutic professions, of course, who claim that the psyche can be trashed just as easily as the body. But leaving aside the affront to therapists, survivors who are medically labelled in this way may end up not survivors at all, but 'victims', thinking that they are 'psychologically scarred', or 'emotionally crippled', or that they are owed compensation, or that some person or authority must rectify whatever misery and fear they may have felt.

This is particularly true if the original 'trauma' is controversially followed by immediate post-incident debriefing (a form of treatment favoured, as we shall see, by the British Medical Association), or by long periods of stress counselling in which the survivor must relive and rehash his original mental anguish. This is why experts opposed to medicalizing the condition prefer to use the simple term 'post incident reaction', so as not to pathologize the psychological process of recovery while the brain sifts and re-examines difficult images and emotions.

PTSD may be distressing, frightening and painful, but if this cluster of reactions is the means whereby the brain comes to terms with distressing events, then this process may well be prolonged by ill-advised intervention. Indeed, immediate aftermath therapy may have a 'nocebo effect'. It may create in the mind of the survivor the idea that his reactions are a sign of mental illness and that he is therefore mentally ill. The survivor is then trapped in a spiral of fear and therapy, just as those who come to dread the fight-or-flight response are trapped in the spiral we have labelled stress phobia.

Getting back to 'normal'

Survivors have rights. One of the most important of these must be the right to be reassured and regarded as 'normal' even after a horrifying incident. To be 'normal' means to have one's losses acknowledged, to have one's feelings respected, and to have what is left of one's life and routines restored as soon as possible, rather than to be consigned to a world of white coats. Yet at the moment this simple human right is frequently flouted – by employers, by health authorities, by doctors, by counsellors and stress therapists who believe that they know best what the survivor needs. Perhaps, even if half his loved ones or comrades are gone, and even if he has sustained terrible losses, the survivor simply wants to be returned to life, work and humanity.

Some survivors, however supported by friends and colleagues, feel unable to do this. They may try to return to normal and fail, because they are overwhelmed by a sense of panic or anger, or because they keep collapsing in tears, and because they think these emotions are 'not right' or not endurable, or a sign that they are mentally ill. These survivors may indeed seek what they think of as 'professional help'. But unless and until they do, it should surely not be foisted upon them.

Normalizing used to be considered a very beneficial and healthy idea. A good – and extreme – example comes from the First World War battlefront. Dr William Johnson, formerly of Guy's Hospital, had spent three years with a field ambulance and won a Military Cross for his bravery during the battle of the Somme, prior to being put in charge at No. 62 Casualty Clearing Station behind the line at Passchendaele. Johnson felt that the climate of belief in shell shock had convinced the troops that it was 'a definite disease and that the term meant some mysterious change in the nervous system'. Such beliefs inevitably inspire both terror and symptoms in men under fire. Johnson's method was to demystify the whole thing:

To the soldier's mind it was as much an entity as scarlet fever, with the further addition that, being incurable, shell shock was more to be dreaded. In quite a number of cases the eradication of this false belief from the patient's mind was all that was needed to effect a rapid recovery from his symptoms. To explain to a man that his symptoms were the result of disordered emotional conditions due to his rough experiences in the line, and not, as he imagined, to some serious disturbance of his nervous system produced by bursting shells, became the most frequent and successful form of psychotherapy ...[13]

Such sane talk and a fortnight's rest in hospital 'not infrequently ended in the man coming forward voluntarily for duty'. Johnson's caseload was not small. During the four months of the Passchendaele campaign during the autumn of 1917, 5,345 men, at an average of about 60 a day, filed through his tent, many of them believing themselves to be shell shocked and showing the most alarming symptoms. Johnson provided what he called 'an atmo-sphere of cure'. His rapid reduction of 'symptoms', for example by asking patients who had lost the power of speech to imitate his breathing with as little effort as possible, phonate on a few words and then go through the alphabet, was seemingly miraculous. With difficult patients who 'trembled all over', Johnson's method was to provide rest and vigorous massage by 'a professional rubber who was accustomed to train men for athletics'.[14] Such simple normal-izing tactics could make the symptoms vanish. In fact Johnson said that the actual methods used were not important in themselves. What mattered was that the patient should trust his judgement that everything was normal, and that the symptoms were not a sign of incipient madness. The soldier was respected as a sane man, merely exhausted and in need of rest, after which he would be fighting fit again.

What modern research exists that compares the benefits of such traditional 'normalization' with post-trauma debriefing in order to test their relative efficacy? Even specialists in the field like Dr Jo

Rick have heard of no such research initiative. Yet normalization might turn out to be not only a useful form of treatment, but a source of optimism and hope for survivors of disasters who want to get better more quickly.

Framing negative expectations

How very different are such optimistic messages from the ones promulgated in the name of stress counselling. Dr David Wainwright, another expert, says: 'It's true that if you get traumatic experiences, then further down the line you may have problems and you may become psychologically damaged. But it's *not* the stressful experience that is responsible for that. It's the fact that you're immersed in this therapeutic ethos where they tell you that you should be disturbed about it . . . It's the people that counsel the victims afterwards, I think, that are doing the damage.'[15] Negative expectations about bad experiences have become part of our culture. Dr Wainwright believes that these should be challenged.

His studies of the sociology of health and illness have shown that there is a wide range of possible responses to adverse experiences, and that these are by no means all negative or damaging. This social scientist is not alone in thinking that we need to move away from a 'health issue' approach altogether and instead explore resilience and the way in which cultural expectations affect coping abilities. After all, he points out, even the 'new and virulent epidemic' of 'work stress' has not happened by accident. Dr Wainwright's book on that subject[16] examines the role of government and the trades union in increasing workers' awareness of it, and how these authorities have 'played a role in defining work stress as a key concern for health and safety'. Disaster counselling is simply another example of negative expectations (about the response to adverse experiences) becoming a self-fulfilling philosophy.

About ten years after the *Herald of Free Enterprise* sank off Zeebrugge en route to Dover in March 1987 with the loss of 188 lives, Dr Wainwright carried out a study of 'work stress' among the Dover population,[17] which included a fair number of cross-Channel ferry workers. He discovered to his surprise that post-disaster stress is, like the Curse of the Yahoobies, highly contagious:

I spoke to the people involved in the counselling service and told the Head of Counselling there that I intended to do some interviews with cross-Channel ferry workers. She said: 'We have had a lot of stressful events. The health service is in crisis and we've had a lot of people coming in with stress. Our counsellors have had severe stress problems as a result of counselling these people. If you carry out interviews with those who have had these stressful experiences, you yourself may suffer stress, and if you want to come back and talk to me, I'll be happy to counsel you.' So there was I, sort of three times removed from the boat sinking, and I'm getting stress third hand. So it's like an infectious disease. They can pass it on to you!

David Wainwright is suspicious of this whole pathologizing endeavour, and the fact that counselling may now be offered to members of the public even 'after a particularly challenging episode of *EastEnders*'. Indeed, the producers of soap operas now have to beware of failing to provide support services for the viewing public after upsetting events on screen. After an episode of *Coronation Street* in which Toyah Battersby (played by Georgia Taylor) was raped, the Independent Television Commission (ITC) upheld complaints from members of the public that ITV had failed to offer a viewer support helpline. Even contestants in TV shows are expected to need emotional salvage. Producers of the American version of *Pop Idol* in 2002 hired a psychiatrist to help unsuccessful wannabes deal with rejection, disappointment and unkind comments from judge Simon Cowell.

'Band-aid' counselling

Unfortunately for those of us keen on sanity as a way of life, the application of post-trauma counselling to survivors of critical incidents has become standard practice. Teams of trained counsellors now stand ready at every major disaster – September 11, Zeebrugge, Hillsborough, the Omagh bombing, the King's Cross fire, Lockerbie. Emergency service crews attending such disasters, although expected to be tougher than most, are now routinely offered or coerced into counselling and time off work. Indeed, their employers may be sued if they fail to provide sufficient counselling, as happened in the case of a young doctor awarded £465,000 after she pricked her finger attending a suspected case of AIDS and subsequently developed 'needle phobia'.

In the year following the World Trade Center attacks in 2001, 9,000 counsellors and therapists descended on New York survivors, three for every person who died. Yet a study of those who witnessed the horrors of September 11 found that counselling had not helped, and had in fact been an 'enormous waste of money'.[18] Janet Maxwell, forty-one, narrowly escaped the destruction of the Twin Towers. She managed to scramble under an ambulance as the skyscrapers sank to earth and was nearly suffocated in the dust storm. She is still startled at loud noises, but found counselling a very negative experience. She went along to a few sessions organized by her employers but soon realized the circular nature of it. 'They wanted to keep rehashing everything and I didn't want to. I just wanted to forget about it and move on.' Another survivor who keeps talking to her about the event gets short shrift from Janet, who replies: 'Get a life'.[19]

The princess and the PTSD man

Princess Anne was roundly condemned by the therapeutic professions after she addressed a Victims' Support conference in Glasgow in 1996. The Princess Royal aired the view that trauma victims should be treated with dignity and respect, rather than as cases exhibiting symptoms, or the subjects of absorbing psychological theories. She said: 'The more information you gather, the more likely you are to stick a label on certain attitudes – which I suspect is where Post Traumatic Stress Disorder came from.' She added: 'It is for the individual to make the difference, not somebody applying a name or a cure.'[20] She thought that survivors needed time to come to terms with their experience, not therapists. 'They seem to fail to understand that people are far more competent than that, and infinitely more intelligent than they are given credit for.'

Glasgow psychologist Dr Jack Boyle was one of many therapists vexed by such remarks. 'Post Traumatic Stress Disorder is recognized throughout Western Europe and America as a genuine condition ... As far as I know, Princess Anne is not qualified in psychology, psychiatry or medicine and, in the absence of these qualifications, she is better to maintain her silence.'[21] It might be added that many stress counsellors do not hold these qualifications either, and that Princess Anne was herself the survivor of a rather 'traumatic' event. In 1974 in London's Mall, she and her husband Mark Phillips were returning to Buckingham Palace in their Rolls-Royce when another car blocked their path. A gunman jumped out, fired six shots and tried to get into the Princess's car to seize her before being arrested. A police officer was shot in the stomach and the Princess's chauffeur and private detective were both wounded. The gunman had intended to hold Princess Anne to ransom for £3 million. Arguably, her knowledge of the needs of 'trauma survivors' is at least as valid as any therapist's.

The BMA favours trauma stress counselling

According to the BMA in 1992, critical incident debriefing modified the emotional effects of attending disasters among rescue workers:

For example, during the Piper Alpha disaster police were provided with detailed induction to their tasks, explaining the importance of what they were doing, their possible reactions, and the need to attend to their own welfare. They worked in pairs with an older, experienced officer in each pair, their shifts were limited, they were debriefed each day, and informal support was available from a psychiatrist. Under this regime they showed no long-term effects from their stress.[22]

Even leaving aside the blithe use of the scientifically insubstantial term 'stress' in a report by the UK's most senior medical authority, whether such benefits were the result of debriefing, or simply of induction and teamwork, is debatable. The BMA adds, citing a study undertaken at Sheffield's Northern General Hospital in 1990: 'Debriefing programmes were also successfully used with health workers after the Hillsborough disaster, where 95 people [96 according to other sources] were crushed to death.'

The BMA in 1992 came down wholly in favour of stress counselling for doctors and medical students: 'Counselling and careers advice should be available to all those within the medical profession co-ordinated by postgraduate deans ... Counsellors should have the ability to refer doctors with particular difficulty on to more specific therapists where a range of treatment options may be available.'[23]

In 2005 The BMA saw no reason to revise its position. Spokesman Steve Harman told me: 'The BMA does a lot of work for doctors suffering from stress.' They provide not only a 24-hour counselling service but an additional support service to provide doctors with advice from *other* doctors about 'health and work-related problems including stress'. In fact, 'We are very much in favour of counselling and provide as much of it as we can.' Therapists working for FirstAssist, the BMA's own service provider, must apparently hold a four-year diploma in counselling, are not allowed to counsel for more than twenty hours per week and 'have to be comfortable on the telephone and be able to use this medium as effectively as if they were face-to-face', according to the same source. Such unqualified and uncritical approval for stress counselling from the UK's premier medical body must lead British doctors to assume that it is indeed a wondrous form of treatment. And if stress counselling is a good thing, it follows that trauma stress counselling must be even more efficacious.

Those against trauma stress counselling

However, not everyone in psychiatry or medicine agrees that debriefing and stress counselling perform such wonders. Professor Richard Mayou and a research team at the Warneford Psychiatric Hospital in Oxford worked with 100 randomly selected road accident victims admitted to hospital to investigate the benefits of counselling. Their follow-up findings were published in 2000 in the *British Journal of Psychiatry*.[24] Talking about their ordeal immediately afterwards did not reduce or prevent post traumatic stress disorder in the survivors, and indeed made some of them worse. Consultant psychiatrist Dr Michael Hobbs told the press that the three-year study highlighted the damage and dangers of debriefing: 'What our research highlights – together with many other studies – is the danger of mental health professionals and counsellors causing serious damage.' Debriefing, it was shown, could disable those it was intended to help. 'Now we know that such an approach can not only be intrusive, but in the worst cases it can exacerbate the mental trauma.'[25]

Dr Martin Deahl, a consultant psychiatrist and senior lecturer in psychological medicine, is another outspoken opponent of debriefing. Some of his research, on UN servicemen who had witnessed atrocities in Bosnia, was published in the *British Journal of Medical Psychology* in 2000.[26] Dr Deahl and a team of army officers found that PTSD could actually be prevented by suitable training before going into conflict. Psychological debriefing following exposure to traumatic events, although it did help to reduce long-term alcohol misuse after returning home, had no effect on the rates of PTSD. The findings showed that there were 'very low rates of PTSD and other psychological illnesses', and the authors think that the training package beforehand (acquainting them with the nature of events they were likely to encounter and briefing them on what to do if they felt any 'symptoms') was probably a factor in the soldiers' ability to cope. Dr Deahl, of Shropshire NHS and formerly St Bartholomew's Hospital in London, had reported in 1998 that those routinely faced with distressing situations, such as emergency workers, were better served by prior training and acclimatization than by counselling after the event, and these findings on the Bosnian conflict certainly support such a view. In Martin Deahl's experience, 'Psychological debriefing is a waste of time.'[27]

A Dutch study published in *The Lancet* analysed similar debriefings, and found little difference in the long-term health benefits between those who had undergone counselling and those who had simply spoken to friends and family. Another study, of Australian fire-fighters, found that the incidence of 'delayed-onset PTSD' was greater in those who had received debriefing.[28] And in 2000, Dr Jo Rick warned the British Psychological Association that a joint study found no evidence of any long-term benefit to survivors: 'At best its efficacy is neutral and at worst it can be damaging.'

Professor Michael King thinks stress counselling interventions may be applied too hastily: 'If you come in there very quickly, like after a football stadium disaster, and you try and debrief people or counsel them, there's now some evidence that those people do badly. They do not do so well as the other people who have been left alone.' Associate Professor in clinical psychology Justin Kenardy, of the University of Queensland, reported in an editorial for the *British Medical Journal*: 'Despite the widespread use of psychological debriefing, serious concerns have been raised about its effectiveness and potential to do harm.'[29]

Debriefing is a 'grassroots' intervention that is popular among many health and allied practitioners ... Organizations such as banks and hospitals are likely to continue using it since there is no comparable broadly acceptable early intervention that is comparatively low cost. The continued use of debriefing might not matter (other than to taxpayers and shareholders) if studies had found that psychological debriefing had no effect or a positive effect on recovery. But this may not be the case. Distress after trauma typically reduces over time, stabilizing at levels that are proportional to the initial traumatic event. For debriefing to be worthwhile it should at least accelerate the downward trajectory of distress. What should concern practitioners, organizations and researchers is that not only does the evidence indicate that this is not happening, but it also indicates that debriefing may prolong the process of recovery.[30]

Academics, medics and psychiatrists who oppose debriefing base their conclusions on research, but there are others who also object on the basis of first-hand experience of frontline work. One of the speakers at the London conference *Stress – A Change of Direction* was former Chief Superintendent and President of the Police Superintendents' Association, Lord Brian Mackenzie of Framwellgate. A powerful opponent of trauma stress counselling in the police force, he believes that after a particularly distressing incident, officers don't need to have their feelings medicalized by being subjected to counselling and therapeutic interventions. Instead they 'should be commended and made to feel good about their role in it'. He thinks that they should be treated as heroes, not patients.

It should not be assumed that those who volunteer for frontline work will become psychologically weak or defenceless when faced with traumatic events, or that their emotions will be rendered damaged or delicate. Many service personnel regard it as part of their job to steel themselves, and Lord Mackenzie points out that this used to be the norm. When an officer witnesses some terrible carnage, as he did the day he became an officer nearly forty years ago, he says: 'You don't panic. You have to deal with the situation.' Such demands on one's emotional strength, according to this more traditional thinking, are hindered rather than helped by a therapeutic culture. Lord Mackenzie wants to see a shift away from therapy towards more traditional values of courage and duty: 'I have long argued that the modern obsession with compensation, the blame culture and "stress" caused simply by doing the job you take on voluntarily, enfeebles the police service and disables the body's natural ability to deal with trauma.'

Another forthright critic of trauma stress counselling is Professor Frank Furedi, of the Department of Sociology at Kent University. He deplores the growth of the 'therapeutic culture' because it pulls the rug from under emergency workers and survivors struggling to stand on their own two feet and deal with their reactions. Furedi points to the Aberfan disaster, in which 144 schoolchildren and villagers were buried beneath the black avalanche that engulfed the Welsh mining village in 1966, as an example of pre-therapeutic coping. A year later, according to local child psychologist Mary Essex, the surviving children 'seemed normal and well-adjusted' and 'the villagers have done admirably in rehabilitating themselves with very little help.'[31] In contrast, said Furedi, we are now overrun with counsellors, one for every victim of misfortune: 'Victims of crime are now urged by the police to undergo counselling. Almost every large employer is expected to offer counselling for every conceivable problem.'[32]

Professor Simon Wessely of the Department of Psychological Medicine, King's College Hospital, says: 'When a glamorous disaster happens I have been promised over 30 trained counsellors immediately. I have to say that makes me a little cross.'[33] He referred to 'the largest and possibly the best conducted' trial of psychological debriefing, by Jonathan Bisson at the University of Wales College of Medicine, Cardiff,[34] on 133 patients with serious burns. Among those who received psychological debriefing, 26 per cent were found to have PTSD thirteen months later, compared with only 9 per cent of those who did not receive it. So the counselled group actually had a significantly higher rate of psychiatric disorder when followed up.

Research published by the Oxford-based Cochrane Collaboration, which provides worldwide guidance for doctors, reviewed the evidence for trauma stress counselling as a means of preventing PTSD in 1999, looking at no less than eight randomized trials. It concluded that such counselling was at best useless and at worst made people more likely to suffer PTSD. It found no evidence that counselling reduced subsequent levels of other forms of mental illness, depression or anxiety.[35] Simon Wessely, who led the review, also completed a study of 3,000 soldiers who served in the Bosnian conflict. He found that only 3 per cent of the servicemen suffered long-term trauma. 'Undoubtedly some people suffer, but most do not. The toxic effect of counselling is that some people begin to see themselves as having a mental health problem when they do not.'[36]

How can talking cures make you worse?

How could a talking cure designed to help people deal with their terrifying experiences possibly make them worse? According to Australian investigator Professor Justin Kenardy: 'It has been suggested that debriefing "medicalizes" normal distress by generating in an individual the expectation of a pathological response.'[37] In other words, if a health authority tells you that you have undergone an experience likely to cause mental illness, you are quite likely to believe you are mentally ill. Another very simple explanation is that rehashing a survivor's bad feelings increases those bad feelings. The study tracking witnesses to the destruction of the Twin Towers, by Assistant Professor George Bonanno of the department of psychology at Columbia University of New York[38] found that: 'There is more data supporting the view that talking about how unhappy you are just makes it worse.'

Another theory is that 'rewarding' symptoms provides a disincentive to recovery. Therapy may create a negative mind-set by constantly reminding the patient of his or her victimhood, and if this is then backed up by the thought of compensation, symptoms may persist for a very long time. Trauma expert Professor Charles Figley, who has treated families of Beirut hostages and written many books on trauma, told a European trauma conference organized by London Transport in September 1997 that some victims fake symptoms in order to cash in on the compensation culture. His remarks on the subject were widely reported in the press. More significantly, he pointed out that others become dependent on compensation, and locked into a victim mind-set. 'If you are given compensation as a result of trauma symptoms, it is more likely the symptoms are going to be repeated.'

Another potential source of damage comes from the PTSD diagnosis itself. Some experts theorize that the term may offer those who have shown psychological frailty a defence, by making them appear to have had no responsibility in the matter. If they failed to react well to a terrible event and were diagnosed as 'suffering from PTSD', the reasons for their failure become medical rather than personal. The emotionally frail may therefore seize upon the diagnosis to protect them from suggestions of cowardice and from uncomfortable thoughts about their own failure to cope.

One of the 'ego defence' theorists was himself a very prominent advocate of the term PTSD. 'Knowledge of PTSD and its symptoms is now so widespread – I blame myself,' says Dr James Thompson, one of the first British psychiatrists to popularize the PTSD diagnosis in the UK. But even he now thinks that the diagnosis may act as an emotional safety blanket. 'There is pressure from people who are stressed and agitated: "Say I am traumatized – I fit the disorder." The motive is clear: which description would you prefer about yourself: "He collapsed because of the extreme stress placed upon him", or "He collapsed because he is a weak, fragile individual who could not cope with life"?'[39] This interpretation has the advantage of emotional intelligence. In human psychology, as in physics, there is a force of gravity. It is always easier to fall, to give in, than it is to remain standing and fighting. Standing and fighting require effort. Falling does not, and when respected authority figures add their weight to psychological gravity, falling becomes even more likely.

Giving survivors the choice

Why then, despite all these professional concerns about the possible dangers of trauma stress counselling, should the survivors of traumatic events have to put up with seeming droves of disaster counsellors determined – indeed authorized – to diagnose them? At a time when their emotions may feel like open wounds, why should vulnerable people be inundated with offers of a form of treatment under such fierce critical scrutiny? According to Charles Figley's 1997 European trauma conference speech, in the wake of the Oklahoma bombing counsellors crawled over victims 'like ants going to a picnic.' Indeed, after one infamous British disaster, counselling critics Dr Jennifer Cunningham and Yvonne McEwan observed: 'In Dunblane, there were more counsellors than victims'.[40] Apparently psychological guides lighted upon even those delivering the floral tributes.

At the very least, survivors of such events should surely be given information on the risks associated with trauma stress counselling, and asked if they still wish to go ahead with the treatment. They may prefer to be left alone. This would certainly have been Frank

McFarlane's preference. Frank emerged from one of the worst traumatic incidents of recent years, the Piper Alpha disaster. He watched workmates in flames jumping off the helicopter deck and was then subjected to trauma stress counselling. He told BBC television medic Dr Phil Hammond: 'As a whole I don't think the counselling helped at all. The people who are giving the counselling are doing their best, but they don't know anything about it. And sometimes you feel worse after it.'[41] In the end, his wife Margaret became so concerned at the harm to Frank that she went round and gave the counsellors a piece of her mind. In her televised interview Mrs McFarlane repeated what she had told them:

Do you know that he comes home after your sessions and the world revolves around him? I work the other hours of the day to make him feel normal, and to try and build up his resilience to all the knocks and problems life presents, and he comes back from your sessions feeling 'Woe is me'. And they said, 'We'll give you some counselling'.

In an age of therapy, the idea that post disaster stress counselling might harm survivors will be difficult for many compassionate people to accept. We have become so accustomed to the safety blanket, the helping hand. How could disaster survivors possibly manage on their own? How could well-intentioned trauma counselling possibly fail them, or prolong their agony of mind? But the evidence is there for all to see.

Even more amazing is another possibility: that the traumatic event itself might eventually prove to be of long-term benefit to the survivor's mental health. In 1999, researchers presented their findings to the 107th Annual Convention of the American Psychological Association in Boston on the long-term psychological effects of one of the most angst-ridden ordeals known to modern man – the plane crash. They found that those who survived were in better psychological shape – in terms of levels of anxiety, depression and PTSD – than passengers whose planes arrived safely.[42] Not only this, but the crash survivors 'reported strong positive changes in their outlook on life'.

What doesn't kill you, it seems, really can make you stronger . . .

CHAPTER SEVENTEEN
NATION SEDATION

All things have rest: why should we toil alone,
We only toil, who are the first of things?
... There is no joy but calm!

Alfred Lord Tennyson, *The Lotos-Eaters*

If arousal were a disease, the best course of action would be to avoid it. Under the aegis of stress management theory, which views all arousal as a risky business, methods of avoidance have therefore proliferated. In fact, so far as is practicable in Britain and America, we are heading for the Land of the Lotos-Eaters, where nobody will get aroused about anything ever again.

Moods may be modified with prescription tranquillizers, sleeping pills and anti-depressants. Then there is self-medication, most popularly with nicotine, cannabis and alcohol. The stress management industry, as we have seen, sells a plethora of calm-downs, nostrums, prophylactics, palliatives and panaceas. And for those who seek shelter from life altogether, there is a bewildering array of 'escapist' activities, from monastic-style retreats and early retirements to multiple holidays, binge-eating, 'stress-busting' foods (such as sprouting seeds and bananas), mind-numbing television and Classic FM, the radio station that presents even the passions of classical music as a form of stress management balm with such catchphrases as 'Forget it all' and 'Relax and escape' (fortunately the music rises above such anodyne nonsense).

Sedating young and old

Nation sedation – arousal management on a national scale – has infiltrated the education system through modular school examinations and continuous assessment to avoid 'exam stress', and crept into geriatric medicine where calming drugs may be used to control the elderly in care homes and make them more tractable to overworked staff. Perfectly normal moods and behaviours such as anxiety, restlessness, wandering and non-cooperation are being modified by the use of chemical tranquillization.

In the UK, prescription tranquillizing of old folk has been widely linked to falls and fractures, yet the practice persists. In February 2003 a survey of more than 900 people in twenty-two British care homes was published in the journal *Age and Ageing*. The research team, led by Alice Oborne and Stephen Jackson from Guy's, King's and St Thomas's School of Medicine in London, found that 24.5 per cent of residents had been given neuroleptic medicines (drugs used for the treatment of mental disorders). In more than 80 per cent of cases, the medicines had been prescribed inappropriately or with inadequate monitoring of side effects. Hypnotic drugs are being liberally handed out in Wales. 'The level of prescribing of hypnotics in Wales is a matter of concern' says a 2003 official bulletin.[1] In the United States between 14 per cent and 40 per cent of elderly Americans are regularly taking, or being given, inappropriate psychotropic drugs including tranquillizers.[2]

According to Professor Steven Rose, director of Brain and Behaviour Research at the Open University, 'There's an epidemic of drug-taking among British schoolchildren',[3] but he refers not to Ecstasy or cannabis, but to the 50,000 children being prescribed SSRI anti-depressants (selective serotonin re-uptake inhibitors), and to what he calls 'the explosion in prescribing' of the behaviour-modifier Ritalin to young schoolchildren from 'no more than a couple of thousand a year in the early 1990s ... to 120,000 a year today'.

The children taking Ritalin have been diagnosed as suffering from Attention Deficit Hyperactivity Disorder or ADHD, the 'symptoms' of which are inattentiveness or disruptive behaviour in class, being beyond parental control, or being generally disorderly. There is no reliable biochemical or physiological test for detecting ADHD, and the same children, most of whom were boys, may once simply have been viewed as naughty. The number of prescriptions for the drug (which paradoxically is a central nervous system stimulant) shot up from 2,000 in 1992 to 92,000 in 1997. In 1998 that figure doubled, whereupon the World Health Organization became involved and the latest Department of Health figures (April 2001 to September 2003) show a curb in prescription.

Over the period covered by these statistics, Ritalin has cost the UK taxpayer £291,953.40 for 20 mg tablets and £1,965,183.91 for 10 mg tablets. However, with European legislation now in place to deter parents from smacking, the use of alternative measures of control may be expected to increase dramatically among parents who 'cannot cope' with disruptive or overactive children, who cannot establish their authority without recourse to physical chastisement, and who consider their children to be a source of stress.

Sedating the American child

However, Britain's Ritalin problem pales into insignificance when one looks to America. In the United States, ADHD is estimated to affect between 3 and 5 per cent of school-age children, although a panel of experts appointed by the National Institutes of Health in 1998 found no consistency either of diagnosis or treatment.[4] The panel called for urgent clarification and research into the long-term effects of Ritalin prescription. At that time it was estimated that more than a million children with ADHD were taking psychostimulants. Since then, ADHD diagnosis and drug treatment in the US have reached epic proportions.

In 2003, a team of scientists from the Center for Pediatric Research, Eastern Virginia Medical School and the University of Nevada School of Medicine, led by Gretchen LeFever, carried out a major review of current practice. They found 'The current American proclivity toward psychiatric drug therapy for behaviour-disordered children began in the 1960s, when the American medical profession deemed it acceptable to use psychostimulants',[5] particularly methylphenidate (Ritalin) for the condition now known as ADHD. Prior to this, medication for behavioural problems was 'an almost nonexistent practice'.

Over the last three decades in the US, the rate of drug treatment for behaviour problems has increased exponentially, culminating in the prescription of ADHD drug treatment for at least 5 to 6 million American children annually.[6] Although over-diagnosis and over-prescription are not considered a problem in every American state, a growing number of communities are thought to be affected, prompting the United Nations International Narcotics Control Board in 1997 to issue a warning to American physicians. Apparently not much notice was taken. During the 1990s, there was a staggering 700 per cent increase in the use of psychostimulants, with the US consuming nearly 90 per cent of the world's supply of the drugs.[7] In a 1999 study of one school year among 30,000 schoolchildren in two districts in Virginia, between 8 and 10 per cent of those between grades two and five were treated with stimulants for ADHD.[8] In a 2002 review in the same Virginia region, an astonishing 17 per cent of all elementary students and 33 per cent of white boys had been diagnosed with ADHD, 'and the vast majority had been medicated for this condition'.[9] In other words, one third of white boys of elementary school age were deemed to be not just misbehaving in class but suffering from a mental disorder.

Use of other psychotropic drugs to modify the behaviour and

moods of American children has also escalated dramatically. Between 1995 and 1998, anti-depressant use increased 74 per cent among children under eighteen, 151 per cent among children between seven and twelve, and 580 per cent among children under six. The use of 'mood stabilizers' increased by 400 per cent among children under eighteen, and medication with anti-psychotic drugs (for severe mental illness) increased by 300 per cent in the same age category.[10]

Professor Hamid Ghodse, Chair of Addiction Psychiatry at St George's Hospital in London, has expressed concern at the liberal use of a drug intended to sedate naughty children in America and Britain and warns in a newspaper article: 'We are medicalizing something that is often not a medical condition.'[11]

Relax or else

There are a number of suggested explanations for this grand-scale sedation of our children and old folk: collusion between the medical and psychiatric professions and the drug companies, convenience medication for high-speed lives, preoccupation with control and prevention of risk, and so on. But one very cogent explanation must be the theory that there is something 'wrong' with emotional arousal, and for this notion we are indebted to stress management.

Calm down or else, the stress management credo goes. Now, there is nothing wrong with relaxation, or with meditation, or gentle music, whale song or herbal baths either. What is questionable is the current obsession with calming down, based on widespread misunderstanding of the body's defence systems. The fight-or-flight mechanism is fashionably seen, not as a vital survival response that springs threatened individuals into action to help themselves and that functions as a burglar alarm, but as a pathological response that triggers mental and physical illness. Put simply, according to stress management theory, when this biological burglar alarm goes off, we should immediately turn down the volume or, if possible, take the alarm off the wall and throw it in the dustbin. Simma Lieberman Associates, leading proponents of stress management in the US, sum up fairly clearly your average practitioner's position on the subject: 'By learning how to manage stress, we can minimize the fight-or-flight response and recuperate from it.'[12]

The stress manager's toolkit, as we have seen, is crammed full of techniques and goodies to help us relax and enjoy our false sense of security while we 'minimize the fight-or-flight response'. And when we sedate our children and our old folk, we are naturally seeking to minimize *their* fight-or-flight response out of concern and care for their well-being. We are soothing the emotions of those for whom we are responsible, in case they hurt themselves, or cause a nuisance to others, or to us.

Avoidance and analgesia

As has already been suggested, the main reason for concern about sedation generally is that those who indulge in it may take their hands off the controls of their lives and become helpless. But giving up and calming down are all the more alluring because once the brain receives instructions to abandon the hard struggle, it can produce remarkable chemical effects all of its own.

The late millionaire zoo-owner John Aspinall was once almost killed by an angry bear. As he lay in a ditch in the bear's enclosure, resigned to the fact that he was about to suffer an ugly fate, he was overwhelmed by a sudden strange sense of relief and tranquillity. Aspinall surmised that this must be some natural mechanism that enables prey animals to face painful and terrifying death. The work of Michael Persinger, Professor of Psychology and head of the Neuroscience Research Group at Laurentian University, Ontario[13] on temporal lobe transients and near-death experiences investigates such crisis neurology. Near-death experiences are known to be associated with sublime calm and beatific visions, except that Professor Persinger can apparently reproduce them in his lab by stimulating the temporal lobes of human volunteers.

Experimental studies have found that resignation in animals appears to give access to morphine-like substances in the brain, such as the enkephalins, discovered by Hans Kosterlitz in Aberdeen. 'Stress analgesia' was observed in 1969 by neurophysiologist D. V. Reynolds in experiments on the brain stem of the rat, and in 1975 came the discovery – which made scientists all over the world very excited – of two pentapeptides in the brain with opiate activity.[14] Under certain terrible circumstances, the brain could *tranquillize itself*.

This particular type of 'stress analgesia' (unlike the analgesia associated with injury in exhilarating activities such as sport) may occur in situations of utter helplessness. As we have seen in Chapter Seven, the term 'learned helplessness' was coined by Martin Seligman and his colleagues in the late 1960s[15] to describe the behaviour of laboratory animals that, subjected to various ordeals, lost the will to help themselves, even when escape became an option. Perhaps, to the animals in learned helplessness experiments, self-destruction might be an option preferable to the experiences they are being forced to undergo. Perhaps this is also true of humans made to endure genuinely uncontrollable and unbearable experiences. In such cases, 'health' may not be possible because it is not desirable. But giving up may provide pain-killing effects at the same time as it undermines survival.

In an earlier chapter it was suggested that 'learned helplessness' is the missing middle term in the 'stress-disease' proposition. The literature on this phenomenon provides ample insight into why disease may frequently follow distressing experiences. The subject, perceiving himself to be unable to control distressing stimuli, does nothing to help himself, gives up and succumbs to the alluring analgesic effects of despair. He therefore gets sick. He therefore may die.

Links have been found between hopelessness and premature death from cardiovascular diseases.[16] A well-publicized example was the tragic case of sixty-eight-year-old Pauline Jefferys, from Kendal in Cumbria, who waited in vain for a hospital bed for her operation. She died of heart failure, as her son described it at the hearing, after 'giving up the will to live.'[17] Sudden and potentially dangerous drops in blood pressure have been recorded in people simply talking about their own helplessness and despair.[18] Bullied children who become docile succumb to health harms currently blamed on stress. Animals used in painful and distressing experiments often become sick or susceptible to disease after resigning themselves. They suffer ulcer formation, increased steroid release, changes in metabolism and later, deadly immune changes. Vital lymphocyte cells are reduced in rats that learn to be helpless. The male rat, introduced into the cage of other males, that turns over on his back to show submissiveness, may avoid a fight but resigns immune functioning. In human studies the same lymphocyte suppression is found in widowers during the first year of mourning for their wives, and in other seriously depressed patients.[19]

Not all dire or distressing experiences trigger the body's numbing self-destruct system, but a helpless, self-tranquillizing outlook may be adopted by those who feel they 'cannot cope' with threats and challenges, and who as a consequence succumb to illness. Helplessness is a maladaptive behaviour that looks for rescue and finds none. It may anaesthetize the individual both from present pain and future action, and make all attempts at self-help appear futile. Such resignation may be counterintuitive, but to anyone who has experienced it, it is a tranquil yet abject state of mind. In its most extreme form, this is the twilight from which few struggle to return. Helpless people are known to favour 'avoidance' strategies, which protect them from consciously confronting the threat. For this reason, sedation is most dangerous to those who are most vulnerable. They, of all people, should avoid avoidance.

Relaxation exercises

Where medically appropriate – as, for example, in the case of remedial training for hyperventilating asthmatics – relaxation exercises may be of great benefit. As a former asthmatic who was often hospitalized, I can vouch for their usefulness in learning to breathe normally. Anyone can experience the improvement relaxation can make to respiration. Try relaxing your nose and throat next time you go to bed congested with a cold, and breathing calmly by slightly opening and shutting your mouth. The effects are startling, because the inflammation and tension gradually subside, unblocking the airways. In contrast, continuously blowing your nose causes further inflammation and tension, and the constriction blocks the airways.

Relaxation exercises may also help those who, although no actual threatening stimulus presents itself, are nevertheless afraid. They may even be useful, in the short term, for victims of the stress ideology who have succumbed to what we might call 'life-fear' – a residual low-level apprehension, worry over information bombardment and a vague sense of dread. When this unease is combined with very widespread misinformation about stress and arousal avoidance, the brain may lose its efficiency at recognizing real threats and challenges. Instead of normal arousal which serves a useful purpose, the brain may instead produce small but uncreative waves of anxiety over trivia. In the long term what is needed to help those affected is emotional education and robustness training. But as an interim measure, people who can no longer distinguish between healthful calm and healthful arousal might benefit from relaxation techniques, properly taught by trained practitioners.

Although scientists used to think that there is one 'relaxation response' and that all relaxation techniques invoke it, this is not the case. There are many different kinds of relaxation. Muscularly orientated methods may have specific somatic effects because they depend on a muscular skill. Cognitive methods may have cognitive effects, autonomically orientated methods may produce autonomic effects and so on. Stress management consultants offering 'relaxation techniques' would need to be competent in several of the appropriate methods: to offer one is hardly sufficient as people differ very much in their requirements.

For some people muscular relaxation – requiring no perceptual adjustment – may be preferred, because it involves no purely psychological intervention. For others, cognitive training may be considered more appropriate because of the need to address complex psychological sources of worry and tension. For yet others wishing to move from 'fight-or-flight' mode to 'digest and rest' mode, relaxation methods that target the autonomic nervous system itself may be the answer. Yet stress management practitioners do not necessarily make any distinction between these different relaxation methods and members of the public may assume they are all the same, as well as all desirable in all circumstances.

It should in any case be emphasized that relaxation exercises are not a cure for the woes and worries of life. In fact, they may even be a 'symptom'. Regarding relaxation exercises as a cure-all may well be a sign of high anxiety about the stress phenomenon, and undue concern about relaxation is a fairly reliable indicator of the stress-phobic personality.

Peace be with you

Everywhere you look, people are trying to pacify themselves. Stress is invariably blamed for this pacifying obsession, rather than stress management and its calm-down culture. We can take a very unscientific snapshot of this cultural trend by looking at some 'human interest' stories in a popular newspaper. Take the case of the young Southampton primary teacher who confessed to spending £80 a week on stress management. Her unorthodox methods included Ecstasy, cannabis and amphetamines. She is quoted as saying of her job: 'The stress is horrendous. If I could not do drugs I would probably go insane.'[20]

The world has evidently become too arousing to sustain life. People must be protected. The parents of young Morris Mitchener, taken to see *Peter Pan* at the West Yorkshire Playhouse in Leeds, began legal action against the show's producers, saying it caused their child to scream and hide behind the seat. As the boy's mother, Amanda, told a reporter: 'It was a terrible ordeal, but we couldn't get out of our seats for 45 minutes until the interval.'[21] Farmers in Surrey have been warned by their county council not to put up 'Beware of the Bull' signs as these are 'too frightening'. Instead they should say: 'Proceed with caution, bull in field.'[22] Two swans terrorized a village in Milton Keynes, Buckinghamshire, by waddling up garden paths. One householder was quoted as saying: 'It's got beyond the joke. They are terrifying.'[23]

In the US, the so-called Better Sleep Council recently conducted a survey revealing that 51 per cent of Americans are 'losing sleep over stress'.[24] Worse, 45 per cent of Americans toss and turn because of their partners losing sleep over stress. And Australians, hitherto famous (to use a couple of Strine idioms) for mutton-punching and sod-busting, as well as wrestling crocs, by all accounts now find their lives too awful to contemplate and long for rest. One in twelve of them, according to the Anxiety Disorders Foundation of Australia, suffers from an anxiety disorder.[25] This would approximate to 1,360,000 robustly bred, economically opulent, sun-blessed people worrying a great deal.

Enter the King of Calm, Sydney advertising executive Paul Wilson. In 1997 his bestseller *Little Book of Calm* sold more than 1.4 million copies worldwide and 450,000 in Britain, and was followed by tapes, CDs, a website, and more books, such as *Calm at Work*. It tells people how to imagine soothing scenes, meditate, hypnotize themselves, daydream (for twenty minutes at a time), burn oils and go into a trance (those using equipment should presumably do so with caution). Another of his peacemakers, *Instant Calm*, offers 'over 100 successful techniques for relaxing mind and body'. One method is to wrap rubber bands round the tops of your fingers 'until your fingertips turn blue'.[26] Another is to whisper your worries to a cotton reel or envelope and 'forget about your worries and anxieties for the time being'.[27] Whether such methods will eventually sedate the nation Down Under remains to be seen. Clearly, people who resort to such desperate measures need help of some sort.

They might prefer twenty minutes in 'fairyland' or nearest earthly approximation. The first Relaxarium in Britain opened at the Feel Good Factory in Goldhawk Mews, London SW11, in 1998. The brainchild of north London firm Inch by Inch, the facility offers dimly lit rooms, lavender oil, and strangely shaped vibrating beds where you look at a starry ceiling and listen to New Age music coming off the wall. You could have the same enchanted world in your spare room for between £8,000 and £10,000.

Or why not withdraw from reality altogether? In twenty-two acres of Herefordshire countryside, the gong echoes through the grounds of the Dhamma Dipa retreat. Withdrawers are asked not to talk as it interferes with the meditative atmosphere. This is one of an estimated 1,000-plus such establishments in the UK, offering everything from massage and pulse-diets to plainsong-chanting, storytelling and circle-dancing. There are themed retreats, yoga retreats, Bach flower retreats. There are Buddhist retreats, like Throssel Hole Abbey in Northumberland. In Dyfed, Wales, there is even a Mongolian nomadic dwelling, called a yurt, where you can lull yourself without benefit of hypnotics. The National Retreat Association reports a steady increase in the number of inquiries. The only downside with escapism is that retreaters generally have to go home, and there waiting for them, unresolved and possibly bigger than before, will be all the problems they left behind.

Of course meditation, taken seriously, may lead to life-changing adjustments and a more spiritual existence. But dabbled in as a means of stress management and escape from reality, it can simply provide the fainthearted with a means of withdrawal from life. Furthermore, to regard meditation itself as a magical panacea would be misguided. Tennis star Arthur Ashe, who famously used transcendental meditation to win Wimbledon in 1975, four years later underwent heart surgery. He died in 1993 at the age of forty-nine. In Cambodia, Saloth Sar, aka Pol Pot, learned to meditate at a Buddhist monastery. He went on to liquidate 1.5 million people.

Drinking as a stress management technique

Research suggests that binge-eating is a maladaptive stress management technique and that sufferers from bulimia nervosa are trying to calm themselves in the face of their worries. What they need instead is 'to acquire adequate coping and problem-solving skills.'[28] Binge-drinking is another version of this calm-down-at-all-costs stress management. Alcohol, actually a depressant, is often taken in an attempt to soothe the mind, and the results are worrying.

The number of middle-aged men dying of alcohol-related diseases has doubled in five years, according to official figures. Alcohol consumption in Britain has increased by 50 per cent since 1970. Troubled women executives are now resorting to alcohol. In a survey of 8,000 government employees, senior women staff were more than three times as likely to be problem drinkers (14 per cent) as those working in the lowest grades. Jenny Head, senior lecturer in epidemiology and public health at University College London, says:[29] 'This is just another way that stress can impact on health.' A 2004 report by senior scientists including Professor Sir Michael

Marmot of the University College, London[30] calls for taxes on alcohol to increase in an attempt to tackle 'runaway alcohol consumption'. Deaths from cirrhosis of the liver have increased ninefold since the 1970s. Alcohol is estimated to cost the NHS £1.7 billion. One in three accident and emergency admissions is fuelled by drink, and the annual cost of drink-related crime and public disorder is estimated at £7.3 billion. Alcohol is far more toxic than heroin. It interferes selectively with neurotransmission and diminishes the ability to recognize novelty. In other words, it deadens and sedates the brain.[31]

Smoking

Another popular method of stress management is smoking. The peace pipe of the second millennium is filled either with tobacco or cannabis. Comforts are both chemical and psychological – from the nicotine or marijuana and from satisfying the need to suckle in times of distress. Of nicotine-related mortality one expert observes: 'Researchers used to think that the death rate in middle age was about twice as high in cigarette smokers as in lifelong non-smokers. Now they know that it is almost three times as high.'[32] Tobacco kills one smoker in two. Its mortal wounds are not only to the lungs and cardiovascular system, but to the mouth, throat, gullet, stomach, pancreas, bladder and rectum. New links have been revealed between smoking and leukaemia. Smokers are heavily taxed by the government to finance their hospital beds. They are paying dear, both to the Chancellor of the Exchequer and to the grim reaper for their small sticks of peace.

Cannabis is the most widely used illicit drug in the UK. It has recently been reclassified (downwards) as a Class C drug in Britain and those reliant upon it have been given hope of their drug's benignity by its use in medicine as a painkiller. Heroin is also used in medicine as a painkiller. This is not a sign of its benignity.

Britain's most senior coroner, Hamish Turner, believes cannabis is behind many deaths currently recorded as accidents and suicides. Of the 100 corpses he has examined, he claims up to 10 per cent ended up in the morgue because of pot.[33] The weed is improving itself: high-quality 'skunk' is being smuggled in from South Africa, according to the National Criminal Intelligence Service, which is ten times more powerful than the joints and roaches of yore.

Mr Turner, president of the Coroners' Society, says: 'Cannabis is a mind-altering drug which has ravaging effects on the brain.' It is a favourite 'rite of passage' drug among children and teenagers and many of them regularly smoke it, along with cigarettes. According to research conducted in 2003 at the London Maudsley Hospital by Dr Michael Farrell, these youngsters are seven times more likely to develop some form of psychiatric disorder later in life. Other research links cannabis with the onset of depression, and with increased risk of head, neck and lung cancers. According to leading British neurologist Susan Greenfield, Professor of Pharmacology at Oxford University, about 7,000 milligrams of alcohol are needed to achieve relaxation, whereas for cannabis the figure is just 0.3 milligrams, and the effect lasts much longer – up to fifty hours for a single joint. Because cannabis reconfigures the neural networks, users are literally 'blowing their minds'. The drug can lead to memory loss, attention-impairment, sudden mood-swings, paranoia, anxiety and panic. 'It may even trigger schizophrenia'.[34] The effects may be long-term and irreversible. Other research links the drug both with psychosis and relapse of underlying illness in those with psychotic disorders. Adverse reactions have been widely documented.

Anodyne television

No review, however cursory, of non-prescription avoidance-and-sedation strategies could possibly omit mention of the anaesthetic effects of popular television entertainment. Perusal of an average evening's top-rated programmes reveals a nation glued to consecutive fictional gobbets woven around mono-dimensional characters known to audiences by their first names and eliciting powerful affiliations without catharsis, without purpose and without hope of resolution. This fantasy land, in which many viewers dwell for entire evenings and indeed many afternoons, has led to the abject expression 'couch potato' to describe the vegetative state of their millions of brains. Yet whilst the converse phenomenon of over-stimulation from television sex and violence has invoked a cascade of scientific research into its possible dangers, the effects of deadening and escapist television remains largely a mystery.

CHAPTER EIGHTEEN

THE CHEMICAL COSH

One of the first duties of the physician is to educate the masses not to take medicine.

Sir William Osler, *Aphorisms* from his *Bedside Teachings*

Emotion alleviators

Thoughts and feelings are not illnesses. Yet every day, millions of people put powerful chemicals in their mouths to modify their brains and inhibit them from functioning normally. Often they may do this on the advice of some health expert, such as a general practitioner, psychiatrist or stress management authority, who has convinced them that their emotions are abnormal, harmful or curable and, as we have seen, those who believe they are suffering from stress will do anything for a quiet life. They have therefore willingly submitted to 'sedatives' and 'tranquillizers' – the difference between the two types of drugs, according to a medical dictionary, being spurious since they are both intended to calm.[1]

Calming drugs have been classified in different ways at different times by different authorities, and even doctors may be unclear on current generic definitions. In the UK, the pacific drug groups, classified by the British National Formulary, are under review. The very latest advice comes from MIND, the mental health charity, who keep a close watch on the changes in order to advise patients. The pacifying drugs are currently classified as follows: all sedatives and tranquillizers are divided into 'major' and 'minor' tranquil-lizers. 'Minor' tranquillizers refer to the barbiturates and benzo-diazepines, and these are collectively known as 'sedative hypnotics'. The 'major' tranquillizers are the neuroleptics, also known as 'anti-psychotics'. However, moves are underway to reclassify the neuro-leptics simply as 'anti-psychotics' and *not* 'tranquillizers'. The reason for this change is that the 'major' tranquillizers do not necessarily tranquillize. They act to control the nerve impulses themselves. Indeed, they may have quite the opposite effect – known as 'paradoxical' agitation. Given this classification, patients who feel they need to be medically calmed could easily become confused, particularly about the meaning of 'tranquillize', and about the word 'minor' when referring to hypnotic and sedative chemicals used to control the brain.

According to a social audit on the safety of medicines, the manufacturer Roche's promotion of their calming benzodiazepines Librium and Valium in the 1960s 'helped to persuade many doctors that there was a real difference between "sedatives" and "tranquil-lizers" – when in fact their similarities mattered much more . . . The main difference between them was that "tranquillizers" were to a great extent promoted and perceived as non-sedating sedatives – seemingly a contradiction, but not in marketing terms.'[2]

The manufacturers wished to promote the fact that the new benzodiazepines were less 'sedating' and safer in overdose than the 'sedative' barbiturates. Indeed, a Roche advertisement for their benzodiazepine sleeping pill Mogadon in 1974 depicted a tombstone inscribed: 'Some patients stay on barbiturates until the day they die. Every day in Britain three patients die after deliberately taking overdoses of barbiturates – a total of over 1,000 a year. Virtually all of these patients could have been transferred to Mogadon, which is much safer, but just as effective against insomnia.'[3] However, just five years earlier another advertisement, for the barbiturate Butisol (sodium butabarbital) that appeared in the *Journal of the American Medical Association*,[4] depicted a smiling young housewife with the caption: 'Now she can cope ... thanks to Butisol, the "daytime sedative" for everyday situational stress.' The manufacturers, McNeil, claimed that their drug was 'still a first choice among many physicians for dependability and economy in mild to moderate anxiety'. So it is clear that such 'sedatives' were being promoted by the manufacturers and prescribed by doctors as appropriate for 'stress' in exactly the same way as the benzodiazepines.

The cost of soothing

In Britain we are paying a very high price indeed for soothing patients and chemically adapting their moods. We can get some idea of the extent of our mood-manipulation by looking at the Department of Health quarterly figures on hypnotics, anxiolytics and anti-depressants prescribed since April 2001.

In America, a storm of criticism is gathering over the way drug companies influence research. Medicine is the biggest business in the US, commanding over $1.5 trillion a year and constituting over 14 per cent of the gross domestic product.[6] In 2000 the prestigious *New England Journal of Medicine* joined other medical authorities in calling for stronger controls on stock ownership and other financial perks for researchers.[7] In a towering editorial the *NEJM* warned: '... these ties will bias research, both the kind of work that is done and the way in which it is reported ... Of even greater concern is the possibility that financial ties may influence the outcome of research studies.' Even the *Journal of the American Medical Association* (JAMA) weighed in, focusing on the way gifts and perks from pharmaceutical giants influence prescribing and the practice of medicine.[8] Put simply, patients are being given drugs by doctors who have been given gifts.

In Britain, the power of the pharmaceutical giants to control what may be written about their products is now, even according to

TRANQUILLIZERS AND ANTI-DEPRESSANTS: THE LATEST PRESCRIPTION PICTURE

Hypnotics and Anxiolytics	items	NIC £
Apr–Jun 2001	4,008,423	9,095,161
Jul–Sep 2001	3,994,441	9,059,594
Oct–Dec 2001	4,157,240	9,495,008
Jan–Mar 2002	4,037,379	9,185,984
Apr–Jun 2002	4,008,476	9,117,345
Jul–Sep 2002	4,076,145	9,217,347
Oct–Dec 2002	4,167,496	9,473,381
Jan–Mar 2003	4,036,021	9,195,031
Apr–Jun 2003	4,025,261	9,173,170
Jul–Sep 2003	4,084,029	9,282,577

Anti-depressants	items	NIC £
Apr–Jun 2001	5,922,098	82,258,198
Jul–Sep 2001	5,943,162	84,084,096
Oct–Dec 2001	6,338,824	90,932,604
Jan–Mar 2002	6,280,890	90,764,830
Apr–Jun 2002	6,435,645	93,325,252
Jul–Sep 2002	6,548,215	94,569,291
Oct–Dec 2002	6,739,679	96,800,439
Jan–Mar 2003	6,615,539	95,361,225
Apr–Jun 2003	6,739,028	96,959,852
Jul–Sep 2003	6,844,738	97,041,998

All CNS drugs*	items	NIC £
Apr–Jun 2001	26,326,131	245,784,277
Jul–Sep 2001	26,336,896	254,331,482
Oct–Dec 2001	27,917,820	273,491,289
Jan–Mar 2002	27,320,410	272,683,235
Apr–Jun 2002	27,548,188	283,615,988
Jul–Sep 2002	27,805,051	291,300,043
Oct–Dec 2002	28,739,007	302,912,921
Jan–Mar 2003	28,104,187	300,652,798
Apr–Jun 2003	28,349,665	311,535,735
Jul–Sep 2003	28,715,159	319,475,798

*also includes drugs used in psychosis and related disorders, CNS stimulants, drugs used to treat obesity, drugs for nausea and vertigo, analgesics, anti-epileptics, drugs used in Parkinsonism and related disorders, drugs used in substance dependence, drugs used in dementia.

Prescription Items

Prescriptions are written on a prescription form. Each single item written on the form is counted as a prescription item.

Net Ingredient Cost (NIC)

NIC is the basic cost of a drug. It does not take account of discounts, dispensing costs, fees or prescription charges income.

This information was obtained from the Prescribing Analysis and Cost Tool (PACT) system, which covers prescriptions prescribed by GP practices and nurses in England and dispensed in the community in the UK. Prescriptions written in England but dispensed outside England are included. Prescriptions written in hospitals/ clinics that are dispensed in the community, prescriptions dispensed in hospitals and private prescriptions are not included in PACT data.

medical editorials, unacceptable. Reporting on evidence to a select committee at the end of 2004, the voice of the *British Medical Journal* echoed that of *The Lancet*:

The relationship between medical journals and the drug industry is 'somewhere between symbiotic and parasitic,' according to the editor of *The Lancet*, Richard Horton. But at the moment it has swung too much towards the parasitic, he told the House of Commons Select Committee on Health last month in his oral evidence on the role of the industry.

He outlined some of the financial incentives that could, potentially, influence a commercially run medical journal to publish a paper. Many of the formal research papers in *The Lancet* are reprinted and bought in bulk by drug companies, which use them for marketing purposes, he explained. The drug companies regularly try to exert pressure on the journal to run a paper by arguing that, if the journal does so, they will buy reprints, which will earn the journal more money, he said.[9]

Clearly in this case, the normal protocols that should protect the public from the profit-making zeal of large manufacturers appear to have broken down, and because the producers of emotion alleviators are significant stakeholders in the stress management industry, the public need to be on their guard.

'Minor' tranquillizers – benzodiazepines

Take, for example, the class of drugs known as the benzodiazepines, which succeeded the (possibly lethal) sedative barbiturates as the drugs of choice for calming down worried and sleepless patients. In his book *The Complete Guide to Psychiatric Drugs: a layman's guide*, Ron Lacey describes the (frequent) inappropriate use of benzodiazepines as 'akin to sitting on a fire and taking pain killers'.

Benzodiazepines are a very popular treatment for anxiety, insomnia and other symptoms and conditions that currently go by the name of 'stress'. In Western societies it is estimated that between 10 and 20 per cent of adults regularly take them.[10] They have by all accounts helped many users, and drug companies can provide testimonies from those for whom these drugs have apparently been beneficial. The mental health charity MIND say they are not against drugs per se, appropriately prescribed, and that some people find them useful in the short term. Whether these same patients might have benefited equally from non-chemical interventions, or emotional education, is of course open to question.

Benzodiazepines are known as 'minor' tranquillizers, although this is misleading. They are 'minor' only in relation to the 'major' tranquillizers or neuroleptics, of which more below. Benzodiazepines are a subset of chemical weapons in your doctor's arsenal for dealing with the troubled mind: others include meprobamate (Equagesic), and buspirone (Buspar), both recommended for short-term use only, and beta-blockers, such as propranolol, which may be used to treat the physical symptoms of anxiety but which may produce their own adverse effects, including sleep problems and nightmares. By far the most common 'remedy' for the worries of this world are the 'benzos': the following (brand-names in brackets) are popularly prescribed: alprazolam (Xanax), clorazepate (Tranxene), chlordiazepoxide (Librium, Tropium), diazepam (Valium, Tensium, Dialar, Diazemuls, Stesolid, Valclair), flunitrazepam (Rohypnol), flurazepam (Dalmane), loprazolam (Dormonoct), lorazepam (Ativan), lormetazepam, nitrazepam (Mogadon, Remnos, Somnite), oxazepam, temazepam.

Librium, the first of its kind, went on the market in 1960. Valium was released for clinical use in 1963 and Mogadon, the sleeping pill, followed in 1965. These were the new 'safe' generation of pacific drugs with which it was extremely difficult to overdose. Doctors started handing them out liberally. They were (and are) prescribed for worry, panic attacks, insomnia, night terrors, sleepwalking, claustrophobia, alcohol withdrawal, drug withdrawal, exam nerves, bereavement, backache, epilepsy, febrile seizures, spasticity, spasmodic torticollis, migraine prophylaxis, tardive dyskinesias, dystonias, irritable bowel syndrome, eclampsia, operative premedication, vertigo and stress (name your effects and causes). Victims of Tranquillizers, one of the groups representing UK addicts, list sixty-six reasons for prescription they have come across, including 'driving test', 'floater in the eye', 'shyness', 'cat died' and 'cooker blew up'.[11]

The drugs themselves are hypnotics (inducing sleep) and anxiolytics (reducing anxiety). But they achieve these effects by acting 'on all areas of the brain, including those responsible for rational thought, for memory, for the emotions, and essential functions, such as breathing.'[12] Yet in 1975, 100 million prescriptions were filled in the US alone. 'In 1981, about one in ten of all men and one in five of all women in Britain had taken tranquillizers for at least several weeks.'[13] The possessive properties of these calming drugs quickly became apparent, at least to the authorities.

Adverse reactions

In Britain, over 200 adverse reactions for Valium were reported by doctors to the MHRA (Medicines and Healthcare products Regulatory Agency) between 1963 and 1997, though information was slow to filter out from the regulatory body to the public. Two hundred adverse reactions was, in medical terms, a worrying figure. These were 200 different bad reactions, not 200 different patients with bad reactions. Since then, the situation has deteriorated. The MHRA provided me in March 2004 with the following list of the number of 'reactions recorded' to different brands of benzodiazepines:

Alprazolam	209
Chlorazepate	185
Chlordiazepoxide	406
Diazepam	1,508
Flunitrazepam	62
Flurazepam	209
Loprazolam	32
Lorazepam	817
Lormetazepam	87
Nitrazepam	741
Oxazepam	123
Temazepam	670
Total	**5,049**

When I asked them about their affiliations with drug companies I was given the following response. The MHRA maintains that it has established 'a rigorous policy that precludes staff holding interests that may give rise to conflict of interest.'[14]. However, the chief executive of MIND, Richard Brook, recently resigned from the MHRA board of advisers over these vested interests and the admitted suppression (since it was first licensed for use in the UK in 1990) of unsafe levels of prescribing of the anti-depressant Seroxat. Seroxat is not a tranquillizer, but anti-depressants are frequently offered to patients trying to escape from tranquillizers. Anti-depressants are also keenly prescribed for stress. The charity issued a press release:

MIND has consistently highlighted the flaws in drugs regulation in this country. In this sorry tale far too little heed has been paid to ordinary people experiencing awful side effects and severe withdrawal symptoms. Far too much attention has been paid to the spin of drugs company marketing departments.[15]

Dependence and withdrawal

Reports of users becoming dependent on benzodiazepines began to filter out as early as 1961, yet it was not until 1980 that the Committee on the Review of Medicines expressed concern. Gradually it was admitted that dependence and withdrawal were serious problems. Current advice from the British National Formulary (BNF) is that hypnotics should not be prescribed for longer than three weeks and preferably for no longer than one week. Yet by 2000 it was estimated that because of benzodiazepines, upwards of half a million people in the UK and perhaps a million Americans (where long-term use is less common) were now involuntary prescription tranquillizer addicts. Many of them had been downing the drugs for twenty or thirty years. In Greece, India and South America, where the drugs can be bought over the counter, the problem is even greater.[16] According to Professor Trevor Norman of the University of Melbourne, Australia:

When initially introduced they were believed to be devoid of dependence-inducing properties. Recent studies suggest that a substantial proportion of patients receiving benzodiazepines will develop some form of dependence, both high and normal doses of the drugs being implicated.[17]

In the UK in the early 1990s, about 17,000 patients began legal proceedings against manufacturers Hoffman LaRoche and John Wyeth & Brother Limited (the UK wing of the makers of Ativan), coordinated by some 300 law firms. The class action was joined initially by a group of Australian litigants. It was the largest civil action of its kind in legal history and collapsed following the withdrawal of legal aid funding.[18] Prominent product liability lawyer Peter Cashman (of Maurice Blackburn Cashman Limited), who represented the Australian users, says the case 'still rankles' with him, particularly as his own mother was addicted to benzodiazepines.[19]

'Beat the Benzos'

The pressure group Beat the Benzos, founded by Barry Haslam and Michael Behan, campaigns on behalf of thousands of addicts and former addicts like themselves and submits written evidence to the Commons Health Select Committee currently investigating the case against the drug companies. Their library of evidence suggests there are in fact 1.2 million long-term addicts in the UK.

Barry Haslam told me: 'I have no memory of the ten years that I spent on Ativan (lorazepam) and other benzodiazepines. I had a wife and two little girls, but I was in a coma. I came out of that long black tunnel into a world full of pain and anger. The anger I've worked out campaigning to help other people, but the pain and illness are permanent as the drugs damage your brain.'[20] In Oldham, where Barry works with the Primary Care Trust to help 5,200 other addicts, they come across people that have been on the drugs for forty years. Beat the Benzos collects the latest research evidence for the Commons Committee. One example is a 2004 data sheet from the Canadian Pharmacists' Association which states: 'Use of benzodiazepines, including lorazepam, may lead to potentially fatal respiratory depression.'

Fellow campaigner Mike Behan was one of the original litigants in the class action against the manufacturers. He has never fully recovered from his addiction either. 'People think you recover when you stop taking the drug. You don't. They damage your brain, your short-term memory, your coordination, your ability to organize. They leave you with permanent fatigue.'[21] He is understandably bitter about the failure of the legal system, accusing the drug companies of 'complicating and extending the proceedings' until the Legal Aid Board, having spent £35 million of taxpayers' money, felt it could no longer fund the action. A reduced number of litigants, many of whom were too ill to pursue their case, went to a higher court but were struck out. 'We stood no chance. They were wheeling out trolley-loads of files and we had no legal training. A small group of us went to the Court of Appeal but they found against us on some technicality. Costs were awarded against us – hundreds of thousands of pounds. We petitioned the House of Lords but got a brief response that the case was "inadmissible". All the hearings were *in camera* so the press were not admitted. The evidence has never actually been heard.'

However, benzo addicts have recently made a small advance on justice. In June 2002, a landmark legal victory was scored with the case of fifty-year-old Raymond Nimmo, who for fourteen years was prescribed benzodiazepines by his doctor following an allergic reaction to an antibiotic given to him for a dental infection. Mr Nimmo descended into a world of itching, sweating, dyspepsia and flu-like symptoms, followed by insomnia, suicidal depression, agoraphobia, panic attacks and addiction. He was awarded £40,000 in recognition of his doctors' clinical negligence in over-prescribing medication that destroyed his life. Other cases – two in Ireland and one in Scotland – are ongoing.

Even politicians have been moved by the plight of the benzo campaigners. In his capacity as Shadow Secretary of State for Health, David Blunkett described it as 'a national scandal'.[22] And according to legal affairs spokesman Paul Boateng, MP, 'Clearly, the aim of all involved in this sorry affair is the provision of justice to the victims of these drugs.'[23]

Because of extreme concern and new prescribing policies, the number of prescriptions issued fell from a peak of almost 31 million in 1979 to 16 million in 1992. But addiction had already claimed many benzo users. Three and a half million people were taking them for longer than four months according to a MORI poll published in 1985, and a survey in the late 1980s revealed that 1.2 million people were taking them continuously for over a year.

Approximately one in four adults in the UK has been prescribed one of these drugs. Women and elderly people are particularly targeted.

In America, consumer champion Ralph Nader claimed in the mid-1970s that 1.5 million Americans were addicted to diazepam, brandname Valium, celebrated in the Rolling Stones' song 'Mother's Little Helper' and in Jacqueline Susann's bestseller *Valley of the Dolls*. Between 1969 and 1982 it was America's most prescribed drug. In 1978 2.3 billion tablets were swallowed in the US. Senate hearings followed and prescription was cut. On 11 September 1979, a panel of doctors and former addicts told a US Senate Subcommittee on Health that Valium, at that time taken routinely by more than 15 per cent of the adult population, was an imprisoning drug, even in moderate doses. The former users testified that when they tried to get off Valium they experienced horrifying withdrawal symptoms, and that their doctors prescribed it without warning them of the drug's addictive risks. According to neuroscientist Professor Colin Blakemore: 'There is little doubt ... that millions of people around the world are still addicted to these drugs.'[24]

In Australia, for example, diazepam is marketed by several pharmaceutical companies under different brandnames – Valium, Antenex, Ducene and Valpam – but in 2002–2003, half of all diazepam prescriptions were for good old Valium. Almost 2 million prescriptions were issued for diazepam in 2002, at a cost of more than $13 million that year.[25] One source puts 'the annual cost to the community' of Australia's general benzodiazepine addiction as high as $55 million because doctors down under have failed to wean patients off the things. Dr Lynn Weekes, head of Australia's National Prescribing Service: 'Yes, we've been nagging the community for years on this one and you'd have to say, without a great deal of success.'[26] Some benzodiazepines, such as Valium and Xanax, come in packs of 50 and 100, and the Commonwealth Department of Health have apparently lost control on repeat prescribing. For all they know, Australians could be drowning in a pacific sea of pills. Lynn Weekes comments: 'It is fair to say we don't have a good picture of what is happening out there.'[27]

The potentially lethal effects of Valium in combination with alcohol and other drugs has been highlighted by a number of celebrity deaths, including that of singer Judy Garland at the age of forty-seven. Her daughter Liza Minnelli has twice been admitted to the Betty Ford clinic in a bid to break free of her own Valium addiction, saying: 'I didn't want to end up like momma.'[28] Elvis Presley was dosing up on Valium and other prescription medication when he was found dead in his bathroom. As we shall see later in this chapter, many others less famous have died with benzos in their bloodstream.

The numbers of prescriptions for benzodiazepines from 1980 to 2000 are listed in the tables. However the number of prescriptions cannot be used to determine the number of patients receiving benzodiazepines. Information is not available on the number of patients considered to be clinically dependent upon benzodiazepines.

Prescriptions (1000)	1980	1981	1982	1983	1984	1985	1986	1987	1988
Temazepam	1,014	1,709	2,431	2,896	3,378	5,133	5,802	6,242	6,129
Diazepam	7,300	6,604	5,812	5,147	4,449	4,374	4,217	4,071	3,622
Nitrazepam	7,362	6,910	6,596	5,912	5,368	5,001	4,657	4,383	3,850
Lorazepam	2,033	2,487	2,928	2,957	2,736	2,590	2,607	2,395	1,756
Chloridiazepoxide	1,834	1,694	1,516	1,294	1,112	1,007	893	816	697
Oxazepam	587	675	654	612	561	609	646	621	511
Lormetazepam	—	32	163	346	442	122	160	191	194
Clonazepam	40	48	55	72	77	93	99	107	111
Loprazolam Mesylate	—	—	—	2	50	19	71	125	127
Clobazam	275	330	381	378	396	109	42	39	48
Triazolam	402	795	855	782	906	1,200	1,468	1,576	1,635
Alprazolam	—	—	—	127	261	63	—	—	—
Bromazepam	—	—	9	76	151	32	—	—	—
Clorazepate Dipotassium	945	930	971	971	1,016	216	—	—	—
Flunitrazepam	—	—	7	86	188	54	—	—	—
Flurazepam Hydrochloride	1,885	1,833	1,860	1,700	1,628	376	—	—	—
Ketazolam	37	105	135	138	118	27	—	—	—
Medazepam	198	176	159	140	108	25	—	—	—
Prazepam	—	—	12	55	55	12	—	—	—
Total	23,912	24,329	24,544	23,962	22,999	21,062	20,662	20,565	18,680
Annual Change (Percentage)	—	1.7	0.9	-2.4	-4.0	-8.4	-1.9	-0.5	-9.2

Addicts' experiences

In Britain, pressure groups like Beat the Benzos and Victims of Tranquillizers champion the cause of patients chronically addicted to prescription pacific drugs, lobbying Parliament and seeking to pursue manufacturers at law. Patients might originally have taken the drugs to calm them down, but then have kept taking them to alleviate their withdrawal symptoms, which include panic and anxiety about not taking the drugs. The manufacturers claim these people are 'psychologically dependent' and the patient groups say their members are physically addicted. They point out that the

House of Commons Official Report
Parliamentary Debates (Hansard)
Benzodiazepines, 4 December 2001.

1989	1990	1991	1992	1993	1994	1995	1996	1997	1998	1999	2000	2001
5,946	5,985	6,428	6,914	6,651	6,345	6,063	5,540	5,252	5,043	4,878	4,697	4,449
3,331	3,147	3,254	3,225	3,220	3,288	3,411	3,600	3,798	3,989	4,108	4,293	4,502
3,523	3,188	3,1863	,074	2,902	2,721	2,582	2,539	2,426	2,333	2,210	2,095	1,963
1,452	1,227	1,137	1,018	932	867	818	785	758	743	728	715	731
604	548	542	503	467	449	438	428	423	414	402	384	368
406	399	378	352	328	311	300	304	306	300	289	272	262
169	163	181	215	218	208	201	234	249	252	246	210	194
111	127	137	144	152	160	168	181	196	213	231	253	278
144	160	195	239	230	219	213	221	215	211	200	191	181
59	53	66	67	67	68	70	74	74	82	85	93	101
1,530	1,513	1,123	—	—	—	—	—	—	—	—	—	—
—	—	—	—	—	—	—	—	—	—	—	—	—
—	—	—	—	—	—	—	—	—	—	—	—	—
—	—	—	—	—	—	—	—	—	—	—	—	—
—	—	—	—	—	—	—	—	—	—	—	—	—
—	—	—	—	—	—	—	—	—	—	—	—	—
—	—	—	—	—	—	—	—					
17,274	16,510	16,626	15,751	15,167	14,638	14,266	13,905	13,698	13,580	13,378	13,204	13,028
-7.5	-4.4		—	-5.3	-3.7	-3.5	-2.5	-2.5	-1.5	-0.9	-1.5	-1.3

same drugs are also prescribed for non-psychological conditions, and some of these users, like Mr Nimmo, become equally dependent. Addicts find themselves in a prescription prison and can't get out. Arguments about whether such imprisonment is physical or psychological do not help those locked inside.

Neuroscientist Colin Blakemore[29] quotes a former addict, Liza Harrison, on her attempts to kick Valium: 'I would experience electric shocks going all over my body, and my skin felt as though I had been scalded with hot water. I felt as though my body was actually falling apart, that my arms and legs would come off, that my chest would just fall open. It was as though my thought processes were rivers, and there were thousands and thousands of these ... There were so many thought processes ... and it was crazy. I couldn't cope with it. It was insanity.'

Dependence on benzodiazepine sleeping pills among MIND's respondents often started in hospital. The charity discovered that at one time a drug company was supplying hospitals with their own brand of benzodiazepines free of charge, and observes: 'Dependence on tranquillizers and sleeping pills can therefore be seen as an iatrogenic (or caused by medical treatment) disease.' Those taking sleeping pills can become addicted after just three or four nights. Rebound insomnia is very likely following discontinuation of benzodiazepines that have a short half-life ('half-life' means the time it takes for the amount of the drug in the body to be reduced by half).[30] In 1988 an editorial in the *British Medical Journal*[31] suggested that about 40–50 per cent of regular users will develop pharmacological dependence, and have withdrawal symptoms when they try to stop taking the drugs. In another study, sudden cessation of use was found to be inadvisable 'due to the risk of seizures or psychosis in extreme cases'.[32]

Prescription addicts unable to kick the benzo habit can't get rehabilitation either: 'The chances of getting residential treatment and rehabilitation is one-fiftieth of that for an alcoholic or illegal drug addict,' says Dr Reg Peart, Victims of Tranquillizers national co-ordinator and himself a former tranquillizer addict.[33] Prescription tranquillizer addicts are treated by the drug companies and the NHS as a sort of shameful problem, to be denied, criticized or brushed under the carpet. According to Dr Peart, the drugs have ruined the lives of many of his members, and because of over-reliance upon them as a treatment option and failure to warn patients of the drugs' possessive properties, prescription rates in the UK are two and a half times higher than in America.

The opium of the masses

Malcolm Lader , Professor of Clinical Psychopharmacology at the Institute of Psychiatry, University of London, is an acknowledged expert on benzodiazepines and the author of over 100 papers on the subject. In 1978 he called these drugs 'the opium of the masses' and in 1981 he warned that in the context of tranquillizer addiction 'there is an epidemic in the making'. In 1999 he was saying: 'It is more difficult to withdraw people from benzodiazepines than it is from heroin.'[34] MIND, representing patients, issue dire warnings on side effects and dependency based on their own Yellow Card user reporting system. C. Heather Ashton, Emeritus Professor of Psychopharmacology at the Royal Victoria Infirmary, Newcastle University, who has written extensively on benzodiazepine withdrawal, dependency and abuse, has published a list of 'socio-economic costs of long-term benzodiazepine use'.[35] These include increased risks from overdose, accidents, attempted suicide and aggression. For twelve years Professor Ashton ran a benzodiazepine withdrawal clinic for people wanting to come off the drugs: 'Much of what I know about this subject was taught to me by those brave and long-suffering men and women.'[36]

An internet search on 'benzodiazepine dangers' produced 4,106 results.[37] Whatever the content or accuracy of information on these sites, the volume of information may be taken as an indication of concern about the risks posed by this class of tranquillizers. One potential danger is that if they are given for bereavement they may interfere with psychological adjustment. Another is the risk to pregnant and breastfeeding women. Yet another is road safety, and another – briefly touched upon in the last chapter – is tranquillizing the elderly.

Among 5,579 elderly drivers in Quebec in the 1990s who were involved in serious car accidents, it was found that long half-life benzodiazepines were associated with a 28 per cent increased risk of a crash. The drugs may impair judgement and slow down reaction time. In the UK: 'A recent study suggested that approximately one in 2,900 people will be admitted to hospital for a traffic accident within two weeks of first taking a benzodiazepine. For every 100 elderly people who take benzodiazepines, about one person is admitted to hospital after a fall.'[38] The old are often less able to metabolize the drugs, resulting in more pronounced effects. Professor Elaine Murphy, of the department of geriatric medicine at Guy's Hospital, London, commenting on inappropriate prescribing of mood-altering drugs for elderly folk in care, said it was 'profoundly concerning' that vulnerable residents, who may not understand or want the medication, should be treated in this way. 'There are an awful lot of elderly people receiving drugs they neither need, want nor that are doing them any good. Nationally, we have a serious problem.'[39]

Side effects and withdrawal symptoms

Experiences with benzodiazepines vary from patient to patient. Use during pregnancy carries risks to the child, including withdrawal symptoms – such as tremor, vomiting and high-pitched crying – floppy muscles, breathing problems, dyslexia, dyspraxia (a movement disorder), ADHD, cleft palate, urinary tract abnormalities, and heart and stomach abnormalities. In adults the commonest side effects include drowsiness, light-headedness, confusion, unsteadiness (especially in elderly people, leading to falls and fractures), memory problems and muscle weakness. Some users may experience increased hostility, aggression or anxiety. Occasional side effects include headaches, vertigo, low blood pressure, changes in saliva production, digestive disturbances, sight problems (such as double vision), diction problems, tremor, changes in sexual desire, incontinence, difficulty urinating, blood disorders and jaundice. After continued use, patients may find it difficult to concentrate, 'and begin to lose confidence in themselves and their abilities. They may feel dulled, slow, isolated, unreal and unable to respond, emotionally, to pleasure or pain. They may develop weight problems, and feel irritable and impatient.'[40]

Tormented by their drug-induced symptoms, patients may ask their doctors to 'get them off'. They then face a different set of symptoms, which again vary from person to person. Some may resemble the patient's original complaint. Some may be different. Some may be worse. Some may be much worse. Symptoms reported to MIND include increased anxiety and depression, insomnia, nightmares, restlessness and inability to concentrate, panic attacks and agoraphobia, cravings for the tablets, loss of interest in sex, loss of appetite and of body weight, muscle tension, tight chest, palpitations, sweating, trembling or shaking, dizziness, headaches, nausea, blurred vision, sore eyes, increased sensitivity to light, noise, touch and smell, tinnitus (ringing in the ears), sore tongue and metallic taste, face and neck pain, tingling in the hands and feet, abdominal cramps and unsteady legs. Severe withdrawal symptoms may include: muscle twitching, burning sensations in the skin, severe depression, hallucinations, paranoia and delusions, confusion, memory loss, fits, depersonalization (feeling strange in familiar surroundings) and derealization (feeling out of touch with reality). Sudden withdrawal may cause confusion, psychosis, fits, rapid heartbeat, and a condition resembling *delirium tremens* triggering sweating, high blood pressure, tremors, hallucinations and agitated behaviour.

It may strike you that a lot of the side effects referred to, and the withdrawal symptoms listed above, are typically mentioned in connection with stress. They may certainly be perceived by the patient as 'stress', and in its severest form. So here we have an interesting phenomenon: a class of drug intended to relieve stress symptoms, and routinely prescribed for the treatment of those symptoms, that actually produces 'stress' symptoms. Yet in spite of all the evidence against them, and in spite of all the warnings from boffins and medics and mental health groups and addicts, benzodiazepines are still the most common treatment for people complaining of anxiety, insomnia and stress, and in 2001 another 12,648,900 prescriptions were filled out for them in the UK.

Unfortunately, the patient doesn't even need to visit his or her doctor now for a prescription. Mood-altering drugs like Valium, Prozac and the calm-down Rohypnol (flunitrazepam, used to sedate victims in recent highly publicized 'date rape' cases) are now available on the internet and can be airmailed direct from Bangkok or from online pharmacies. So it is unlikely that the problem can now be sorted at the supply end. The only solution is to alert potential users to the true cost of the so-called 'minor' tranquillizers.

'Major' tranquillizers – the neuroleptics

The so-called 'major' tranquillizers are the neuroleptics. Although these drugs are soon to be officially reclassified as 'anti-psychotics' rather than tranquillizers – partly to clarify their chemical actions and partly to customize their use for patients suffering from severe mental illness – neuroleptics have been considered appropriate in the treatment of extreme anxiety, and this covers a wide remit. They may still be prescribed to calm down patients presenting with severe agitation or distress, and not a few of these patients have become tragically addicted to their medication, as we shall see. Some addicts have complained of their doctors' casual prescribing habits and diagnoses of 'extreme anxiety', 'distress' and 'severe stress' have been notoriously imprecise.

Although manufacturers and their researchers argue that these drugs are not habit-forming, MIND's Yellow Card monitoring system reached far different conclusions. The vast majority of the charity's user respondents believed that they did not receive enough information (87 per cent) and that they were not warned of possible adverse effects (86 per cent). While many reported benefits, less than half (46 per cent) were convinced of the drugs' overall helpfulness. Worse, many users submitted unequivocal reports that their medication was extremely damaging both to mental and physical health.

MIND concluded that 'there is a lack of acknowledgement, for example, of tardive dyskinesia (TD), a disorder of the central nervous system linked to neuroleptic drugs', which involves abnormal and uncontrollable muscular movements, usually beginning with the face but also extending to the limbs and trunk. The risk of this adverse reaction, sometimes irreversible, increases with dose and length of use. One study showed two thirds of long-term users of neuroleptics exhibited signs of TD. MIND is also concerned to highlight 'sudden deaths associated with neuroleptics (there are no hard figures for this but a rate of one death a week has been estimated)' and 'the lack of alternatives available – for example talking treatments, facilities for the drug-free management of severe distress . . .'[41]

MIND recorded adverse reactions to anti-psychotic drugs as follows: muscular side effects, including painful muscle spasms (dystonias), involuntary movements, stiffness, shuffling, twitching, frowning, tremor, leg swinging and intense restlessness, inner tension or mental itching (akithisia). Some dystonias affect ability to speak and breath. One respondent reported being only able to grunt, while others reported feelings of suffocation and strangulation. Adverse effects on mood and alertness included tiredness, lethargy, feeling like a zombie, feeling in a 'chemical straitjacket', confusion, loss of concentration, depression, flattened emotions, anxiety and panic attacks. There were also reports of large weight gain, eyesight problems, disrupted menstruation, loss of sexual appetite and impotence, as well as dry mouth, skin sensitivity, sleeplessness and night sweats, indigestion and sickness, irregular heartbeat, ache in the kidneys, dribbling, headaches, hallucinations, nightmares, jaundice and asthma.

One respondent commented: 'A sort of cerebral cloud descends which wraps your brain in no-pain sellotape. Whether this is a benefit is open to interpretation.' Over half those reporting adverse effects to their general practitioner found the doctor unhelpful, rising to 62 per cent among those receiving depot dosage (long-acting doses injected on a fortnightly or monthly basis). Nineteen were told: 'it's the price you have to pay'. Another user described the drug experience as 'very damaging to me – I have been humiliated, crippled, made suicidal, and the chances of ever leading a normal life have been drastically reduced'. Another said: 'the major tranquillizers are not short of torturous in my view', and yet another complained: 'I'd have a life without it, it totally suppresses your life'.

One user described the treatment as 'legalised savagery'. Another was more philosophical: 'I've been on medication all my adult life so have nothing to compare it with.' MIND's report concluded: 'The Yellow Cards reveal a shocking lack of information being made available to people who are given very potent drugs which can have devastating effects with a far-reaching impact on people's lives.' Where anti-psychotic drugs are being used to chemically cosh individuals who are understandably anxious about serious problems, or who are thought to be suffering from severe stress, the charity's recommendations surely have particular urgency.

Tranquillized to death

The most adverse effect of all tranquillizing drugs that may be prescribed for anxiety and stress is that they can be used, alone or in combination with other prescription drugs or alcohol, to commit suicide. They may also themselves cause death by adverse reaction. A very significant aspect of the treatment of vulnerable patients with pacifying chemicals lies in the drug mortality statistics, of adverse reaction, accidental overdose and suicide.

The patients' group Beat the Benzos, extrapolating from official Home Office statistics, says that: 'In the period 1990–1996 (excluding 1994), benzos were responsible for 1,810 deaths in the UK ... benzos also induce suicidal tendencies and may have accounted for many more deaths by other methods. Some 761 regular users of benzos are known to have committed suicide during this period.'[42] The figure of 1,810 deaths between 1990 and 1996 is endorsed by Professor Ashton of the University of Newcastle, whose research also shows that 'a total of 170 cases of fatal outcome due to suspected adverse reactions to benzo-diazepines were reported on the Yellow Card scheme up to 2004 ... Extrapolation of [Home Office] data to the period 1964–2004 would suggest a figure of 12,000 such deaths ... Adding the observation that benzodiazepines cause 110 road accident deaths per year, the estimated figure for total benzodiazepine-related deaths rises to around 17,000. According to Home Office 1990–1996 figures, benzodiazepine-related deaths exceed the number of deaths attributed to all Class A drugs put together.'[43]

Prescription tranquillizers are often used in suicide bids. One of the possible reasons why drug-takers – and especially addicted or dependent drug-takers – may commit suicide is that they feel their drugs are a last resort, and that they can neither manage with them nor without them. Furthermore, were these patients not on tranquillizing drugs, they might not have considered suicide using those drugs, which offer a method readily to hand. In a study of trends between 1976 and 1989, it was found that most overdoses involved medicinal drugs, and that self-poisoning was also used in 86.5 per cent of attempted suicides. Among females, minor tranquillizers and sedatives were used in 259 or 14 per cent of suicides attempts among ten- to nineteen-year-olds. Among males between the ages of ten and nineteen, minor tranquillizers and sedatives were used in 104 attempts, or 17.3 per cent.

Drug-related deaths as reported by coroners in a 2001 Review[44] showed that in 53 per cent of all drug-related deaths in Scotland, benzodiazepines were the principal substance implicated. Hypnotics and sedatives, alone and in combination with other drugs, were mentioned in 207 cases. A table of suicides and pre-scribed psychoactive medication for July to December 2001 shows that over the six-month period 446 of those who committed suicide were on prescribed mood-altering drugs. Of these almost half were on hypnotics and sedatives, and in almost 33 per cent of cases hyp-notics and sedatives played a part in their deaths.

Mortality figures for young adults in the UK as a whole show that in women, although suicide accounted for less than 10 per cent of deaths between 1961 and 2001, a slight increase that occurred in the 1970s may be attributed to 'the high level of tranquillizers pre-scribed to women during this period.'[45] Between 1993 and 2001, again according to official figures, a steep rise in drug-poisoning deaths occurred in the UK among men, from 982 in 1993 to 1,526 in 2001. Of those 1,526 male drug suicides, 133 involved benzo-diazepines and a further 129 involved anti-depressants.

Actually the rise is worse than that. If we take the figures from 1979 to 2001, drug-related poisoning mortality tripled in young men. It accounted for 13 per cent of all mortality in young adult men and 7 per cent in young adult women in 2001. And these figures reflect only cases where the drugs are specifically cited. Mood medication must also be seen as contributing to the 30,622 suicides in 2001 in the US, where on average one American died by his or her own hand every 17.2 minutes. Self-poisoning was used in 17 per cent of those deaths.

In the stark face of such figures, the obvious must not be overlooked. Many of these statistics refer to young people. Many of these deaths involved drugs prescribed by doctors to calm them down. All of these deaths were potentially avoidable.

Depressants and anti-depressants

Another mood-altering class of drug frequently prescribed for stress is the anti-depressant. This same group of drugs is also frequently recommended for patients trying to withdraw from tranquillizers, in an attempt to modify their depression. Calming drugs work by chemically suppressing and slowing down the activity of the brain. So do tranquillizers actually *cause* depression? I put this question to the Department of Health: '*Are tranquillizers depressant?*' Spokesman Steve Ryan responded that 'tranquillizers are not a class of drug recognized by the DOH as such because there are different types, such as hypnotics, anxiolytics and 'barbiturates, but that in so far as drugs are intended to calm people down, then ultimately the answer is yes – they *are* depressant'.[46]

The American Medical Association is quite specific on the subject, and in 1999 warned of the dangers:

Depressants include barbiturates (such as Amytal, Nembutal and Seconal), benzodiazepines (such as Valium, Librium and Rohypnol), and methaqualone (Quaalude). Depressant drugs, commonly known as tranquillizers or sleeping pills, are prescribed by doctors to relieve anxiety and sleeplessness. In controlled doses these drugs produce a feeling of relaxation and well-being. Large doses result in intoxication similar to drunkenness.

All depressants have a high potential for abuse. Tolerance to depressants develops quickly and may lead to physical and/or psychological dependence. These drugs work by temporarily shutting down some areas of the central nervous system; the user who takes increasingly large doses as tolerance develops risks the central nervous system shutting down entirely. This risk becomes particularly acute when depressants are combined with alcohol, which produces a synergistic effect – a phenomenon best understood as 'one plus one equals three.' Because the lethal dose of depressants remains the same as tolerance increases, a person taking heavy doses of depressants or mixing them with alcohol risks coma or death. [47]

So here we have a problem for the stress industry, and it is not small. It has implications way beyond the use of mood-altering drugs themselves. Could stress management, with its panoply of techniques for calming people down, actually *depress* them? If this were so, then what we have termed Nation Sedation, whether by chemical or other means, would be likely to increase depression in the general population and we would therefore expect to see, in a tranquillizing culture, increases in the numbers of people who say they are depressed.

The depression pill epidemic

In the US, among those under thirty, 'major depression has doubled over the past 25 years'[48] and depression is projected to become the second highest cause, after heart disease, of disability in the country. Ten million American children use anti-depressants. In 2000, over 43 million American prescriptions were filled for the top six brands. Between 1987 and 1997, according to a 2002 investigation by Columbia University, the number of Americans being treated for depression rose from 1.8 million to 6.3 million.

More than 6 million people in the UK regularly take the drugs. In Britain, prescriptions for anti-depressants have rocketed in the past decade from 10 million in 1992 to 26 million in 2002. The NHS bill for anti-depressants has increased from £18 million in 1992 to £380 million in 2002. One in three GP appointments now involves patients reporting depression. In 2004, 250 GPs were surveyed by Norwich Union Healthcare.[49] They found that eight out of ten doctors admitted that they were over-prescribing anti-depressants and three quarters said they were prescribing more of the drugs than they did five years ago. The excuse given was a 'dire shortage' of counsellors.

US prescription and efficacy

In the US in 2000, the six most widely prescribed anti-depressants were (brand name first, generic name in brackets):

Zoloft (sertraline)	10.7 million prescriptions
Paxil (paroxetine)	10.49 million
Prozac (fluoxetine)	10 million
Celexa (citalopram)	5.29 million
Effexor (venlafaxine)	4.2 million
Serzone (nefazodone)	2.34 million[50]

Do they work? A (US) Freedom of Information Act request from two psychologists, Thomas Moore and Irving Kirsch of the University of Connecticut, led to the publication of a review[51] of forty-seven studies used by the US Food and Drug Administration (FDA) for approval of the six most commonly prescribed anti-depressants between 1987 and 1999. Overall, the anti-depressants performed 18 per cent better than placebos. More than half of the forty-seven studies found that patients on anti-depressants improved no more than those swallowing sugar pills. According to Irvin Kirsch: 'They should have told the American public about this.'[52]

The 'sunshine' drug

The 1990s saw the emergence of a new generation of anti-depressants, known as SSRIs (Selective Serotonin Reuptake Inhibitors), hailed, like all new-generation pharmaceuticals, as 'without the harmful side effects of the previous generation'. SSRI prescription has soared. In 1997, around 6.5 million prescriptions were issued for SSRIs, but by 2002 this had risen to 13.3 million. In the US, more than 142 million prescriptions were dispensed in 2003, up from the 98 million in 2000. This represents a staggering 45 per cent increase in America in three years. Among this new generation of drugs were Prozac and Seroxat. Some patients swear by them, and some believe that they have been saved from suicide by these drugs. American Professor Dr Peter D. Kramer, in his bestseller *Listening to Prozac*, offers testimonies from the drug's advocates and claims it can make people not only well, but 'better than well'. Others are not so sure. Critics worry that normal moods are suddenly being medicated. Author and psychologist Dr Paula Caplan, from the Pembroke Center for Teaching and Research on Women, Rhode Island says: 'It's as if there's no such thing as normal behaviour anymore.'[53] She thinks that unhappiness and negative emotions are being pathologized.

Like tranquillizers, 'happy' pills are not infrequently used by the severely depressed to kill themselves. According to a recent study in the *British Journal of Psychiatry*: 'Deaths from anti-depressants continue to account for a substantial proportion of drug-related deaths.'[54] In young women in England and Wales in 1993, for example, 'anti-depressants were the most frequently mentioned substance appearing on 30 per cent of drug-related poisoning death certificates'.[55]

As soon as it was licensed in the US in 1988, millions began swallowing Prozac, the so-called 'sunshine drug' manufactured by Eli Lilly – for depression, for stress, for everyday troubles. And since then, some 200 cases have come to court in the US blaming Prozac for suicide and violence. Psychiatrist Dr David Healy, director of North Wales Department of Psychological Medicine and one of the world's leading experts on anti-depressants, launched a £4.3 million lawsuit in 2001, claiming his £180,000-a-year appointment at Toronto's Centre for Addiction and Mental Health had been rescinded after he linked Prozac with higher suicide rates.[56] Dr Healy, author of a comprehensive history of anti-depressants, *The Antidepressant Era*[57] maintained: 'I was only saying what I should be saying – I am telling people what the hazards are.'[58] In a lengthy 2003 briefing paper on anti-depressants and suicide, citing a wealth of statistical and medical evidence, he writes:

There is a long clinical tradition of recognizing anti-depressant-induced suicidality. Traditional and company methods of assessing cause and effect leave little doubt that SSRIs can induce suicidality. Companies have failed to report in full their clinical trial data on suicidal acts. Current clinical trial data on the relative risk of suicidal acts on anti-depressants in either children or adults points to comparable elevations in the risk of suicide induction on active agent compared with placebo – an approximately 2.5 times greater risk, not including any risk that might stem from withdrawal effects.[59]

According to the Australian Board of Statistics [Social Trends 2001, Health: Mortality and Morbidity] in 1999:

In 1999, opiates were involved in 63 per cent of accidental drug-related deaths, while benzodiazepines were involved in 27 per cent. Opiates were involved in the highest proportions of accidental drug-related deaths of both males and females (67 per cent and 50 per cent respectively). However, the accidental deaths of females were more likely to involve benzodiazepines (35 per cent) and anti-depressants (28 per cent) than those of males (25 per cent and 10 per cent respectively).

The drugs used most commonly in suicides were benzodiazepines, anti-depressants and opiates, with each involved in a third of all suicides by drugs ... Alcohol was also used in combination with other drugs in 19 per cent of suicides by drugs, although was not the underlying cause of the death.

Self-harm and Prozac

Although the manufacturers strenuously deny any link, numerous investigative reports have connected Prozac with self-harm, and a recent study of 2,776 consecutive cases of DSH (deliberate self-harm) attending an accident and emergency department in 2000 found that occurrence 'was highest with fluoxetine (Prozac)'.[60] In one American court case, seventy-six research papers were cited to demonstrate that Prozac causes violence and suicide.[61]

In just three years after Prozac was licensed, suicides while on the drug numbered 198 in the US and 94 elsewhere. Of course, some of these depressed people might have committed suicide anyway, but some might not. Since then, doctors of around 38 million patients worldwide have written out a prescription for this drug. One of those patients, Joseph Wesbecker, a print worker from Louisville, shot eight colleagues, injured another sixteen and then turned the gun on himself. Another, Bill Forsyth, a retired car rental company owner from California, took Prozac for twelve days and then stabbed his wife fifteen times and impaled himself on the kitchen knife he had used. Ten days into his prescription course, Reginald Payne, a retired Cornish teacher, suffocated his wife and threw himself off a cliff.

In some Prozac compensation cases, there have been mega-dollar settlements out of court. Manufacturer Eli Lilly's position is always to blame the depression not the drug, but the company's internal documents revealed in court that they had known about the risks of explosive tension and violent agitation (akathisia) since the drug's clinical trials in 1978. Plaintiffs claimed that Prozac had caused balanced individuals with mild depression to become suicidal killers. Anti-psychotic drugs have long been associated with akathisia and doctors are usually alert to the risks, but Prozac is a general purpose anti-depressant, taken with little supervision. The German licensing authority, the Bundes Gesundheit Amt (BGA), subsequently insisted that a suicide warning appear on the label.

Prozac's sisters

Prozac's sister drugs are also widely prescribed. SSRI anti-depressants have been given to children – an estimated 50,000 in the UK alone. They are 'indicated' for a growing spectrum of psychiatric illnesses beyond depression and stress. Because of their relative safety in overdose compared with other anti-depressants such as the tricyclics (TCAs), SSRIs may be the pills of choice for patients most at risk.[62] Because such people might simply be looking for a means to their end, it is difficult for courts to determine in suicide cases, and the drug manufacturers, like tobacco companies, are well able to defend themselves. However, in 2001 there was a landmark court ruling in the US in the case of Donald Schell, a retired oil-rig worker who had been taking the SSRI antidepressant Paxil for two days when he shot and killed his wife, daughter and granddaughter and then turned the gun on himself. The jury found that Paxil, made by GlaxoSmithKline, 'can cause some individuals to commit suicide and/or homicide' and awarded the surviving family members $8 million in damages.

Other patients and their families have been told that tragedies like these are due to the original condition rather than the anti-depressant, but if this were the case, then the drug must surely have failed to act, or to act sufficiently quickly, or with sufficient efficacy. At all events, in 2004, the US Food and Drug Administration asked the manufacturers of ten popular anti-depressants to add suicide warning labels to their products. The drugs cited are Celexa, Effexor, Lexapro, Luvox, Paxil, Prozac, Remeron, Serzone, Wellbutrin and Zoloft. Long-suppressed research in the UK linking certain anti-depressants with suicide among children and teenagers[63] had rung alarm bells in America. The advice from the UK Committee on Safety of Medicines (CSM) is now to 'contraindicate' the use of most SSRI anti-depressants in patients under eighteen. Of the seven drugs under review – Celexa, Effexor, Lexapro, Luvox, Paxil, Prozac and Zoloft – four (Zoloft, Celexa, Paxil and Effexor) were found to increase the rate of self-harm. Two (Lexapro and Luvox) had no clinical trial data available.

Seroxat

The best-selling anti-depressant in the UK is Seroxat, manufactured by chemical giant GlaxoSmithKline. The Committee on Safety of Medicines advises that patients should initially be given only 20 mg a day, but in 2003 it became apparent that 17,000 patients had been started on higher doses, which could seriously increase the risk of side effects. In fact Seroxat had been prescribed at unsafe levels since it was first licensed for use in the UK in 1990.[64] The British drug regulatory body, the MHRA, is now investigating other reported problems with Seroxat – dubbed the 'anti-shyness pill' – such as anxiety, nausea, violent rages and suicidal thoughts. Spokesperson Janice Simmons of the Seroxat Users Group was reported as saying in 2004: 'Prescribing of these drugs has become absolutely scandalous. They are powerful drugs and have been shown to have severe side effects.'[65] While Health Minister Lord Warner had announced at about the same time: 'It's important to ensure that health professionals are reminded to follow the recommended safe dosage for patients receiving Seroxat for the first time so that patient safety is not compromised.'[66] In 2002 hundreds of patients had been complaining of distressing withdrawal symptoms and they are now planning a legal fight for compensation. Their solicitor Mark Harvey of Hugh James and Company said: 'I have 850 cases and more coming in every day.'[67]

The latest development comes in the form of warnings from two of the UK's leading drug-monitoring authorities. The National Institute for Clinical Excellence cautioned doctors in December 2004 to exercise more care in prescribing anti-depressants, and advised that at the outset of treatment in cases of mild depression the drugs should not be used at all. Commenting on the new guidelines, Andrew McCulloch of the Mental Health Foundation observed: 'The group of people who will benefit from these drugs is smaller than some GPs think.'[68] At the same time the Medicines and Healthcare Products Regulatory Authority called for stronger warnings on SSRIs such as Prozac and Seroxat: according to an analysis of published and unpublished data by the Committee on Safety of Medicines, there was 'a modest increase in the risk of suicide from SSRIs compared to placebos' in adults.[69]

The future for psychiatric medication

If you think all this is bad, consider the future. A record number of psychiatric medications are in research and development. In America alone, 50 million people have been diagnosed with some form of mental illness. The drug companies are very busy. In 2000, 103 drugs were under development to treat moods and emotions like depression, anxiety and whatever goes by the name of stress.

But what justification can there be for all these drugs to alter the brain chemistry of people who are not seriously deranged or a danger to themselves or others? Perhaps we should *not* keep taking the pills. Perhaps we should resist trying to mood-manipulate, soothe ourselves, stress-manage, run from the risk of reality – and look at our reasons for doing these things. Because such avoidant behaviour might in itself turn out to be very abnormal indeed.

Psychiatrist M. Scott Peck certainly thinks so: 'This tendency to avoid problems and the emotional suffering inherent in them is the primary basis of all human mental illness.'[70]

Part Five THE ALTERNATIVES

Note to Part Five

So must pure lovers' souls descend
T'affections, and to faculties,
Which sense may reach and apprehend,
Else a great prince in prison lies.

   John Donne, *The Extasie*

The last part of this book, although short, is in a way the most important and has been the focus of my research for twenty-five years, long before 'stress management' became the faith of the day. The final indictment of the 'stress' ideology comes not from me, nor from any boffin or writer or medic or researcher pleading for a review of the stress concept. The final indictment comes from a much more formidable foe – the human brain.

The brain is magnificent and wise. Its capacities, its powers, its workings, even to neuroscientists at the cutting edge of research – inspire respect and awe. Those who seek to subdue it, whether by chemical or psychological means, presume too much. As John Donne observes in his famous poem about the value of real human experience, they put a great Prince in prison.

So in this last section we shall be looking at how to let him out again.

CHAPTER NINETEEN

INUREMENT

Courage is being scared to death – but saddling up anyway.

John Wayne

If stress management doesn't work, what can be done to help those millions of people who believe themselves to be suffering from stress? How can we release these people from fear and restore sanity?

The theme of this book has been that these goals can only be achieved by tackling the problem of stress at source, which means providing science-based, clear and logical information on the stress ideology itself, to explain where the theory of stress management came from, and why it does not and cannot work. It is hoped that this information will empower 'stress sufferers' to begin taking responsibility for their own emotional health, rather than leaving it to a therapeutic industry. However, this would not be enough in itself. People also need to know what they can do *instead* when they are unhappy, worried, tense, frustrated or scared.

Emotional education

So in this last section we shall be looking at how to achieve emotional wisdom, resilience, courage and creativity without stress management. Before that ideology set off the wave of stress phobia that has disabled millions, there was a far different school of thought, dating back to the Romans, based not on *avoiding* negative emotions such as fear and tension, but on *rehearsing* them. Children were taught resourcefulness and mental strength by 'character-forming pursuits' that developed fortitude and self-mastery. By using the opposite of stress management – emotional rehearsal, emotional experimentation, emotional exploration – our ancestors made themselves psychologically more robust.

The word 'peril', and the words 'experience', 'experiment' and 'expert', all derive from the Latin *experiri*, meaning to 'try thoroughly' or 'put to the test'. Negative emotions including fear and tension are part of the rich cerebral process that makes possible our creativity, our peak experiences and our joy. Perhaps the underlying tragedy of stress phobia is that its victims are being robbed of these gifts.

Childhood dares, games and contests, sport and adventure activities, the arts – all provide emotionally challenging experiences that help people to understand and season their own sensations and feelings, and take them through unpleasant emotions in order to achieve a resolution, an epiphany, a pay-off or a reward. All of these activities require tension to produce a climax. Many involve the fight-or-flight response and reward with pleasure and satisfaction.

Human sexuality works on the same principle and conforms to the same pattern of neural and physiological activity as all the other leisure rites of passage we shall be examining. Arguably, these are the methods whereby people have always been 'trained' by society, or by the brain itself, in emotional competence and creativity.

Living under the stress dogma, people have perhaps lost sight of how alien and unnatural it is. According to this strange creed, emotions are seen as dangerous and wrong. Feelings are high risk. Humans must be calm, and remain calm. They must chill. Cool is beautiful. Even physical traces of emotion should ideally be obliterated. The unlined face, particularly in the female, must be achieved by creams, injections, tucks and surgery. Feelings are not beautiful. Do not look as though you have experienced things. Do not appear to have laughed or wept or frowned. Hide your grey: people may think you have worried. Airbrush it all out.

But human emotions are *not* wrong: they are important. Rather than being artificially smothered or tranquillized they need to be understood, and moderated by experience. Emotional maturity, emotional literacy and control, a sense of perspective about the relative importance of events and respect for the feelings of others – these may all be learned through the process of exposure and social support that half-decent parenting and schooling ought to provide. Temper tantrums are tempered. Egos are secured and stored out of sight. Irrational fears are vanquished. Everyday worries and frights are seen as problems to be faced and dealt with. Love and friendship are worth being hurt for.

The major religions of the world do not regard suffering as meaningless. They see it as having a purpose. In fact suffering – in the form of fasting, going up into high mountains, self-flagellation, hairshirts, poverty, solitude and painful rites of passage – may actually be encouraged as a means to 'enlightenment' (the shedding of light in the brain). Suffering is actually a tenet of some faiths. Christianity has at its heart the symbol of a Saviour flayed and crucified. The first of the Four Noble Truths taught by Buddha was: 'Life is suffering'.

In some cultures, suffering may be 'taught': children, apprentices and novices may be exposed to hardship in order to be accepted as seasoned members, or as mature adults. Bullying, fagging (the ritual humiliation of new pupils by older boys in the British public school system) and 'hazing' (a similar rite in American sporting and military team-bonding) are all part of this ruthless agenda. Astronauts, the Special Air Service (SAS), Marines, martial artists, Roman legionaries, American Indian braves and English public schoolboys have all been subjected to training that is not simply rigorous, but painful, punishing, frightening and arguably cruel.

The purpose, depending on the discipline involved, is to toughen them up, to force them upon their inner resources, to push them beyond their mind barriers towards self-discovery, to link them emotionally with their comrades, and even to give them transcendent experiences.

In Britain, such harsh education used to be called 'character-training' and was seen as the backbone of the Empire. This was the seminary of Sir Winston Churchill's 'lion-hearted nation' that endured the 'blood, toil, tears and sweat' of the Blitz, blackouts and rationing, slept on Underground platforms and dodged doodlebugs to get to work. With the advent of stress management it has been largely abandoned in favour of protection. The moral argument is compelling: that the weak may not survive, or be rendered tough by such training; they may simply be broken. The strong must therefore be protected along with the weak, in order to safeguard the weak. But this is a specious argument, because strength and weakness are in all likelihood not fixed character traits. They may simply be emotional experiences that we all pass through. A small child knows what it feels like to be a hero. A hero knows what it feels like to be a coward. Many a decorated soldier will tell you: 'Don't call me a hero – I was as scared as the next man.'

Whether we act out our feelings of weakness or strength is, one might argue, largely up to us. It depends what we are willing to experience. The stress management ideology seeks to protect us from emotional pain, fear, grief, tension and anxiety. Even hurt feelings (as, for example, by racist or sexist remarks) are seen as 'unbearable' and worthy of compensation. Many people are therefore currently unwilling to experience unpleasant emotions. They expect someone to cure their pain and fear without delay.

The most unwilling to experience unpleasant emotions are younger people who have grown up in, and been persistently exposed to, the stress ideology. We know this because evidence is emerging all over the world that the younger generation falls prey to stress propaganda more readily than their hardened elders. In the

US, according to the National Council on Compensation Insurance, almost 60 per cent of claims reported are from workers under the age of forty. In Australia, in the old days when tranquillizer addiction affected relatively few, typically the addict was over forty. Now addicts are usually aged between twenty and twenty-nine, and their numbers have increased dramatically.[1] Findings from the largest longitudinal study on women's health ever undertaken were presented at the 4th Australian Women's Health Conference in Adelaide in 2001. Results on stress surprised the researchers. They had expected middle-aged women to 'have the highest stress levels', but instead they found that young women between the ages of eighteen and twenty-three were most 'stressed'.[2]

Fighting or flying

There is powerful scientific evidence that those who voluntarily engage in harsh and dangerous pursuits involving negative emotions gain psychological robustness, and that those who pluck up the courage to take part in activities involving fear and pain may encounter the most rewarding joy – so much joy, in fact, that they are willing to risk their lives to re-experience it.

We are all afraid of something. We can choose to 'face the monster' or run: the fight-or-flight mechanism will serve for either. But whereas running can morally disembowel us, guts can make us great. In professional sport, for example, many years of research have demonstrated that when contestants have equal abilities, the winner will be the person willing to endure fear and tension and yet perform. Champions experience 'pressure' – the competitors' expression for unpleasant sensations in the head – but do not succumb: they brave it out.

In contrast, technically skilled contestants who somehow fail just short of winning – or 'choke artists' as they are cruelly labelled by their fellow competitors – are *not* willing to undergo this mental anguish. They back off on 'pressure' points. They recede from the mounting tension as the match crisis approaches, or let loose mistakes on the threshold of victory, bow their heads and head for the safety of the locker room. They are not, as the public imagine, simply 'unlucky'. Technical skill does not make you a champion. Technical skill plus willingness to endure fear and tension does. Modern sports training therefore includes a high psychological component: it teaches competitors how to withstand 'pressure', how to perform when they are extremely tense and nervous, and how to rise above, ignore or use these emotions. Learning to cope with fear is vital to winning.

In the armed forces, fear training is absolutely crucial. All soldiers are human and some may suffer battle fatigue and emotional reactions if they are expected to remain indefinitely in a war zone. Consequently there have been many interventions in recent years by military psychologists to monitor and modify abreactions, aimed at protecting combatants from distress. Psychologists wield enormous power, and their theories have great credence among vulnerable people exposed to danger. 'Syndromes' such as PTSD have now entered the vernacular, even between the soldiers themselves. Whether these 'symptoms' are normal, abnormal or the result of suggestion, and whether this effort to protect serving soldiers really makes them more resilient, or more self-vigilant, anxious and fearful, is a question that could only be settled by genuinely disinterested research.

Roman generals believed that you minimized fear and tension in the soldier by taking away the option to escape. Julius Caesar thought this important. Before one of his greatest battles he had all the horses taken away, including his own. He reasoned that his troops would then fight for their lives without having second thoughts.[3] Some of his enemies, including the Helvetii and Vercingetorix, shared this view, and burned their own towns and villages prior to a campaign so that soldiers could not think of escape in critical situations.

Consultant gastroenterologist and nutritional expert Dr Mike Stroud is expedition partner to Sir Ranulph Feinnes and recently accompanied Sir Ranulph on his 'seven marathons in seven days on seven different continents' endurance feat. He also acted as adviser to endurance performer David Blaine before his 'Above the Below' fasting challenge. Dr Stroud has written extensively on extreme survival challenges, and was called in as a consultant during a television training experiment involving twenty-four fit civilians, to see whether they could endure the notoriously harsh SAS training in the Namibian desert. Dr Stroud watched the super-fit competitors breaking down mentally and physically, and commented: 'It's not like a real survival situation, where you all carry on whatever happens. Here you can give up. And that makes it harder in many ways.'[4] Whereas for real 'Specials' in combat, as for Caesar's legionaries, there is no escape, no anxious choice. Syndromes like PTSD and shellshock, whatever else they may do, offer escape routes out of warfare. Ironically, they may, therefore, make the soldier's job more tense and fearful.

But whatever your views on military syndromes, it is widely accepted that combatants will be better able to cope with their experiences if they have been fittingly trained. So how do you steel men for the terrors of war? There are two distinct theories, and they are diametrically opposed. The first method is based on the principle of protection and relaxation, and the second is based on the principle of exposure and rehearsal. You either choose to protect them and teach them, by some artificial technique, to keep calm, so that they will not be frightened when they go into combat. Or you progressively expose them to harsh conditions, so that they get used to their fear and learn to master it. By the latter method they become calmer anyway because they are gradually inured to the experience. Soldiers who have learned to perform *through* fear are referred to as 'seasoned' – exposed to the elements.

The first method – of seeking to keep one's troops calm and avoid frightening them unduly – is based on the currently fashionable concept of stress management. But, so far as we know, not one army has used it, although the ultra-tough Royal Marines, faced with a recruitment shortfall and high failure rate at their base in Lympstone, Devon, *are* currently experimenting with a more protective approach. Since 2001 they have been sending their instructors on management courses to learn to curb their harshness with the trainees and issuing boots early to avoid giving the new recruits blisters.

The second method, of exposure to fear, is the one traditionally favoured by armed forces the world over. It has been tried and tested for thousands of years. The Spartans swore by inurement. At the age of seven, Spartan boys were enrolled in a military academy known as an *agoge*. Their regimen gave us the word 'spartan' – a life acid-dipped of every comfort, with little food other than pig blood stew, and naked, barefoot training in the bitterest cold. They grew into warriors of awesome courage. In August 480 BC, 300 Spartans died beside King Leonidas at Thermopylae, a fifty-foot gap in the mountains, fighting with spears, swords, shields, fists and teeth to resist 200,000 Persians while their own Greek forces regrouped.

The SAS, of whom Adolf Hitler complained, 'These men are dangerous', have been inurement-trained in combat-survival since the Second World War. Recruits are toughened psychologically to withstand fear and fatigue, as well as physically to live off the land behind enemy lines. Their training goes the extra mile. It includes what used to be called a 'sickener factor'[5] (the SAS equivalent of 'beastings' or punishment drills). Already exhausted recruits, sleep-deprived and force-marched over deadly terrain with mighty backpacks in extreme temperatures, are then subjected to sensory deprivation and realistic interrogation, and expected to carry out complex military assignments. Those who complete the training are emotionally competent to deal with the most extreme physical and psychological hazards.

So deeply did the Romans themselves believe in inurement

training, even for the general populace, that they plunged alternately into extremely hot and cold baths, 'hardening' their bodies on the same principle as tempering steel, and made the beating heart of their world the Colosseum. Men, women and children watched brutality to curdle the stomach of even the most avid fan of modern screen violence. Although Seneca and the Christian emperors dismissed the Games as barbaric, many others, including Symmachus, the poet Martial, Pliny the Younger and Cicero, praised them because they instilled contempt for pain and death. Cicero thought that watching gladiators taught Romans to regulate their own fear:

Look at the gladiators, who are either ruined men or barbarians ... See how men who have been well trained prefer to receive a blow rather than basely avoid it! ... What gladiator of ordinary merit has ever uttered a groan or changed countenance? Such is the force of training, practice and habit. Shall then the Samnite, filthy fellow, be capable of this, and shall a man born to fame have any portion of his soul so weak that he cannot strengthen it by systematic preparation?[6]

The all-conquering Roman Army endured from 750 BC until the Siege of Constantinople in 1453. Its success could not have been achieved without soldiers of indomitable courage, efficiency, order and high morale. The Romans made a science of warfare, of rigorous drills, battle analysis and stable tactics. But above all, the men were harshly and fittingly trained. Their exercises, as historian Josephus commented, were just like battles without the blood, so that their real battles were like exercises with blood.[7]

This principle has guided armies ever since. It was the inspiration behind the so-called Battle Schools set up all over Britain under the direct control of General Sir Bernard Paget, Commander-in-Chief of the Home Forces in 1942. After Dunkirk, many officers realized that the British soldier needed more realistic training to face the might of the German *Blitzkrieg*. The aim was: 'the training of men in the circumstances as near as may be of actual battle, so that when they are confronted with the "real thing", they well know instinctively what to do and how to do it.'[8]

Another British wartime inurement school, Outward Bound, was established by Gordonstoun headmaster Kurt Hahn and ship-ping line manager Laurence Durning Holt as a character-training course for young Merchant Navy recruits, among whom there had been very high combat casualties. Raw cadets in the heat of battle tend to panic and make mistakes that may cost them their lives. Outward Bound provided emotional training in the form of testing and potentially dangerous adventure activities. It was so successful that the scheme is still running and now includes a commercial division, Outward Bound Professional. A sister programme, the inspirational Duke of Edinburgh Award Scheme, was founded in 1956 and promotes 'the spirit of adventure and discovery'[9] through challenge-based activities for young people between the ages of fourteen and twenty-five. There are currently around 200,000 participants in the UK, learning by carefully controlled exposure to danger how to access their hidden resources and how to be courageous, self-disciplined and resilient in their lives.

De-sensitization and embracing fear

But what has all this character-training to do with the rest of us? The answer lies in the principle of fear exposure. What applies to the SAS soldier or the Spartan youth applies just as much to the agoraphobic, afraid to venture outside the front door. Unlike the hardened soldier, the agoraphobic has used avoidance of fear as a life tactic. Normal tasks and challenges causing a little apprehension, instead of being accepted, are avoided because of the fear involved. But then that fear, because it has been avoided, becomes an unknown quantity. Its quantity might be very great. It might unhinge the mind or prove fatal – the agoraphobic simply does not know. Apprehension therefore builds up about this fear, and the ability to cope with it. It attaches to all contact with the world that caused the original fear, and then to all actions leading up to that contact, and then to everything else, until finally the sufferer realizes that he/she is completely disabled and asks for help.

One form of cognitive behaviour therapy that has been found particularly effective in treating agoraphobics is de-sensitization. Patients are asked by the therapist to grade their fear on a scale of one to ten as they try to perform certain tasks: going towards the door, grasping the door-handle, opening the door, and so on. They are asked to talk through their level of fear, and observe it going up or down. Gradually, they learn that they can cope with quite high levels and still go ahead with the task. And as they face and conquer these feelings, their levels of arousal go down. The patient becomes inured, or de-sensitized. He or she can then walk out of the front door like everybody else.

The same process of inurement or habituation goes on all the time in our daily lives. The horror film that scared you years ago makes you laugh now. The novice motorist may initially find his knees knocking under the dashboard having to negotiate traffic, but gradually becomes so unfazed by driving that he may ignore traffic hazards, thunder through speed limits and even nod off at the wheel on the motorway out of sheer boredom. Fear exposure is a natural process. Pedestrians are so inured to traffic that, as we walk along the pavement, enormous lorries can speed past just inches from our elbow and we hardly notice. The phenomenon is well known to scientists. Laboratory animals used in 'taming' research exhibit less and less fear the more they are handled. Their brains adapt and alter their structure. This is why the best way of mastering fear is not avoidance, but practised exposure. In fact, many of our key leisure pursuits are a means of practising fear in relative safety.

Susan Jeffers' 1987 book *Feel the Fear and Do It Anyway* took the idea of making fear your friend and turned it into an international bestseller. The theme was to live life, 'push the envelope', break out of comfort zones.

I suggest that each day you do something that widens that space for you. Call someone you are intimidated to call, buy a pair of shoes that costs more than you would ever pay in the past, ask for something that you want that you have been too frightened to ask for before. Take a risk a day – one small or bold stroke that will make you feel great once you've done it.[10]

It is no accident that our fiction and mythology are devoted to the idea of turning and facing the monster, and the rewards that courage can bring. Walking towards fear (rather than running away from it) is presented as a life-enhancing experience: George simply must fight the Dragon. Adult fiction pulsates with heroism. Movies of every sort pit some protagonist against the odds, or a terrifying foe, and the cinema-goer invests emotions in the endangered hero and shares in his triumph.

Intriguingly, most children's fairy stories have heroic challenge as a theme, from 'Jack and the Beanstalk' and 'Sinbad the Sailor' to the chilling 'Hansel and Grethel'. For true tension and terror, adult horror movies can scarcely hold a candle to some of these stories told to generations of kids, who often ask for the grisly bits to be re-read.

Despite our desire to censor and protect, youngsters instinctively recognize the need for what Peter Pan calls 'an awfully big adventure'. This is why, of their own volition, they dare one another to perform acrobatic and illegal feats, put coins on railway lines, let off thunderous fireworks, eat worms, watch horror films and read what are known as 'gruesome spewsome' comics (such as the *Spine-Chiller Collection* and *Toxic*, with gunge-exuding freaks and free 'scary stick-on scars'). Computer games favoured by children are not for the faint-hearted either. Parents who think they are safeguarding their little ones from fear by shutting them in their rooms with a small screen should take a look at their PlayStation games. Grendel's Mother might tremble, but children find such fright-ridden entertainment thrilling.

Or look at their preferred reading. Harry Potter has to face many a knee-wobbler ('Harry and Ron thought that meeting the three-headed dog had been an excellent adventure, and they were quite keen to have another one').[11] In J. R. R. Tolkien's *Lord of the Rings*, scared Hobbit Frodo Baggins must return the ring to the place where it was made, venturing after hundreds of pages into Mordor, lair of the evil Sauron. Such is our 'tender age' literature. Children appear to relish the 'adrenalin rush' that comes from entering a fictional world of terror and darkness. Yet according to the stress management ethos we should do our best to protect these youngsters and shield their delicate sensibilities by banning conkers and softening the ends of nursery rhymes like 'Humpty Dumpty' to avoid fictional contact with catastrophe.

Children like to entertain themselves with derring-do, but even they are not as daring as our joy-riding, drug-experimenting, speed-loving, sex-absorbed, thrill-seeking, white-knuckle-riding, authority-challenging teenagers. Male adolescents are renowned for inhabiting life's dangerous edge, no matter how much parents warn them off. Adolescent girls may, on the surface, appear less adventurous, although a growing number of young women are engaging in dangerous sports. But whereas a male youth might prefer to hang-glide, speed or bungee-jump in order to gain peer recognition, avoid being picked on and challenge his fear, girls may choose to encounter peril in a different way, by involving themselves with dangerous and unsuitable males. The more unsettling the men, the more exciting and compelling these relationships may seem. Indeed, a minority of these young women may return repeatedly to be threatened and even beaten up by their perilous partners, a phenomenon well known to agony aunts, refuge campaigners and the police. It seems that wild horses could not drag such danger-loving females to safety.

Of course, not all young people are fascinated by fear, but those who are not tend to remain shy or get bullied, with all the misery that this entails. The estimated one in five bullied children of the stress management millennium may well have been singled out precisely *because* of their sensitivity, 'stress'-avoidance, poor communication skills, signs of weakness and unwillingness to undergo courage tests – difficulties that might ironically be helped by a judicious set of challenges. For most, there is a collective credo that those who dare, win, that faint heart never won fair maid, and that fears have to be faced if life is not to be sad, mundane and 'middle-aged'. Such juvenile relish for danger and fear can hardly be accidental. By such activities, the young learn to inure themselves to the threats and perils of life. When the going gets tough, the tough will be those who, either gladly or through peer pressure, have braved such inurement training.

CHAPTER TWENTY
'EMERGENCE'

> Here it was again: order. Order for free. Order arising naturally from
> the laws of physics and chemistry. Order emerging spontaneously from
> molecular chaos and manifesting itself as a system that grows.
>
> M. Mitchell Waldrop, *Complexity*

We are all familiar with the sweat mantra, *no pain, no gain*. The
West is obsessed with physical fitness. A multi-billion-dollar
industry offers strenuous workouts for every part of the human
body *other* than the brain. By a strange logic, taxing the body is
seen as the key to physical fitness (and even mental fitness), while
taxing the mind is seen as the key to physical and mental illness.
Odd, because some of the stress research itself shows that gruelling
physical training may have far more dramatic effects on immune
functioning than 'psychological stress', however defined.[1]

This is the Age of Body Fit, Brain Flab. Some allowance is made
for improving the IQ by doing quizzes and brain-teasers. There is
also a concession on avoiding senility, with the elderly being advised
to 'use it or lose it'. Otherwise we should all be careful. Stress
management policy on the brain is fairly clear. Use it in modera-
tion, or you may cause it to break down.

Those advocating brain workouts are in a tiny minority. Organ-
izers of the Mind Sports Olympiad, held annually in London,
foster brain contests like chess, Go (the Chinese game), back-
gammon, bridge and Scrabble. NASA, in the 1960s, found that you

could help pilots to respond faster on experimental X15 rocket planes by doubling the speed of the flight simulators. Real speed was then a jolly. They also found that NASA wives who played the piano could get better faster by turning up the metronome when practising. Tony Buzan, co-founder of the Mind Sports Olympiad and inventor of 'mind maps', believes that even the most disruptive child can 'unlock his or her natural genius', provided the youngster's brain is suitably exercised and extended.[2]

Some scientists contend that dangerous sports may be viewed as brain workouts in that they require fast learning curves and present a form of 'risk exercise'.[3] This may be the real reason why those who participate in them are more alive, creative and efficient. Indeed, *any* emotionally challenging experience could give the bored brain something to do. Californian human relations specialist Dr Michael Cavanagh says: 'Stress should not be avoided and, in fact, it often should be judiciously sought out. Humans need both physical and psychological workouts to continue to grow and remain in good shape.'[4] Director of UCLA's Neuropsychiatric Institute, Professor Peter Whybrow, agrees: 'Stress is like mental callisthenics. It forces you, in a way, to shape and make more precise your ideas about how you can cope with the world.'[5]

Exercising the brain

The normal adult brain weighs between 1400 and 1500 grams. In it, 'the surface of the cerebral hemispheres is deeply infolded, so as to cram the vast area of the cerebral cortex into the space under the skull.'[6] 'We can show that each of the ten billion neurons [nerve cells] in the human brain has a possibility of connections of one with 28 noughts after it.'[7] 'Cerebral Blood Flow is 50–60 ml per 100 g brain tissue per minute, so that total brain flow is about 750 ml per minute or 15 per cent of the total cardiac output.'[8] 'The human neocortex contains some tens of billions of neurons, comparable in number to all the stars in our galaxy. Some of these connections between neurons are local ... but others leave the cortical sheet and travel some distance before entering another part of the sheet or going elsewhere. These longer connections are often covered by a fatty sheath, made of a material called myelin, that enables the signal to travel faster ...'[9] If a neuron is excited, it fires by sending an electrical impulse (known as a spike) down its output cable or axon, which may be microscopic or several feet long. Firings vary between 1 and 5 Hertz (cycles per second) up to 50–100 Hertz but may go as high as 500 Hertz. And so on. There are no manuals on how to operate this staggering piece of equipment.

Scientists are leery of theorizing about how the whole brain works, perhaps because of past blunders. Theories of the brain as a telephone exchange, or more recently a computer, have lost kudos. Dr Franz Josef Gall's anatomical head maps became a curiosity. Aristotle (384–322 BC), an acknowledged genius, believed that the brain was a device for cooling the blood. Then for centuries scientists theorized that thoughts and feelings swam about like tadpoles in the fluid that surrounds and bathes the brain.

Millions of experiments later, although aspects of the brain's functioning have been clarified, scientists still do not know what causes consciousness. Neuropharmacologist Dr Susan Greenfield, giving a 1994 Royal Institution Christmas lecture, said scientists have long believed that when we think a thought, there must be some part of the brain acting like the captain on the bridge of the Starship Enterprise. Sadly, 'a hundred years or more of exploration through the universe inside our heads have failed to find it'.[10] Neurologist Dr Adam Zeman of Addenbrooke's Hospital, Cambridge says: 'There is no single compelling theory of consciousness.'[11] Nobel-prizewinning co-discoverer of the structure of DNA, Francis Crick, writing in 1994: 'There does not appear to be one set of ideas that click together in a convincing way to make a detailed neural hypothesis that has the smell of being correct.'[12]

The brain as a complex system

One group of scientists, however, is looking at the brain in a radically different way. Chaos theory – the idea that the universe is an ever-exploding Big Bang of complexity – worried scientists very much. If everything in the universe really were chaotic and random, why practise science? Experimental results must be meaningless as well. So in the 1980s at the newly founded Santa Fe Institute, New Mexico, a number of Nobel laureates, including physicists Murray Gell-Mann and Philip Anderson and economist Kenneth Arrow, put their heads together. They were joined by other distinguished scientists from a variety of disciplines who would not normally collaborate. They began prying into the secrets of complex systems. They had been inspired, among other things, by non-linear dynamics – the science of what doesn't 'add up', such as why the whole may be greater than the sum of its parts – and by the discovery of an amazing phenomenon known as *emergence*.

In 1977 a Nobel Prize had been awarded to Belgian physicist Ilya Prigogine for his work in the field of self-organizing structures. These are common in nature: a tornado, a wasp swarm, a storm cloud, a pile of sand, a living cell, a laser beam are all complex systems that adapt and exhibit seemingly 'intelligent' transitions, spontaneously grouping themselves in an orderly way. Cellular automata – programmes for generating patterns on a computer screen – at a particular critical point exhibit a 'phase transition', just on the edge of chaotic complexity, where you get beautiful, self-generating, splitting and recombining patterns that appear to have a life of their own. Or take a pan of heating water. Water molecules, as they begin to warm up, become more and more unstable and behave increasingly randomly until suddenly, as though at the throwing of a switch, they organize themselves into a hexagonal convection pattern – and simmer. On the edge of apparent chaos they act coherently. Order just emerges, as if by magic.

Emergence has implications for all sorts of complex systems, and ecosystems. The money markets, for example: emergence could explain their crises, booms and busts. And if other complex systems behave like this, then why not the brain? So the Santa Fe Institute turned its collective consciousness on neural networks, to investigate whether the brain exhibits these peculiar phase transitions as well. The research is ongoing, but complexity scientists like John H. Holland already believe that 'The mind is an emergent property'.[13] So does Nobel laureate Francis Crick: 'Much of the behaviour of the brain is "emergent" – that is, behaviour does not exist in its separate parts, such as the individual neurons. An individual neuron is in fact rather dumb. It is the intricate interaction of many of them together that can do such marvellous things.'[14]

Emotional crisis and psychological tension

What a pity the sciences don't any longer talk to the arts. Years before I read about the Santa Fe research, as a student of English literature in the 1970s, I wanted to know why all great works of fiction were apparently about emotional crises. Why was there always a build-up of tension in the storyline which eventually reaches a climax or crisis point, followed by a fictional resolution? I thought at the time that perhaps writers were people whose heads contained a lot of unresolved conflicts, and who needed to find 'closure' artificially, in the form of stories, plays and poems. But there was more to it than this. Many of our leisure pursuits focus on crisis situations of one sort or another, in which we either participate ourselves in the emotional loop, or watch others experiencing it.

Take professional sport. What exactly is it that so fascinates millions of fans? In 1979, after several years of research and interviews with top-level sportsmen, my first book was published, on 'pressure' in sport. It said that spectators wanted to see how people perform in crisis. Sport enables this to happen, providing arenas, seating and media coverage, prize money, time limits and rules to ensure high motivation and intense competition between those under scrutiny. Fans could identify with participants, invest in their mental experiences, share their fate. The behaviour and thoughts of contestants could then be analysed at length, not only by spectators but in the back pages of every newspaper, to find out what made them tick, or not tick, or go all to pieces.

Something intriguing was also going on in post-match interviews. I noticed that competitors used a lot of metaphorical expressions to describe mental states, such as 'rush of blood', 'pressure', 'on tenterhooks', 'hot under the collar', 'tight', 'pumped up' and so on. Sportsmen are very alert to psychological states under intense competition, so they use hundreds of these little word-balls. We all use them, in fact. I discovered that the expressions were not random, either, but extremely specific. The whole patois refers to pressure, heat, expansion, high tension and fusion. 'Pressure' and 'tension', though literally opposites (one meaning compressing and the other stretching), were always tangled up together in this odd metaphorical language. I speculated, though I could not prove, that it referred to a process of ever-increasing pressure and tension building up to a crisis point, followed by resolution and an emotional high. In a paper I suggested that perhaps this language might be giving us a glimpse of the brain's own processes.[15]

Tension is inherent in neural activity. A pyramidal neuron (the style of cell found most commonly in the neocortex) looks like a tiny bare tree in winter, with fibrous branches and roots. One long fibre, the axon, extends like a cable for carrying electrical signals. Professor Susan Greenfield, talking about the wet electricity of the brain, describes the brain's signalling system:

The moist environment of the brain contains ions (charged particles) of many different elements ... These ions can go backwards and forwards across the cell membrane through tailor-made pores, or channels, but only if the channels are open. If the membrane always allowed all the ions to pass through, eventually there would be equal concentrations of the different ions on each side of the membrane. This would mean that each side would have equal charge and no electricity would flow. However, the cell actively pushes sodium ions out and lets extra potassium in. The result is that the outside of the cell is more positively charged than the inside: sodium ions want to come in, and potassium ions want to get out. The cell membrane holds everything where it is, like a dam holding back a river. This is called 'resting potential'.[16]

When a cell gets a signal telling it to fire, the electrical potential across the cell membrane, after being held under enormous micro-tension, switches suddenly from negative to positive as charged ions rush through the cell walls. The 'action potential' then moves in a wave along the nerve cable until it reaches the terminals, where it triggers the release of chemical transmitters that carry the message across the 'synaptic gap' on to the rest of the network and if necessary to other circuits. None of this is theoretical. It is scientific fact.

Tension in the 'fight-or-flight' mechanism

Now, the fight-or-flight mechanism, in Dr Johnson's phrase, 'concentrates the mind wonderfully'; it increases activity inside your head. We know this because when we feel threatened, the heart speeds up and blood pressure increases. Blood supply to less essential areas, like the digestive system and the extremities, is diverted to the large muscles (for fighting or running away), and to the brain, which is about to boost up its own power using oxygen and glucose.

Dr Pim van Lommel, whose research on brain activity during near death experiences was published recently in *The Lancet*, told me: 'As far as I know, vasodilation occurs in the brain, the main proximal muscles and the heart with tachycardia during "stress" as a result of the release of epinephrine and norepiphedrine, with vasoconstriction of the digestive system and peripheral extremities. This happens through autoregulation by the autonomic nervous system.'[17] In order to avoid a dangerous rise in pressure on the artery walls, then, the brain's blood vessels *dilate*, ready to receive the influx. This is part of the brain's minutely orchestrated monitoring system for controlling its own blood pressure. (It can also constrict the blood vessels when the supply is interrupted, or too low – a mechanism known as the ischaemic reflex.)[18]

So, challenging situations fashionably referred to as 'stressful' intensify neural processing. And if these dramatic changes are taking place, the brain surely cannot fail to be aware of them. With its exquisitely monitored increase in blood supply, the brain may actually experience 'a rush of blood' and an increase in 'pressure'. When vasodilation occurs in its busiest networks, the brain may experience tension, because its nerve fibres are literally being expanded and stretched, particularly major axons, several feet in length, spanning different circuits. And if the brain is aware of these changes, it is conceivable that it may transmit this awareness to us through the language that we use to describe our feelings in highly charged situations. That language is both very distinctive and very descriptive.

The language of the brain

Here then are some examples of what we might call the language of the brain. The process to which it surely refers, amid the tension and pressure of its billions of neurons synchronised at full power, is emergence.

The first group of expressions are to do with arousal:

a heated argument, about to burst, blow a gasket, bloody hell, bloody minded, boiling with rage, burning desire, don't burst a blood vessel, feeling the pressure, fit to bust, he nearly exploded, his blood was up, hot under the collar, hot-blooded, hothead, if you can't stand the heat get out of the kitchen, in the heat of the moment, in the hot seat, an inflammatory remark, it went to his head (i.e., the blood), let off steam, livid, pressure situation, pumped up, ruddy, rush of blood, she inflamed his desires, we saw red, when the heat is on, and so on.

The second group of expressions refer to the apparent chaos and dislocation caused by the brain's networks 'expanding'. The feeling of being about to crack up or burst, although not unnatural, is illusory:

a shattering blow, all over the place, beside myself, coming apart at the seams, crackers, cracking up, crackpot, crazy (like crazy paving), disjointed, driven to distraction, falling apart, going to pieces, having a breakdown, he blew up, he just crumbled, inarticulate, incoherent, inner conflict, it blew my mind, it broke her heart, nerves shot to pieces, non compos mentis, potty (from crackpots), splitting headache, tearing me apart and so on.

The third group describe being stretched taut and pulled asunder. These feelings are even more unpleasant than the second lot, but may simply be describing *literal* nervous tension:

distracted (from the Latin for 'pulling asunder'), distraught, distress, overextending oneself, frayed nerves, haywire (stretched like lengths of wire for binding hay), snapping under the strain, highly strung, keyed up, nerve-racking (stretched as on a torture rack), nervous tension, on tenterhooks (stretched like cloth on a frame), strain, stress (a shortened form of 'distress' from 'pulling asunder'), strung out, taut, tense, tight as a bowstring, under a lot of strain, uptight, wound up, wired and so on.

Then suddenly there is an alchemical change. At a moment of high tension (and perhaps optimum heat), the brain, fully charged, undergoes a phase trasition. Tiny channels flick open in thousands of neuron walls, as millions of charged particles swarm through the locks and the electrical potential across thousands of membranes switches suddenly from negative to positive. A surge of power travels down thousands of axons, held under tension, linking hundreds of networks, transmitting electricity across the galvanized, living brain. Depending on the importance of the pressure situation, millions, perhaps billions of connections may be involved in the lightning power surge.

How might such dramatic cerebral changes be mediated psychologically? What would we be feeling and thinking at the very climax of this neural activity? It seems not unreasonable to suggest that this is the moment when we get the buzz, the relief and thrill of resolution, the feeling of being 'at one' with creation. That this is the source of our goosebumps, the moment when we experience the wave of recognition, the making of connections, the out-of-body sense of concentration and focused thought, when everything becomes suddenly bright, brilliant and crystal clear. This may be why we often come away from personal crises having learned something that we will value for the rest of our lives. The fusions that the brain makes under high tension come forth in our minds as important ideas and insights. They create our music, our scientific breakthroughs, our art. They give us our sense of meaning, our focus and our goals. Indeed, these diamonds of the mind may be the *point* of the whole 'pressure' process. Arguably, this is how the brain makes sense of experience.

Of course, this is all only a theory. The metaphors that we use to describe being 'under pressure' may not mean anything at all. But if the language *did* correspond to events in the brain, then everything we understand by the word *stress*, and all those unpleasant feelings of tension and pressure, are part of a natural process, a means to an end. It might even be that the brain *enjoys* emergence, and requires it to happen fairly often, which would explain why most key leisure pursuits glory in it. And if that were true, then stress management, because it calls for interruption of arousal and tension, may disappoint and disable every cell in our heads. What the brain really needs is *not* relaxation, but resolution. That may be what it dreams of all the time. Dreams are, after all, widely regarded by neuroscientists as the brain's method of processing unresolved information while we sleep.

'Peak experiences'

There is too much evidence of a connection between epiphanies, emotional 'highs' and the pressure process to dismiss the theory of neural 'emergence' out of hand. In near death experiences, at the climax of tension, pain and terror of approaching death, subjects report sudden feelings of beatific peace and calm. In the martial arts the concept of *kirikaeshi* – the moment of highest tension when one strikes the killer blow – is fundamental. In the classic *Zen in the Art of Archery*,[19] apprentice of the Japanese longbow Eugen Herrigel is told to draw and wait at the moment of highest tension until '*it* shoots'. Not him but '*it*'. At the height of arguments, people may experience catharsis and relief. In Dr Michael Persinger's research, 'God Experiences' happen during temporal lobe transients, particularly during fluctuations in blood supply to these sensitive regions of the brain. God experiences are typically associated with 'personal stress'.[20]

In the research of Dr Aaron Antonovsky on concentration camp survivors, those who made it through hell on earth had a 'sense of coherence'.[21] Artists and writers, often struggling against emotional pain, see themselves as making 'magical fusions'[22] in the midst of personal crises (Graham Greene achieved them by playing Russian roulette with his brother's revolver). These are the 'peak experiences' created by the brain's own alchemy. Bearing in mind that brainwaves can turn switches on and off and even work small machines,[23] we should not be too surprised at the brain being able to accomplish these things. I leave you with Russian psychic Nelya Mikhailova, working in a laboratory under scientific supervision in 1968 (the italics are mine):

Mrs Mikhailova was able to displace light objects of plastic material and metals of weight from ten to fifty grams. At the moment of occurrence of phenomena, registrations were observed by means of several electrodes, in EEG, and cardiographic apparatus and also recordings were obtained by an apparatus at a distance without direct contact, indicating an electrostatic fluctuating field; *the latter appeared at the moment of brain tension.*[24]

CHAPTER TWENTY-ONE
THE CEREBRAL CLIMAX (CC)

> ... O my soul's joy!
> If after every tempest come such calms,
> May the winds blow till they have waken'd death!
> And let the labouring bark climb hills of seas
> Olympus-high, and duck again as low
> As hell's from heaven! If it were now to die,
> 'Twere now to be most happy, for I fear
> My soul hath her content so absolute
> That not another moment like to this
> Succeeds in unknown fate.

William Shakespeare, *Othello*, Act II

Why is it that, despite the modern obsession with avoiding 'work-place stress', many people nevertheless devote their leisure hours to activities more or less guaranteed to produce tension, tears and fears? The pursuits we are talking about may expose participants unwillingly or accidentally to this distress (e.g. rock-climbing, hang-gliding, potholing), but often they voluntarily expose themselves and often the activity is virtually designed to produce this emotional exposure. Consider the following selection of leisure-time activities constructed by the author:

CHILDREN AND JUVENILES	ADULTS
childhood dares	fiction classics
fiction and fairy stories	thrillers and chillers
'gruesome spewsome' comics	drama and theatre
'extreme' computer games	horror movies
teenage daredevil pursuits	poetry (extreme words)
fighting and arguing	quizzes (extreme questions)
'recreational' drugs	'punchline' jokes
romance and sex	hunting
rites of passage	spectator sports (watching professionals)
	participant sports (amateur competitive)
	'extreme' sports (e.g. free-falling, base-jumping)
	racing (either watching or taking part)
	martial arts
	'white knuckle' rides
	adventure activities (e.g. rock-climbing, hang-gliding, potholing)
	'drumroll' circus acts
	gambling
	classical music
	challenges (mental and physical)
	romance and sex

Of course I am not personally recommending every leisure pursuit on these lists. One or two are self-destructive. Some, though exhilarating, are very dangerous, to be undertaken at one's own risk. Yet seen as a whole, these activities tell us something about what the brain wants and needs, and what it will do of its own volition in order to achieve its objectives. The conventional wisdom is that we are all simply motivated by the pursuit of pleasure, but our leisure activities are much more complex than that. Indeed, they may hold the key to understanding the brain as an emergent system.

Depending upon the quality and degree of involvement, the activities listed above will often facilitate a so-called 'adrenalin rush', an arousal curve, tension, climax and resolution. They give us our highs, our catharsis, our 'peak experiences'.[1] They are a minor version of the climactic revelations of religious faith, of near death experiences, of the Zen concept of *sartori* (enlightenment) and the martial arts concepts of *kirikaeshi* (highest point of tension or exhaustion) and *mushin* ('no mind' or 'total physical/ spiritual contraction and then relaxation').[2] These more extra-ordinary experiences are generally encountered by an emotional elite: those who are willing, or forced by extreme discipline or circumstances, to undergo the ordeal of a particularly large, particularly tense and particularly gruelling Cerebral Climax.

The cerebral climax (CC)

People have always been willing to endure tension, tears and fears, so long as there is a climactic experience at the end of it. Falling in love can be highly distressing; as the late Elvis Presley put it, one's heart beats so it scares one to death. One is all shook up. But few would forgo the amazing cerebral climaxes that a love affair can give. Or consider the 1970s personal development phenomenon known as EST (Erhard Seminar Training), the brainchild of Werner Erhard. Adopting the often abusive and demeaning approach of Zen master training, EST stripped away every layer of belief from trainees until they discovered within themselves a liberating, ego-less state known as 'It'. For some participants the seminars were a truly harrowing emotional ordeal, but many thousands experienced a life-changing epiphany. These are but two examples of the discomfort that people are willing to undergo in order to have a cerebral climax.

Cerebral climaxes are so valuable to human beings that we are willing to pay for them, and pay dear. It should be emphasized at this point that CCs are not some minor version of, or substitute for, sexual climaxes. They are better than sex. We know this because many religious devotees have foresworn sexuality to experience them, and adventurers regularly put their very lives at risk for a close encounter of the CC kind. Indeed, sex is a version of what cerebral climaxes are, because the body serves the brain, and in all its sub-systems recognizes its master. Sigmund Freud's theory that sex underpinned consciousness, however influential until recently, was arguably a case of tail wagging dog.

The need for the cerebral climax is very prevalent in human society. It may explain (explain not forgive) certain self-destructive and anti-social acts: the gambler staking the housekeeping on a bet, the Ecstasy-popping teenager, the shoplifter who takes things from a store and then discards them at home in their packaging. Dabbling in the forbidden and almost getting caught ensures, for some under-aroused individuals, the requisite 'high'. With the erosion of sexual taboos, the forbidden must become ever more exotic, and the fear of getting caught and disgraced sought out in ever more extreme ways. Many such CC-seekers end up in prison, unable to explain why they have behaved so badly. For some, getting caught is the only possible respite from the need that drives them.

For most of us, such experiences are obtained more easily: by taking part in leisure activities that provide them. The horror movie builds tension to a crisis of fright and gore until finally the terror is vanquished and survivors walk away older and wiser. The white-knuckle ride ratchets up fear and nausea to a climax after which riders clamber off the machinery thinking: 'Phew – that was good!'

The nip-and-tuck of a close sporting duel builds pressure to its apex amid gasps and moans, and then resolves all the tension and uncertainty in a result. The horseracing commentary canters along, rises to a frantic crescendo as front-runners pass the post, and then tails off as they saunter into the winners' enclosure. The more extreme the activity the higher the curve, but the pattern is always the same.

Thrill-seekers

Thrill-seekers are generally *not* trying to kill themselves. The hang-glider's risk of death is in fact 1 in 560, compared with the 1 in 4 general risk of death from a heart attack. But having your canopy tumbled by alarming turbulence amid the elements you, the edge-technician, the danger-controller, may get a cerebral climax. Former world hang-gliding champion and world paragliding champion Judy Leden, after her 41,300-foot world record glider descent from beneath a hot air balloon over Jordan, described what she calls 'those incredible experiences, that are very much like a photograph – they're so clear in your mind':

All your senses are working at their absolute maximum and that's an incredible feeling ... There is a kind of calmness about it, but there's an extreme exhilaration knowing that you're firing on all cylinders, and you couldn't ever make better decisions than you are making right now, because you're thinking so clearly. It's as though the blinkers have been taken off.[3]

Mountaineers *dance* with mountains. Listen to climber Bernard Amy, writing in 1985 about his experiences in a fictionalized autobiography (the character Laurent is a composite of himself and other mountaineers):

In the very depths of the stilled happiness that possessed him, Laurent sensed an immense swaying. Immobile until that moment, the mountain and all its stone began to change. In the slow and measured movements which Laurent created, a new life of rock and void intermingled. On coming into contact with the stone, Laurent touched what there is of perfection within it: its serene endurance.[4]

Adventurers recall the Tibetan adage: 'Better to live one day as a tiger than a whole life as a sheep.' They quote Nietzsche's famous aphorism: 'What doesn't kill you makes you stronger.' My former business partner Rob Moss is a fairly typical example of the transferable skills and courage of the thrill-seeker, because his relish for high-pressure work situations has made him a very successful corporate and academic consultant. In his spare time Rob enjoys skiing and falling out of planes. I watched him freefall at North London Parachute Club, strapped to an instructor. The plane door flung open, an encouraging voice yelled: '*See* ya, wouldn't want to *be* ya!' and out he plunged. On the ground, or at work, he is the most well-balanced person I know. Rob is just one of hundreds of thousands of adventure-seekers who keep themselves in mental trim like this.

Going for those CCs may be done by anyone willing to freefall, sky-dive, fly, water-ski, leap or climb; it may be achieved by the surfer boring through the coil of a wave, or by the skier or speeding motorcyclist, senses forced against the wind, just on the knife-edge of control. You may come across it as you plummet 100 feet through an explosive 5.5 g-force or submit to cyclonic forces on a raging vortex ride or a vertical drop rollercoaster. You may see it loom up as you descend from one of your four BASE jumps (the acronym stands for Building, Antenna, Span and Earth), like this: 'The adrenalin has been and gone. I find that I am very calm and focused. Being on the edge that fraction of a second before you jump, there is a wonderful feeling of commitment, composure, and freedom. The edge is a great place to be – things on the edge make sense.'[5]

No wonder such 'adrenalin junkies', as they are ignorantly labelled, are shown by research to be more emotionally robust than the rest of us.[6] They know, with Ernest Hemingway, that 'place beyond fear' to which all adventurers are drawn, a place of catharsis, ego-release, timeless beauty and tranquillity.

Sport

You could experience a cerebral climax simply by watching sport, and for many fans, this is the high point of their lives. Unfortunately, although most spectator sports attain a result and therefore provide the all-important fusion or closure, a few do not. Some low-scoring games, like football and American ice-hockey, may simply produce a technical result or no result at all. Because of the excitement involved, these sports may build up a great deal of pressure and tension as the match progresses, but without ever resolving them. Fans on the edge of their seats are often left high and dry. These sports are associated with crowd violence.

For the *real* sporting CC, you have to participate. You need to pour your youth into honing your skills, stake your reputation on those skills, and pit yourself against your equals under the global spotlight. What keeps most international sports performers in the high pressure cooker of professional sport is ultimately not the prize-money or the adulation; it is the cerebral climax. Sport enables the competitor, by its very pressures, to transcend him or herself:

Every once in a while, a sportsman suddenly produces a glittering display which comes as a shock, not only to the spectators, but to himself ... If he consciously tries to reproduce it, he cannot. It comes and it goes, like a mystical experience, and each time it happens, the sportsman feels himself to be truly alive, truly exhilarated. There is an odd, even chilling feeling of having been possessed, of having dreamt the whole thing, of having been in another world.[7]

Tennis players talk of 'playing unconscious' or 'in the zone', of playing or being 'spacey', or producing 'no-brainers' – shots not of their making. There are similar ecstatic moments in all sports. In golf, you can *see* the shot you need to make: you simply pick up the club and reproduce it. This is called 'playing like God's professional' or 'playing out of your skin'. Some sportsmen find the experience alarming. They do not want to feel like a medium or conduit for higher things. They prefer to maintain control, whatever the blight on their potential.

At the other extreme there are athletes who take performance-enhancing drugs to try to boost their chances of winning. Arguably they miss the point of sport, which is really an interior contest. They certainly miss the out-of-body experience that comes with cerebral climaxing:

My thin shirt clung to me, and I felt like a skeleton flying down a wind tunnel. My times at the mile and two miles were so fast that I almost felt I was cheating, or had taken some unfair advantage. It was like getting a new body that no one else had heard about. My mind was so crystal clear I could have held a conversation.[8]

Scientists are working on sport's transcendent experiences but so far haven't solved the mystery. They think the cerebellum may be involved, and/or alpha brainwave rhythms.[9] But sporting CCs need to be seen in context with other cerebral climaxes, and some of these have nothing whatever to do with competitive exertions, or even moving about.

Extreme games, extreme television

The Japanese, connoisseurs of the cerebral climax in their martial arts, have long favoured extreme television entertainment – contests involving tarantulas down pants and teetering across snake pits. The Chinese, until very recently, enjoyed extreme games in their wildlife parks, with live prey animals being fed to lions and tigers to entertain the goggling multitudes. Spaniards favour the bullfight. The Ancient Romans would have liked all of the above, but especially relished their *ludi*: gladiatorial combat, animal bloodbaths and (less barbarous but equally stimulating) chariot-races. In the Colosseum their guinea pigs saluted the emperor: *Ave, Imperator, morituri te saluntant* ('Hail, Caesar, those who are about to die salute thee') before they fought and died. Exploration of extreme emotions – 'pressure' experiments if you like – have always played a part in public entertainment. Modern spectator sport is a version of this, with the deaths mostly airbrushed out.

With the proliferation of competitive channels, Western television is fast moving towards 'snuff movie' style viewing. In so-called 'reality' shows, contestants are put under emotional and physical duress whilst being monitored and questioned about their feelings. On the more ruthless talk shows, producers work up an audience and go for the 'money shot' when someone sobs or goes berserk on camera. Endurance shows – such as *Big Brother* house confinement, heat-of-the-kitchen training or jungle survival – feature contestants who must bear all (or bare all) or be voted off by the viewer. In 2000 there were only two such shows (*Castaway* on BBC1 and *Big Brother* on Channel 4). In 2003 there were thirteen, and in 2004 there were twenty-eight. The 'reality' genre appears to be taking over television. Sky One tastefully led the way with a ten-part series entitled *Shock Treatment*, in which contest-ants were confined in the former padded cells of a derelict Victorian mental asylum and subjected to realistic-seeming psychological tortures, including being forced to administer 'shocks' to a screaming man in an electric chair, and having nails surgically inserted in their noses.

Television quizzes are exquisitely designed to produce a graduated tension arc with climax, resolution and pay-off for the successful. They place contestants under the microscope as

Sex and frisson

Everyone recognizes the thrill of the chase; very few connect it with the brain's compulsion for cerebral climaxes. The word 'frisson' (although it can mean other things) is used for that inexplicable tension at the heart of forbidden relationships that has been a feature of illicit affairs down the centuries. Without that tension, sex can become staid, in need of 'spicing up' with unusual underwear, challenging rebuffs, fiery rows or secret trysts, because these are seen as increasing tension, desire and ultimate satisfaction.

The allure of the half-concealed is traditionally seen as more provocative and tantalizing to men than simple female nudity, and tension has always had a role in human sex appeal. Indeed, some of our most enduring symbols of allure have been jarringly imperfect to look at, creating a kind of visual frisson and fascination. Shakespeare complains in the Sonnets that when he sees his mistress, his heart and eye are at mortal war, and the Bard immortalizes the Lady's physical faults as well as his passionate desire for her. The expression *jolie laide*, famously used to describe the sex appeal of former French tennis star Suzanne Lenglen, means 'ugly yet compellingly attractive', holding the viewer in thrall. Cleopatra, according to contemporary accounts, was very far from beautiful, yet she was striking and fascinating enough to seduce a Caesar and generations of admirers. Such tension may also explain the magnetism of male sex icons, such as Dracula and the Phantom of the Opera, who despite being extremely ugly hold mesmerizing sexual power over womankind. How can we account for such mysteries, other than to see them as examples of the brain enjoying its frisson?

So tension, generally viewed as unhealthy in a stress management culture, is defiantly and definitely sexy. Even more intriguingly, the human penchant for sexual tension may be unique to us. Frisson is not, so far as we know, a normal feature of animal sexuality. Human beings are the only creatures on the planet that have apparently turned sexual concourse into an art form and cultivated its tensions with such sophistication. Other animals, it seems, simply use it for making little animals. Having sex is generally good for the heart, but having illicit sex, perhaps because it involves more excitement and tension, presents a greater risk of heart attack.[11] Indeed, anyone with pre-existing disease who goes in pursuit of the cerebral climax in any situation should really take medical advice.

Sex is one of the body's many systems that are peristaltic in nature: childbirth and digestion follow the same pattern, so do the lungs and the heart. 'Dilation, high tension, closure' make up the underlying natural rhythm of so much of human physiology. Arguably this is not because all these other systems imitate the reproductive system, but because they imitate the brain.

The arts

Consider the high point or best feature of your favourite work of art. We might say of it that its climax causes a fusion in the mind. It is the point at which a work of art makes total sense, or makes love to your imagination. It is a visceral experience: it can cause the tingle down the spine, the goose-bumps, the rush of blood. It takes the breath away. It may even have a cathartic effect, coalescing and releasing confused or pent-up emotions and moving you to tears. There has been a great deal of speculation among academics about how such catharsis works. When we witness such intense expression and resolution, emotions that have been 'dammed up' or held in check by denial and inhibition may simply break through at last, bringing relief. Perhaps the great work of art offers some long-awaited, final connection that enables the brain to fire and equalize magnetic tension through its synapses and circuits, and discharge that energy in some satisfying way. We do not know. But we all recognize, instinctively, how important it is.

A prime and ancient example of this 'arts effect' is in the theatre. Aristotle believed that the whole point of theatre and acting was the build-up of tension to the moment when the drama delivers its resolution, relief and 'catharsis'. He divided a play into four parts: *protasis* (the showing of the characters); *epistasis* (working up the plot and expectations); *catastasis* (the climax or height of the play), and *catastrophe* (or unravelling, in which everything is resolved and settled). We use 'tragedy' and 'catastrophe' now to mean any old disaster. Aristotle was much more specific. He thought that the dramatist must arouse two chief emotions in an audience: pity, to draw them towards the hero and the action, and fear, to repel them. These opposite emotions built the necessary tension in the theatre to produce a *catastasis* and a *catastrophe*. The audience then went away purged of their emotions, at peace with themselves and ennobled by the experience.

Geniuses who create our art are masters of high-tension crystallization, resolution and fusion, using expressions and artefacts that are packed and loaded with meaning, and that carry a charge. Our greatest arts professionals produce lots of what we might call 'diamonds of the mind' that are recognized as brilliant and beautiful. They scintillate with condensed emotional and intellectual power.

The circumstances necessary to make such important crystallizations may have to do with personal conflict needing to be resolved, or levels of stimulation which are unusual or acute, or an awareness of deep antitheses in reality. Often, though not always, these circumstances may be the same as those which cause pain, anguish, loneliness and despair. And since those who are renowned for their brilliance at making connections, fusions and crystallizations often come to be classified as 'geniuses', this may give us a glimmer of insight into the clichéd view of the genius as an unhappy, tortured, half-mad creature whose only repose is in his work.

The arts are predicated upon tension and resolution. Usually, as in fiction, ballet, opera, cinema and theatre, this is delivered through a storyline that builds to a climax. But even paintings and sculpture manifest its impact. Stand before a masterpiece like Van Gogh's *Sunflowers* or Rodin's *The Kiss* and what do you see? Concentration of powerful emotions invoked by consummate skill and locked together in tense harmony. Very often the resolution has cost the artist dear and this sacrifice is reflected in its power. Modern 'conceptual' art, with its encased animal parts, dung daubs and unmade beds, undoubtedly aims at this complex tension and resolution, crystallized to explode in the mind of the onlooker. Whether such art is successful, or simply empty and shocking, is a matter of angry debate.

Horror movies

You may not think of the horror movie as an art form. But to understand the tension and resolution so typical of the cerebral climax, study the horror movie: all of its patterns and devices are there.

Alfred Hitchcock was known as the 'master of suspense'. As a boy waiting for the strap from his Jesuit teachers, he discovered a formula relating tension, time and terror: 'There is no terror in the bang, only in the anticipation of it.' Hitchcock had little need for special effects and was certainly no gore-merchant. Instead his movies focus on unsettling the viewer and ratcheting up tension, shooting a key scene in *Rope* in what appears to be one continuous take. Hitchcock wanted to 'always make the audience suffer as much as possible'. The resolution, when it came, was then that much more satisfying. In fact he boasted how people thanked him for scaring the daylights out of them and one of his most famous anecdotes concerned a woman cinema-goer who came up and praised him for giving her 'a good cry'.

Another horror master, Tobe Hooper (*The Texas Chainsaw*

Massacre), observes that the genre is a marvellous inurement medium, 'to get the dream world out of your mind and experience fear in safeness'. An important part of this process is the build-up of pressure and tension in the movie-goer's head. According to horror director John Carpenter: 'In a horror movie you know something's going to happen. The question is, when? Is it going to happen now? That's the kind of tension that you want your audience to feel.'[12] Quentin Tarantino, publicizing *Reservoir Dogs*, warned his audiences that they would be trapped with his desperate characters in a warehouse to endure what they endured. Referring to that fulcrum of all good horror movies, he commented: 'We're gonna sell you this seat but you're only gonna use the edge of it.' Half of the frightened movie-goer wants to escape, while the other half wants to stay and see the resolution. The resulting tension can then be built to a climax that provides release and joy.

Those who believe horror movies turn fans into psychotic killers are, according to Wes Craven (*Nightmare on Elm Street*), quite wrong. For the great majority, the films have a salubrious effect: 'They come out like just chattering and laughing and slapping each other on the back ... enjoying themselves in some strange, wonderful, giddy way.' Mark Kermode, presenting an excellent documentary on horror for Channel 4, summed it all up: 'When I was a teenager I went to see slasher films *in order* to scream, and although precious few of them actually delivered the goods, the ones that did made me feel alive, exhilarated, even ecstatic. Now tell me – where's the harm in that?'[13]

Poetry and fiction

The Romans called the poet *vates* – diviner, prophet. In Chaucer's day he was a 'maker', a creator. Many poets claim not to have written their lines themselves, but to have acted as a conduit. Their brains produce brilliant crystallizations, and their work is written in short lines on the page, to signify that it is not like ordinary language but condensed, powerful and explosive. It fuses multiple meanings.

Ezra Pound used the German term for poetry – *Dichtung* (condensation) – to describe it. Dr Johnson said of the metaphysical poets, of whom he disapproved: 'the most heterogeneous ideas are yoked by violence together'.[14] Such dramatic fusion is a feature of all great poetry. In the classic treatise *On the Sublime*, written in the first century AD, the author theorizes that when we read such words, 'we are filled with a proud exaltation and a sense of vaunting joy'. The poet 'selects and fuses the most extreme and intense manifestations' of our emotions.[15] T. S. Eliot felt that a poet must extinguish his own personality. His brain was merely a crucible in which the following alchemy could take place:

The poet's mind is in fact a receptacle for seizing and storing up numberless feelings, phrases, images, which remain there until all the particles which can unite to form a new compound are present together ... For it is not the 'greatness', the intensity, of the emotions, the components, but the intensity of the artistic process, *the pressure, so to speak, under which the fusion takes place, that counts*. (My italics.)[16]

The poet-philosopher Samuel Taylor Coleridge devoted much of his literary life to exploring the creative process. According to Coleridge, the poet 'brings the whole soul of man into activity ... He diffuses a tone and spirit of unity that blends and (as it were) fuses, each into each, by that synthetic and magical power, to which we have exclusively appropriated the name imagination. This power ... reveals itself in the balance or reconciliation of opposite or discordant qualities.'[17]

All of the above are descriptions of the literary cerebral climax – the way in which it occurs, and the way in which it transmits to the reader. Great novelists use the same high-tension, fusing power for their audiences, but ultimately perhaps for themselves, seeking to mend their own minds by their art. Some fail. Virginia Woolf, whose long battle with mental illness ended in suicide, said that she was beset by 'a shock-receiving capacity' and that this was what made her a writer. When she suffered an emotional blow, she had to write about it in order to connect up and crystallize the experience:

It is only by putting it into words that I make it whole; this wholeness means that it has lost its power to hurt me; it gives me, perhaps because by doing so I take away the pain, a great delight to put the severed parts together. Perhaps this is the strongest pleasure known to me. It is the rapture that I get when in writing I seem to be discovering what belongs to what; making a scene come right; making a character come together. From this I reach what I might call a philosophy; at any rate it is a constant idea of mine; that behind the cotton wool is hidden a pattern; that we – I mean all human beings – are connected with this; that the whole world is a work of art; that we are parts of the work of art.[18]

Because writers undertake to explore extreme emotions, they often find themselves narrating their characters' crises and torments, and they take their readers through these as well, in order to achieve a resolution. Here is Kafka, in one of his most unsettling stories, describing the plight of a prisoner subjected to torture under the harrow:

But how quiet the man grows at the sixth hour. Enlightenment comes to the most dull-witted. It begins around the eyes. From there it radiates. A moment that might tempt one to get under the harrow with him.[19]

Near death experiences are renowned for producing moments of epiphany, and they are apparently becoming increasingly common. They are estimated to occur in about 45 per cent of adults and up to 85 per cent of children who have had life-threatening illnesses.[20] Kafka may not have known this, but his genius told him that in extreme emotional situations the brain of an ordinary man may suddenly convulse its powers and produce something rapturous, just as great writers do.

Perhaps the most famous example of this kind of fictional epiphany comes from a very great writer indeed – Charles Dickens. In *A Christmas Carol* his hardened miser Scrooge is subjected to disturbing hauntings and visions, one of them particularly harrowing because it concerns his own death. Scrooge is converted by all this terror into a joyous fellow who feels the need to celebrate Christmas, give his money away and stand on his head.

We need to be reminded here that according to stress management theory, extreme emotions are to be avoided, either because they are a source of 'stress', or because they *are* 'stress', and therefore harmful to health. Such censorship of emotional life makes nonsense of great literature and art, which set out to *produce* powerful emotions. Stress management may not only deter people from freely experiencing great literature. It may prevent them from fully appreciating the benefits of high-tension resolutions in art, and in themselves, and this is dangerous to their happiness.

Crises out of drama

What effect has the stress ideology had on the acting profession? Nerves are a besetting problem for actors, particularly stage actors who fear that they may forget their lines during a performance, and some have avoided the ordeal by abandoning their craft. Because stress management theory presents nervousness as something to be feared and avoided, we can only suppose that it increases anxiety among these sensitive and vulnerable actors about their ability to withstand all the emotional exigencies of the job. In the spring of 2000, a stress audit was mailed out to Britain's actors by *The Stage* and the British Performing Arts Medical Trust in association with BUPA. Called the Entertainment Industry Health Questionnaire, it stated: 'Life as a performing artist is undoubtedly stressful, both physically and mentally. Undue stress impairs performance and may lead to mental and physical illnesses.' This is frightening stuff. Yet fear and stage fright have traditionally been viewed as a needful part of the acting process. As David Lean famously put it: 'Only the jerks are confident.' So why should a medical authority like the BPAMT be telling actors to beware of the dangers of stage fright, when previously great actors have used it to advantage?

Sir Laurence Olivier, as we have seen, refused to take tranquillizers and channelled his terror into his work. Dame Judi Dench wrote to me, saying: 'I was interested to read about your articles on "stress", which I think is a much over-used word and often attributed to circumstances which are more exhilarating than stress-inducing. Many actors suffer from "First Night Nerves", but this can very often give an "edge" to their performance.'[21] The mesmerizing Harvey Keitel, a former US Marine who served in the Lebanon, knows the value of fear: 'When I work with the right people, we have such a wonderful experience together, descending into what we're scared of.'[22] The great Meryl Streep exorcizes her own demons during her performances: 'Acting is what keeps me sane . . . I can put all my neuroses to good use. Acting has saved a lot of money on therapy.'[23]

Yet, since the advent of stress management, this more robust view of stage fright has apparently given way to more angst. Indeed, there has been a spate of incidents in which British actors have suddenly left the stage, fearing for their mental and physical health. John Alderton and his wife Hannah Gordon both withdrew from a West End production of *On Approval* in 1994 because of nervous exhaustion and stress. Alderton said: 'I don't think I have ever suffered stress like that,' adding that he had consulted his doctor about the matter. 'He told me, "You haven't had a heart attack but you are in a terrible state". He said my breathing was wrong and I would have to stop what I was doing immediately or I really would have a coronary. I had a constant feeling I was in a nightmare. My doctor put me to sleep with pills that knocked me out for three or four days. I really needed it.'[24] Alderton was actually asleep when the play opened with Jeremy Sinden and Kate O'Mara in the leading roles.

Stephen Fry walked out of another West End play, *Cell Mates* in 1995 and fled to Belgium, saying: 'I can only offer cowardice, embarrassment and distress as excuses for such absurd behaviour ... After realizing how inadequate my performance in *Cell Mates* was, I'm afraid I suffered a dreadful attack of what golfers call the yips and actors call stage fright and I slunk away rather than cause a scene in public. Basically, I couldn't stand the heat, so I escaped from the kitchen.'[25] He complained that the producer 'does not accept medical reports which made it quite clear that I was not a well person', and despite describing his own condition as nothing more than 'stage fright' has since undergone psychotherapy in the US.

John Sessions made a brief but unscheduled stop at the Criterion Theatre during *My Night with Reg* after forgetting a line. He explained: 'I was just like a rabbit in the headlights ... A lot of stuff was churning around in my head.'[26] Daniel Day-Lewis, brilliant actor son of the poet laureate Cecil, fled the stage during a National Theatre performance of *Hamlet*, having been troubled by childhood visions. He was sent to a psychiatrist, who diagnosed 'stress syndrome'.[27]

Perhaps efforts to warn actors of the 'dangers' of stage fright have undermined their resilience and set them worrying unduly about the emotional demands of an acting career. At all events, it is very difficult to see how a stress phobic actor, if any such there be, could possibly fulfil his or her true potential.

'Transformation' acting

Actors, whether they work in the medium of theatre or cinema, clearly have a stake in highly charged drama. They are psychological frontiersmen. Their job is to inhabit different identities in order to work through an emotional journey. The hugely influential

Polish director and theatre guru Jerzy Grotowski devised training techniques to break the actor out of his shell. He believed that actors needed to be: 'searching for the things which can hurt us most deeply, but which at the same time give us a total feeling of purifying truth that finally brings peace'.

One must give oneself totally, in one's deepest intimacy, with confidence, as when one gives oneself in love. Here lies the key. Self-penetration, trance, excess, the formal discipline itself – all this can be realized, provided one has given oneself fully, humbly and without defence. This act culminates in a climax. It brings relief.[28]

Constantin Stanislavski likewise trained actors to transform themselves. His influence has been pivotal and gave rise indirectly to 'Method' acting. According to Stanislavski, the actor must discipline his mind and body to produce: 'Something that lifts the spectator off the ground ... There is no room here for reasoning and analysing – there can be no doubt about the fact that this unexpected something has surged up from the well springs of organic nature. The actor himself is overwhelmed and enthralled by it.' This 'event of a lifetime' does not come cheap:

Our art seeks to achieve this very result and requires that an actor experience the agony of his role, and weep his heart out at home or in rehearsals, that he then calm himself, get rid of every sentiment alien or obstructive to his part. He then comes out on the stage to convey to the audience in clear, pregnant, deeply felt, intelligible and eloquent terms what he has been through.[29]

The schools of acting popularized by Stanislavski in Moscow, and later by Richard Boleslavsky in New York, by Lee Strasberg in the Actors' Studio and by Jerzy Grotowski in the Poor Theatre, have been hugely influential in international stage and film work, and have produced actors of outstanding merit who engage with their characters at a very intimate level. The degree of emotional engagement these schools demand from an actor is exacting and even punishing, and any actor unwilling to undergo this process should perhaps have chosen a less emotionally demanding profession.

Audiences are left to consider whether they like watching actors who are trained to take them on an emotional roller-coaster ride, or whether they prefer the more technical theatre of Bertolt Brecht, who mistrusted the power of performers (such as Hitler, whom he had seen) to stir up an audience, and who deliberately sought to detach theatre-goers from the action on stage by means of what he called 'alienation effects'. But the former, it is suggested, would be more in keeping with the principles of Aristotle's cathartic theatre, and more likely to give you a cerebral climax.

Gratifying your grey matter – the Mozart effect

However, perhaps the art form most associated with mood manipulation is music. From blues to brass bands, from Vera Lynn to Wagner, music has sustained human beings through some of their darkest hours. Even in Auschwitz it provided a shaft of light.

One of the things that music can undoubtedly do is to soothe the savage breast. Classic FM, the UK's largest independent radio station, has done much to popularize classical music – for which huge praise – but as a form of stress management. It presents Bach, Brahms and Beethoven as 'Smooth Classics', and as a means of 'chilling out'. Bach and Brahms would have been startled to hear their mighty works characterized in this fashion. Beethoven, whose ferocious temper was impartially unleashed on prince and pauper alike, and who shook his fist at a thunderstorm on his deathbed, may well have firebombed the building.

The truth is that classical music has been composed by geniuses over hundreds of years to invoke the cerebral climax. In so doing it may include tranquil passages and movements. It may even make you cry and sob (opera is notorious). But its complex notations are a formula, exquisitely developed, for producing tension and pressure in sounds and sequences, climbing, falling back and then climbing ever higher – to one cerebral climax after another. Listeners can both hear them and feel them. In a concert hall the end result is almost palpable. The hushed audience suddenly breaks into deafening applause. Staid citizens stamp, laugh, weep and generally behave strangely.

Classical music doesn't care what century it is, or what country it is in. Outstanding performers may hail from Japan or Jerusalem, Birmingham or Berlin. The music can produce its effects across wide cultural and linguistic divides because it speaks directly to the brain. In fact there is now scientific evidence: classical music is good for you. The work of Frances H. Rauscher and colleagues at the University of California-Irvine, who published their initial findings in the journal *Nature* in 1993, showed that the brain functioning of college students altered and that their ability to perform paper-and-pencil spatial-temporal tasks improved after listening for ten minutes to Mozart's Sonata for Two Pianos in D Major, K448. The Mozart group performed significantly better than either the control group or those who listened to a relaxation tape. [30]

Other experiments have shown that Mozart can help spatial reasoning and route-finding in a series of computer-simulated rooms, suggesting more practical applications,[31] and that listening to Mozart and Bach can improve the spatial learning of school-children.[32] In fact, scientific research on 'the Mozart Effect' and the benefits of classical music has spawned an industry. Florida Senate Bill 660 requires that early child-care centres receive state funds to expose toddlers to classical music. In Georgia, State Governor Zel Miller teamed up with Sony Classical to offer a free classics CD to every mother.

The effects of music on the cardiovascular reactivity of surgeons, on the emotional equilibrium of soldiers, on the learning abilities of schoolchildren, on epilepsy, Parkinson's disease, autism and coma have excited scientists all over the world. In six London primary schools, daily doses of Verdi's *Requiem* and other classical pieces toned up the concentration, intelligence and behaviour of 2,000 pupils and improved their grasp of maths, English and science.[33] Short bursts of Mozart have been found to decrease epileptic fits: Professor John Jenkins of the University of London, a member of the Royal College of Physicians, says: 'Listening to Mozart could just hold some hope in the treatment of epilepsy.'[34]

Professor Susan Hallam, of the Institute of Education, University of London, has carried out experiments to show that Albinoni improves concentration and behaviour in schoolchildren, whereas modern jazz does not.[35] Professor Hallam, who is one of the world's leading experts on the psychology of music, says the classics can alter the mood of even recalcitrant schoolchildren: 'There has been some work carried out in Wales with children of difficult behaviour. Mozart was played to them and it lowered their temperature, heart-rate, pulse and breathing rate.'[36] These and other remarkable effects may only be the tip of the iceberg. The great composers may actually *compose* your braincells, literally.

For those unfamiliar with classical music, here is a 'starter pack'. It is not necessary to understand the niceties of musical notation – the climbs and climaxes announce themselves. I have generally listed whole pieces as the composer intended you to hear them that way, but where sharply defined cerebral climaxes appear in particular movements I have indicated these as well. It may take a bit of practice before your brain begins to tune in and respond, but once it does you will know at least one way of giving your brain the climaxes it deserves.

CLASSICAL CLIMAXES – STARTER PACK
Bach: Toccata and Fugue in D Minor
Beethoven: practically everything (try the *Egmont* Overture,
    Choral Symphony Finale, or the fourth Symphony,
    especially the 4th movement)

Brahms: Piano Concerto No. 1 (especially the Finale)
Bruch: Violin Concerto in G Minor (especially the Finale)
Dukas: *The Sorcerer's Apprentice*
Elgar: *Enigma Variations* (especially Nimrod)
Grieg: Hall of the Mountain King
Haydn: *The Creation*
Handel: *The Messiah* (especially the Alleluia chorus)
Holst: *The Planets Suite* (especially Mars)
Khachaturian: *Spartacus*, Adagio
Mendelssohn: Violin Concerto
Mozart: Mass in C Minor, K427 Kyrie
Mozart: Symphonie Concertante, K364 (especially the first movement)
Mozart: Overture to *The Marriage of Figaro*
Orff: O Fortuna, from *Carmina Burana*
Prokofiev: Classical Symphony
Rachmaninov: 2nd Piano Concerto
Ravel: Bolero
Richard Strauss: *Also Sprach Zarathustra*
Rodrigo: Guitar Concerto (especially 2nd movement)
Rossini: Overtures, *The Barber of Seville*, *The Thieving Magpie*
Saint-Saëns: Organ Symphony No. 3 in C Minor (especially the Finale)
Shostakovich: Piano Concerto Number 2
Sibelius: 5th Symphony
Tchaikovsky: Piano Concerto No. 1 in B-flat minor (especially the Finale)
Tchaikovsky: Rose Adagio, *Sleeping Beauty*
Tchaikovsky: *Swan Lake*, Finale
Tchaikovsky: *Pathetique* Symphony (3rd movement)
Tchaikovsky: 1812 Overture
Vaughan Williams: *The Lark Ascending*
Wagner: *Tannhäuser* Overture
Wagner: *Tristan und Isolde*, Liebestod

Arts medicine

There are now international congresses on the benefits of the arts to mankind, from psychodrama in prisons to poetry therapy for autistic children. In an age so dominated by the sciences, the arts are beginning to re-emerge as needful to human health and sanity. Student nurses at Brisbane's Griffith University are now required to read classic novels to give them more insight into the emotions of their patients. Tyneside Metro found that playing music by Delius and other classical composers on their stations prevented vandalism. In January 1998 the then culture secretary Chris Smith commended a ballet performance programme that had transformed the lives of boys on a run-down Bristol estate.

Arts Medicine, as it is called, is increasingly seen as a valuable therapy. There are now liberal arts health promotion courses and medical papers written 'on the role of the arts in physician stress management'.[37] In Britain in 2004 the mental health charity SANE lent its support to an innovative programme called Mad for Arts, aimed at increasing the arts involvement of people with mental health problems. In America, the work of pioneers like Dr Richard Lippin, president of the International Arts Medicine Association and corporate medical director of ARCO Chemical Company, have influenced many occupational health programmes. Dr Lippin challenges what he calls 'the relaxation gurus' of stress management. His work promotes 'responsible pleasures' such as laughter, crying, hitting and kicking exercises, sexuality and the arts as a means of providing 'the active and healthy resolution of the stimulus arousal curve'. Such pursuits he sees as 'releasing' or 'venting' stress.[38]

The arts and sciences are two halves of a whole, like the right and left hemispheres of the brain. They should complement each other to form a unified vision. In Britain, while generous funds and lottery money have been pumped into science and technology, the arts have been steadily starved of cash. Outgoing chairman of the Arts Council, Lord Gowrie, denounced this execrable neglect in 1998, saying: 'The funded arts are in their worst revenue crisis of my adult lifetime.'[39]

Without the arts, a society can have no integrity. It becomes unbalanced, unhealthy, brutal and mechanized. In cerebral terms, it lurches towards the left. 'Stress management' is in many ways the technical, left-brain theory of how to manage emotions and keep them under control. But emotions make up the richness of human experience, and they need to be understood, not lobotomized. A society becomes emotionally educated in various ways, but chiefly through the arts, which are specifically designed to facilitate this process. If we steep ourselves in the arts we shall have little need of stress management – and better even than that, a 'great Prince' will get out of jail.

In looking back over the alternatives suggested in this last section – inurement training, adventure activities and challenges, and the arts – it is important to understand that these pursuits are not being recommended as ways of 'managing stress'. Nor do they represent a 'quick fix' cure for emotional suffering, which is endemic to the human condition. What these pursuits do offer is a way of achieving emotional education and strength of character: a means of gradually discovering hidden resources and coping skills, and making sense of our experiences. Such activities provide not just relaxation – the mantra of stress management – but resolution, which is infinitely more satisfying.

The case presented in this book has sometimes been referred to in the media as my new theory about stress. But character training and emotional education are not some theory of mine, and they are certainly not new. They enabled our ancestors to survive privations and torments that we would find it hard to imagine, let alone bear. Such traditional strategies and activities are time-honoured. Stress management, on the other hand, is not. In fact if there is a new hypothesis, it is the theory of stress

APPENDIX
Definitions of 'Stress'

Longer definitions

1. 'Stress is essentially the rate of wear and tear on the body.' Hans Selye, *The Stress of Life*, McGraw-Hill, 1956/1976, p. 1.
2. 'In any event, wear and tear is only the result of all this; hence now we define stress as the non-specific response of the body to any demand.' Hans Selye, *The Stress of Life*, McGraw-Hill, 1956/1976, p. 55.
3. 'Stress is the state manifested by a specific syndrome which consists of all the nonspecifically-induced changes within a biological system.' Hans Selye, *The Stress of Life*, McGraw-Hill, 1956/1976, p. 64.
4. Stress should be seen as 'resulting from a misfit between individuals and their particular environment'. British Medical Association, *Stress and the Medical Profession*, p. 7.
5. 'I define stress as a preoccupation with emotional upsets.' Derek Roger, Director of the Work Skills Centre and Senior Lecturer in Psychology, University of York, on BBC Radio 4's *Patient Progress*, October 2000.
6. 'Stress is the natural reaction people have to excessive pressures or other types of demand placed on them.' HSE website, 1 November 2000.
7. 'The adverse reaction people have to excessive pressure or other types of demand placed upon them.' HSE website, in 2003.
8. 'Stress is people's natural reaction to excessive pressure – it isn't a disease.' HSE, *A Short Guide*, website on 18 April 2001.

9. 'Stress is the reaction people have to excessive pressures or other types of demand placed upon them. It arises when they worry that they can't cope.' HSE, *Stress at Work: a Guide for Employers*, HSE Books, 1995.

10. 'Stress is people's natural reaction to excessive pressure – it isn't a disease … But when demands and pressures become excessive, they lead to stress. And it's clear from the recognised symptoms of stress that it's actually bad for you.' HSE, *Help on Work-Related Stress, A Short Guide*, August 1998.

11. 'It can involve both physical and behavioural effects but these are usually short-lived and cause no lasting harm. When the pressures recede, there is a quick return to normal … Stress is not therefore the same as ill-health. But in some cases, particularly where pressures are intense and continue for some time, the effect of stress can be more sustained and far more damaging, leading to longer-term psychological problems and ill-health.' HSE, *Stress at Work*, 1995.

12. 'In particular there is the notion that stress entails a sequence of events that include the presence of demand, a set of evaluative processes through which that demand is perceived as significant (in terms of threat, and in terms of its impact on individual resources or requiring of the individual something other than normal functioning), and the generation of a response that typically affects the well-being of the individual.' HSE, *A 'management standards' approach to tackling work related stress – Part I, Rationale and Scientific Underpinning*, 2004.

13. 'Stress is probably best conceived as a state of the total organism under extenuating circumstances.' M. H. Appley and R. Trumbull. 'On the concept of psychological stress,' in M. H. Appley and R. Trumbull (eds), *Psychological stress: Issues in research*, New York: Appleton-Century-Crofts, 1987, p. 11.

14. Work-related stress: 'the emotional, cognitive, behavioural and physiological reaction to aversive and noxious aspects

of work, work environments and work organizations. It is a state characterized by high levels of arousal and distress, and often by feelings of not coping.' European Commission, Directorate-General for Employment and Social Affairs, *Guidance on work-related stress: Spice of Life – or Kiss of Death*, 1997.

15. 'Unfortunately to answer the question "what is stress", let alone work-related stress, is difficult. This is because the same stressor may act differently on different people. Therefore, no single definition of the term "stress" can be offered. Academic and professional texts tend to focus their discussion – and definitions – within the "school" of psychology they follow.' D. A. Grayham, *Journal of the Royal Society of Health*, April 1997, vol. 117, no. 2.

16. 'We are in the midst of an epidemic of stress that is causing illness and even death, but few agree about how to define stress.' C. L. Sheridan and S. A. Radmacher, *Health Psychology: Challenging the Biomedical Model*, Chichester: John Wiley, 1992, p. 148.

17. 'What happens is that each individual constructs his own reality of stress. Adopting this phenomenological approach, the person who feels stress is under stress and will show signs or symptoms of stress.' D. A. Grayham, quoting p. Berger and T. Luckmann, *Social Construction of Reality: Treatise in the Sociology of Knowledge*, Harmondsworth: Penguin, 1991.

18. 'Stress isn't rocket science.' Professor Tom Cox, Director, Centre for Organizational Health and Development, Nottingham University, IBC Conference paper, London, 30 April 1998.

19. 'Stress, it is argued, can only be sensibly defined as a perceptual phenomenon arising from a comparison between the demand on the person and his or her ability to cope. An imbalance in this mechanism, when coping is important, gives rise to the experience of stress, and to the stress response.' T. Cox, *Stress*, Basingstoke: Macmillan Education, 1978.

20. 'Workplace stress is explained in line with a transactional model of stress emphasizing the dynamic properties of the concept as well as the role of subjective processes such as appraisal and coping.' Cary L. Cooper, Helge Hoel and Kate Sparks, *The Cost of Violence/Stress at Work and the Benefits of a Violence/Stress-Free Working Environment*, Report commissioned by the International Labour Organization (ILO) Geneva, ILO website, 2001.

21. 'Job stress can be defined as the harmful physical and emotional responses that occur when the requirements of the job do not match the capabilities, resources, or needs of the worker.' *Stress at Work*, United States National Institute of Occupational Safety and Health, Cincinnati, 1999.

22. 'There is increasing consensus around defining work-related stress in terms of the "interactions" between employee and (exposures to hazards in) their work environment. Within this model stress can be said to be experienced when the demands from the work environment exceed the employees' ability to cope with (or control) them. Defining stress in this way focuses attention on the work-related causes and the control measures required.' T. Cox *et al.*, *Research on Work-Related Stress: Summary of Agency Report*, European Agency for Safety and Health at Work, 2000.

23. 'The 20th Century Epidemic.' 1992 United Nations Report.

24. 'I'm right in the middle of a study at the moment: we're literally stopping people on the streets of London and actually asking them what they think stress is. And they're answering a questionnaire about how they get stressed and how they don't get stressed, and how they deal with stress. And when it comes to asking them what they think stress is, or how they recognize it in themselves, they have far more difficulty dealing with this. So it's a very global concept that people have been applying to many situations, but when you actually ask them what it actually means to them, they're not so clear.' Stephen Palmer,

Centre for Stress Management, BBC Radio 4, *Patient Progress: Stressed Out*, 2000.

25. 'Stress is the psychological, physiological and behavioural response by an individual when they perceive a lack of equilibrium between the demands placed upon them and their ability to meet those demands, which, over a period of time, leads to ill-health.' Stephen Palmer, Occupational Stress, *The Health and Safety Practitioner*, 7 (8), pp.16–18.

26. 'Stress occurs when pressure exceeds your perceived ability to cope.' Cary Cooper and Stephen Palmer, *Conquer Your Stress*, Institute of Personnel and Development, 2000, p. 5.

27. 'When pressure exceeds your ability to cope with it, then you're in the stress arena.' Cary Cooper, *The Science of Stress*, Equinox, Channel 4, 2000.

28. 'Excess of perceived demands over perceived abilities.' J. M. Atkinson.

29. 'The word "stress" has acquired a vague, catch-all meaning, used by different people to mean different things. It is used to describe both physical and mental conditions, and the pressures which cause those conditions. It is also used to describe stress which is beneficial and harmful both in its sources and its effects.' Health Education Authority, *Stress in the Public Sector – Nurses, Police, Social Workers and Teachers*, 1988.

30. 'Stress is a process that can occur when there is an unresolved mismatch between the perceived pressures of the work situation and an individual's ability to cope.' Report of the Education Service Advisory Committee of the Health and Safety Commission, *Managing Occupational Stress: A Guide for Managers and Teachers in the Schools Sector*, 1990.

31. 'When the demands and pressures placed on individual workers do not match the resources available, or do not meet the individual's needs and motivations, stress can occur and endanger that person's health and well-being. In the

short-term, stress can be debilitating; in the long-term, stress can kill.' The London Hazard Centre, *Hard Labour: Stress, Ill-Health and Hazardous Employment Practices*, 1994.

32. 'Stress per se is not an actionable injury. The first hurdle a claimant must surmount in a stress at work claim is to establish that they are suffering from a positive psychiatric illness, not merely grief, stress or any other normal emotion ... The distinction between what constitutes mere mental stress and symptoms that amount to a recognizable psychiatric illness is not always clear or well defined.' Dr Martin Baggaley, Consultant Psychiatrist and Honorary Senior Lecturer, *Stress-Related Psychological Illness: medical aspects and causation*, Berrymans Lace Mawer Occupational Disease Series, 2003.

33. 'Stress occurs where demands made on individuals do not match the resources available or meet the individual's needs and motivation ... Stress will be the result if the workload is too large for the number of workers and the time available. Equally, a boring and repetitive task which does not use the potential skills and experience of some individuals will cause them stress.' TUC, in International Stress Management Association, *Stress News*, October 2000, vol. 12, no. 4.

34. 'Many individuals are confused as they believe that pressure and stress are one and the same. They are not. Stress will result from an inappropriate level of pressure, whether real or perceived ... In reality stress can and will affect each and every one of us both directly and indirectly.' Caroline Raymond, 'Stress – The Real Millenium [*sic*] Bug', *Stress News*, October 2000, vol. 12, no. 4.

35. 'Stress is a collective bargaining issue.' *TUC Newsletter*, 9 February 2002.

36. 'Stress is an unavoidable consequence of life. Without stress, there would be no life. However, just as distress can cause disease, there are good stresses that offset this, and promote wellness. Increased stress results in increased productivity – up

to a point. However, this level differs for each of us.' The American Institute of Stress, *Stress – America's Number One Health Problem*, Symbiosisonline.com, 2003.

37. 'Hans Selye discovered stress in 1935 as a syndrome occurring in laboratory rats ... His findings were rejected by physiologists until the 1970s.' Russell Viner, University of London, An International Review of Research in the Social Dimensions of Science and Technology, *Social Studies of Science Journal*, vol. 29, issue 3, June 1999.

38. 'When Dr Selye was asked to present a paper in France, it was found that there was no word in French for stress, so they coined one: Le Stress. Similarly, when asked to speak in Germany, there was no German word for stress, so it was named *Der Stress*. He is therefore, without doubt, the founder of the concept of stress.' Dr Hans Selye, *The Stress Doctor*, Foreword, reprinted on <http://www/sstressdoctor.com>, Dr Brian J. Gorman, 2003.

39. 'It's a real problem, difficult to define. It's a hypothetical construct.' Rosemary Anderson, Chair, International Stress Management Association, July 2003.

40. 'No, look – some people spend their lives trying to stop people using split infinitives. We call this stress because that's what people know it as. No one is getting compensation for that. What people are getting compensation for is real illness and it doesn't help those people to tell them they haven't got it just because they haven't got the name right.' Owen Tudor, TUC Senior Health and Safety Officer, Radio Five Live, *Drive Time*, February 2002.

41. 'The sum of the biological reactions to any adverse stimulus, physical, mental, or emotional, internal or external, that tends to disturb the organism's homeostasis. Should these compensating reactions be inadequate or inappropriate, they may lead to disorders. The term is also used to refer to the stimuli that elicit the reactions.' HeSH classification (Medical

Subject Headings, a hierarchical structure of medical concepts from the National Library of Medicine), June 1999.

42. 'Stress arises when individuals perceive that they cannot adequately cope with the demands being made on them or with threats to their well-being.' R. S. Lazarus, *Psychological Stress and the Coping Process*, New York: McGraw-Hill, 1966.

43. 'Stress occurs when a human experiences any threat either to his or her physical integrity or mental well-being.' Professor Stafford Lightman, endocrinologist, Bristol University, *The Science of Stress*, Equinox, Channel 4, 2000.

44. 'We've been involved in an intensive programme to design a pill which can counter the effects of stress. And the way to do this is to block the first chemical made by the hypothalamus in the brain which actually controls the whole of the stress response ... So if we can do this the whole part of the cascade starting in the hypothalamus which causes you to respond to stress by producing cortisole for instance can be blocked right at the central level in the brain.' Professor Stafford Lightman, *The Science of Stress*, Equinox, Channel 4, 2000.

45. 'The chemistry of the brain is very similar in patients who are depressed and patients who have chronic stress.' Professor Stafford Lightman, BBC Radio 4, *Patient Progress: Stressed Out*, 2000.

46. 'The stress response is perfectly normal. It's a physiological response that is there to adapt us to a challenge in our environment. You need to have stress hormones in order to survive the challenges of the world.' Jonothan Settle, endocrinologist, BBC Radio 4, *Patient Progress: Stressed Out*, 2000.

47. 'I think we're very poor at defining it and there's a very interesting story here, that the man who did much of the original research in stress, Hans Selye, was in fact a non-English speaker. And his idea was to make a parallel between the effects of human stress and stress in engineering terms ... And his idea was to apply this to mammalian systems where

the "stress" was the external event, while "strain" was the way that the body responded. But because of his poor English he mixed up the words "stress" and "strain", and so as a result of this we've got a rather poor idea of understanding stress.' David Phillips, epidemiologist, BBC Radio 4, *Patient Progress: Stressed Out*, 2000.

48. 'Everyone uses the word stress in a different way. I use it to mean the activation of one of the two main stress response systems of the body.' Professor Vivette Glover, perinatal psychobiologist, Imperial College, London, *The Science of Stress*, Equinox, Channel 4, 2000.

49. 'Stress is an internal experience, an emotional or physical threat to the survival of the organism.' Professor Carolyn M. Mazure, psychiatrist, Yale School of Medicine, *The Science of Stress*, Equinox, Channel 4, 2000.

50. 'When an animal or a person is exposed to a change in the environment that requires work in order to get back to their usual function, that is in fact stress.' Professor Charles Nemeroff, psychiatrist, Emery University, Atlanta. *The Science of Stress*, Equinox, Channel 4, 2000.

51. 'Stress results from an imbalance between demands and resources.' R. S. Lazarus and S. Folkman, *Stress, Appraisal and Coping*, New York: Springer, 1984.

52. 'In the present context, "stress" refers to any natural or experimentally contrived circumstances that (intuitively, at least) pose an actual or perceived threat to the psychobiological unity of the individual.' R. Ader, and N. Cohen (1993), 'Psychoneuroimmunology: Conditioning and stress', *Annual Review of Psychology*, 44, pp. 53–85.

53. 'In lay terms, stress is used on a daily basis to mean almost anything. Everyone will have their own understanding of the word, but it becomes very confusing and very difficult to understand what a person means when they say that they are stressed or something is stressful. General consensus is that

stress is something we suffer from, but what it is exactly remains very unclear.' Dr Jo Rick *et al*. 'Stress: Big issue, but what are the problems?' *IES Report* 331, Summary, 1997.

54. 'For all its apparent relevance to everyday life, stress is a concept beleaguered by problems of definition. It is very much an umbrella term which covers a wide range of very different aspects of work and life.' Dr Jo Rick *et al*. Ibid.

55. 'We find stress a difficult subject to talk about because there are probably as many definitions of it as there are psychologists.' Frank Davies, in his capacity as Chairman of the Health and Safety Commission, *HSC Newsletter* 114, August 1997.

56. 'Occupational stress results from negative harmful stress or distress.' Australian National Occupational Health Commission, ANOHSC website, Hazards and Solutions, July 1998.

57. 'Stress is the misfit between a worker's needs and capabilities and what the workplace offers and demands.' State of Victoria OHS (Occupational Health and Safety) Reps website, 'Stress at work', July 2003.

58. 'Stress is any change we have to adjust to.' Simma Lieberman, Simmer Lieberman Associates website, 'What is stress?' 24 June 2004.

59. 'Stress is a physical or mental challenge.' Dr Eric Brunner, University of London on *The Money Programme, Burnt Out Britain*, BBC2, February 2004.

60. 'A bucket of fog.' The Nerve Centre, May 2005.

Shorter definitions

The following is a list of states and conditions, internal and external, to which the term 'stress' has been applied in the research literature, in the media, in audits, interviews, workshops and elsewhere. (The list is by no means all-inclusive.)

INTERNAL

1. abjectness
2. affront
3. aggravation
4. agitation
5. agony
6. alienation
7. ambitious drives
8. ambivalence
9. anger
10. angst
11. anguish
12. animosity
13. apprehension
14. 'attitude'
15. avoidance
16. bad dreams
17. being highly strung
18. being nagged
19. being upset
20. bereavement
21. bile
22. bitterness
23. boredom
24. burnout
25. butterflies
26. chagrin
27. chip on the shoulder
28. compensation consciousness
29. cowardice
30. dauntedness
31. defeatism
32. degradation
33. dejection
34. demoralization
35. depression
36. desire for recognition
37. desire for revenge
38. desolation
39. despair
40. desperation
41. despondence
42. disappointment
43. discomfort
44. discomposure
45. discontent
46. disgrace
47. disgust
48. dishonour
49. disillusionment
50. dislike of colleagues
51. dislike of job
52. dismay
53. disquiet
54. dissatisfaction
55. distraction
56. distress
57. dolour
58. doubtfulness
59. dread
60. edginess
61. embarrassment
62. emotional immaturity
63. emotional pain
64. emptiness
65. enmity

66. envy
67. exasperation
68. exhaustion
69. faint-heartedness
70. fatigue
71. fear of action
72. fear of ageing
73. fear of death
74. fear of failure
75. fear of future
76. fear of illness
77. fear of loss
78. fear of madness
79. fear of physiological changes
80. fear of physiological mechanisms
81. fear of rejection
82. fear of 'stress'
83. fear of unemployment
84. feeling abandoned
85. feeling appalled
86. feeling brow-beaten
87. feeling crestfallen
88. feeling cut up
89. feeling demeaned
90. feeling disheartened
91. feeling disrespected
92. feeling downtrodden
93. feeling driven
94. feeling frantic
95. feeling hell-bent
96. feeling ill-used
97. feeling insulted
98. feeling neglected
99. feeling nerve-racked
100. feeling overwhelmed
101. feeling overwrought
102. feeling paralysed
103. feeling petrified
104. feeling rattled
105. feeling scorned
106. feeling sickened
107. feeling stricken
108. feeling stunned
109. feeling suicidal
110. feeling tainted
111. feeling threatened
112. feeling thwarted
113. feeling trigger-happy
114. feeling troubled
115. feeling unlucky
116. feeling unmanned
117. feeling unnerved
118. feeling useless
119. feeling victimized
120. feeling worthless
121. feeling wounded
122. fieriness
123. fractiousness
124. fret
125. fright
126. frustration
127. fury
128. gall
129. general anxiety
130. gloom
131. grief

132. grudge
133. guilt
134. haggardness
135. hatred
136. health worries
137. heart sickness
138. heartache
139. heartbreak
140. helplessness
141. homesickness
142. hopelessness
143. horror
144. hostility
145. humiliation
146. hurt feelings
147. hurt pride
148. hysteria
149. ignominy
150. ill humour
151. ill will
152. immaturity
153. impatience
154. inability to communicate
155. inability to cope
156. inability to express feelings
157. inability to face reality
158. inadequacy
159. indignation
160. inexperience
161. inferiority
162. insecurity
163. intensity
164. intimidation
165. intolerance
166. irascibility
167. irresolution
168. irritation
169. isolation
170. jadedness
171. jealousy
172. jitters
173. jumpiness
174. lack of concentration
175. lack of confidence
176. lamenting
177. lethargy
178. libidinousness
179. loneliness
180. longing
181. loss of confidence
182. loss of face
183. loss of faith
184. loss of reputation
185. loss of status
186. lovelessness
187. low self-esteem
188. low spirits
189. lugubriousness
190. malevolence
191. malice
192. martyrdom
193. melancholy
194. misanthropy
195. misery
196. misogyny
197. moodiness
198. morbidity

199. moroseness
200. mortification
201. mournfulness
202. nervousness
203. numbness
204. obsession
205. offence
206. oppression
207. over-involvement
208. over-sensitivity
209. panic
210. perplexity
211. perturbation
212. petulance
213. pique
214. prostration
215. querulousness
216. rage
217. rancour
218. rattiness
219. recklessness
220. regret
221. rejection
222. religious doubt
223. remorse
224. resentment
225. resignation
226. restlessness
227. revulsion
228. sadness
229. satiety
230. self-loathing
231. self-pity
232. self-reproach
233. sense of failure
234. sense of futility
235. sense of grievance
236. sense of worthlessness
237. sensitivity
238. sentimentality
239. shame
240. shock
241. shyness
242. sleeplessness
243. smart
244. snappishness
245. sorrow
246. specific anxiety
247. spiritual torment
248. spite
249. spleen
250. staleness
251. strain
252. stupor
253. suffering
254. sulkiness
255. sullenness
256. tearfulness
257. temper
258. tension
259. terror
260. tiredness
261. torment
262. touchiness
263. turbulence
264. umbrage
265. unhappiness
266. venom

267. vexation
268. victim mentality
269. virulence
270. vulnerability
271. weakness
272. weariness
273. world-weariness
274. worry
275. wretchedness
276. yearning
277. zenophobia

EXTERNAL

1. abandonment
2. abuse
3. accommodation problems
4. ageing
5. anti-depressant addiction
6. anti-depressants, habituation
7. anti-depressants, side effects
8. assault off duty
9. assault on duty
10. authority problems
11. awaiting outcome
12. bad blood
13. bad company
14. banishment
15. being beaten
16. being blamed
17. being left in suspense
18. being lied to
19. being made a scapegoat
20. being made to look stupid
21. being overshadowed
22. blemished record
23. brainwashing
24. bullying
25. burdening
26. capture
27. career barriers
28. caring for disabled relative
29. caring for sick relative
30. change affecting family
31. change affecting self
32. change of colleagues
33. change of workplace
34. childbirth problems
35. childlessness
36. chores
37. class issues
38. combat
39. commuting
40. compensation claim
41. compensation culture
42. complexity
43. computer angst
44. conscience, issue of
45. conflicts with spouse/partner
46. contraception problems
47. criticism
48. crowding
49. cruelty, experience of
50. cruelty, witness to
51. cultural starvation

52. culture clash
53. culture shock
54. damage to property
55. deadlines
56. dealing with the public
57. death of companion animal
58. death of loved one
59. debt
60. deformity
61. demanding boss
62. demotion
63. dereliction of duty
64. derision
65. dieting
66. digestive illness
67. disciplinary measures
68. discovery of guilt
69. disfigurement
70. dislike of weapons
71. disorganization
72. disputes over property
73. disputes over rights
74. divorce
75. doing dirty work
76. domestic upheaval
77. drink
78. drugs, abuse of
79. drugs, addiction to
80. effort not rewarded
81. enclosed spaces
82. epileptic fit
83. equipment problems
84. exclusion
85. expensive lifestyle
86. exposure to criminality
87. exposure to disease
88. exposure to fumes
89. exposure to noxious substance
90. exposure to poison
91. exposure to radiation
92. exposure to strobe lighting
93. extremes of temperature
94. failure to arrest
95. falling in love
96. family demands
97. feuds
98. financial deadline
99. form-filling
100. gambling addiction
101. gambling debts
102. getting married
103. going on holiday
104. going underground
105. grassing or being grassed
106. grievances, real or imagined
107. hardship
108. hearing horrific accounts
109. heights
110. holiday problems
111. hopes dashed
112. hospitalization
113. hunger
114. hurtful remarks
115. identification with case/client

116. ill-fitting footwear
117. illicit affair
118. illness
119. illness in family
120. imminent retirement
121. imprisonment
122. inadequate social skills
123. incomplete task
124. increased responsibility
125. industrial conflict
126. infringement of rights
127. injustice
128. in-laws, problems with
129. institutionalization
130. insubordination
131. intellectual inadequacy
132. intellectual starvation
133. intolerable conditions
134. irregular shifts
135. isolation
136. issue unresolved
137. job at risk
138. job change
139. judgement
140. job hassles
141. lack of attention
142. lack of consideration
143. lack of evidence
144. lack of exercise
145. lack of guidance
146. lack of praise
147. lack of recognition
148. lack of representation
149. lack of support
150. lack of training
151. lack of work
152. lack or loss of leadership
153. lack or loss of leisure
154. lack or loss of norms
155. landlord problems
156. lateness
157. legal disputes
158. loss of colleague(s)
159. loss of equipment
160. loss of friend(s)
161. loss of hearing
162. loss of mobility
163. loss of privacy
164. loss of rank
165. loss of sight
166. macho pressures
167. malpractice, experience of
168. malpractice, witness to
169. management change
170. management practice
171. marital infidelity
172. mental challenge
173. miscarriage (self or partner)
174. misinformation on 'stress'
175. missed transport
176. misunderstanding
177. mobile phone angst
178. modern world angst
179. money worries
180. monotony
181. motoring offence

182. moving house
183. needs not met
184. new baby
185. new practices
186. nicotine addiction
187. noisy neighbours
188. noisy working environment
189. obesity
190. open spaces
191. operational difficulties
192. ostracism
193. over-promotion
194. over-protection
195. oversleeping alarm
196. overtime pressures
197. parenting pressures
198. parents, problems with
199. peer pressure
200. pension worries
201. persecution
202. personal crossroads
203. physical challenge
204. physical depletion
205. physical disability
206. physical inadequacy
207. physical injury
208. physical pain
209. political correctness
210. political interference
211. poor eating habits
212. poor hierarchy position
213. poor scheduling
214. power disputes

215. pregnancy (self or partner)
216. prolonged absence from partner
217. prolonged contact with partner
218. promotion
219. prostitution, real or figurative
220. protocol dispute
221. provocation
222. puberty
223. punctuality problems
224. punishment
225. race issues
226. racial abuse
227. racial prejudice
228. rape
229. reading horrific accounts
230. red-light district, caught in
231. red tape
232. redundancy
233. rejection of work
234. relationship difficulties
235. religious issues
236. relocation problems
237. rent arrears
238. responsibility
239. restrictions on social life
240. return to work
241. rivalry
242. roadworks
243. rows

244. seeing horrific sights
245. seeking closure
246. sensory deprivation
247. sexual abuse
248. sexual impotence
249. sexual inadequacy
250. sexual prejudice
251. shoplifting
252. shopping angst
253. skeleton in the cupboard
254. skill deficit
255. sleep disturbance
256. sleeping pills, addiction
257. sleeping pills, habituation
258. sleeping pills, side effects
259. soul-destroying tasks
260. speech impediment
261. staying home to mind children
262. street dispute
263. stroke, self or family member
264. suicide in family
265. suicide, witness to
266. surgery
267. sunlight deprivation
268. taxed abilities
269. technological pressures
270. theft of ideas
271. theft of property
272. therapy problems
273. thirst
274. threat to life
275. threat to masculinity

276. threat to safety
277. time pressures
278. toothache
279. traffic accident
280. tranquillizer addiction
281. tranquillizers, habituation
282. transquillizers, side effects
283. transport problems
284. travel pressures
285. ugliness
286. unacceptable conditions
287. unclear rules
288. unemployment
289. unfair dismissal
290. unfair treatment
291. unpleasant working environment
292. unrealistic demands
293. unrequited love
294. unsympathetic colleagues
295. unwanted pregnancy
296. unwanted childbirth
297. urban lifestyle
298. violence at home
299. violence at work
300. war
301. weight loss
302. weight gain
303. work absence problems
304. workload
305. workplace rows
306. worries over childcare
307. worries over parenting
308. youth culture issues

NOTES

IS THIS PERSON QUALIFIED?

1. A. Patmore, *Playing On Their Nerves: The sport experiment*, Stanley Paul, 1979.
2. Lawrence Olivier, *Confessions of An Actor*, Coronet edition, 1984, p. 301.
3. Stephen Overell, 'Stress shibboleth comes under attach, *Daily Telegraph*, 14 May 1998.
4. Workplace Stress, EuroForum, 28 March 1996, Grosvenor House Hotel, London.
5. Carole Spiers Associates contact literature, 30 June 1999.

DEFINITION?

1. Health and Safety Executive website, updated July 2003.
2. J. Cassel, 'The contribution of the social environment to host resistance', *American Journal of Epidemiology*, 104, 1976, p. 108.
3. S. V. Kasl, 'Methodologies in stress and health: Past difficulties, present dilemmas, future directions', in S. V. Kasl and C. L. Cooper (eds.), *Stress and Health: Issues in Research methodology*. Chichester: John Wiley, 1987, p. 312.
4. L. R. C. Haward, 'The subjective meaning of stress', *British Journal of Medical Psychology*, 33, 1960, p. 185.
5. G. Pickering, 'Language: The lost tool of learning in Medicine and Science', *The Lancet*, 15 July 1961, p. 116.
6. J. W. Mason, 'A historical view of the stress field (parts 1 and 2)', *Journal of Human Stress*, vol. 1, 6–12, 22–36, 1975.

7. K. Pollock, 'On the nature of social stress: Production of a modern mythology', *Social Science and Medicine*, 26, 1988, p. 390.

8. B. Wilks, 'Stress management for athletes', *Sports Medicine*, 11 (5), 1991, p. 290.

9. H. Weiner, *Perturbing the Organism: The biology of stressful experience*, University of Chicago Press, Chicago and London, 1992, p. 1.

10. Dr Edward C. Hamlyn, letter to the author, 28 September 1999.

11. C. Cooper, 'Stress? It's as old as the hills', *Independent*, 8 May 1996.

12. L. Hardy, 'Psychological stress, performance and injury in sport', *British Medical Bulletin*, 48 (2), 1992, pp. 615–29.

13. *Probe*, BBC Radio 4 science magazine, 8 September 1996.

14. Centre for Stress Management website, <http://www.managingstress.com> 22 July 2003.

15. Stephen Palmer, speaking on BBC Radio 4's *Patient Progress* series: *Stressed Out*, 2000.

16. Joe Macdonald Wallace, chairman ISMA, *Stress News*, 2 (2), September 1990.

17. 'When stress makes you fat', Eleanor Bailey. *Shape*, June 1999. 'How stress piles the pounds on a woman', James Chapman, *Daily Mail*, 23 September 2000.

18. 'Stress in pregnancy can make your child naughty', James Chapman, *Daily Mail*, 5 July 2003.

19. 'Children fed on junk food as a cure for stress', Beezy Marsh, *Daily Mail*, 2 August 2003.

20. 'Are you guilty of stress addiction?' Louise Bray, *Daily Mail*, 9 June 1997.

21. 'Stressed out – but quids in?' Hashi Syedain, *Observer*, 11 July 1999.

22. International Labour Organization, *Safework*: ILO webpage, 8 July 2003.

23. 'Mother of all stress', Laura Clark, *Daily Mail*, 12 February 2000.

24. 'Rats in a rage', Rob Walker, *Slate* webpage, 16 January 2001.

25. 'Cary Cooper, in 'Stressed out – but quids in?' *Observer*, 11 July 1999.

26. *Employee burnout: causes and cures*, Part 1: Employee stress levels, Northwestern National Life Assurance, Minneapolis, 1992.

27. 'Job Stress', <http://www.stress.org/job.htm> 8 July 2003.
28. Cary Cooper, 'Strains over stress', Judy Jones, *Observer*, 25 February 1996.
29. Tim Field, *Bully OnLine*, National Workplace Bullying Advice Line, 2 July 1999, 1.
30 Stress UK 97, <http://www.stress.org.uk/what.htm>
31. British Heart Foundation statement, 6 May 1998.
32. Email to the author, August 2004
33. Letter to the author, 7 October 1998.
34. Dr David Costain, in answer to my question, 'How do BUPA define stress?' at the Winnicott Clinic symposium: *Stress: Understanding it, managing it, the role of therapy,* 11 May 1999.
35. *Stress and the Medical Profession*, BMA, June 1992, p. 7.
36. A. Meyer, *Collected Papers* (ed. E. Winters), Baltimore: John Hopkins Press, 1951 and 1952
37. H. G. Wolff, S. G. Wolf and C. C. Hare (eds), *Life stress and bodily disease*. Baltimore: Williams and Wilkins 1950.
38. H. G. Wolff, *Stress and disease*, Springfield, Illinois: C. C. Thomas, 1953.
39. T. H. Holmes and R. H. Rahe, 'The social readjustment rating scale', *Journal of Psychosomatic Research,* 1967, 11, pp. 213–18.
40. Derek Roger and Poppy Nash, Workplace Stress, *Training Officer*, March 1994, issue 30, p. 2.
41. Email to the author, 6 June 2001.

Part One **THE DISEASE**

ONE
STRESS PHOBIA

1. European Agency for Safety and Health at Work, *Working on Stress*, European Week 2002 Information Resources.
2. 1995 Australian Workplace and Industrial Relations Survey, National Occupational Health and Safety Commission, Australia.
3. *Stress at Work*, National Institute for Occupational Safety and Health (NIOSH), USA.

4. BBC Radio 4, *Patient Progress II*, 10 October 2000.

5. Paul J. Rosch, in *Stress Remedies*, Carl Sherman (co-author), Rodale Press: Pennsylvania, 1997, p. x.

6. See e.g. M. E. P. Seligman, *Helplessness: On Depression, Development and Death*, Freeman: San Francisco; M. E. P. Seligman and G. Beagley, Learned helplessness in the rat, *Journal of Complementary Physiology and Psychology*, 88, 1975, pp. 534–41.

7. Jane Austen, *Pride and Prejudice*, 1813, chapter XLVII.

8. Ben Shephard, *A War of Nerves*, Jonathan Cape, London, 2000, pp. 5–20.

9. T. C. Allbutt, 'Nervous diseases and modern life', *Contemporary Review 67*, 1895, pp. 210–31.

10. Hay Management Consultants, 26th *Annual Survey of Employee Benefits*.

11. *Daily Telegraph*, 14 May 1998.

TWO
SPREADING THE INFECTION

1. *Working on Stress*, *HSE Action Pack* for European Week 2002.

2. Cary L. Cooper and Stephen Palmer, *Conquer Your Stress*, Institute of Personnel and Development, 2000, p. 6.

3. BHS *Patient Information Factsheet* and booklet *Understanding High Blood Pressure*.

4. P. G. Kaufmann *et al.* and HIPP Investigators, 'Hypertension intervention pooling project', *Health Psychology*, 7 (Supplement), 1988, pp. 209–24.

5. Blood Pressure Association National Blood Pressure Testing Week, Rapid Survey 2002.

6. T. Truelsen *et al.*, *Self-Reported Stress and Risk of Stroke: the Copenhagen City Heart Study,* Institute of Preventive Medicine, Kommune Hospitalet, Denmark, 2002.

7. 1963 film clip of Arthur Miller, in BBC TV's *Century of the Self*, Part 3, 2002.

8. M. Peterson, and J. F. Wilson, 'Work stress in America', *International Journal of Stress Management*, 11, 2, 2004, pp. 91–113.

9. Sperling's BestPlaces New Stress Index ranking 331 Metro Areas, 9 January 2004.

10. Gordon Rayner, 'Tony's stressbuster', *Daily Mail,* 10 January 2004.

11. See e.g. R. Voelker, 'Nocebos contribute to a host of ills', *JAMA*, 1996, 275, 345; Arthur J. Barsky *et al.*, 'Non-specific medication side effects and the Nocebo phenomenon', *JAMA*, 287, 2002, pp. 622–27; Robert A. Palmer *et al.*, 'When are medication side effects due to the Nocebo phenomenon?' *JAMA*, 287, 2002, pp. 2502–4.

12. Hazel Claire Weekes, MB, DSc, FRACP, *Self-Help for Your Nerves*, Angus and Robertson, 1962, p. 8–9.

13. BBC Radio 4, *Patient Progress* Series, 10 October 2002.

14. 'Time to Put Up and Shut Up', *Independent On Sunday*, 10 October 1999.

15. OHS Reps website, 'Stress at work', July 2003.

16. ACCI press release, 'Stress as a community and workplace issue', 11 January 2002.

17. NOHSC website, 'Hazards and solutions', July 1998.

Part Two **THE SCIENCE THAT SPAWNED AN INDUSTRY**

THREE
PARADIGM

1. In *The Structure of Scientific Revolutions*, 1962, originally published in the *International Encyclopaedia of the Unified Sciences*.

2. E. Fromm, *The Fear of Freedom*, London: Routledge and Kegan Paul, 1942.

3. The History of Phrenology on the Web, Dr John van Wyhe, <http://pages.britishlibrary.net/phrenology/overview.htm>

4. H. Selye, *The Stress of Life* (revised edition), McGraw-Hill, 1976, p. 90.

5. R. Ader (ed.), *Psychoimmunology*, New York: Academic Press, 1981.

6. L. E. Hinkle, 'The concept of stress in the biological sciences', *Stress in medicine and man*, 1, 1973, pp. 31–48.
7. *Stress and the Medical Profession*, British Medical Association, 1992, pp. 1, 5.
8. H. Burnham, 'The study of adolescence', *The Pedagogical Seminary*, 1 (2), 1891, pp. 174–95.
9. M. Mead, *Coming of Age in Samoa*, Harmandsworth: Penguin, 1928.
10. Ben Shephard, *A War of Nerves*, London: Jonathan Cape, 2000, p. 349. H. Selye, *The Stress of Life* (revised edition), 1976, p. 50.
11. S. Brown, By dint of force. *The Life of Stress: seeing and saying dysphoria*. Doctoral thesis, Department of Psychology, University of Reading, 1997, 1:5.
12. B. Shephard, op. cit., p. 457.
13. R. Viner, 'Putting Stress in Life: Hans Selye and the making of stress theory', *Social Studies of Science,* 29, 1999, pp. 391–410.

FOUR
PROVENANCE

1. H. Selye, 'Interactions between systemic and local stress', *British Medical Journal*, 22 May 1954, 1167–70.
2. H. Selye, *The Stress of Life* (revised edition), McGraw-Hill, 1976, p. 17.
3. H. Selye, 'A syndrome produced by diverse nocuous agents', *Nature*, 138, 1936, p. 32.
4. H. Selye, *Stress: the physiology and pathology of exposure to stress*, Montreal: Acta Medica, 1950.
5. H. Selye, 'Confusion and controversy in the stress field', *Journal of Human Stress*, 1 (2), 1975, pp. 37–44.
6. H. Selye, op. cit., 1976, p. xvii.
7. H. Weiner, *Perturbing the Organism: The biology of stressful experience*, University of Chicago Press, 1992, p. 2.
8. P. S. Hench, E. C. Kendall *et al.*, 'The effect of a hormone of the adrenal

cortex and of pituitary adrenocorticotrophic hormone on rheumatoid arthritis', *Proceedings of Staff Meetings,* Mayo Clinic, 1949.

9 A. Munck, p. M. Guyre and N. Holbrook, 'Physiological functions of glucocorticoids in stress and their relation to pharmacological actions, *Endocrinology.* Rec. 5, 1984, pp. 25–44.

10. H. Selye, 'The evolution of the stress concept', *American Scientist,* 61, 1973, pp. 692–9.

11. R. Viner, 'Putting Stress in Life: Hans Selye and the Making of Stress Theory', *Social Studies of Science: An International Review of Research in the Social Dimensions of Science and Technology,* 29, 1999, p. 3.

12. H. Selye, 'The stress concept: Past, present and future', in C. L. Cooper (ed.), *Stress research: Issues for the eighties*, Chichester: John Wiley, 1983.

13 McGraw-Hill Higher Education website <http:///www.dushkin.com/connectext/psy/ch12/bio12.mhtml>

14. E. S. Deevey, 'The Hare and the Haruspex: A cautionary tale', *The Yale Review,* Winter, 1960, pp. 571–90. Quoted in Steven Brown, *The Life of Stress: Seeing and saying dysphoria.* University of Reading Department of Psychology thesis, 1997.

15. W. B. Cannon, 'The interrelations of emotions as suggested by recent physiological researchers', *American Journal of Psychology,* 25, 1914, pp. 256–82. W. B. Cannon, 'Physiological regulation of normal states: Some tentative postulates concerning biological homeostatics', *Jubilee Volume for Charles Richet,* 1926, pp. 91–93.

16. W. B. Cannon, 'Voodoo death', *American Anthropologist,* 44 (2), 1942, pp. 169–181.

17. W. B. Cannon, *The Wisdom of the Body*, Norton & Company, New York, 1932 (revised and enlarged) edition, Norton Library, 1963.

18. The French physiologist Claude Bernard delivered a classic series of lectures at the College de France in Paris in the late ninetenth century on the *milieu intérieur.* His concept was that all living things maintain a constant internal equilibrium despite changes in their surroundings.

19. H. Weiner, op. cit., p. 21.

20. J. W. Mason, 'A re-evaluation of the concept of "non-specificity" in stress theory', *Journal of Psychiatric Research*, 8, 3–4, 1971, pp. 323–33; Mason, 'The scope of psychoendocrine research', *Psychosomatic Medicine*, XXX, 1968, pp. 565–75; Mason, 'A review of psychoendocrine research on the pituitary-adrenal cortical system', *Psychosomatic Medicine* XXX, 1968, pp. 576–607; Mason, 'Organization of the multiple endocrine responses to avoidance in the monkey', *Psychosomatic Medicine* XXX, 1968, pp. 774–90.

21. L. E. Hinkle, 'The concept of "stress" in the biological and social sciences', *Science, Medicine and Man*, 1, 1973, pp. 31–48.

22. J. W. Mason, 'Emotion as reflected in patterns of endocrine integration', in L. Levi (ed.), *Emotions: Their parameters and measurement*, New York: Raven, 1975.

23. Mason, op. cit., 1968, pp. 781–3.

24. Mason, op. cit., 1971, p. 332.

25. e.g. H. Anisman and R. M. Zacharko, 'Depression as a consequence of inadequate neurochemical adaptation in response to stressors', *British Journal of Psychiatry*, 160 (Supp. 15), 1992, pp. 36–43. N. Shanks and H. Anisman, 'Strain-specific effects of anti-depressants on escape deficits induced by inescapable shock', *Psychopharmacology*, 99, 1989, pp. 122–8. R. M. Zacharko *et al.*, 'Strain-specific effects of inescapable shock on intracranial self-stimulation from the nucleus accumbens', *Brain Research*, 426, 1987, pp. 164–8.

26. D. M. Gibbs, 'Vasopressin and oxytocin: Hypothalamic modulators of the stress response', *Psychoneuroendocrinology*, 11, 1986, pp. 131–40.

27. Mason, op. cit., 1971, p. 326.

28. R. R. Grinker and J. P. Spiegel, *Men Under Stress*, New York: McGraw-Hill, 1945.

29. N. H. Pronko and W. R. Leith, 'Behaviour under stress: a study of disintegration', *Psychological Reports*, 2, Monographic supplement 5, 1956, pp. 205–22.

30. D. Steven Brown, *The Life of Stress: Seeing and saying dysphoria*, Department of Psychology, University of Reading, 1997, p. 1.

FIVE
PSYCHONEUROIMMUNOLOGY

1. Steven D. Brown, *The Life of Stress: seeing and saying dysphoria*, doctoral thesis, Department of Psychology, University of Reading, 1997, p. 5.
2. R. Ader, and N. Cohen, 'Behaviorally conditioned immuno-suppression, *Psychosomatic Medicine*, 37 (4), 1975, p. 333–40.
3. Talking on BBC TV, *Horizon: Mind over Body*, February 2000. See also D. L. Felten *et al.*, 'Noradrenergic sympathetic innervation of the spleen: Nerve fibers associate with lymphocytes and macrophages in specific compartments of the splenic white pulp', *Journal of Neuroscience Research*, 18, pp. 1987, 28–36.
4. J. E. Blalock, E. M. Smith and W. J. Meyer, 'The pituitary-adrenocortical axis and the immune system', *Clinics in Endocrinology and Metabolism*, 14, 1985, pp. 1021–38.
5. Interview, BBC TV, *Horizon: Mind over Body*, February 2000.
6. H. O. Besedovsky, E. Sorkin *et al.*, 'Changes in blood hormone levels during immune response', *Proceedings of the Society for Experimental Biology and Medicine*, 150, 1975, pp. 466–70. R. Dantzer *et al.*, 'Behavioral effects of cytokines: An insight into mechanisms of sickness behavior', in E. B. DeSouza (ed.), *Neurobiology of cytokines*, San Diego: Academic Press, pp. 130–51.
7. S. F. Maier, L. R. Watkins and M. Fleshner, Psychoneuroimmunology: the interface between behavior, brain and immunity, *American Psychologist* 49, 1994, p. 12.
8. J. K. Kiecolt-Glaser, R. Glaser *et.al.*, 'Marital quality, marital disruption, and immune function', *Psychosomatic Medicine*, 49, 1987, pp. 13–25. J. K. Kiecolt-Glaser, R. Glaser *et al.*, 'Marital Stress: immunologic, neuroendocrine and autonomic correlates', *Annals of New York Academy of Science*, 1 May, 840: 1998, pp. 656–63.

9. J. K. Kiecolt-Glaser and R. Glaser, 'Mind and immunity', in D. Goleman and J. Gurin (eds), *Mind/Body Medicine*, New York: Consumer reports, 1993, pp. 39–59.

10. See e.g. J. K. Kiecolt-Glaser *et al.*, 'Chronic stress and age-related increases in the proinflammatory cytokine IL-6', *Proc. National Academy of Sciences USA*, 22 July; 100 (15), 2003, pp. 9090–5. R. Glaser, 'The effects of stress on the immune system: implications for health', Summary of Presentation on 17 December 1996, Science Writers' Briefing, OBSSR and Amerian Psychological Association, 1996. J. K. Kiecolt-Glaser, R. Glaser, 'Psychological stress and wound healing', *Advances in Mind Body Medicine*, winter 2001; 17, (1), 1995, pp. 15–16.

11. Jan Glaser, *Horizon* interview, February 2000.

12. Maier, Watkins and Fleshner, op. cit., 1994, pp. 1004–17.

13. A. O'Leary, 'Stress, emotion, and human immune function', *Psychological Bulletin*, 108 (3), 1990, pp. 363–82.

14. R. Ader and N. Cohen, 'Psychoneuroimmunology: Conditioning and stress', *Annual Review of Psychology*, 44, 1993, pp. 53-85.

15. *Equinox: the Science of Stress*, Channel 4, November 2000.

SIX
PATHOLOGISING EMOTION

1. H. Selye, *The Stress of Life*, revised edition, McGraw-Hill, 1976, p. 183.

2. V. E. Frankl, *Man's Search for Meaning*, Pocket Books, New York, 1963.

3. J. B. Rotter, 'Generalized expectancies for internal versus external control of reinforcement', *Psychological Monographs: General and Applied*, 80, 1, 1966, p. 609.

4. S. C. Kobasa, 'Stressful life events, personality and health: An inquiry into hardiness', *Journal of Personality and Social Psychology*, 42, 1979, pp. 707–17. S. C. Kobasa, 'The hardy personality: Towards a social psychology of stress and health', in *Social Psychology of*

Health and Illness (G. S. Sanders and J. Suls, eds) Lawrence Erlbaum, Hilldale, New Jersey, 1982, pp. 3–32.

5. A. Antonovsky, *Health, Stress and Coping*, Jossey-Bass, San Francisco, 1979. A. Antonovsky, The sense of coherence as a determinant of health. In *Behavioral Health: A handbook of health enhancement and disease prevention*, J. D. Matarazzo, (ed.), John Wiley, New York, 1984, pp. 114–29.

6. J. J. Lynch, K. E. Lynch and E. Friedmann, 'A cry unheard: Sudden reductions in blood pressure while talking about feelings of hopelessness and helplessness', *Integrative Physiological and Behavioral Science*, 27, (2), 1992, pp. 151–69.

7. See e.g. W. Linden, 'A microanalysis of autonomic activity during human speech', *Psychosomatic Medicine*, 49, 1987, pp. 562–78. J. J. Lynch *et al.*, 'Blood pressure changes while talking', *Journal of Nervous and Mental Disease*, 168, 1980, pp. 526–34. G. Naring, H. DeMey and C. Schaap, 'Blood pressure response during verbal interaction: Review and prospect', *Curr. Psychological Research Rec.* 7, 1988, pp. 187–98. D. Silverberg and J. Rosenfield, 'The effect of quiet conversation on the blood pressure of hypertensive patients', *Israeli Journal of Medical Science*, 16, 1980, pp. 41–3. C. H. Tardy, W. R. Thompson and M. T. Allen, 'Cardiovascular response during speech: Does social support mediate the effects of talking on blood pressure?', *Journal of Language and Social Psychology*, 8, 1989, pp. 3–4.

8. J. J. Lynch *et al.*, op. cit., 1992, p. 160.

9. PTED was discovered in *Psychotherapy and Psychosomatics*, 72: 2003, pp. 195–202. Email to the author, 23 June 2003.

SEVEN
PERPLEX

1. Lord Charles Wilson Moran, *The Anatomy of Courage*, London: Constable and Company, 1945, 2nd edition 1966.

2. Ibid., p. 175

3. A. Patmore, *Playing On Their Nerves: The Sport Experiment*, Stanley Paul, 1979.

4. M. Scott Peck, *The Road Less Travelled*, Arrow edition 1990, pp. 13–14.

5. A. Patmore, *Killing the Messenger: The pathologizing of the stress response*, Centre for Environmental and Risk Management, University of East Anglia, 1997 (now published by The Nerve Centre).

6. 'Tragedy of man with only TV to live for', *Daily Mail,* 19 April 1997.

7. M. E. P. Seligman and S.F. Maier, 'Failure to escape traumatic shock', *Journal of Experimental Psychology*, 74, 1967, pp. 1–9.

8. M. E. P. Seligman, *Helplessness: On depression, development and death*, San Francisco: Freeman, 1975.

9. 'London', from *Songs of Innocence and Experience* by William Blake, Oxford University Press, 1967, p. 46.

10. HSE, 'A "management standards" approach to tackling work-related stress – Part I, Rationale and scientific underpinning', 2004, p. 14.

11. J. Head, p. Martikainen, M. Marmot *et al. Work environment, alcohol consumption and ill health: The Whitehall II Study*, HSE Contract Research Report 422/2002, Sudbury: HSE Books, 2002.

12. A. Patmore, *Killing the Messenger*, op. cit., p. 30.

13. Kobasa, S. C. Stressful life events, personality and health: An inquiry into hardiness. *Journal of Personality and Social Psychology*, 42, 1979, pp. 707–17.

14. V. E. Frankl, *Man's Search for Meaning,* New York: Pocket Books, 1963.

EIGHT
PROOF POSITIVE

1. Charles Rycroft, *Anxiety and Neurosis,* Baltimore: Penguin, 1968.

2. H. Weiner, *Perturbing the organism: the biology of stressful experience*, Chicago and London: University of Chicago Press, 1992.

3. Ibid., p. 29.

4. H. Anisman and R. M. Zacharko, 'Depression as a consequence of

inadequate neurochemical adaptation in response to stressors', *British Journal of Psychiatry*, 160 (Supp. 15), 1992, pp. 36–43.

5. R. J. Servatius and T. S. Shors, 'Exposure to inescapable stress persistently facilitates associative and nonassociative learning in rats', *Behavioral Neuroscience*, 108 (6), 1994, pp. 1101–6. T. Shors, C. Weiss and R. F. Thompson, 'Stress-induced facilitation of classical conditioning', *Science*, 257, 1992, pp. 537–9.

6. C. Stanford, 'Why stress gets on your nerves', *New Scientist*, 123, 1989, p. 1679.

7. H. Selye, *The Stress of Life*, revised edition, McGraw-Hill, 1976, p. 433.

8. B. Wilks, 'Stress management for athletes', *Sports Medicine*, 11 (5), 1991, pp. 289–99.

9. C. Blakemore, *The Mind Machine*, first published BBC Books, 1988, Penguin edition 1994, pp. 166–7.

10. See e.g. R. Mace and D. Carroll, 'Stress inoculation training to control anxiety in sport', *British Journal of Sports Medicine*, 20 (3), 1986, pp. 115–17.

11. A. Patmore, *Playing on Their Nerves: The Sport Experiment*, Stanley Paul, 1979, pp. 125–44.

12. J. Heider, 'Catharsis in human potential encounter', *Journal of Humanistic Psychology*, 14, 1974, pp. 26–34.

13. Abraham H. Maslow, *Towards a Psychology of Being*, second edition, Princeton: Van Nostrand, 1968, pp. 71–114.

14. M. Persinger, *Neuropsychological Bases of God Beliefs*, New York and London: Praeger, 1987.

15. B. Simpson, 'Stressing the positive', *Management Today*, November 1987.

16. Dr Anthony Daniels, 'Stress? It's positively good for us', *Daily Mail*, 1 September 1998.

17. Elizabeth Summerhayes, 'Thank God it's Monday', *The Times*, 17 October 1998.

18. Dr Robert Brine, in Elizabeth Summerhayes, 'Thank God it's Monday', *The Times*, 17 October 1998.

19. Rannia M. Leontaridi and Melanie E. Ward, 'Dying to Work: an investigation into work-related stress, quitting intentions and absenteeism', presented at the Royal Economic Society's 2002 Annual Conference at the University of Warwick.

20. Aparna Malhotra, 'Stress is not all bad, say workers', 22 August 2003, BusinessEurope.com.

21. B. C. Amick *et al.* (2002), 'Relationship between all-cause mortality and cumulative working life course psychosocial and physical exposures in the United States labor market from 1968 to 1992', *Psychosomatic Medicine*, 64, pp. 370–81.

22. A. Patmore, *Killing the Messenger: The pathologizing of the stress response*. Centre for Environmental and Risk Management, University of East Anglia, 1997, now published by The Nerve Centre.

23. M. Popplestone, telephone interview with the author, 1996.

24. Dr Raj Persaud, 'Is boredom making you ill?', *Daily Mail*, 9 October 2000.

25. Research and Teaching Showcase, Wadsworth Publishing Company website, <http://psychstudy.brookscole.com>, December 2000.

26. B. Burchell, 'The effects of labour market position, job insecurity and unemployment on psychological health', *Social Change and Economic Life Initiative*, Economic and Social Research Council, Oxford, 1990.

27. M. Jahoda *et al.*, *Marienthal – The sociography of an unemployed community*, London: Tavistock, 1972. M. Jahoda, *Employment and unemployment: a social-psychological analysis*, Cambridge: Cambridge University Press, 1972.

28. J. K. Morris, D. G. Cook, and A. G. Shaper, 'Loss of employment and mortality', *British Medical Journal,* 308, 30 April 1994.

29. I. Delisle, 'Le suicide a l'age de la retraite', *Canadian Nurse*, 88 (5), May, 1992, pp. 39–41.

30. David Wilkes, 'Staying at work is a recipe for longer life', *Daily Mail*, 9 March 2002.

31. Janice M. Horowitz, 'Say yes to stress', *Time Magazine*, 12 November

2001. Elizabeth Summerhayes, 'Thank God it's Monday', *The Times*, 17 October 1998.

32. M. E. Cavanagh, 'What you don't know about stress', *Personnel Journal*, July 1988.

33. M. Bland, 'A new approach to management of stress', *Industrial and Commercial Training*, 31 (2), 1999, pp. 44–8.

34. J. Houston, 'Tend and befriend: Women's reactions to stress', *Trancetime Quarterly Newsletter*, March 2002.

35. P. H. McCrea, 'Trends in suicide in Northern Ireland 1922–1992', *Irish Journal of Psychological Medicine*, March, 13 (1), 1996, pp. 9–12.

36. 'Life expectancy to soar', BBC News, 9 May 2002.

37. Marios Kyriazis, Stress makes you live longer. *Daily Mail*, 3 May 2005.

Part Three COSTS

NINE
WORK SICKNESS

1. Harris Interactive/Marlia Company, *Attitudes in the American Workplace VII*: 7th Annual Labor Day Survey.

2. Reuters, <http//www.msnbc.com/news2003> The estimate originated with Dr Paul Rosch, President of the American Institute of Stress.

3. John de Graaf, (ed.) *Take back your time*: *Fighting overwork and time poverty in America*, San Francisco: Berrett-Koehler, 2003.

4. Rats in a Rage, *Slate*, 16 January 2001, <http://slate.msn.com/id/1006885>

5. 'Job Stress', 8 July 2003, <http://www.stress.org/job.htm>

6. Institute for Management Excellence online newsletter, October 2002.

7. Research on work-related stress, European Agency for Safety and Health at Work, 2000.

8. K. J. Lennane, 'Employers blamed for workplace stress', *NSW Doctor*, February, 1994, pp. 15–16.

9. Clive Hamilton, *Overconsumption in Australia: the rise of the middle-class battler*, Australian Institute Discussion Paper 49, November 2002.

10. John Naish, 'Stress', *The Times*, 11 November 2004.

11. *ILO examines mental health in the workplace*, International Labour Organization Press Release, 10 October 2000.

12. Helge Hoel, Kate Sparks and Cary L. Cooper, *The Cost of Violence/Stress at Work*, Report commissioned by the ILO, Geneva.

13. European Agency for Safety and Health at Work, *Working on Stress*, European Week 2002 Information Resources.

14. European Agency for Safety and Health at Work, *Europe under stress*, news release, 19 June 2000.

15. 'Work-related stress – the consequences', HSE website, 1 November 2000.

16. Confederation of British Industry's 15th Annual Absence Survey, *Pulling Together,* published in association with PPP Healthcare, May 2001.

17. A. Smith, S. Johal *et al.*, *The Scale of Occupational Stress: The Bristol Stress and Health at Work (SHAW) Study*, Contract Research Report 265, 2000. Also HSE website, 'Work-related stress – myths and facts', November 2000.

18. HSE, *The costs to Britain of work place accidents and work-related ill health in 1995/96*, HMSO, J. R. Jones, C. S. Huxtable *et al.*, *Self-reported work-related illness in 2001/02: Results from a household survey*, Sudbury: HSE Books, 2003.

19. Gaby Hinsliff, 'Stress becomes the No. 1 complaint of British workers', *The Observer*, 31 October 2004.

20. *Sign Up*, HSE/Department of Health, Issue 10, Autumn 2002, p. 6.

21. *Sign Up*, Issue 8, Winter 2001, p. 6.

22. Dan Roberts, 'Workplace stress blamed as sick day rate doubles', *Financial Times*, Home UK, 11 December 2002.

23. Sean Poulter, 'Sicknote epidemic', *Daily Mail*, 27 January 2003.

24. Online *Hazards* bulletin, <http//www.hazards.org/workedtodeath> *Hazards* is a TUC-backed publication.

25. Dean Nelson, 'Brown driver complained of stress at work', *Observer*, 27 June 1999.

26. Ibid.

27. 'Drop Dead', *Hazards* Factsheet 83, August 2003, <http//www. hazards.org/workedtodeath>

28. Email to the author, 5 August 2003.

29. J. Head, p. Martikainen, M. Marmot *et al.*, *Work Environment, Alcohol Consumption and Ill-health – The Whitehall II Study*, HSE Contract Research Report 422, 2002, pp. 26–7. *See also* S. Stansfeld, J. Head and M. Marmot, *Work-related factors and ill-health: The Whitehall II Study*, HSE Contract Research Report 266, 2000.

30. In their 2004 paper: *A Management Standards approach to tackling work-related stress,* p. 13.

31. Samaritans, *Stressed Out* Survey, Mori Omnibus, April 2003.

32. Presentation by senior occupational physician Dr Mark Popplestone, 1996 Euro Forum *Workplace Stress* conference.

33. Alexandra Frean, 'Managers warped by stress', *The Times*, 26 July 1999.

34. A. Ferriman, 'Overwork: the Nineties Disease', *Independent on Sunday*, 29 January 1995.

35. Emails to the author, 24 December 2002, 9 May 2003.

36. Pat McGuinness, 'New work, new stress', *Industrial Society Policy Paper*, 2000, p. 7.

37. Channel 4, *Stop, Go Home* Series, *Stressed Out*, October 2000.

TEN
LITIGATION

1. OHS Reps: State of Victoria Occupational Health and Safety Representatives' website, 'Stress at work', July 2003.

2. American Institute of Stress: <http://www.stress.org/job.htm>

3. Jon L. Gelman, 'Stress in the workplace: the availability of workers' compensation benefits', *New Jersey Law Journal*, 123, 7, 16 February 1989.

4. 'Stress at work 1: statutory and common law duties of care', Guidance Note 40140, *Industrial Relations Law Bulletin* 527, August 1995, p. 5, 2004.
5. Ibid.
6. Berrymans Lace Mawer: *Occupational Disease Series*, Chapter 1: 'Stress at Work Claims – an Introduction'.
7. *Sutherland v Hatton* [2002] IRLR 272, Court of Appeal
8. *Barber v Somerset County Council*, [2004] 2 All ER 385.
9. K. O'Hanlon, barrister, 'Employer's liability for psychiatric injury caused by stress at work', *The Independent*, 25 January 2005.
10. Summary Judgement Approved by the Court for Handing Down, *Sutherland v Hatton and Others*.
11. HSE website: <http://www.hse.gov.uk/pubns/stress.1.htm> 'Work-related stress – myths and facts', 1 November 2000.
12. 'HSE publishes report on employee assistance and workplace counselling programmes', Press Release E40:98, 6 March 1998.
13. Berrymans Lace Mawer, op. cit.,Conclusion.

ELEVEN
DAMAGED WORKERS

1. 'Stress at Work 1: statutory and common law duties of care', Guidance Note 40140, *Industrial Relations Law Bulletin*, 527, August 1995.
2. *Page v Smith* [1996] AC 155
3. Jeffrey Masson, *Against Therapy*, Harper Collins, 1997, p. 37.
4. Dr Martin Baggaley, consultant psychiatrist and honorary senior lecturer, 'Stress-Related Psychological Illness: medical aspects and causation', in Berrymans Lace Mawer, *Occupational Disease Series*, Chapter 5, 2002.
5. *International Classification of Mental and Behavioural Disorders; Clinical Descriptions and Diagnostic Guidelines*, Geneva; World Health Organization, 1992.
6. *Diagnostic and Statistical Manual of Mental Disorders*, 4th edition, Washington, American Psychiatric Association, 1994.

7. Jennifer Smith, *An employer's guide to stress at work litigation*, IBC Conference Report, 30 April 1998.
8. *Walker v Northumberland County Council* [1995] IRLR 35, Queen's Bench Division.
9. D. A. Grayham, 'Work-related stress; implications for the employer', *Journal of the Royal Society of Health*, April 1997, vol. 117, no. 2, pp. 81–7.
10. *Health and Safety at Work: duty to take reasonable care*, Contracts of Employment 39364, IDS Brief 533, January 1995.
11. *Walker v Northumberland County Council* [1195], 741.
12. *Daily Mail*, 27 April 1996.

Part Four THE INDUSTRY

TWELVE
HEAD-HELP HONCHOS

1. Google search, 21 July 2003.
2. A. Huzil, email to the author, 11 July 2003.
3. Email to the author, 11 July 2003.
4. *Market for Stress Management Programs, Products and Services*, September 1996. Marketdata Enterprises Inc., MarketResearch.co. website.
5. *Century of the Self,* four-part series written and produced for television by Adam Curtis for BBC 2, screened between 17 March 2002 and 7 April 2002.
6. B. Wiseman, *Psychiatry – The Ultimate Betrayal*, Freedom Publications, Los Angeles, 1995.
7. P. Braggin, *Toxic Psychiatry: a psychiatist speaks out*, New York: St Martin's Press, 1991.
8. Jeffery Masson, *Against Therapy*, London: HarperCollins, 1989.
9. D. Impastato, 'The story of the first electroshock treatment', *American Journal of Psychiatry*, 116, 1960, pp. 1113–14.
10. National Association for Consumer Protection in Mental Health Practices press release.

11. Online letter from Judith Ramirez on behalf of the Ontario Association for Marriage and Family Therapy to G. Kumagai, RHPA Project, Ministry of Health and Long-Term Care, Toronto, 1 May, 2002.

12. D. C Caulfield, M. F. Dollard and C. Elshaug, 'A review of occupational stress interventions in Australia', *International Journal of Stress Management*, 11, 2, 2004, pp. 149–66.

13. 'Best practice self-regulatory model for psychotherapy and counselling in Australia', discussion paper, Psychotherapy and Counselling Federation of Australia, January 2004.

14. BACP membership figures: 1991: 7,713; 1995: 12,208; 2000: 17,396; 2003: 21,892.

15. Angela Couchman, BACP Research Department statistical paper, updated March 2003.

16. BACP, *Counselling in primary care in the context of the NHS quality agenda – the facts*.

17. According to Lewis Edwards, BACP.

18. BBC2 *Horizon*, 'Mind Over Body', 18 September 1997.

19. Translations of practitioners' abbreviations available on the website of the Complementary Health and Alternative Medicine Information Service, CHIS UK.

20. Email to the author, 2 January 2004.

21. Channel 4 *Stop Go Home* Series 'Stressed Out', December 2000.

22. Phone interview, 11 February 2004.

23. Phone interview, 23 February 1997.

24. Speaking on Radio 4 *Patient Progress* documentary 'Stressed Out' in 2000.

25. Ibid.

26. London Hazards Centre, *Hard Labour*, Part 3, section 1, 1994.

27. BBC 2, *Trust Me I'm a Doctor*, 'Stress-Busting', 15 March 2000.

28. *Heart of the Matter*, 'Bully for you', BBC 2, 1999.

29. R. Briner and S. Reynolds, 'Stress management at work: with whom, for whom, and to what ends?', *British Journal of Guidance and Counselling*, 22, no. 1, 1994, p. 75.

30. R. Briner and S. Reynolds, 'Bad theory and bad practice in occupational stress', *Occupational Psychologist*, 19 April 1993, p. 6.

31. *BBC News* Online, 2 January 2001.

32. R. Lancaster, A. Pilkington and R. Graveling, 'Evaluation of the Organisational Stress Health Audit', Institute of Occupational Medicine, on behalf of the Health Education Board for Scotland and HSE, 1999.

33. A. Wilson and J. Bostock, 'Evaluation of stress management', *Occasional Papers of the Royal College of Practitioners*, 61, August 1993, pp. 30–35.

34. BBC Radio 4, *Patient Progress*, 'Stressed Out', 2000.

35. R. Briner and S. Reynolds, op. cit., 1994, p. 87.

36. S. W. Rabkin, 'Non-pharmacologic therapy in the management of hypertension: an update', *Canadian Journal of Public Health*, 1194, 85 (Supplement 2), 1994, pp. 544–7.

37. A. Wilson and J. Bostock, op.cit., 1993, p. 30.

38. M. A. Shearn and B. H. Fireman, 'Stress management and mutual support of groups in rheumatoid arthritis', *American Journal of Medicine*, 78, 1985, pp. 771–5.

39. P. G. Kaufmann *et al*. and HIPP Investigators, 'Hypertension intervention pooling project', *Health Psychology*, 7 (Supplement), 1988, pp. 209–24.

40. R. G. Jacob *et al*, 'Relaxation therapy for hypertension', Annals of Behavioral Medicine, 13, 1991, pp. 5–17.

41. Channel 5, *Scary Animals, Super Creeps*, Catspaw Productions, 24 September 1998.

42. Chaudhary Vivek, 'Call for stricter guidelines on hypnotism', *Guardian*, 8 November 1995.

43. J. H. Schultz and W. Luthe, 'Autogenic methods', in W. Luthe (ed.). *Autogenic Therapy*, vol. 1, New York and London: Grune and Stratton, 1969, p. 20.

44. C. S. Adler and S. Morrisey-Adler, 'Strategies in general psychiatry', in J. Basmajian (ed.), *Biofeedback: principles and practice for clinicians*, Baltimore: Williams and Wilkins, 1983.

THIRTEEN
GADGETS AND GIZMOS

1. <http//www.fitech.co.uk/stress_counsellor.html>
2. Email to the author, 2 March 2004.
3. Quoted in Colin Adamson, 'Cyber counselling: the new face of therapy', *Evening Standard*, 17 July 2000.
4. Simone Cave, 'Is the key to stress on the tip of your tongue?', *Daily Mail*, 5 January 1999.
5. Stafford Lightman, *Daily Mail*, 5 January 1999.
6. Euan McColm, 'Stress buster', *Scottish Daily Record,* 16 July 1999.
7. Interview with the author, 5 January 2004.

FOURTEEN
WORKPLACE INTERVENTIONS

1. <http://symbiosisonline.com/stress.htm> 16 July 2003.
2. 'Stress is problem for most Americans', *Research Alert* 1996: 14 (21):1.
3. Peter Chowka, 'A year to remember', NaturalHealthLine website, 15 January 2001.
4. Jo Revill, 'Life makes you sick', *Observer*, 12 October 2003.
5. ISMA leaflet distributed at the HSE Standards launch, *You can do something about stress.*
6. *Observer*, 12 October 2003.
7. Phone interview, 18 June 2004.
8. *Observer*, 12 October 2003.
9. HSE, *A 'management standards' approach to work-related stress – Part I, Rationale and scientific underpinning*, 2004.
10. Ibid., p. 3.
11. Ibid., p. 5.
12. C. L. Cooper, p. J. Dewe and M. P. O'Driscoll, *Organizational stress*, Thousand Oaks, London: Sage Publications, 2001.
13. P. B. Warr (1990), 'Decision latitude, job demands and well-being', *Work and Stress,* 4, no. 4, pp. 285–94.

14. A. A. Milne, *The House at Pooh Corner*, Methuen, 1928, Chapter 3.

15. HSE, op. cit., 2004, p. 10.

16. The theory deriving from R. A. Karasek (1979), 'Job demands, job decision latitude, and mental strain: implications for job redesign', *Administrative Science Quarterly*, p. 24.

17. J. Rick, L. Thomson, R. B. Briner *et al.*, *Review of existing supporting scientific knowledge to underpin standards of good practice for work related stressors – Phase I*, HSE Research report 024, Sudbury: HSE Books, 2002.

18. HSE, op. cit., 2004, p. 16.

19. T. Cox, 'Work-related stress: from environment exposure to ill-health', in *Legge – The Changing Nature of Occupational Health*, Sudbury: HSE Books, 1998.

20. J. Rick and R. B. Briner, 'Psychosocial risk assessment: problems and prospects', *Occupational Medicine*, 50, 2000, pp. 310–14.

21. HSE, op.cit., 2004, p. 21.

22. Ibid., p. 25.

23. R. B. Briner and S. Reynolds, 'The costs, benefits and limitations of organizational level stress interventions', *Journal of Organizational Behaviour*, 20, 1999, pp. 647–67.

24. N. K. Semmer, 'Job stress intervention and organization of work', in J. C. Quick and L. E Tetrick (eds), *Handbook of Occupational Health Psychology*, Washington, DC: American Psychological Association, 2003.

25. S. Reynolds, 'Interventions: what works, what doesn't?', *Occupational Medicine*, 50, 2000, pp. 315–19.

26. HSE, op.cit., 2004, p. 27.

27. Letter to the author, 11 November 1999.

28. Published in the summer of 2002 in the French analytical journal *Futuribles*.

29. HSE, *Stress at work: a guide for employers*. HS (G) 116, Sudbury: HSE Books, 1995.

30. *The Times*, 30 August 1999.

31. Dr David Wainwright interviewed at the Department of Social Medicine, University of Kent, 23 Ocober 1999.

32. Ruth Lea, 'The "Work-Life Balance" and all that – The re-regulation of the labour market', IOD Policy Paper, April 2001, p. 36.

33. Ibid., p. 42.

34. Frank Furedi, 'Diseasing the workplace', *Occupational Health Review*, December 1999.

35. Aired on Channel 4 on 4 November 2002.

36. *The Money Programme*: 'Stress in the workplace', editor Diarmuid Jeffreys, 1998.

37. T. Cox, *Stress research and stress management: Putting theory to work*, CRR 61, HSE Books, 1993, in *Health and Safety Information Bulletin* 220, April 1994.

38. Rob Briner, 'Stress management 2: effectiveness of interventions', IRS, December 2000.

39. M. L. Wassel, 'A stress management incentive program for nursing staff during Operation Desert Storm', *American Association of Occupational Health Nurses*, 41 (8), 1993. pp. 393–5.

40. R. B. Briner and S. Reynolds, 'Bad theory and bad practice in occupational stress', *Occupational Psychologist*, 19 April 1993, p. 6.

41. J. Rick and A. Guppy, 'Coping strategies and mental health in white collar public sector employees', *European Work and Organizational Psychologist*, 4 (2), 1994, pp. 121–37.

42. J. Rick *et al.*, 'Stress: Big issue, but what are the problems?', *IES Report* 331, 1997.

43. John Carvel, 'Teaching crisis – half plan to quit', *Guardian*, 29 February 2000.

44. Letter to the author, 22 May 2000.

45. *Lost Time: The management of sickness absence and medical retirement in the Police Service*, HMIC Thematic Inspection Report, 1997, p. 59.

46. Touche Ross, evidence to the Joint Staff Association Working Group, 1991.

47. *Lost Time*, op. cit., p. 56.

48. *Daily Mail*, 2 August 2003.

49. Quoted in Michael Clarke, 'The vanishing police', *Daily Mail*, 20 December 1999.

50. Opinions of the Lords of Appeal for Judgement in the Cause, *White and Others v Chief Constable of South Yorkshire and others*, 3 December 1998, para. 7.

51. Ibid., paras 11–12.

52. Myranda Mowafi, 'From BBC bosses to staff, the bottom line in how to relax', *Daily Mail*, 12 February 2001.

53. Email to the author, 13 March, 2001.

54. Email to the author, 16 March 2001.

FIFTEEN
COUNSELLING

1. CounsellingResource.com: Finding counsellors and therapists, 30 June 2004.

2. Ibid.

3. Frank Furedi, 'A curse on counselling!' *Daily Mail*, 14 October 2003.

4. British Association for Counselling, Information Guide, May 1997.

5. Ruth Lea, 'Healthcare in the UK: the need for reform', IOD Policy paper, 2000, p. 40.

6. *Lost Time: the management of sickness absence and medical retirement in the police service*, HMIC Thematic Inspection Report, 1997, p. 56.

7. Colin Feltham, *What is Counselling?*, London: Sage, 1995, p. 2.

8. See e.g. 'In Dunblane, there were more counsellors than victims'. LM99, April 1997.

9. Colin Adamson, 'Cyber counselling: the new face of therapy', *Evening Standard*, 17 July 2000.

10. Brian Thorne, *Norwich Centre Counselling Service for Norwich Union*, Report, December 1996.

11. Jeffrey Masson, *Against Therapy*, London: HarperCollins, 1997, p. 19.

12. Brian Thorne, *Person-Centred Counselling: Therapeutic and spiritual dimensions*, London: Whurr Publishers, 1991, p. 27.

13. C. R. Rogers, 'In Retrospect: forty-six years', *American Psychologist*, 2, 1974, p. 116.

14. J. Masson, *Against Therapy,* op. cit., p. 245.

15. B. Thorne, op. cit., p. 24.

16. Ibid., p. 18.

17. Dave Mearns and Brian Thorne, *Person-Centred Counselling in Action,* 2nd edition, London: Sage Publications, 1999, p. 41.

18. Bruce Charlton, 'Life before health (against the sentimentalising of medicine)', in Anderson and Mullen (eds), *Faking it: The sentimentalisation of modern society*, London: Penguin Press, 1998.

19. A. Roth and p. Fonagy, *What works for whom? A Critical Review of Psychotherapy Research,* Guildford Press, 1996.

20. Ingrid Seward, *The Queen and Di*, London: HarperCollins, 2000, p. 62.

21. Ibid., p. 165.

22. Ibid., p. 69.

23. 'Therapy damaged Diana, says her mother', *Daily Mail*, 2 September 2000.

24. Dorothy Rowe, *The Successful Self* and *Breaking the Bonds*, London: HarperCollins.

25. Anna Maxted, 'Does therapy work?' *Shape* magazine, June 1999, p. 83.

26. Interviewed on BBC 2, *Heart of the Matter*, 'Bully for you', 1999.

27. *Survey of Employee Benefits*, Hay Management Consultants, October 2000.

28. Frank Furedi, 'A curse on counselling', *Daily Mail*, 14 October 2003.

29. Andrew Bolger, 'Wise counsels can cut costs', *Financial Times* 'Guide to Business Health and Safety', 25 October 1999.

30. Ibid., p. 25.

31. T. Allison, C. L. Cooper and P. Reynolds, 'Stress counselling in the workplace: the post office experience', *The Psychologist*, 2, 1989, pp. 384–8. J. A. Firth and D. A. Shapiro, 'An evaluation of psychotherapy for job-related distress', *Journal of Occupational Psychology*, 59, 1986, pp. 111–19.

32. T. Newton *et al.*, *'Managing' Stress: emotion and power at work*, London: Sage, 1995.

33. Email to the author, 12 May 2000.

34. Brian Thorne, 'Stress in a Changing Culture', Norwich Union seminar, 25 September 1996.

35. Brian Thorne, December 1996.

36. Ruth Lea, 'Healthcare in the UK: the need for reform', IOD Policy Paper, February 2000, p. 40.

SIXTEEN
'TRAUMA' STRESS COUNSELLING

1. *Stress and the Medical Profession*, British Medical Association, June 1992, p. 16.

2. Report of the Law Commission, no. 249, para. 3.4.

3. Al Colombo's US Veteran Information website, 30 June 2004.

4. Ibid.

5. *Veterans Benefits News and Resources*, official website of Vietnam Veterans of America. WA's guide on PTSD, 30 June 2004.

6. A. B. Adler *et al.*, 'US Soldier peacekeeping experiences and well-being after returning from deployment in Kosovo', Army Medical Research Unit, Europe. Technical Report, September 2000.

7. Keith Tennent, *The Aussie Digger* website, 'The home of all Australian ex-service and serving members', 25 June 2004.

8. Ibid.

9. J. Rick and R. Briner, 'Trauma management *vs.* stress debriefing: What should responsible organizations do?', Institute of Employment Studies, January 2000, p. 4.

10. 'Help at Hand: Information and advice for anyone who has been involved in a distressing experience', 1990s NatWest Group staff leaflet on preventing PTSD.

11. Quoted in Brian Moynihan, 'Not all it's cracked up to be', *Sunday Times Magazine*, 25 May 1997.

12. J. Rick and R. Briner, op. cit., 2000, p. 2.

13. Dr William Johnson, RWOCIS, 81–2, quoted in Ben Shephard, *A War of Nerves,* London: Jonathan Cape, 2000, p. 59.

14. Ibid., p. 60.

15. Interviewed at the Department of Social Medicine, University of Kent, May 1998.

16. David Wainwright and Michael Calnan, *Work Stress: the Making of a Modern Epidemic*, Milton Keynes: Open University Press, 2002.

17. Ibid.

18. According to George Bonanno, Assistant Professor of Psychology at Columbia University in New York, who led the research.

19. Sarah Baxter and Lois Rogers, 'Stiff upper lip beats stress counselling', *Sunday Times*, 2 March 2003

20. David Fletcher, 'More common sense, less counselling, says Princess Royal', *Daily Telegraph*, 24 February 1996.

21. Greg Hadfield and Simon Houston, 'Anne blasts the boom in stress counsellors', *Daily Mail*, 24 February 1996.

22. *Stress and the Medical Profession,* British Medical Association, June 1992, p. 17.

23. Ibid., p. 72.

24. R. A. Mayou, A. Ehlers and M. Hobbs, 'Psychological debriefing for road traffic accident victims: Three-year follow-up of a randomised controlled trial', *British Journal of Psychiatry*, 176, 2000, pp. 589–93.

25. Colin Adamson, 'Cyber counselling: the new face of therapy', *Evening Standard*, 17 July 2000.

26. M. Deahl, M. Srinivasan *et al.*, 'Preventing psychological trauma in soldiers: the role of operational stress training and psychological debriefing', *British Journal of Medical Psychology*, 73 (1), 2000, pp. 77–86.

27. M. Deahl and S. Wessely, 'Psychological debriefing is a waste of time', *British Journal of Psychiatry*, 183, 2003, pp. 12–14.

28. A. Macfarlane, 'The longitudinal course of post-traumatic morbidity: The range of outcomes and their predictors', *Journal of Nervous and Mental Disease*: 176, 1, 1988, pp. 30–39.

29. J. A. Kenardy *et al.*, 'Stress debriefing and patterns of recovery

following a natural disaster', *Journal of Trauma Stress*, 9, 1996, pp. 37–49.

30. J. A. Kenardy, 'The current status of psychological debriefing', *British Medical Journal*, 321: 2000, pp. 1032–3.

31. Frank Furedi, 'A curse on counselling!' *Daily Mail*, 14 October 2003.

32. Ibid.

33. Interview with Dr Phil Hammond, 1999, BBC2, *Trust Me, I'm a Doctor,* produced by Adelene Alani.

34. J. Bisson, P. Jenkins *et al.*, 'Randomised controlled trial of psychological debriefing for victims of acute burn trauma', *British Journal of Psychiatry*, 171, 1997, pp. 78–81.

35. S. Wessely, S. Rose and J. Bisson, 'A systematic review of brief psychological interventions (de-briefing) for the treatment of immediate trauma-related symptoms and the prevention of post traumatic stress disorder', in *Cochrane Collaboration*, Cochrane Library, 4. Oxford: Update Software, 1999.

36. Sarah Baxter and Lois Rogers, 'Stiff upper lip beats stress counselling', *Sunday Times*, 2 March 2003.

37. J. A. Kenardy, op. cit., 2000, p. 1033.

38. *Sunday Times*, 2 March 2003.

39. Quoted in Kevin Toolis, 'Shock tactics', *Guardian Weekend,* 13 November 1999.

40. Cover story by Dr Jennifer Cunningham and Yvonne McEwan, *LM Magazine*, April 1997.

41. Interview with Dr Phil Hammond on *Trust Me I'm a Doctor*, op. cit.

42. G. Capobianco and T. Patelis, 'Long-term psychological effects of airplane crash survival', Presentation to the American Psychological Association, 1999.

SEVENTEEN
NATION SEDATION

1. Welsh Medicines Resource Centre Bulletin, 10 October 2003, p. 3.
2. J. R. Mort and R. R. Asparasu, 'Inappropriate prescribing for the elderly: Beers' criteria review', *Annals of Pharmacotherapy*, 34 (3) 2000, pp. 338–46. R. R. Asparasu, J. R Mort and A. Asparasu, 'Inappropriate psychotropic agents for the elderly', *Geriatric Times*, 2, March–April 2001, p. 2.
3. S. Rose, 'Ritalin: the UK's hidden drug epidemic', *Socialist Teachers' Alliance News* website, 3 December 2003.
4. F. Charatan, 'US panel calls for research into effects of Ritalin', *British Medical Journal*, 5 December 1998.
5. G. B LeFever, A. p. Arcona and D. O. Antonuccio, 'ADHD among American schoolchildren: evidence of over-diagnosis and overuse of medication', *Scientific Review of Mental Health Practice,* vol. 2, 2003, p. 1.
6. L. Diller, *Running on Ritalin: a physician reflects on children, society, and performance in a pill*, New York: Bantam Books, 1998; G. Sinha, 'New evidence about Ritalin: what every parent should know', *Popular Science*, June 2001, pp. 48–52.
7. P. Mackey and A. Kipras, 'Medication for attention deficit/ hyperactivity disorder (ADHD): An analysis by federal electorate', <http://www.aph.gov.au/library/pubs/cib/2000-01cib11.html>, 2001; E. Marshall, 'Epidemiology: Duke study faults overuse of stimulants for children', *Science*, 289, 2000, p. 721.
8. G. B. LeFever, K. V. Dawson and A. L. Morrow, 'The extent of drug therapy for attention-deficit/hyperactivity disorder among children in public schools', *American Journal of Public Health*, 89, 1999, pp. 1359–64.
9. G. B. LeFever, M. Villers *et al.*, 'Parental perceptions of adverse educational outcomes among children diagnosed and treated for ADHD: a call for improved school/provider collaboration', *Psychology in the Schools*, 39, 2002, pp. 63–72.

10. L. Diller, 'Kids on drugs', *Salon* website, 9 March 2000, <http://dir.salon.com/health/feature/2000/03/09/kid_drugs/index.html>

11. Quoted in *Daily Mail*, 31 May 2003.

12. Simma Lieberman Associates website: 'What is stress?' 24 June 2004.

13. M. A. Persinger, *Neuropsychological Bases of God Beliefs*, Praeger, 1987; M. A. Persinger, 'Religious and mystical experiences as artefacts of temporal lobe function: a general hypothesis', *Perceptual and Motor Skills*, 57, 1983, pp. 1255–62.

14. J. Hughes, T. W. Smith, H.W. Kosterlitz *et al.*, 'Identification of two related pentapeptides from the brain with potent opiate agonist activity', *Nature*, 258, 1975, pp. 577–9.

15. J. B. Overmier and M. E. p. Seligman, 'Effects of inescapable shock upon subsequent escape and avoidance behavior', *Journal of Complementary Physiology and Psychology*, 63, 1967, pp. 23–33; S. F. Maier and M. E. P. Seligman, 'Learned helplessness: theory and evidence', *Journal of Experimental Psychology* (Gen), 105, 1976, pp. 3–46; S. F. Maier, M. E. P Seligman and R. L. Solomon (1969), 'Pavlovian fear conditioning and learned helplessness', in B. A. Campbell and R. M. Church (eds), *Punishment and Aversive Behavior*, New York: Appleton-Century-Crofts; M. E. p. Seligman, *Helplessness: On Depression, Development and Death*, San Francisco: Freeman, 1975.

16. J. J. Lynch, *The Broken Heart: the medical consequences of loneliness*, New York: Basic Books, 1977.

17. Rebecca Paveley, 'Waiting lists grow', *Daily Mail*, 9 March 2002.

18. J. J. Lynch, K. E. Lynch and E. Friedmann, 'A cry unheard: sudden reductions in blood pressure while talking about feelings of hopelessness and helplessness', *Integrative Physiological and Behavioral Science*, 27 (2), 1992, pp. 151–69. J. J. Lynch, *The Language of the Heart: the human body in dialogue*, New York: Basic Books, 1985. J. J. Lynch, S. A. Thomas *et al.*, 'Blood pressure changes while talking', *Journal of Nervous and Mental Disease*, 168, 1980, pp. 526–34.

19. Colin Blakemore, *The Mind Machine*, London: Penguin, 1994, pp. 169–70.

20. 'Woman admits £80-a-week habit to help cope with stress', *Daily Mail*, 3 April 1996.

21. Anne Shooter, 'Watch out, Peter Pan, for the legal crocodiles', *Daily Mail*, 2 March 1996.

22. Bill Mouland, 'Beware of the PC bull', *Daily Mail*, 24 January 1998.

23. 'Families in flap at door-to-door terror of two hungry swans', *Daily Mail*, 18 November 1995.

24. 'More stress, less rest in America', <http//www.mental-health-matters.com>, 29 June 2004.

25. Anxiety Disorders Foundation of Australia (NSW Branch) website, 30 June 2004.

26. Paul Wilson, *Instant Calm*, London: Penguin, 1995, p. 195.

27. Ibid., p. 218.

28. See e.g. R. G. Laessle, P. J. V Beumont *et al.*, 'A comparison of nutritional management with stress management in the treatment of bulimia nervosa', *British Journal of Psychiatry*, 159, 1991, pp. 250–61.

29. 'Stressed women reach for alcohol', *BBC News On Line*, 1 March 2004.

30. *Calling Time*, Academy of Medical Sciences, March 2004.

31. A. Patmore, op. cit., 1997, p. 37.

32. P. Brown 'Tobacco kills one smoker in two', *New Scientist*, 15 October 1944, 144: pp. 1947.

33. Ben Taylor, 'Top coroner warns on cannabis, the silent killer', *Daily Mail*, 3 November 2003.

34. Susan Greenfield, 'Cannabis: the case against', *Daily Mail*, 24 October 2001.

EIGHTEEN
THE CHEMICAL COSH

1. E. A. Martin (ed.), *Concise Medical Dictionary*, 2nd edition, Oxford University Press, 1985.

2. Charles Medawar, *Power and Dependence: Social Audit on the safety of medicines*, Social Audit Ltd, 1992, p. 93.

3. Roche advertisement reproduced in ibid., p. 96.

4. On 24 March 1969.

5. Yahoo Finance/Reuters Industry browser, 15 March 2004.

6. According to a National Academy of Science's Institute of Medicine Report, issued 10 January 2001.

7. Dr Marcia Angell, 'Is academic medicine for sale', *New England Journal of Medicine*, 18 May 2000.

8. Robert M. Tenery Jr, editorial, *Journal of the American Medical Association*, 19 January 2000. Dr Tenery is a member of the American Medical Association's Council on Ethical and Judicial Affairs.

9. Lynn Eaton, News Roundup, *British Medical Journal,* 330, 2005, p. 9.

10. Trevor R. Norman, *et al.* (1998), 'Benzodiazepines in anxiety disorders: Managing therapeutics and dependence', *Medical Journal of Australia*. eMJA 0150179, <http//www.mja.com.au/public/mental health/articles/norman.html>

11. R. F. Peart, 'Tranquillizer addiction – a medically induced epidemic', Presented at the conference: *Stress – A Change of Direction*, 1998.

12. MIND, 'Making sense of minor tranquillizers', information online, 16 March 2004.

13. Colin Blakemore, *The Mind Machine*, London: Penguin edition, 1994, p. 106.

14. Letter to the author, 26 April 2004.

15. MIND press release, 11 March 2004.

16. Heather Ashton, *Benzodiazepines: How they work and how to withdraw*. University of Newcastle School of Neurosciences, 2002, p. 2.

17. T. Norman, Op. cit., 1998.

18. M. Lader, 'History of benzodiazepine dependence', *Journal of Substance Abuse Treatment*, 8, 1991, pp. 53–9; Julie-Anne Davies, 'Accidental addicts', online article, <http//www.theage.com.au> (Australia), 16 June 2003.

19. Ibid.

20. Telephone interview, 22 February 2005.

21. Telephone interview, 22 February 2005.

22. David Blunkett, Letter to Barry Haslam, 24 February 1994.

23. Paul Boateng, Letter to Barry Haslam, 25 April 1994.

24. C. Blakemore, op. cit., p. 107.

25. Clara Pirani, 'Anxious and addicted', *The Australian*, 26 July 2003.

26. Quoted in Julie-Anne Davies, op. cit.

27. Ibid.

28. Paul Bracchi, 'Health fear for Liza as UK tour is axed', *Daily Mail*, 30 May 1998.

29. C. Blakemore, op. cit., p. 107.

30. J. C. Gillin, C. L. Spinweber and L. C. Johnson, 'Rebound insomnia: a critical review', *Journal of Clinical Psychopharmacology*, 9, 1989, pp. 161–72.

31. P. Tyrer, 'Prescribing psychotropic drugs in general practice', editorial, *British Medical Journal*, 296, 1988, pp. 588–9.

32. J. Morrison, 'Withdrawal from Tranquillizers', *The Practitioner*, September, vol. 235, 1991, pp. 684–8.

33. R. F. Peart, 'Tranquillizer addiction – a medically induced epidemic', 1998, p. 4.

34. Malcolm H. Lader, 'CV and Quotations', <http//www.Benzo.org.uk>

35. H. Ashton, in *Psychiatric Annals*, 25, 3, 1995, pp. 158–65.

36. H. Ashton, 2002, p. 5.

37. MSN search, February 2003.

38. MIND, 'Making sense of minor tranquillizers', online, 16 March 2004.

39. Martyn Halle, 'Homes are keeping up to a quarter of old folk on drugs', *Sunday Telegraph*, 26 April 1998.

40. MIND, 'Making sense of minor tranquillizers', op. cit.

41. MIND 'Yellow Card Scheme reporting the adverse effects of psychiatric drugs', First report, 1996, p. 2.

42. Barry Haslam, '"Beat the 'Benzos": a call for EU guidelines on the prescribing of Benzodiazepines', 2004.

43. H. C. Ashton, Letter to Phil Woolas MP, 31 January 2005.

44. Published October 2002.

45. I. Waldron, 'Increased prescribing of Valium, Librium and other drugs – an example of the influence of economic and social factors on the practice of medicine', *International Journal of Health Services*, 7 (1), 1977, pp. 37–62.

46. Department of Health, Information Line, 7 April 2004.

47. American Medical Association, Medical Library, 1999.

48. D. Shelton, 'New psychotropics under development', Amednews. com, 21 August 2000.

49. Norwich Union Healthcare Mental Health Report, commissioned January 2004, conducted by Doctor Foster Research.

50. IMS Health, published in *USA Today*, 'Health and Science', 7 July 2002.

51. In *Prevention and Treatment*, an e-journal of the American Psychological Association, 15 July 2002.

52. Quoted in 'Health and Science', *USA Today*, 7 July 2002.

53. Quoted in 'Are we hooked on happy pills?' LHJ.com (*Ladies' Home Journal* online), July 2004.

54. S. Cheeta, F. Schifano *et al.*, 'Antidepressant-related deaths and antidepressant prescriptions in England and Wales, 1998–2000', *British Journal of Psychiatry* 184, 2004, pp. 41–7.

55. *Trends in the mortality of young adults aged 15–44 in England and Wales*, 1961–2001, p. 29.

56. D. Healy, *Anti-depressants and suicide*, Briefing Paper, 20 June 2003.

57. D. Healy, *The Antidepressant Era*, Cambridge, MA: Harvard University Press, 1999.

58. 'Academic in Prozac job row seeks £4m', *Daily Mail*, 26 September 2001.

59. 'Anti-depressants and Suicide', Briefing Paper, 20 June 2003.

60. S. Donovan, and R. Madeley, 'Deliberate self-harm and anti-depressant drugs', *British Journal of Psychiatry*, 177, 2000, pp. 551–6.

61. *Forsyth v Eli Lilly in the US District Court of Hawaii*, 5 January 1998.

62. J. C. Markowitz, 'Anti-depressants and suicide risk', *British Journal of Psychiatry*, 178, 2001, p. 477.

63. 'FDA asks drug manufacturers to include suicide warnings', *Insight*, On the News, 22 March 2004.

64. MIND press release, 11 March 2004.

65. Maxine Frith, 'Prozac nation, UK', *The Independent*, 30 March 2004.

66. 'Warning on antidepressant doses', BBC News online, 11 March 2004.

67. 'Patients "hooked on the shy pill"', *Daily Mail*, 17 September 2002.

68. 'GPs get new anti-depressant rules', BBC News online, 6 December 2004.

69. Ibid.

70. M. Scott Peck, *The Road Less Travelled*, Arrow edition, 1990, p. 14.

Part Five THE ALTERNATIVES

NINETEEN
INUREMENT

1. Julie-Anne Davies, 'Accidental addicts. Online article', <http//www.theage.com.au> (Australia), 16 June 2003.

2. 'Young Australian women failing the stress test', <http//www.MyDoctor.com.au> Professionals' site builder, 20 February 2001.

3. Julius Caesar, *The Conquest of Gaul*, 1982 edition, edited by J. Gardner, London: Penguin, p. 40.

4. BBC 2, *SAS Desert: Are You Tough Enough?*, 15 February 2004.

5. Tony Geraghty, *Who dares wins: The story of the SAS 1950–1980*, Fontana, 1981, p. 264.

6. Cicero, *The Tusculan Disputations*, translated by J. E. King, Cambridge, MA: Harvard University Press, 1927.

7. F. Josephus, *Eye-Witness to Rome's First-Century Conquest of Judea*, Macmillan: London, 1993 edition, p. 87.

8. 'Battle School: The "real thing" in training', *The War Illustrated* Volume 6, 131, June 1942, p. 14.

9. F. Johnson, S. Williams and S. M. Stoney, *The Duke of Edinburgh's Award Qualitative Study, Final Report*, National Foundation for Educational Research, 1998, p. 1.

10. Susan Jeffers, *Feel the Fear and Do It Anyway*, Arrow edition, 1991, p. 43.

11. J. K Rowling, *Harry Potter and the Philospher's Stone*, Bloomsbury, 1997, p. 121.

TWENTY
'EMERGENCE'

1. See e.g. A. Patmore, *Killing the messenger: the pathologizing of the stress response*, CERM/UEA and the Nerve Centre, 1997, p. 26–8; L. Hoffman-Goetz and B. K. Klarlund Pedersen, 1994, 'Exercise and the immune system: a model of the stress response?', *Immunology Today*, 15 (8), August pp. 382–7; R. Bahr, p. K. Opstad *et al.*, 'Strenuous prolonged exercise elevates resting metabolic rate and causes reduced mechanical efficiency', *Acta Physiologica Scandinivia*, 141, 1991, pp. 555–63.

2. Tony Buzan, *Brain Child: How smart parents make smart kids*, London: Harper Collins, 2003.

3. S. R. Rosenthal, quoted in T. Klen, 'Accidents in the Arctic: a psychological point of view', *Arctic Medical Research* 1992, 51, (Supplement 7), 1967, pp. 71–6.

4. M. E. Cavanagh, 'What you don't know about stress', *Personnel Journal*, July, 1988, pp. 53–9.

5. Quoted in T. Lott, 'Unlocking our secret self', *The Times*, 7 April 1998.

6. Colin Blakemore, *The Mind Machine*, London: Penguin, 1994, p. 21.

7. Moscow University's Prof. Petr Kouzmich Anokhin, veteran of sixty years of brain research, quoted in Tony Buzan, *The Mind Map Book*, BBC Books, 1993, p. 29.

8. J. Smith and J. Kampine, *Circulatory Physiology*, Williams and Wilkins: Baltimore, 1990, p. 187.

9. Francis Crick, *The Astonishing Hypothesis*, London: Simon and Shuster, 1994, p. 82.

10. Susan Greenfield, *Journey to the Centre of the Brain*. Study Guide to

the Royal Institution of Great Britain Christmas Lectures, BBC Education, 1994, p. 6.

11. Adam Zeman, 'Will we ever make sense of awareness?', *The Times*, 23 January 1995.

12. F. Crick, op. cit., p. 250.

13. M. Mitchell Waldrop, *Complexity: The emerging science at the edge of order and chaos*, London: Penguin, 1994, p. 82.

14. F. Crick, op. cit., p. 1.

15. A. Patmore, 'StressSpeak: a message from the mind', *Network: The Scientific and Medical Network Review*, 64, August 1997, pp. 17–19.

16. Greenfield, op. cit., p. 17.

17. Email to the author, 28 May 2004.

18. Cerebral Blood Flow (CBF) controls are still somewhat mysterious even to neurologists, and I consulted three during research for this chapter. Dr Julian Miller told me: 'It's one of the great mysteries how the brain shifts blood from one active region to another. The most popular view is that local circulation is controlled locally.' For the CNS ischemic reflex and other factors producing vasodilation and vasoconstriction in the brain, see e.g. J. Smith and J. Kampine, *Circulatory Physiology*, Baltimore: Williams and Wilkins, 1990, pp. 174–253.

19. Eugen Herrigel, *Zen in the Art of Archery*, London: Routledge,1953.

20. M. Persinger, *Neuropsychological Bases of God Beliefs*, Praeger, 1987, p. 31–2.

21. A. Antonovsky, *Health, Stress and Coping*, Jossey-Bass: San Francisco, 1979.

22. TV dramatist Andrew Davies describing his fellow-writers, *Huw Weldon Memorial Lecture*, BBC 2, 2 January 1995.

23. See e.g. S. Ostrander and L. Shroeder, *PSI: Psychic Research behind the Iron Curtain*, Abacus, 1976, p. 368ff.

24. Ibid., p. 399.

TWENTY-ONE

THE CEREBRAL CLIMAX (CC)

1. A. Maslow, *Toward a Psychology of Being*, Princeton: Van Nostrand, 1962. On catharsis see e.g. J. Heider, 'Catharsis in human potential encounter', *Journal of Humanistic Psychology*, 14, 1974, pp. 26–34.

2. Karate Club at USF website, <http//www.ctr.usf.edu/shotokan/mushin.html> 5 June 2004.

3. Interview with the author, 26 March 1996.

4. Bernard Amy, 'The Rhythm of Things', from *La Provence en Archipel* translated by Eric Davidson, 1985.

5. BASE jumper Rupert, quoted by Malcolm Burgess in *Equinox, Living Dangerously*, Channel 4 information booklet, 1999, p. 27.

6. See e.g. M. Zuckerman, *Sensation-Seeking: Beyond the Optimal Level of Arousal*, Hillsdale, New Jersey: Erlbaum,1979. M. Zuckerman, *Biological Bases of Sensation-Seeking: Impulsiveness and Anxiety*, Hillsdale, New Jersey: Erlbaum, 1983. T. Klen, 'Accidents in the Arctic: a psychological point of view', *Arctic Medical Research* 51, Supplement 7, 1992, pp. 71–6. A. Patmore, *Killing the Messenger: the pathologizing of the stress response*, CERM/UEA and The Nerve Centre, 1997, pp. 11–13.

7. A. Patmore, *Playing On Their Nerves: The sport experiment*, Stanley Paul, 1979, p. 125.

8. Syracuse University distance runner Mike Spino quoted in Jack Scott, *The Athletic Revolution*, Free Press, 1971, p. 222ff.

9. Equinox, *Losing It,* Channel 4 documentary, 10 November 1997.

10. 'In Millionaire Mania', *Daily Mail*, 11 September, 1999.

11. According to research by Prof. Shah Ebrahim presented at the World Stroke Congress in Melbourne in 2000 and a Toyko study of fatal strokes by Dr Izumi Toyoda.

12. *Scream and Scream Again*, written and presented by Mark Kermode for Channel 4, 28 October 2000.

13. *Scream and Scream Again*, October 2000.

14. Mona Wilson, *Johnson, Poetry on Prose*, London, Rupert Hart-Davis, 1968, p. 798.

15. *On the Sublime,* traditionally attributed to Longinus, in T. S. Dorsch, *Classical Literary Criticism: Aristotle, Horace, Longinus.* London: Penguin, 1965 translation, pp. 107, 114.

16. T. S. Eliot, *Tradition and the Individual Talent*, II, London: Faber.

17. Samuel Taylor Coleridge, *Biographia Literaria*, XIV.

18. Virginia Woolf, *Moments of Being.*

19. 'In the Penal Settlement', translated by Willa and Edwin Muir, in *Penguin Complete Short Stories*, London: Penguin, p. 150.

20. For an excellent scientific analysis of NDEs see Dr Pim van Lommel's paper in *The Lancet*, 15 December 2001, 358, pp. 2039–45.

21. Letter to the author, 22 February 1996.

22. Interviewed in *Esquire*, November 1993.

23. Clare Goldwin, 'The Review', *Daily Mirror*, 15 February 2003.

24. 'My Nightmare: "dream team" reunion took Alderton to the brink of a breakdown', *Daily Mail*, 9 April 1994.

25. '"Forgive me – I'm a silly old fool" says Fry', The Press Association, 24 February 1995.

26. 'Exit Sessions, stage fright', *Daily Mail*, 30 December 1994.

27. Garry Jenkins, *Daniel Day-Lewis: The fire within*, London: Sidgwick & Jackson, 1994.

28. Jerzy Grotowski, *Towards a Poor Theatre*, Methuen Paperback, 1968, pp. 38, 42.

29. Constantin Stanislavski, *Building a Character*, Methuen Paperback edition, 1950, pp. 74, 298.

30. F. H. Rauscher, G. L. Shaw and K. Ky, 'Music and spatial task performance', *Nature*, 365, 1993, p. 611.

31. C. S. Jackson and M. Tlauka, 'Route-learning and the Mozart Effect', *Journal of Music*, 32(2), 2004, pp. 213–20.

32. V. K. Ivanov and J. G. Geake, 'The Mozart Effect and primary school children', *Psychology of Music*, 31 (4), 2003, pp. 405–13.

33. Helen Ward, 'Verdi hits right note for pupil behaviour', *Times Educational Supplement*, 1 March 2002.

34. Prof. John Jenkins interview on <http//www.bbc.co.uk> 2 April 2001.

35. S. Hallam, J. Price and G. Karsarou, 'The effects of background music on primary school pupils' task performance', *Educational Studies*, 28, (2), 1 June 2002.

36. Interviewed in Sharon Hendry, 'How the Mozart Effect can fine tune young brains', *Daily Mail*, 3 April 1999.

37. S. Kramer and D. Hughes, 'The role of the arts in physician stress management', *North Carolina Medical Journal*, 54, 1993, p. 2.

38. R.A. Lippin, *How the arts inform occupational medicine*. Presented at the Australian and New Zealand Society of Occupational Medicine's Annual Scientific Meeting. Manly, Australia, 13 October 1998.

39. 'Cash-strapped arts world "is lottery loser"', *Daily Mail*, 17 January 1998.